LEGAL RESEARCH AND WRITING

SECOND EDITION

Other books in the *Essentials of Canadian Law* Series

ESSENTIALS OF CANADIAN LAW

LEGAL RESEARCH AND WRITING

SECOND EDITION

TED TJADEN

Faculty of Law and Faculty of Information Sciences
University of Toronto

Legal Research and Writing, Second Edition
© Irwin Law Inc., 2004

Published in 2004 by

Irwin Law Inc.
347 Bay Street
Suite 501
Toronto, Ontario
M5H 2R7
www.irwinlaw.com

ISBN: 1-55221-098-7

Library and Archives Canada Cataloguing in Publication

Tjaden, Ted
    Legal research and writing / Ted Tjaden. — 2nd ed.

(Essentials of Canadian law)
Includes bibliographical references and index.
ISBN 1-55221-098-7

1. Legal research—Canada. 2. Legal composition—Canada.
I. Title. II. Series.

KE250.T53 2004   340'.072'71   C2004-906488-6
KF240.T53 2004

The publisher acknowledges the financial support of the Government of Canada through the Book Publishing Industry Development Program (BPIDP) for its publishing activities.

Printed and bound in Canada.

1 2 3 4 5   08 07 06 05 04

SUMMARY
TABLE OF CONTENTS

DETAILED
TABLE OF CONTENTS

CHAPTER 9:
SELECTING AND ACQUIRING LEGAL RESOURCES

CHAPTER 10:
LEGAL RESEARCH AND WRITING MALPRACTICE

LIST OF FIGURES

---

*   Reprinted by permission of Quicklaw Inc.

†   Reprinted by permission of Carswell, a didvision of Thomson Canada Limited.

‡   Reprinted by permission of Canada Law Book.

LIST OF TABLES

PREFACE

To the Second Edition

Much has changed in legal research over the last few years since the publication of the first edition of this book. Some of the changes incorporated in this second edition include:

- Updates to reflect a new edition of the McGill Guide (5th ed.).
- Over 70 new cases added on the recoverability of online search charges (Chapter 1), legal research and writing malpractice (Chapter 10) and occupier's liability and waivers (Chapter 12, sample problem).
- Updated copyright analysis of the Supreme Court of Canada decision in *CCH Canadian Ltd. v. Law Society of Upper Canada* and its impact on legal research.
- Expanded coverage of Australian legal research (in addition to Canadian, American and British coverage).
- Updates to reflect the LexisNexis Canada takeover of Quicklaw and expanded online coverage of WestlaweCARSWELL and CCH's *LegislativePulse* and the introduction of a new edition of Carswell's *Canadian Abridgment*.
- New and updated illustrations and tables.
- Expanded and updated coverage of Internet law-related resources.
- An increase in the number of topics in Chapter 8 — Legal Research by Topic — from 34 topics to 45 topics, including the addition of the following 11 new topics: alternative dispute resolution (ADR), charities and not-for-profit law, competition and anti-trust law, introduction to law/legal systems, legal practice, media law/defamation, occupational health and safety, pension law, privacy law, sports and entertainment law, workers' compensation law. In addition, there are over 500 new book titles added to this chapter, resulting in a listing of over 800 leading Canadian law-related books in Chapter 8.

- Expanded legal writing resources and added a section on consequences of sloppy drafting.
- Completely re-written sample legal research memo based on an occupier's liability problem involving bungee-jumping and the enforceability of waivers of liability.

Thanks as always go to all of my colleagues at the Bora Laskin Law Library and particularly to John Papadopoulos for his helpful comments and insights on legal research and writing. Esmé Saulig also helped with finding resources and reviewing drafts of the book. I have, I am sure, also borrowed some of the content in this book from my colleague Shikha Sharma during our co-teaching of "Legal Research on the Internet" at the Professional Learning Centre at the University of Toronto, Faculty of Information Studies, and I thank her for her ongoing work and contributions in that course.

I am also indebted to the group of Toronto-based legal research lawyers who tolerate my presence at their informal meetings. They are too many of them to thank individually but special thanks should go to each of Simon Chester and Bonnie Fish for their participation in a number of legal research panels at various continuing legal education seminars. Thanks also must go to each of Wendy Bellack-Viner, Ruth Wahl and Shelley Obal for their teaching of legal research and writing at the law school and our many discussions of legal research and writing issues.

I am indebted to all of these people for their ideas, their teachings and their commitment to legal research and writing. I have borrowed liberally from all of them, not all of which can be properly documented; hence this form of general acknowledgement.

A special word of thanks to Angela Long whose expertise in editing and knowledge of legal research and writing made this second edition much better than when I started it. Finally, thanks also to Jeff Miller, Aimee Coueslan, and Heather Raven of Irwin Law. I cannot imagine a better publisher — I am extremely impressed by the dedication of the Irwin Law staff and the quality of their publications.

Ted Tjaden
October 2004
Toronto, Ontario

INTRODUCTION TO LEGAL RESEARCH AND WRITING

Legal research is a practical skill needed by lawyers, law students, paralegals, judges, law librarians, and members of the public who must find and use law-related information such as court cases, legislation, commentary, sample court documents, and agreements. With the advent of the Internet, online legal databases, and CD-ROMs, legal research now encompasses the need to use and master both print and online resources. Computer technology has in fact changed much in legal research in Canada with the increase in the amount of law-related information available online and improvements in search and retrieval software. With these changes comes the need for many to learn new techniques and new sources for finding law-related information.

Related to legal research is legal writing, also a practical skill that requires clarity, precision, and an understanding of some basic legal writing requirements. Legal writing involves the drafting of a number of law-related documents including legal research memos, opinion letters, business agreements, court pleadings, and factums. Fortunately, much has been written about legal research and writing in the past few years, which should assist those teaching it in law schools to improve how it is currently taught. In addition, this book provides readers with a brief overview of effective legal writing.

For many lawyers and law students, legal research and writing is a bad memory of first-year law school library exercises that did not always make sense and were easily forgotten. For first-time legal researchers, finding relevant cases and legislation can be difficult;

1

ensuring that a particular case or statute has not been reversed or amended can be seemingly impossible for the uninitiated (it is not). Finding and drafting relevant and effective court documents and other law-related documents poses its own challenges. While the introduction of computer technology has in many cases improved access to legal information, computer technology also introduces the spectre of "information overload" and the danger of being bogged down with too much information. The need now is to be able to sift effectively through this mass of information to distill the particular information relevant to the question being researched.

This book — aimed at lawyers, law students, paralegals, judges, law librarians, and members of the public — seeks to explain the practical skills needed for print and online legal research, as well as for legal writing. It provides a current and comprehensive look at the topic, consolidating information on legal research and writing into one handy, easy-to-use resource. This chapter introduces legal research and writing by (1) arguing its importance to the legal profession; (2) discussing some basic legal research techniques and resources; (3) introducing legal citation; and (4) discussing some basic copyright issues.

A. THE IMPORTANCE OF LEGAL RESEARCH

There should be no need to argue the importance of legal research and writing, but given the short shrift it is often given in law school, it is understandable that some lawyers may not regard legal research as important as other skills, such as advocacy and negotiation, for example. In fact, much has been written on the reasons why law schools graduate students with such poor legal research and writing skills.[1] Many law stu-

---

1   See Emily Grant, "Toward a Deeper Understanding of Legal Research and Writing as a Developing Profession" (2003) 27 Vt. L. Rev. 371; Maureen F. Fitzgerald, "What's Wrong with Legal Research and Writing? Problems and Solutions" (1996) 88 Law Libr. J. 247; Donald J. Dunn, "Why Legal Research Skills Declined, or When Two Rights Make a Wrong" (1993) 85 Law Libr. J. 49; Ron M. Mersky, "Rx for Legal Research and Writing: A New Langdell" (1991) 11 Legal Ref. Serv. Q. 201; Joan S. Howland & Nancy J. Lewis, "The Effectiveness of Law School Legal Research Training Programs" (1990) 40 J. Legal Educ. 381; Christopher G. Wren & Jill Robinson Wren, "The Teaching of Legal Research" (1988) 80 Law Libr. J. 7; Helene S. Shapo, "The Frontiers of Legal Writing: Challenges for Teaching Research" (1986) 78 Law Libr. J. 719; Leonard L. Baird, "A Survey of the Relevance of Legal Training to Law School Graduates" (1987) 29 J. Legal Educ. 264 at 273, Table 3; Robin K. Mills, "Legal Research Instruc-

dents are able to graduate from law school without having done very much original research. First-year students, for example, are provided pre-made casebooks containing much of the law they need to read, lessening or eliminating the need to find their own relevant cases. In addition, since legal research and writing is often taught on a "pass-fail" basis, many students will regard such courses as being less important than the substantive, graded courses they are required to take. And since most law school courses are taught as discrete subjects, there is a false sense given to students that legal problems fall nicely into well-defined categories when in fact the reality is that legal problems are not always so easily categorized, problems that in real life must be correctly analyzed if the research being performed is to be meaningful and effective.

1) Competent Lawyers Know How to Research

What is it then that lawyers do and why would legal research and writing be so important to their work? Simply put, lawyers are licensed professionals who are given a monopoly to provide legal advice to clients. Given that modern society is unfortunately complex with numerous (and sometimes conflicting) rules that govern relationships between individuals, there is a role to be played by lawyers in helping people understand their legal rights and structure their affairs to comply with these complex rules. The role that lawyers play therefore involves two basic tasks: (i) *understanding* the law, which requires legal research skills; and (ii) *communicating* the law to the clients or to judges, which requires, among other things, legal writing skills.

The Competence Task Force of the Law Society of Upper Canada has in fact recognized the importance of legal research and writing in its 1997 Final Report[2] in its definition of the attributes of a competent lawyer:

> A competent lawyer has and applies relevant skills, attributes, and values in a manner appropriate to each matter undertaken on behalf of a client. These include:

---

tion in Law Schools, the State of the Art or, Why Law School Graduates Do Not Know How to Find the Law" (1977) 70 Law Libr. J. 343; Sandra Sadow & Benjamin R. Beede, "Library Instruction in American Law Schools" (1975) 68 Law Libr. J. 27; Robert A.D. Schwartz, "The Relative Importance of Skills Used by Attorneys" (1973) 3 Golden Gate U.L. Rev. 321.

2   Law Society of Upper Canada, "Competence Task Force — Final Report" (28 November 1997), online: Law Society of Upper Canada <http://www.lsuc.on.ca/services/comp_final_en.jsp>.

i. *knowing general legal principles and procedures, and the substantive law and procedure* for the areas of law in which the lawyer practices;

ii. *investigating facts, identifying issues, ascertaining client objectives, considering possible options*, and developing and advising the client as to appropriate course(s) of action;

iii. implementing the chosen course of action through the application of appropriate skills including:

(a) *legal research,*

(b) *analysis,*

(c) *application of the law to the relevant facts,*

(d) *writing, and drafting,*

. . .

(h) problem solving ability as each matter requires . . . .

[emphasis added]

With this definition of a "competent lawyer," the Law Society of Upper Canada is recognizing that legal research and writing are basic skills for all lawyers.

2) Recovery of Costs and Disbursements for Legal Research

The importance of legal research has also been recognized in a number of cases in which the court or taxing officer has commented on the importance of legal research[3] or allowed a party to recover the costs of legal research, including the cost of Quicklaw online search charges.[4]

---

3   See Lisa A. Peters, "Recovery of Legal Research Expenses in Taxations and Assessments of Costs" (1997) 55 Advocate (B.C.) 79 at 80–81, citing, among other cases, *Xidos v. Tim Hill and Associates* (1990), 97 N.S.R. (2d) 212 (T.D.) ¶ 15–17, where the court encouraged lawyers to conduct research since it helps the court in its decision-making.

4   See *Coleman Fraser Whittome & Parcells v. Canada (Department of Justice)*, [2003] N.S.J. No. 272 (S.C.) [online search charges allowed, but reduced; research involved case law and case reports that would not normally be expected to be in the office library of the law firm]; *McNulty v. Noordam*, [2003] B.C.J. No. 2166 (Prov. Ct.) [online search charges allowed]; *Lawyers' Professional Indemnity Co. v. Geto Investments Ltd.* (2002), 17 C.P.C. (5th) 334 (Ont. S.C.J.) [Quicklaw expenses are time- and cost-effective and efficient, allowed]; *Oliver & Co. v. Choi*, 2002 BCSC 152 [Quicklaw search charges allowed but reduced since excessive and no agreement with client]; *Fasken Martineau DuMoulin LLP v. Bastion Development Corp.*, 2001 BCSC 1694 [online searches provide a benefit to client, costs allowed but reduced because excessive]; *Early Recovered Resources Inc. v. Gulf Log Salvage Co-Operative Assn.*, 2001 FCT 1212 [computer assisted

In *Sellors v. Total Credit Recovery Ltd.*,[5] for example, the court allowed Quicklaw charges on the basis that they were cost and time effective and efficient:

> The Quick Law research expense is a legitimate solicitor and client disbursement. I could be tempted in calling the charges items of over-

---

research of $110.29 allowed]; *Boots v. Mohawk Council of Akwasasne*, [2000] F.C.J. No. 312 (T.D.) [*Boots*]; *Girocredit Bank Aktiengesellschaft Der Sparkassen v. Bader* (1999), 118 B.C.A.C. 204 [especially at the appellate level]; *Nordlander v. Nordlander Estate (Executor and Trustee of)*, [1999] O.J. No. 117 (Gen. Div.) [but reduced by the court]; *Lang Michener Lawrence & Shaw v. Hui*, [1999] B.C.J. No. 2505 (S.C.) [unusual legal issues]; *Pharmacia Inc. v. Canada (Minister of National Health and Welfare)*, [1999] F.C.J. No. 1770 (T.D.) [online research necessary because of a "change of research needs and techniques"]; *Ager v. International Brotherhood of Locomotive Engineers*, [1999] F.C.J. No. 909 (C.A.) [allowed, but reduced due to lack of evidence on necessity of online research]; *Keddy v. Western Regional Health Board*, [1999] N.S.J. No. 464 (T.D.) [reasonable amount for Quicklaw searches allowed, online research is generally cost-effective]; *Maison des pâtes Pasta Bella Inc. v. Olivieri Foods Ltd.*, [1998] F.C.J. 1171 (T.D.) [online searches allowed as reasonable, represent a change in research needs and techniques]; *Atkinson v. McGregor* (1998), 66 Alta. L.R. (3d) 289, 227 A.R. 376, 23 C.P.C. (4th) 166 (Q.B.) [*Atkinson* cited to Alta. L.R.]; *Canada v. W. Ralston & Co. (Canada) Inc.*, [1997] F.C.J. No. 291 (T.D.); *C & B Vacation Properties v. Canada*, [1997] F.C.J. No. 1660 (T.D.); *Marchese (c.o.b. Dooney's Café) v. Hix*, [1997] O.J. No. 3186 (Gen. Div.); *LDR Contracting Inc. v. Filion*, [1996] O.J. No. 2768 (Gen. Div.); *Gaudet v. Mair*, [1996] B.C.J. No. 2547 (Prov. Ct.); *Canastrand Industries Ltd. v. Lara S (The)*, [1995] F.C.J. No. 1157 (T.D.) [computer-aided research was essential]; *Parsons v. Canada Safeway Ltd.*, [1995] B.C.J. No. 1947 (S.C.) [Quicklaw disbursements of $214.30 allowed for occupier's liability research, many unreported decisions are available only on Quicklaw]; *CNR v. Norsk Pacific Steamship Co.*, [1994] F.C.J. 1293 (T.D.) [costs allowed for online searches where the decision to incure the cost was a prudent representation of the client, even if nothing of use was found in the search]; *Lau v. Tung*, [1994] O.J. No. 1873 (Gen. Div.) [Quicklaw search charges allowed, "reasonably necessary for the conduct" of litigation]; *Denzler v. Aull* (1994), 19 O.R. (3d) 507, 29 C.P.C. (3d) 99 (Gen. Div.) [Quicklaw disbursements of $118.55 allowed on solicitor-client cost award]; *Prouvost S.A. v. Munsingwear Inc.*, [1994] F.C.J. No. 1289 (T.D.); *Wenden v. Trikha* (1992), 1 Alta. L.R. (3d) 283, 124 A.R. 1, 6 C.P.C. (3d) 15 (Q.B.) [allowed for the physical cost of putting information into a computer and transmitting it to counsel]; *Kawartha Feed Mills (1980) Inc. v. Goldie*, [1992] O.J. No. 3739 (Gen. Div.); *Holmes (Re)* (1991), 80 Alta. L.R. (2d) 373, 121 A.R. 170, 7 C.B.R. (3d) 82 (Q.B.) [disbursements for computer research allowed]; *Westco Storage Ltd. v. Inter City Gas Utilities Ltd.*, [1988] 4 W.W.R. 396, 53 Man. R. (2d) 130 (Q.B.) [computer research costs of $1,593.52 held to be reasonable]; *Re Solicitor*, [1973] 1 O.R. 870 (T.O.) [fifty hours of research reasonable for complicated criminal defence]. See also Mark M. Orkin, *The Law of Costs*, 2d ed., looseleaf (Aurora, ON: Canada Law Book, 1987) ¶ 219.6(9).

5   [2001] O.J. No. 2337 (S.C.J.).

head consumed in the time-keeper's hourly rate and simply the cost of doing business. It is an interesting argument.

I believe that these particular disbursement expenses are created for a specific client in a specific proceeding touching on issues and law specifically relating to that client's case. Quick Law is generally time and cost effective and efficient. The incurrence of the expense is neither unreasonable nor unnecessary.

Involvement with this cost is specifically for the benefit of the client. All reasonable and necessary disbursement expenses within the four corners of this litigation should be assessable. Quick Law research disbursement expense is not overhead expense within the meaning and intent of a solicitor and client award of costs.[6]

Likewise, in *Boots*[7] the court allowed Quicklaw disbursements on the basis that the research was necessary and the costs were reasonable:

As to the matter of disbursements, and as I explained at the assessment, an issue has arisen from time to time about computer research costs, in this case Quicklaw searches, and whether they are distinguishable from the overhead costs of a law firm, the premise being that overhead costs are already reflected in counsel fees. I am satisfied from counsel's explanation, however, that the research conducted in respect of this particular counterclaim was necessary and the costs claimed by the Defendant were reasonably incurred. The other disbursements are supported by the evidence contained in the affidavit of K. Melanson sworn on July 5, 1999. They appear to be reasonable and necessary in the circumstances of these proceedings and are allowed with the following exceptions . . . .[8]

In *Atkinson*[9] the court thought that online research, where necessary, should be promoted within the industry by allowing the recovery of online search fees:

I agree with the decision in *Parsons*: charges for Quicklaw are a cost of doing business for lawyers. Since a law firm might charge a disbursement for legal research done by an outside agency; it does seem odd that a law firm that has the capacity to do in-house research cannot claim the computer charges. Indeed, as I said in *Kelly v. Lundgard*, a memorandum on costs issued on 1997 [sic] which did not find its

---

6   *Ibid.* ¶ 56–58.
7   Above note 4.
8   *Ibid.* ¶ 8.
9   Above note 4.

way into Quicklaw, it is a cost which should be encouraged because it improves the quality of research at a very minimal cost to the client. I issued that decision as a Memorandum, and not Reasons, because I was of the view that the issue of charges for computer research was not a new topic in Alberta, having already been discussed in *Wenden*. In *Kelly*, I said:

> . . . there is a strong public policy argument for supporting com-
> puter research and by making that support practical by awarding
> costs for access to computerized legal research. Done responsibly,
> computer access to data bases will give lawyers, and therefore lit-
> igants, much quicker access to applicable case law than can be
> achieved by the traditional, labour intensive, methods of legal
> research. The dramatic savings in time spent result in major sav-
> ings to the clients. In addition, computerized legal research gives
> access to current case law, months before any of those cases
> would be published by traditional means. It may be too soon to
> declare that the normative standard for legal research is comput-
> er research, but the day on which courts will make that pro-
> nouncement cannot be far off.
>
> That is not to say, however, that costs for computer
> research, like all other costs, will never be excessive. We are
> entitled to assume that lawyers have not only some general
> background in law, but that they have some general back-
> ground in obtaining information from electronic data bases
> and are using appropriate means to acquire that information.

Moreover, as pointed out in *Parsons*, Quicklaw contains many decisions which are not otherwise reported . . . .[10]

To the contrary, however, are several cases in which the courts have not allowed legal research costs or have reduced the costs to be award-ed for legal research where the research was held to be unnecessary or not conducted in a reasonable manner.[11] In particular, Alberta courts

---

10   Above note 4 at 293–94 (emphasis added).

11   *Milsom v. Corporate Computers Inc.*, [2003] 9 W.W.R. 269, 2003 ABQB 609 [dis-
     bursement to a legal research firm not allowed, cost already built into tariff in
     the form of trial preparation]; *Mitchell v. Canada (Minister of National Revenue)*,
     2003 FCA 386 [Quicklaw searches allowed but not the cost of outside counsel
     retained to conduct the searches]; *Boyne Clarke v. Steel*, [2002] N.S.J. No. 186
     (T.D.) [online search charges not allowed, research involved Supreme Court of
     Canada cases and other materials easily available in print]; *Bank of Montreal v.
     Scotia Capital Inc.* (2002), 211 N.S.R. (2d) 107, 2002 NSSC 274 [not appropriate
     for party and party costs]; *Rankin v. Menzies*, [2002] O.J. No. 1280 (S.C.J.)

tend to be the most restrictive on the basis that online charges are already covered in that part of the costs tariffs dealing with trial preparation. Some of these decisions where online search charges have not been allowed must be taken with some caution. There is a difference between not allowing online search charges where the cost is unreasonable or unnecessary (something which makes sense) versus not allowing online search charges simply because they represent some "new fangled technology" (something which is backwards-looking and out of touch with the way law is and will be practiced). In some of the decisions where the court refused to order the losing party or client to pay the cost of the online research charges a comparison is made to the general overhead costs that lawyers or law firms carry to maintain a print law library, costs that are not generally charged to a client on spe-

---

[Quicklaw charges not allowed where student credited with 15.8 hours of legal research under tariff]; *Jeff (Guardian ad litem of) v. Kozak*, 2002 BCSC 103 [Quicklaw searches not properly attributable to losing party where purpose of the search was to check out judge assigned to the hearing]; *Edmonton (City) v. Lovat Tunnel Equipment Inc.*, [2002] A.J. No. 1440 (Q.B) [computer search charges not allowed since included in the costs awarded for trial preparation]; *Standquist v. Coneco Equipment*, 2000 ABCA 138 [online search charges not allowed, a substitute for lawyer's work covered elsewhere in tariff]; *Hughes v. Gillingham*, 1999 ABQB 747 [not allowed since a technological substitute for the time spent in trial preparation]; *Kuchma v. 1028719 Ontario Ltd. (c.o.b. Ryland Homes)*, [1999] O.J. No. 3068 (S.C.J.) [amounts not shown to be reasonable]; *Nebete Inc. v. Sanelli Foods Ltd.*, [1999] O.J. No. 859 (Gen. Div.) [Quicklaw disbursements not allowed since should be included in the lawyer's hourly rate]; *Elliott v. Nicholson* (1999), 179 N.S.R. (2d) 264 (S.C.) [part of office overhead]; *Hennings v. Hennings* (1999), 49 R.F.L. (4th) 295 (S.C.J.) [not allowed due to lack of evidence regarding whether necessary]; *Zwicker v. Schubert*, [1999] 12 W.W.R. 273, (1999) 184 Sask. R. 35 (Q.B.) [no reasons given]; *Royal Bank of Canada v. Hayter*, [1999] O.J. No. 1621 (Gen. Div.) [no reasons given]; *Moin v. Collingwood (Township)*, [1998] O.J. No. 1522 (Gen. Div.) [no reasons given]; *Dornan Petroleum Inc. v. Petro-Canada* (1997), 199 A.R. 334 (Q.B.); *Lalli v. Chawla* (1997), 53 Alta. L.R. (3d) 121, 203 A.R. 27 (Q.B.) [not allowed in this particular case]; *Powar v. British Columbia (Ministry of Transportation and Highways)*, [1995] B.C.J. No. 706 (S.C.); *Re Briand* (1995), 10 E.T.R. (2d) 99 (Ont. Gen. Div.), aff'd (1999), 122 O.A.C. 295, (1999) 28 E.T.R. (2d) 302 (Div. Ct.) [legal research costs for estate work reduced as not being justified]; *Sidorsky v. CFCN Communications Ltd.* (1995), 167 A.R. 181, 35 C.P.C. (3d) 239, 27 Alta. L.R. (3d) 296 (Q.B.), rev'd in part on other grounds (1998), 206 A.R. 382, 156 W.A.C. 382, 53 Alta. L.R. (3d) 255 (C.A.) [*Sidorsky* cited to C.P.C.]; *Argentia Beach (Summer Village) v. Warshawski and Conroy* (1990), 106 A.R. 222 (Alta.C.A.) [not allowed here, but might be allowed due to extent or difficulty of research]; *Knight v. Millman Estate* (1990), 66 Man. R. (2d) 275 (Q.B.); *Lee v. Leeming* (1985), 61 A.R. 18 (Q.B.) [no reasons given].

cific files. But there is a major difference between the general costs of maintaining a print law library, which will be used repeatedly for a variety of research tasks over time, versus a specific charge for a specific client at a particular point in time, a charge that is related to the file at hand and involves research that is not likely of benefit to other lawyers or clients at the firm. As such, online search charges are not like the costs to maintain a print law library and should be recoverable.[12] Moreover, it has been argued that not allowing recovery of these online charges may result in unequal access to the law since poorer clients may be reluctant to incur these online charges if they will not be reimbursed by the losing party if successful at trial.[13] Finally, the commercial online databases are sometimes the only source of case law or other information or can be the only effective way of locating particular items (through advanced online searches that would be impossible to replicate using print resources); in these situations, the costs of online searches should clearly be recoverable.

Thus, where a party is seeking to recover the solicitor-client costs of research or the disbursement cost of online searches, it will be necessary to show that the research conducted was reasonable and necessary. Even though there are these contradictory decisions regarding whether online computer search charges should be allowed as taxable disbursements to be paid by the losing party, it is clear that courts will allow such charges, and the costs of conducting any type of print or online legal research, where it can be established that the research was necessary and that the costs or time incurred was reasonable under the circumstances given the applicable issues facing the lawyer. In seeking to recover legal research costs and online search disbursements, the lawyer should be prepared to lead evidence regarding the necessity and complexity of the research, the advantages of using online research databases for the research, and the agreement of the client to incur such costs.

B. SOME BASIC LEGAL RESEARCH TECHNIQUES

If legal research is an essential skill for all lawyers, what are some of the legal research techniques that researchers should use to help ensure the

---

12   Peters, above note 3 at 85.
13   *Ibid.*

quality of their legal advice? This section of the book sets out some basic legal research techniques, all of which are touched upon or discussed in more detail throughout the book.

Primary resources versus secondary resources. As a starting point, it helps to understand that law-related information can be divided into two basic categories: primary legal resources versus secondary legal resources. Primary legal resources consist of legislation (statutes and regulations) and case law (the decisions of courts and administrative tribunals). Secondary legal resources, on the other hand, are background materials that comment on or help explain how to use or find primary legal resources. Secondary legal resources include such things as textbooks, legal journals, encyclopedias, case law digests, dictionaries, word and phrases services, Web guides, and current awareness tools. While secondary legal resources may carry some persuasive value with courts, it is ordinarily only primary legal material that will bind a court and directly affect a person's legal rights. Thus, just as a doctor will not diagnose a patient without first conducting a physical examination of the patient, a lawyer should not render a legal opinion to a client without having at least consulted primary legal resources. Having said this, however, smart legal researchers will *start* their legal research with secondary legal resources (because of their broad overview and identification of relevant cases or legislation) and then *finish* their research by consulting and verifying primary sources of law.

Use of dictionaries and words and phrases. Legal dictionaries and words and phrases services are discussed in more detail in Chapter 2 and are useful for not only defining Latin and legal phrases, but in some cases, for also finding cases or legislation in which particular terms have been defined. For those who cannot afford the cost of the hardbound version of these dictionaries, the publishers of these dictionaries usually offer softcover, abridged versions of their dictionaries at a cheaper price (see Chapter 2 for a list of some of these pocket dictionaries).

Identifying the issue; starting broad. A critical first step in legal research is correctly identifying the relevant factual and legal issues that one must research. Sometimes, the issue will be obvious or specific, such as "On what grounds can the police search a car trunk without a warrant?" In other cases, the issue may be less obvious and require some analysis to ensure that one has identified the relevant areas of law. It is also important to keep the initial analysis and research broad. There can be a danger in too quickly narrowing one's legal research in case one has overlooked other possible relevant considerations.

Legal research as a three-step process. Another useful technique is to realize that most legal research involves a three-step process, regardless of the particular resources being used:

1. *Finding.* The first step involves finding the relevant information by using an index, table of contents, catalogue, or other finding tool for print resources and by typing in your keywords or search criteria for online resources.
2. *Reading.* The second step is to then read the relevant material found using step one above. The information read in this step could include a case, a statute, or a passage from a book or encyclopedia, for example.
3. *Noting up.* The third and final step in most legal research is to "note up" the information consulted in step two above. Noting up involves verifying your information by ensuring that the information, be it a case, a statute, or a passage from an encyclopedia, has not been reversed or amended, as the case may be. The technique of noting up is discussed in more detail later in the book. For now, it is sufficient to realize that noting up might entail different procedures or techniques, depending on the particular resources being used and whether it is in print or online format. For some print, looseleaf resources, such as the *Canadian Encyclopedic Digest*, noting up involves checking supplemental yellow pages at the front of the tab or book. Other material involves consulting a cumulative supplemental volume. Many American resources have a "pocket" on the inside of the back cover that contains a cumulative paper update. Online resources, on the other hand, are often already up-to-date or simply offer a "button" or "link" on which one can click to note up the information being researched.

Online computer skills. Like it or not, the world has moved in the direction of computer technology and lawyers increasingly will need to become computer literate to access online information. Fortunately, with the improvement in computer software, computers are becoming more intuitive to use. Basic keyboarding skills, the ability to use and control a mouse, and a flexible attitude are the basic online computer skills that lawyers and others conducting legal research will need to have.

Practise, practise, practise. For most people, legal research and writing is an applied skill that only improves through regular use and practise. Reading a book about how to play the piano or attending a lecture on playing the piano will not make you a good piano player unless you put to use what you have read or learned through hands-on practice. It is the same with legal research and writing.

The legal research process. There is a tendency to treat legal research as a discrete activity involving various techniques on how to use law books. In reality, however, legal research is not just the application of techniques in using a particular resource but the process that one takes in first correctly analyzing the facts and issues related to the problem being researched and correctly applying the research to those facts and issues. Unlike in law school when legal research problems are often given in discrete subject areas (a "criminal law" problem, for example), real-life problems do not come bundled in a box with all of the relevant facts and issues set out in advance.

The legal research process is often described in the legal literature as a multi-step process that requires the researcher to think systematically about what is being researched. A common approach is to break the research process into the following steps, described by Fitzgerald as the "FILAC" approach (based on the first letter for each of the five steps):[14]

Facts: The first step in this legal research process is to correctly identify the relevant facts. In some research situations, the relevant facts will be obvious or will be provided and can be taken as a given. In other situations, the relevant facts may not be so obvious and may only be identified after one has gotten further along in the research process, thereby requiring the researcher to maintain a flexible attitude and a willingness to continually "run through" this research process in search for new, different information. The relevance of facts will also vary from problem to problem. In a breach of contract problem, the age of one of the parties is likely irrelevant (unless the party is an infant) but in a wrongful dismissal problem, the age of the employee may be relevant if the employee is older, a long-time employee, and unlikely to be easily re-hired. Section E of Chapter 11 discusses writing legal research memos and suggests that an important aspect of a research memo is briefly setting out the relevant facts so that the person reading the memo can have some context for the opinion that is being provided.

---

14   Maureen F. Fitzgerald, *Legal Problem Solving: Reasoning, Research and Writing*, 3d ed. (Toronto: Butterworths, 2004) at 2–4, c. 2, 3, 10. See also Christopher G. Wren & Jill Robinson Wren, *The Legal Research Manual: A Game Plan for Legal Research and Analysis*, 2d ed. (Madison, WI: Legal Education Publishing, 1986).

Issues: After the relevant facts have been identified in step 1, the next step is for the researcher to identify the relevant issues to be researched. These issues will quite obviously arise from the facts identified and should ordinarily be stated in the form of legal questions that the client needs answered. In some research situations, the issue may be fairly broad — is there a common law tort for the invasion of privacy in Ontario? More often, the issue to be identified will be narrower and specific to the client's situation: what are the procedures, if any, to appeal a decision by a University to expel a student for an alleged violation of the University's e-mail policies? Like the situation in identifying relevant facts, identifying relevant issues can be a fluid process where the issues may change slightly as the research is undertaken and new approaches or issues are identified.

Law: Once the facts and issues are identified, the researcher must find the relevant law, a process described in detail throughout this book. Ordinarily, it is prudent to begin the finding process using secondary resources (such as books, journal articles, and encyclopedias) to gain a broad overview of the applicable law. This is then followed by narrowing in on relevant primary sources of law (legislation and case law). The competent researcher keeps a checklist or notes of the resources consulted to make it easier to later update the research or to allow a different researcher to carry on the work.

Analysis/Application of law to facts: The next step in the legal research process is to apply the relevant law to the facts to analyze the way in which a judge would decide the matter given the same set of facts. At this stage, if the researcher is preparing a memo, it is usually wise to analyze the facts and the law from multiple viewpoints, not just from the viewpoint of the client. This allows one to anticipate the arguments to be made by the opposing party and to assess the strengths and weaknesses of those arguments.

Conclusions: If the foregoing steps have been followed, it should ordinarily be quite easy to answer the questions raised in the legal research problem. In some cases, the researcher can be relatively confident of the conclusions reached by speaking in terms of a "strong likelihood" of success. In other situations, the law may be unsettled and the conclusions reached must be couched in appropriate terms that identify the unsettled nature of the law and the relevant factors that might influence the outcome one way or the other.

Understanding the legal research process is a very important part of being an effective legal researcher. There is a short legal research checklist in Chapter 10, section E to help researchers be systematic in the approach they take to legal research. Another important aspect of legal research is to understand correct legal citation.

C. LEGAL CITATION

Legal citation involves standardized rules for the way in which one refers to court cases, legislation, and other legal materials. For example, in Canada, it is standard to cite a court case in the following pattern: case name (in italics), year (in square brackets or round parentheses, depending on the reporter), volume number of reporter, reporter name, reporter series (if any), page number of the first page of the decision, and then the jurisdiction and level of court:

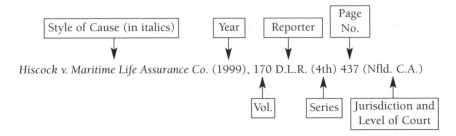

Standardized legal citation is important for several reasons: (i) information from the citation can be used to quickly identify whether the material is worth pursuing, for example, by looking at the year of the case and the level of court; (ii) the citation can be used to easily retrieve the full text of the material from the shelf or from an online database such as Quicklaw; and (iii) using proper citation lends credibility to your written work and makes it easier for readers to find the information being cited.

In Canada, the leading style guide is the *Canadian Guide to Uniform Legal Citation*,[15] known by its more common name — the "McGill Guide" — since it is a publication by the editors of the *McGill Law Journal*. In the United States, legal researchers use *The Bluebook: A Uniform System of Citation* (the "Bluebook").[16] Rules between the McGill

---

15   5th ed. (Toronto: Carswell, 2002).

16   17th ed. (Cambridge, MA: Harvard Law Review Association, 2000). There is an online equivalent of *The Bluebook* called *Introduction to Basic Legal Citation* — see <http://www.law.cornell.edu/citation/>. An alternative American citation guide that is gaining popularity due to its simpler approach is Darby Dickerson,

Guide and the Bluebook vary and are fairly specific to each jurisdiction. The McGill Guide does explain how Canadian legal researchers should cite American and British materials and should therefore usually be used as a standard by Canadian legal researchers.

The McGill Guide covers a wide range of citation questions, including rules on footnoting (Rule 1.3), citing legislation (Chapter 2), citing case law (Chapter 3), citing government documents (Chapter 4), citing international materials (Chapter 5), and citing secondary materials (Chapter 6). The McGill Guide is published as one book in both English and French and contains a number of useful appendices, including information on courts, court levels, case law reporters, and their abbreviations. For matters of citation not included in the McGill Guide, refer to more general style guides such as *The Redbook: A Manual on Legal Style*,[17] *The Chicago Manual of Style*,[18] or *A Manual for Writers of Term Papers, Theses, and Dissertations*.[19]

In recent years, especially with the proliferation of online case law, there has been a move towards "neutral citation" that provides for a standard citation for court decisions by case name, year, court, decision number, and paragraph numbers:

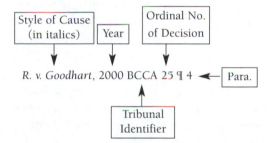

The Canadian Citation Committee has developed these neutral citation formats, which are being adopted by Canadian courts and which are expected to be more widely seen over the next few years.[20] In addition, the Supreme Court of Canada has special rules governing the citation of electronic versions of decisions of the Supreme Court of Canada and

---

ALWD Citiation Manual: A Professional System of Citation, 2d ed. (New York: Aspen, 2003).

17   (St. Paul, MN: West Group, 2002).

18   15th ed. (Chicago: University of Chicago Press, 2003).

19   Kate L. Turabian, 6th ed., revised by John Grossman & Alice Bennett (Chicago: University of Chicago Press, 1996).

20   See the Web page of the Canadian Citation Committee at <http://www.lexum.umontreal.ca/ccc-ccr/index_en.html>.

other courts.[21] Quicklaw also provides information on citing material found on Quicklaw databases.[22]

What follows next in this section is a list of answers to the most frequently asked questions about legal citation:

Do I need to italicize the "v." in the style of cause?

The "v." (or "c." in French) in the style of cause is an abbreviation for "versus" (*Smith v. Jones*) and is pronounced "v" or "and." Rule 3.2.2 of the McGill Guide now authorizes (for the first time) the reader to italicize the "v.", something which many authors and publishers already did since the names of the parties in the style of cause must also be italicized, making it easier while word processing to also italicize the v. (or "c." in French) as well.

When citing a case, when do I use square brackets vs. round parentheses for the year?

This is, somewhat surprisingly, the most confusing citation issue for law students and those new to legal research. **Round parentheses** are used for the year when citing cases that are reported in case law reporters that are published by the volume number — in other words, use round parentheses to indicate the year of the decision: McGill Guide, Rule 3.2.3.1. The comma follows the round parentheses. Example (emphasis added): *Bingo Enterprises Ltd. v. Plaxton* **(1986)**, 41 Man. R. (2d) 19 (C.A.). **Square brackets** are used for the year when citing cases that are reported in case law reporters that are published annually or by the year — in other words, use square brackets to indicate the year of the reporter: McGill Guide, Rule 3.2.3.2. The comma precedes the square brackets. Example (emphasis added): *R. v. Noble*, **[1997]** 1 S.C.R. 874.

Table 1.1 sets out a list of some popular Canadian case law reporters that use either square brackets or round parentheses:

---

21   Supreme Court of Canada, *Bulletin* (6 October 2000), online: University of Montreal <http://www.lexum.umontreal.ca/csc-scc/en/bul/2000/html/00-10-06.bul.html>.

22   See online: LexisNexis Canada <http://www.lexisnexis.ca/ql/en/about/citations.html>.

Table 1.1
Sample Citations: Square Brackets vs. Round Parentheses

Popular Canadian Case Law Reporters Published by Year [Use Square Brackets]	
Reporter	**Example**
Supreme Court Reports [1923–current]	*Douglas v. Tucker*, [1952] 1 S.C.R. 275
Federal Court Reports [1923–current]	*"Donnacona II" (The) v. Montship Lines Ltd.*, [1961] Ex. C.R. 249 or *Feherguard Products Ltd. v. Rocky's of B.C. Leisure Ltd.*, [1993] 3 F.C. 619 (C.A.)
Dominion Law Reports [1923–1955]	*Canadian Performing Rights Society Ltd. v. Ming Yee*, [1943] 4 D.L.R. 732 (Alta. Dist. Ct.)
Western Weekly Reports [1923–1955] [1971–current]	*Bradshaw v. Epp*, [1937] 3 W.W.R. 577 (Man. C.A.) or *Waldron v. Royal Bank*, [1991] 4 W.W.R. 289 (B.C.C.A.)
Ontario Reports [1931–1973]	*Mitchell v. Jolly*, [1960] O.R. 470 (C.A.)
Popular Canadian Case Law Reporters Published by Volume (Use Round Parentheses)	
Reporter	**Example**
Supreme Court Reports (1867–1922)	*Francis v. Allan* (1918), 57 S.C.R. 373
Exchequer Court Reports (1875–1922)	*Canadian Vickers Ltd. v. "Susquehanna" (The)* (1919), 19 Ex. C.R. 116 (C.A.)
Dominion Law Reports (Vol. 1, 1912–Vol. 64, 1922) (Vol. 1, 1956–Vol. 70, 1968) (2d) (Vol. 1, 1969–Vol. 150, 1984) (3d) (Vol. 1, 1985–current) (4th)	*Pratt v. Lovelace* (1913), 11 D.L.R. 385 (Sask. C.A.) *Morrison v. Mills* (1963), 38 D.L.R. (2d) 489 (Alta. T.D.) *R. v. Zaduk* (1978), 98 D.L.R. (3d) 133 (Ont. C.A.) *Wadsworth v. Hayes* (1996), 132 D.L.R. (4th) 410 (Alta. C.A.)
Western Weekly Reports (Vol. 1, 1912–Vol. 10, 1916) (Vol. 1, 1951–Vol. 75, 1970) (N.S.)	*Drinkle v. Regal Shoe Co.* (1914), 7 W.W.R. 194 (B.C.S.C.) *Gordon v. Hipwell (No. 2)* (1952), 5 W.W.R. (N.S.) 635 (B.C.C.A.)
Ontario Reports (1974–current)	*Boehmers v. 794561 Ontario Inc.* (1995), 21 O.R. (3d) 771 (C.A.)
Note 1: This chart is not an exhaustive list of reporters.	
Note 2: Some reporters, such as the *Dominion Law Reports*, *Ontario Reports*, and *Western Weekly Reports*, have changed over time from publishing by year [square brackets] to publishing by volume (round parentheses).	
Note 3: All Quicklaw unreported decisions use square brackets around the year of the decision — example: *Parsons v. Canada Safeway Ltd.*, [1995] B.C.J. No. 1947 (S.C.).	

What are parallel citations and do I need to use them?

Many important cases are published in print in multiple case law reporters (and online). A decision on tort law from the Supreme Court of Canada that arose in British Columbia would likely be reported in the *Supreme Court Reports*, the *Dominion Law Reports*, the *British Columbia Law Reports*, and the *Canadian Cases on the Law of Torts*. Rule 3.2.8 of the McGill Guide requires the researcher to include citations to multiple case law reports where possible. This is done as a courtesy to the reader who may have access to only one of the several case law reporters listed in the citation. Thus, in a parallel citation, what is being cited is one single decision, a decision that has been reported in a string or list of multiple case law reporters. It is not necessary to consult each version of the case in the list of reporters. An example of a parallel citation is as follows: *Wenden v. Trikha* (1992), 1 Alta. L.R. (3d) 283, 124 A.R. 1, 6 C.P.C. (3d) 15 (Q.B.) — in this example, the same trial decision in *Wenden v. Trikha* is reported in three different case law reporters (i.e., the *Alberta Law Reports*, the *Alberta Reports*, and *Carswell's Practice Cases*).

How do I cite unreported decisions?

Increasingly, lawyers and judges regularly use and cite decisions from online databases. If the case is unreported (i.e., not available in a print case law reporter), the McGill Guide sets out rules on how to cite unreported decisions, whether by citing to the court file (Rule 3.2.12) or to an online database (Rule 3.11). The format follows the general pattern for reported cases (style of cause, year, "source," and jurisdiction and level of court). Unfortunately, the McGill Guide does not provide examples for every possible source of online law-related materials.

A typical decision on Quicklaw that is not reported in a print case law reporter would be cited thus (where "O.J." represents the Ontario Judgments database on which the case was found and the "No. 1723" being the unique number Quicklaw has assigned to that case for that database for that year):[23]

R. v. *Zborovsky*, [1992] O.J. No. 1723 (Prov. Ct.).

I used an online database to find a case — can I cite to only the online version even if the case is also published in print?

Where a case is available in print and online, Rule 3.1 of the McGill Guide requires the researcher to cite to the print version (and also to

---

23   As discussed in note 22 above, Quicklaw's Web site has a fairly exhaustive list of how to cite a wide range of materials found on its databases.

cite to the electronic database). The rationale for this is obvious: not all readers will have access to the online version and not all online versions of material allow for easy "pinpoint" citations if there are no paragraph numbers provided in the online version; as a courtesy to the reader, therefore, one should prefer a citation to print material. The suggestion in the McGill Guide to cite to both the print and the online version is good but is not always done in practice since most sophisticated researchers will know (or readily assume) whether a particular case in print is available online, so it is usually sufficient to cite to only the print version.

A few final tips on legal citation:

- Don't guess and don't be lazy — look it up in the McGill Guide if you are not certain.
- You can often safely rely upon the way in which a reputable publisher has cited a case or a statute in its publication by simply copying how the publisher has cited the material. If your document is important, however, check the McGill Guide.
- Appendix G (case law reporters) and Appendix H (periodicals and yearbooks) to the McGill Guide provide examples of how to abbreviate titles.

D. COPYRIGHT ISSUES

Related to issues of citation are issues of copyright law. In Canada, copyright law is governed by the *Copyright Act*.[24] Under that Act, the owner of the copyright in a literary work (i.e,. a legal textbook) has the sole right to produce or reproduce the work or any substantial part thereof in any material form.[25] Users are given relatively limited rights to copy protected works. One exemption to copyright is the defence of "fair dealing" for the purpose of research or private study (with various conditions attached).[26] For legal researchers, the issue that therefore arises is determining when permission from the copyright owner is needed for the use of law-related resources.

For government works, the issue is affected by the concept of Crown copyright, a concept that the government retains copyright in any work that has been prepared or published by or under the direc-

---

24   R.S.C. 1985, c. C-42.
25   *Ibid.*, s. 3(1).
26   *Ibid.*, s. 29.

tion or control of Her Majesty or any government department.[27] The notion that the government would insist upon Crown copyright over legislation and cases has been criticized by academic commentators.[28] A more preferable viewpoint would be that all works produced under authority of the government are in the public domain for the benefit of all to use, subject possibly to the right of the government to claim any "moral rights" in its works when necessary to protect the accuracy or representation of the work.[29] Alternatively, if the government insists on maintaining a Crown copyright in its works, an argument could likely be made on philosophical grounds that all citizens, as taxpayers, have an implicit, royalty-free licence to use government works.

Fortunately, the Canadian federal government has largely resolved some of these issues as they affect legal research materials through its issuance of the *Reproduction of Federal Law Order*,[30] which allows cases and legislation issued under authority of the government to be freely used so long as any reproductions are accurate and not represented as official versions:[31]

> Anyone may, without charge or request for permission, reproduce enactments and consolidations of enactments of the Government of Canada, and decisions and reasons for decisions of federally-constituted courts and administrative tribunals, provided due diligence is exercised in ensuring the accuracy of the materials reproduced and the reproduction is not represented as an official version.

For private legal publishers, the issues are slightly different. Most, if not all, of these publishers will own copyright in their textbooks, case law reporters, and other law-related publications. Technically, unless one

---

27   *Ibid.*, s. 12.

28   See, e.g., David Vaver, *Intellectual Property Law* (Toronto: Irwin Law, 1997) at 59–60. Available on Quicklaw (database identifier: VAIP).

29   This is in fact consistent with Recommendations 10, 11, and 12 of the House of Commons Standing Committee on Communications and Culture, *Report of the Sub-Committee on the Revision of Copyright: A Charter of Rights for Creators* (Ottawa: Supply & Services, 1985) at 10–12.

30   SI/97-5.

31   The Ontario government also has a policy on copyright of legal materials that allows any person "to reproduce the text and images contained in the statutes, regulations and judicial decisions without seeking permission and without charge" but the materials "must be reproduced accurately and the reproduction must not be represented as an official version." A copyright notice in favour of the Queens Printer for Ontario must also be provided. See Ontario, "Policy on Copyright on Legal Materials," online: Government of Ontario <http://www.gov.on.ca/MBS/english/common/copypolicy.html>.

were able to rely upon the "fair dealing" provisions of the Act — which are relatively narrow — it would be necessary, for example, to obtain the permission of the applicable publisher to photocopy material for court or to cite passages in one's court factum from a publisher's textbook. As a practical matter, legal publishers have not pursued copyright infringement claims against individual lawyers or law firms, although Access Copyright,[32] the national copyright collective in Canada that represents authors, has in the past announced a collective photocopying licence that it intends to negotiate with law firms that would, for a negotiated flat fee, give permission for lawyers and employees at the firm to photocopy from published works. The Federation of Law Societies of Canada, however, has taken a cautious approach to such licences.[33]

Of particular interest to the legal community is the recent Supreme Court of Canada decision arising from a ten-year dispute between several Canadian legal publishers and the Law Society of Upper Canada.[34] The publishers alleged, among other things, that the photocopying service provided by the Law Society's law library infringed the copyright of these legal publishers.

Chief Justice McLachlin, speaking for the Court, ruled largely in favour of the Law Society. It was held that, although copyright existed in the publishers' works under consideration, the copying done by the Great Library was fair dealing with the publishers' works. In addition, the Court ruled that the Great Library did not authorize copyright infringement by the mere fact of supplying self-service photocopiers in its library. The Court also ruled that fax transmissions of photocopy requests to individual patrons were not "communications to the public."

On the issue of the extent of copyright in the court decisions and headnotes, McLachlin C.J. adopted a test of "skill and judgment" in defining the degree of "originality" a work must have to be subject to copyright:

> For a work to be "original" within the meaning of the *Copyright Act*, it must be more than a mere copy of another work. At the same time, it need not be creative, in the sense of being novel or unique. What

---

32 See online: Access Copyright <http://www.accesscopyright.ca>.

33 The Federation of Law Societies of Canada has information for the legal profession on copyright matters on the Web page of its Copyright Committee at <http://www.flsc.ca/en/committees/copyrightNotices.asp>.

34 *CCH Canadian Ltd. v. Law Society of Upper Canada*, 2004 SCC 13, rev'g [2002] 4 F.C. 213, 224 F.T.R. 111, 2002 FCA 187 (C.A.), rev'g (1999), 169 F.T.R. 1, 179 D.L.R. (4th) 609, 2 C.P.R. (4th) 129. See Daniel J. Gervais, "Canadian Copyright Law Post-CCH" (2004) 18 I.P.J. 131.

is required to attract copyright protection in the expression of an idea is an exercise of skill and judgment. By skill, I mean the use of one's knowledge, developed aptitude or practised ability in producing the work. By judgment, I mean the use of one's capacity for discernment or ability to form an opinion or evaluation by comparing different possible options in producing the work. This exercise of skill and judgment will necessarily involve intellectual effort. The exercise of skill and judgment required to produce the work must not be so trivial that it could be characterized as a purely mechanical exercise. For example, any skill and judgment that might be involved in simply changing the font of a work to produce "another" work would be too trivial to merit copyright protection as an "original" work.[35]

In looking at the exercise of "skill and judgment" needed to compile reported judicial decisions, the Court concluded that the compilation of the headnotes, case summaries, topical index, and reported judicial decisions in issue met this test and that the legal materials in this case were "original" works covered by copyright.[36]

On the issue of whether the Law Society authorized infringement of copyright by providing self-service photocopiers in the Great Library, however, the Court ruled in favour of the Great Library:

[A] person does not authorize copyright infringement by authorizing the mere use of equipment (such as photocopiers) that could be used to infringe copyright. In fact, courts should presume that a person who authorizes an activity does so only so far as it is in accordance with the law. Although the Court of Appeal assumed that the photocopiers were being used to infringe copyright, I think it is equally plausible that the patrons using the machines were doing so in a lawful manner.

. . . . The Law Society's posting of the notice over the photocopiers does not rebut the presumption that a person authorizes an activity only so far as it is in accordance with the law. Given that the Law Society is responsible for regulating the legal profession in Ontario, it is more logical to conclude that the notice was posted for the purpose of reminding the Great Library's patrons that copyright law governs the making of photocopies in the library.

Finally, even if there were evidence of the photocopiers having been used to infringe copyright, the Law Society lacks sufficient control over the Great Library's patrons to permit the conclusion that it sanctioned, approved or countenanced the infringement. The Law

35   *Ibid.* ¶ 116.
36   *Ibid.* ¶ 29–36.

Society and Great Library patrons are not in a master-servant or employer-employee relationship such that the Law Society can be said to exercise control over the patrons who might commit infringement . . . . Nor does the Law Society exercise control over which works the patrons choose to copy, the patron's purposes for copying or the photocopiers themselves.[37]

Even though copyright existed in the works in question, the Court took a broad view of "fair dealing" and held that the photocopying done by the Great Library constituted fair dealing in these circumstances. In so deciding, the Court made a number of significant rulings:

- The scope of fair dealing must not be interpreted restrictively.[38]
- The section 29 fair dealing exception is always available to a defendant: "Simply put, a library can always attempt to prove that its dealings with a copyrighted work are fair under section 29 of the *Copyright Act*. It is only if a library were unable to make out the fair dealing exception under section 29 that it would need to turn to section 30.2 of the *Copyright Act* to prove that it qualified for the library exemption."[39]
- If the copying is being done for the purpose of "research," the meaning of "research" must be given a large and liberal interpretation in order to ensure that users' rights are not unduly constrained, even where the research is "for profit" (as in the practice of law).[40]
- To determine whether the copying (or "dealing") of the work is "fair," the Court has proposed that a number of factors be considered: "(1) the purpose of the dealing; (2) the character of the dealing; (3) the amount of the dealing; (4) alternatives to the dealing; (5) the nature of the work; and (6) the effect of the dealing on the work."[41]

In concluding that the Great Library dealt fairly with the publishers' works, the Court placed a considerable degree of emphasis on the fact that the Great Library's "Access to the Law Policy" placed self-imposed restrictions on the library to help ensure compliance with copyright law:

> The factors discussed, considered together, suggest that the Law Society's dealings with the publishers' works through its custom photocopy service were research-based and fair. The Access Policy places appropriate limits on the type of copying that the Law Society will do.

37 *Ibid.* ¶ 43–45.
38 *Ibid.* ¶ 48.
39 *Ibid.* ¶ 49.
40 *Ibid.* ¶ 51.
41 *Ibid.* ¶ 53.

It states that not all requests will be honoured. If a request does not appear to be for the purpose of research, criticism, review or private study, the copy will not be made. If a question arises as to whether the stated purpose is legitimate, the Reference Librarian will review the matter. The Access Policy limits the amount of work that will be copied, and the Reference Librarian reviews requests that exceed what might typically be considered reasonable and has the right to refuse to fulfill a request. On these facts, I conclude that the Law Society's dealings with the publishers' works satisfy the fair dealing defence and that the Law Society does not infringe copyright.[42]

Although there were a number of other procedural rulings by the Court on issues between the parties, one additional ruling, albeit likely in *obiter*, was that the Great Library was entitled to rely upon the "library exemption" under section 30.2(1) of the *Copyright Act*, which allows a library to copy a work on behalf of a patron where that patron was able to rely upon the fair dealing exceptions:

In 1999, amendments to the *Copyright Act* came into force allowing libraries, archives and museums to qualify for exemptions against copyright infringement. Under s. 30.2(1), a library or persons acting under its authority may do anything on behalf of any person that the person may do personally under the fair dealing exceptions to copyright infringement. Section 2 of the *Copyright Act* defines library, archive or museum. In order to qualify as a library, the Great Library: (1) must not be established or conducted for profit; (2) must not be administered or controlled by a body that is established or conducted for profit; and (3) must hold and maintain a collection of documents and other materials that is open to the public or to researchers. The Court of Appeal found that the Great Library qualified for the library exemption. The publishers appeal this finding on the ground that the Law Society, which controls the library, is indirectly controlled by the body of lawyers authorized to practise law in Ontario who conduct the business of law for profit.

I concluded in the main appeal that the Law Society's dealings with the publishers' works were fair. Thus, the Law Society need not rely on the library exemption. However, were it necessary, it would be entitled to do so.[43]

---

42   *Ibid.* ¶ 73.
43   *Ibid.* ¶ 83–84.

With the increase in online legal resources, many publishers are protecting their intellectual copyright through licences that their customers must sign in order to use their products. In most of these agreements, the vendors contractually restrict the use of their data by their customers and control the downloading, storage, and use of the data. Persons or organizations who enter into these licence agreements for online legal resources should take some care in ensuring that the terms of the licence conditions are understood by all persons within the organization who will be accessing the information. Chapter 9, section E provides more information on negotiating licences for law-related resources in electronic format.

E. CONCLUSIONS

Legal research and writing is an important skill. Finding, applying, and communicating the relevant law for a particular issue is a basic function of lawyering. Fortunately, the basic techniques of legal research are relatively straightforward. What follows in the next chapter is a discussion of secondary or background legal resources — such as textbooks, legal journals, encyclopedias, case law digests, and other reference tools — usually a good starting point for all legal research.

F. LEGAL RESEARCH GUIDES

Banks, Margaret A. *Using a Law Library: Canadian Guide to Legal Research*. 6th ed. Toronto: Carswell, 1994.

Berring, Robert C. *Finding the Law*. 11th ed. St. Paul, MN: West Publishing Co., 1999.

Campbell, Enid Monda, Poh-York Lee, and Joycey Tooher. *Legal Research, Materials and Methods*. 4th ed. Sydney: Lawbook, 1996.

Castel, Jacqueline R. and Omeela K. Latchman. *The Practical Guide to Canadian Legal Research*. Rev. ed. Scarborough, ON: Carswell, 1996.

Cohen, Morris L. *Legal Research in a Nutshell*. 8th ed. St. Paul, MN: West Group, 2003.

Elias, Stephen and Susan Levinkind. *Legal Research: How to Find and Understand the Law*. 10th ed. Berkely, CA: Nolo Press, 2002.

Fitzgerald, Maureen F. *Legal Problem Solving: Reasoning, Research and Writing*. 3d ed. Toronto: Butterworths, 2004.

George Washington University Journal of International Law and Economics. *Guide to International Legal Research*. 4th ed. Newark, NJ: LexisNexis Matthew Bender, 2002.

Gordon, Suzanne and Sherifa Elkhadem. *The Law Workbook: Developing Skills for Legal Research and Writing*. Toronto: Emond Montgomery, 2001.

Jacobstein, J. Myron and Roy Mersky. *Fundamentals of Legal Research*. 8th ed. Westbury, NY: Foundation Press, 2002.

Kerr, Margaret. *Legal Research: Step by Step*. Toronto: Emond Montgomery, 1998.

Kunz, Christina et al. *The Process of Legal Research*. 5th ed. New York: Aspen Law & Business, 2000.

LeMay, Denis. *La recherche documentaire en droit*. 5th ed. Montreal: Wilson & Lafleur, 2002.

MacEllven, D. et al. With special assistance by Denis LeMay. *Legal Research Handbook*. 5th ed. Toronto: Butterworths, 2003.

McCallum, Margaret E. et al. *Synthesis: Legal Reading, Reasoning and Writing in Canada*. Toronto: CCH Canadian, 2003.

Nemes, Irene and Graeme Coss. *Effective Legal Research*. 2d ed. Sydney: Butterworths, 2001.

Rehberg, Jeanne and Radu Popa. *Accidental Tourist on the New Frontier: An Introductory Guide to Global Legal Research*. Littleton, CO: F.B. Rothman, 1998.

Sinclair, Mary Jane T., ed. *Updating Statutes and Regulations*. 4th ed. Toronto: Carswell, 1995.

Thomas, Phillip A. et al. *How to Use a Law Library: An Introduction to Legal Skills*. 4th ed. London: Sweet & Maxwell, 2001.

Watt, Robert. *Concise Legal Research*. 5th ed. Sydney: Federation Press, 2004.

Wren, Christopher G. and Jill Robinson Wren. *The Legal Research Manual: A Game Plan for Legal Research and Analysis*. 2d ed. Madison, WI: Legal Education Publishing, 1986.

Yogis, John A. and Innis M. Christie. By Michael J. Iosipescu and
    Michael E. Deturbide. *Legal Writing and Research Manual*. 6th ed.
    Toronto: Butterworths, 2004.

Zivanovic, Aleksandra. *Guide to Electronic Legal Research*. 2d ed.
    Markham, ON: Butterworths, 2002.

CHAPTER 2

SECONDARY LEGAL RESOURCES

The goal of legal research is to find relevant legislation or judicial decisions (i.e., primary legal resources) that apply to the particular legal problem being researched. Finding relevant statutes and cases, however, can be a challenge for first-time legal researchers.

An effective legal research technique when starting to research a particular problem, therefore, is to first consult secondary legal resources to gain a broad overview of the topic. Secondary legal resources include such things as textbooks, law journals, encyclopedias, case law digests, Web guides, and other reference tools. Using secondary legal research resources first has several advantages:

- secondary legal resources generally provide a good synopsis of the law and provide footnotes or links to relevant legislation or case law;
- they are usually written by experts in a particular field, allowing the researcher to take advantage of someone else's work;
- most materials are relatively current, especially if they are in loose-leaf format or online; and
- some secondary legal resources, such as leading textbooks or well-researched law journal articles, can be highly persuasive in court.

This chapter provides a brief overview of secondary legal resources, emphasizing Canadian materials, with discussion of British, American, and Australian materials, where relevant, since these other jurisdictions are the most important comparators for Canadian legal researchers.

A. TEXTBOOKS

Lawyers, judges, academics, and other researchers have written books on most, if not all, legal topics imaginable. If you find a relevant book covering the topic of your research, you will have saved yourself a lot of time by taking advantage of someone else's work.

You can find law-related textbooks at most courthouse, law society, and law school law libraries. In addition, many law firms own their own law-related textbooks relevant to their own areas of practice (for information on selecting or acquiring law-related resources, see Chapter 9). Searching for law-related textbooks has been made easy with the advent of the Internet. Catalogues for major law libraries in Canada (and throughout the world) can now be found online (see Table 2.1). Searching these online library catalogues by author, title, subject, or keyword can help you identify relevant materials for your topic to help you decide if you want to try to borrow the material or buy it for yourself.

Table 2.1
Chart of Online Library Catalogues Containing Law-Related Material

Law Library	WWW Address for Catalogue
Diana M. Priestly Law Library (U. Vic.)	<http://voyager.law.uvic.ca>
U.B.C. Law Library	<http://www.library.ubc.ca>
B.C. Courthouse Library Society	<http://ipac.bccls.bc.ca/ipac-cgi/ipac.exe>
University of Calgary Law Library	<http://osiris.lib.ucalgary.ca>
John A Weir Memorial Law Library (University of Alberta)	<http://www.library.ualberta.ca>
University of Saskatchewan Law Library	<http://sundog.usask.ca>
E.K. Williams Law Library (University of Manitoba)	<http://www.umanitoba.ca/libraries>
U. of Western Ontario Law Library	<http://www.lib.uwo.ca>
U. of Windsor Law Library	<http://cronus.uwindsor.ca/library/>
Osgoode Hall Law School (York U.)	<http://www.library.yorku.ca>
Law Society of Upper Canada	<http://library.lsuc.on.ca>
Bora Laskin Law Library (U. of Toronto)	<http://webcat.library.utoronto.ca>
Supreme Court of Canada Law Library	<http://catalog.sup.bibliomondo.com>
William R. Lederman Law Library (Queen's University)	<http://library.queensu.ca>
University of Ottawa Law Library	<http://137.122.27.99/library/index-e.php>
Nahum Gelber Law Library (McGill U.)	<http://muse.mcgill.ca>
University of Montreal Law Library	<http://www.atrium.bib.umontreal.ca:8000>
University of Sherbrooke Law Library	<http://www.usherbrooke.ca/biblio/catalo/>

Law Library	WWW Address for Catalogue
University of Laval Law Library	<http://arianeweb.ulaval.ca>
Gerald V. La Forest Law Library (U.N.B.)	<http://quest.unb.ca>
University of Moncton Law Library	<http://www.umoncton.ca/cdem/ bibliotheques.html>
Sir James Dunn Law Library (Dalhousie University)	<http://www.library.dal.ca>
National Library of Canada	<http://amicus.collectionscanada.ca/aaweb/ amilogine.htm>

Searching online library catalogues is relatively straightforward, depending on the search engine being used by the library. Many non-librarians may fail to appreciate the value of searching on the "controlled vocabulary" used by library cataloguers in the catalogue to describe materials held by the library. Library of Congress Subject Headings are one of the more common controlled vocabularies. If, like most people (including some librarians), you are not sure of the Library of Congress Subject Heading for your topic, try conducting a "title keyword" search to find any relevant record in the catalogue. Once you find an item of interest, browse through the detailed catalogue record for that item to see what the Library of Congress Subject Headings are for that item and then conduct a "related search" by clicking on the Library of Congress Subject Heading link (if you are in a Web browser version of the catalogue) or by re-typing the *actual* Library of Congress Subject Heading (e.g., "Human rights — Ontario") and re-running your search. This will then result in a list of *all* materials held by that library on that topic. Chapter 8 provides a list of Library of Congress Subject Headings for the major law-related topics, along with a list of the leading textbooks in Canada, arranged by topic.

Another useful technique when searching online library catalogues is to sort your search results by *reverse chronological order* (if this option is available on the catalogue) on the assumption — generally true for legal materials — that more recent material is better than older, dated material.

There are a number of criteria that can be applied in assessing the quality of law-related textbooks. Some of these criteria include

- the *content* of the material: is the law applicable to your jurisdiction or area of practice?
- the *expertise of the author* — what credentials, experience, or reputation does the author have?
- the *currency* of the material — how recent is the book? If it is a looseleaf or in electronic format, how often is it updated?

- the *format* of the material — does the material have an index or table of contents? If so, is the index or table of contents detailed, accurate, and easy to use? If the resource is in electronic format, how easy is it to search or save search results?
- the *publisher* of the material — does the publisher have a reputation for quality?

Some of the leading publishers in Canada of print law-related textbooks include Butterworths, Canada Law Book, Carswell, CCH Canadian, E. Montgomery, Editions Yvon Blais, Irwin Law, Maritime Law Book, and Wilson and LaFleur, although there are also a number of other important publishers of law-related material, including the various provincial and federal bar associations and the federal and provincial governments. Law reform commission reports are an excellent source of legal information since lawyers or researchers acting on behalf of the law reform commission have already done fairly exhaustive research on your behalf. These reports are usually prepared on legal topics of general interest and can be found in library catalogues of academic law libraries or by searching the Web site of the British Columbia Law Institute, which has an excellent online database of law reform commission reports from jurisdictions around the world.[1]

Important publishers of British secondary legal materials include Ashgate, Butterworths U.K., Cavendish, CCH, Hart, Jordan, LLP, Oxford University Press, and Sweet & Maxwell. In Australia, there is Butterworths Australia, Cavendish, CCH, Federation Press, and Lawbook, with the two major publishers being Butterworths (part of the Reed Elsevier family) and Lawbook (part of the Thomson family). In the United States, there is Aspen Law, Bureau of National Affairs, Inc., CCH, Matthew Bender, Oceana Publications, and West Publishing, to name a few.

The American Association of Law Libraries has a useful page setting out information and links on the major international legal publishers (Thomson, Reed Elsevier, and Wolters Kluwer and their various local subsidiaries), including an explanation of the relationship among various publishers within the three major groups and including a list of other independent publishers.[2]

---

1   See British Columbia Law Institute, *Law Reform Database*, online: British Columbia Law Institute <http://www.bcli.org>. See also Manas Media Inc., *World Law Reform Collection: Jurisdiction and Subject Index* (Kanata, ON: Manas Media Inc., 1991) [periodically updated].

2   See *A Legal Publishers List: Corporate Affiliations of Legal Publishers*, 2d ed., online: American Association of Law Libraries <http://www.aallnet.org/committee/criv/resources/tools/list/>.

Increasingly, publishers are willing to publish their textbooks in electronic format, either on CD-ROM or through their commercial online databases. Some recent Canadian examples of online textbooks include the following:

- **Irwin Law textbooks**: There are currently over thirty-five Irwin Law law-related titles available in full-text on Quicklaw. It is possible to search the full-text of these publications by keyword or to browse through the books via a "clickable" Table of Contents. These books are included in the list of law-related material organized by topic in Chapter 8.
- **Carswell textbooks**: Carswell makes a number of the textbooks published by its authors available on its subject-based "Partner Product" CD-ROMs in such areas as bankruptcy and insolvency, employment law, corporate law, civil procedure, and family law, to name a few. It is also possible to search the full-text of these textbooks by keyword or by browsing through a "clickable" Table of Contents. Carswell is now making several of its textbooks available through its "LawSource" products on WestlaweCARSWELL, its Internet subscription service, in the areas of criminal law, family law, bankruptcy and insolvency, and securities law.
- **CCH Canadian**: CCH has published on CD-ROM and through CCHOnline several of its print publications that contain both primary legal resources and commentary thereon in a number of topics, including corporate and securities law, employment law, and taxation, to name a few.
- **Canada Law Book**: The popular Brown and Beatty textbook, *Canadian Labour Arbitration*, is available on CD-ROM and via a Web subscription, as are several other titles.

It is therefore important not to overlook the advantages of first consulting a textbook (in print or electronic format) when beginning your legal research.

B. LAW JOURNALS

Law journals are another excellent source of background material on law-related topics. Articles can range from very practitioner-oriented, often written by lawyers or judges, to more theoretical or policy-based, often written by academics or other scholars. Regardless of the type of article, most cite some law, be it case law or legislation, and can be a great way to take advantage of someone else's research. Law journals are published in print and online by law schools, by law societies and bar associations, by commercial legal publishers, and by special interest groups. Print law journals can be found in most academic and court-house libraries. There has recently been, and will continue to be, an increase in the availability of law journals in electronic format. Quick-law, a Canadian commercial online database vendor discussed in more detail in Chapter 6, provides access to over thirty full-text Canadian law journals, in addition to numerous "netletters" that function as a practi-tioner newsletter/current awareness services (see Figure 2.1 for a par-tial list of the full-text journals available on Quicklaw). Both LexisNexis and WestlaweCARSWELL have extensive full-text journal databases that contain law-related journal articles from the United States and around the world, including some from Canada. Another excellent commercial database of online journals is HeinOnline,[3] a database that provides PDF access to a large number of law journals, most dating back to the first volume for each journal on the database. Individual journal publishers, such as Oxford University Press,[4] also make recent volumes of their law journals available online by subscription.

Finding law journals is best done through journal indices, many of which are increasingly in electronic format, which allow for keyword searching by author, title, and subject. Regardless of whether the jour-nal index is in print or electronic format, it allows the researcher to find citations to relevant law-related journal articles, is extremely easy to use, and usually contains its own user guide. Since most online jour-nal indices only catalogue journal articles from the mid 1980s to the present, researchers must not overlook the need to use older print for-mat journal indices to help locate pre-1980s journal articles.

In Canada, there are two main journal indices:

- *Index to Canadian Legal Literature*. Toronto: Carswell, 1981. [updat-ed quarterly]. Available in print (as part of Carswell's *Canadian Abridgment*) and online through WestlaweCARSWELL (database identifier: ICLL) or Quicklaw (database identifier: ICLL).
- *Index to Canadian Legal Periodical Literature*. Montreal: Canadian Association of Law Libraries, 1963. [updated irregularly] Available in print only.

---

3   Online: HeinOnline <http://heinonline.org>.
4   See, e.g., Oxford University Press's list of online journals at <http://www3.oup.co.uk/jnls/fields/law/online.html>.

Quicklaw also has a database called the Canadian Law Symposia Index (database identifier: CLSI), which provides an index to papers presented at law-related seminars and legal education workshops since January 1986.

Figure 2.1
Partial List of Journals Available on Quicklaw

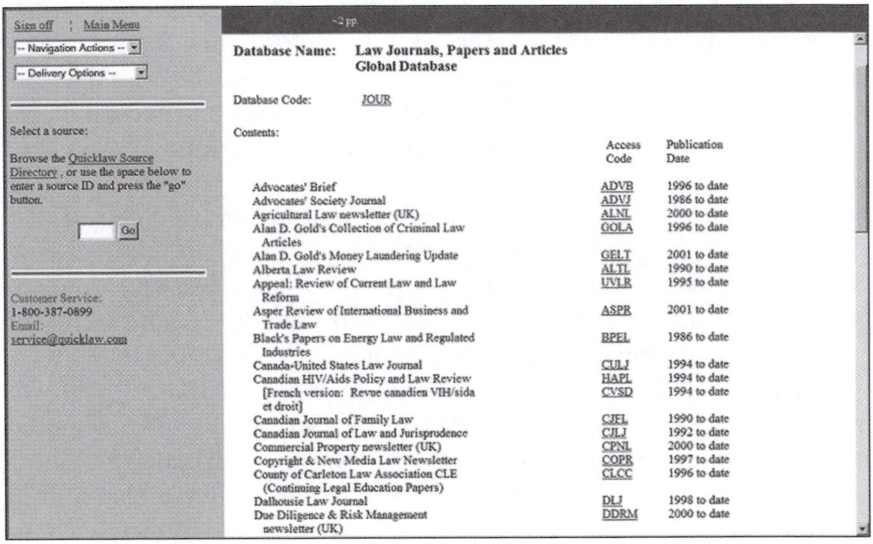

Reprinted by permission of Quicklaw Inc.

Canadian journal literature is also indexed in Wilson's *Index to Legal Periodicals & Books*, available in print and online. This index, which provides coverage from 1981 to present, also provides extensive citations to American legal journal literature, as well as coverage of journals from Australia, Canada, Great Britain, Ireland, New Zealand, and Puerto Rico. Similar journal coverage, including Canadian, is also provided by *Legal-Trac*, an online law journal index published by the Gale Group and available in print as the *Current Law Index* (online coverage from 1980).

Legal Journals Index, available in print and via online subscription from Sweet & Maxwell and available on WestlaweCARSWELL (database identifier: LJI), indexes more than 430 law journals from or about the United Kingdom and the European Union.

One of the major Australian and New Zealand law journal indices is *AGIS: Attorney-General's Information Service*, available in print and via online subscription (held by many major academic law libraries).

The *Index to Foreign Legal Periodicals*, produced by the American Association of Law Libraries, provides access to legal literature outside of the United States, England, Canada, and Australia, covering the period from 1985 to present. It is available in print, on CD-ROM, and online.

In addition to finding relevant journal articles by searching in a print or online journal index, it is also possible to search the full text of journals on Quicklaw (using the JOUR global database or individual journal databases), LexisNexis, or WestlaweCARSWELL. When searching full-text law journal databases, however, it is important to realize that you are usually never searching the entire "universe" of law journal articles since even the most extensive online law journal database does not have every law journal and even for the ones that have a large collection online, they often do not go back very far.[5] Hence the advantage of starting your law journal research with several of the journal indices discussed above, since these indices try to index the entire "universe" of law journals for the time period indicated.

Another potential disadvantage of searching full-text journals is the risk of getting "false hits" unless your search criteria are precise and accurately set out. A useful technique when searching full-text law journals is to search by "field" or "segment" to limit your search terms to a particular part of the article such as title or author. For example, searching full-text law journals on the word "Internet" may retrieve articles where the main focus is not the Internet (simply because the word "Internet" is mentioned somewhere in the text), whereas searching the word "Internet" in the title field or segment will more likely retrieve articles focusing on the issue of the Internet on the assumption that an article where the search term appears in the title will likely be on that topic.

C. LEGAL ENCYCLOPEDIAS

Legal encyclopedias are another excellent starting point for legal research because of their relatively exhaustive scope and broad overview of law-related topics.

In Canada, the *Canadian Encyclopedic Digest* (3d ed.), known as the CED, is published by Carswell as a looseleaf in two separate editions, a

---

5   However, if you are searching on fairly specific keywords — such as a case name or author — a full-text law journal database search can sometimes find discrete references, where your keywords appear in a footnote, for example, resulting in hits that you might not likely find using law journal indices.

brown Western edition and a green Ontario edition, although some titles from both editions, such as administrative law, are identical. The CED contains Volume 1 (Absentees to Agency) to Volume 34 (Weights and Measures to Young Offenders), plus a Research Guide and Key; each topic can be found under a "tab" (called a "title"). Each topic or "title" is written by a lawyer who has some expertise in that area; hence, (i) titles are updated on an *ad hoc* basis, title by title; and (ii) the quality can vary from title to title, although the overall quality of the CED is quite good. The text is supplemented by yellow update sheets, found at the front of each title; thus, to note up your CED research, you must check the relevant paragraph number in the yellow supplemental sheets.

First-time users should consult the Research Guide and Key to obtain an overview of the publication, which is very simple to use. Access is most often by subject, via the index; if you have a case name on point, you can check the Table of Cases from the relevant title for that case and then refer to the paragraph cross-references where the known case is mentioned in the text and find other (similar) cases that may be relevant to your research.

The CED is also available on CD-ROM, a version that has a number of advantages over the print product:

* the CD-ROM contains both the Western and Ontario editions
* there is no need to update the CD-ROM since it does not have print looseleaf pages that require updating
* the CD-ROM is easy to search and does not take up shelf space

More recently, Carswell has also published the CED on WestlaweCARSWELL that has the added functionality over both the print and CD-ROM version in that cases mentioned in the footnotes on the WestlaweCARSWELL version are "clickable" and will launch the full text of the decision (see Figure 2.2 for a sample entry from the CED on WestlaweCARSWELL).

For researching British law, *Halsbury's Laws of England* is an authoritative encyclopedia published by Butterworths that dates back to 1907. Currently available in print in a brown fourth edition, it is also now available on the Internet by online subscription at Butterworths U.K. as *Halsbury's Laws Direct*.[6] Like the CED, *Halsbury's Laws of England* in print is a multi-volume encyclopedia, arranged by topic alphabetically. Each topic is organized into numbered paragraphs with extensive footnotes that provide links to supporting case law and legislation from England and the European Union. Some Canadian aca-

---

6   Online: Butterworths <http://www.butterworths.com/butterworths.asp>.

demic law libraries may still subscribe to the green third edition of *Halsbury's Laws of England*, which has two advantages for Canadian legal researchers. First, the third edition tends to emphasize more British common law whereas the newer fourth edition tends to highlight more of the legislative developments in England in recent years, something of less interest to most Canadian legal researchers. Second, the third edition has "Canadian converter" volumes which provide citations to Canadian case law, that can be useful for some legal research topics that are based on common law principles.

Figure 2.2

Sample entry from Carswell's *Canadian Encyclopedic Digest* on WestlaweCARSWELL

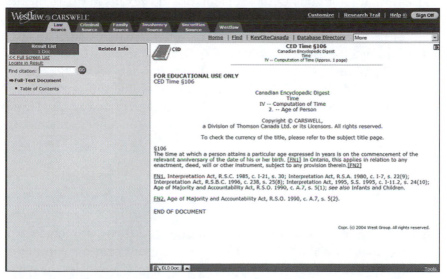

Reprinted by permission of Carswell, a division of Thomson Canada Limited.

For researching American law, there are two major enyclopedias:

- *Corpus Juris Secundum* (West Publishing): The "CJS," as it is known, is available in print in a multi-volume set, organized alphabetically by topic. Information is kept current by annual, cumulative "pocket parts" in the back of each volume. Information is organized by numbered topics, supported by extensive footnotes to case law and legislation, with "key-number" references to the West Digest system to find more case law by topic.
- *American Jurisprudence* (Lawyers Cooperative): "AmJur" is another American legal encyclopedia, originally published by the Lawyers Cooperative that was recently acquired by West Publishing. It is avail-

able in print, on CD-ROM, and on WestlaweCARSWELL (AMJUR). Rather than attempting to provide an exhaustive list of supporting case law, the summaries provide links to only leading cases.

Another "encyclopedic" American work is the series *American Law Reports* (West Publishing). This series provides a collection of articles and annotations of important or leading cases. There is both a federal and state version; it is available in print and on WestlaweCARSWELL. The print Index is relatively easy to use and goes into a fair degree of detail (e.g., "Automobiles and Highway Traffic — Air bag systems defective, product liability"). If one is able to identify one's topic in the Index, one is led to a fairly exhaustive article covering all relevant U.S. case law, legislation, and other authorities on point. Articles are kept current by way of updates or supplements in the "pocket part" at the back of each individual volume.

For researching Australian law, there are two major Australian law-related encyclopedias: (1) *Halsbury's Laws of Australia* (Butterworths, print and online subscription), mirrored after *Halsbury's Laws of England*; and (2) *Laws of Australia* (Thomson, print and online subscription).

Encyclopedias can therefore provide a quick overview of most legal topics and links to relevant case law, legislation, or other commentary on the topic.

D. CASE LAW DIGESTS

Case law digests contain summaries of court cases, usually organized by topic, that allow the researcher to locate relevant case law within the jurisdiction. Unlike legal encyclopedias, which may only refer the reader to significant or leading cases, case law digests usually attempt to provide an exhaustive list of cases for the particular jurisdiction. In print, these case law digests can be quite formidable, due to the volume of case law, which is always increasing with time. Fortunately, there are also a number of case law digests in electronic format that can be searched by keyword or sometimes browsed by topic.

In Canada, the most comprehensive print case law digest is the *Canadian Abridgment* (2d ed.), a multi-volume black and red set published by Carswell, which is also available on CD-ROM and as LawSource through WestlaweCARSWELL, an online Internet subscription (with LawSource, it is possible to link to the full text of most decisions). The *Canadian Abridgment* in print is in fact more than just a service providing digests of case law; there are various components:

- *Canadian Case Citations*: in print, this red, multi-volume component acts as a "noter upper" for Canadian cases, providing case history, judicial treatment, and citation information.
- *Canadian Statute Citations*: in print, this grey, multi-volume component provides summaries of Canadian cases that have considered or applied particular sections of Canadian federal and provincial statutes and rules of practice (as well as selected international treaties).
- *Index to Canadian Legal Literature*: in print, this green, multi-volume component — discussed above in more detail — provides an index to major Canadian law journal articles and other Canadian legal literature.
- *Words & Phrases*: in print, this blue, multi-volume component — discussed below in more detail — provides extensive definitions of words and phrases as defined by Canadian courts.

It is possible to buy individual components or even individual volumes only on specific legal topics. The case law coverage in the *Canadian Abridgment* dates back to the 1800s. Access is primarily by topic using the *Key and Research Guide* or by keyword using the *General Index*. Once the topic is found using either resource, the user is led to the main volume for that topic and paragraph number range; to update the research, the user then consults the paper supplements, which typically include a cumulative supplement and individual monthly supplements. Indices are found in the back of every volume, including supplements.

In 2003, Carswell started to publish the third edition of the *Canadian Abridgment* in new green and blue volumes. The new third edition will be released gradually over five years. One major change with this new edition is an updating and consolidation of the subjects or topics into which case summaries are organized. The new third edition is expected to be a major improvement, but pending its completion, it may be confusing for researchers who sometimes need to consult either or both the second or third edition, depending on the topic being researched and whether that topic has yet been reconsolidated into the new edition.

The *Canadian Abridgment* contains its own classification system that organizes cases into broad topics (e.g., Motor vehicles) and then breaks down the broad topic into ever more discrete sub-topics (e.g., Motor vehicles — Rules of the road — Traffic signs — "Yield"). These topics are assigned classification numbers that are a combination of letters, numbers, and Roman numerals. For example, assume you have been asked to research the issue of mobility rights under the *Canadian Charter of Rights and Freedoms* and you want to find some cases on that topic. If you browse through the Table of Classification in Volume 24 of the *Canadian Abridgment* (3d ed.) under the topic of "Constitutional Law," you will see the following breakdown:

Constitutional Law
XI. Charter of Rights and Freedoms
    3. Nature of rights and freedoms
        e. Mobility rights
           i. General principles

See Figure 2.3 for a sample entry in the print version of the *Canadian Abridgment* (3d ed.), for this topic.

For all future cases involving this topic, the editors of the *Canadian Abridgment* will continue to classify or group cases involving general principles of mobility rights under the *Charter* under this category, which can be summarized by its classification numbers derived from the Table of Classification: Constitutional Law XI.3.e.i. To update the main volume (i.e., to find more recent cases) from the *Canadian Abridgment,* one must use this classification number to find more recent cases in the softcover supplement.

The *Canadian Abridgment* on WestlaweCARSWELL has several advantages over the print and CD-ROM versions. The Internet version is both browsable by topic and searchable by keyword using templates, natural language, or Boolean operators. With the Internet version, a case summary can be clicked on to launch the full text of most decisions (which then allows the researcher to click on the "note up" feature to note up the case). Figure 2.4 sets out a sample entry from the *Canadian Abridgment* on WestlaweCARSWELL for the topic "Education law — Colleges and universities — Students — Discipline."

Another extensive online case law digest is the *Canadian Case Summaries* database on Quicklaw (database identifier: CCS). This database, originally published by CCH in print prior to 1990 as the *Dominion Report Service*, has been continued online by Quicklaw and contains over 360,000 documents. It is possible to access the full text of most case law summaries in CCS by clicking on the appropriate link.

In addition to the *Canadian Abridgment* and the CCS database on Quicklaw, there are a number of other Canadian subject-specific case law digests in print, such as Maritime Law Book's *National Reporter Digest and Index*,[7] the *Charter of Rights Annotated*,[8] and the *Weekly Criminal Bulletin*,[9] to name a few.

---

7   (Fredericton, NB: Maritime Law Book, 1974) [regularly updated].
8   Looseleaf (Aurora, ON: Canada Law Book, 1982).
9   (Aurora, ON: Canada Law Book, 1977) [regularly updated].

Figure 2.3
Sample Entry from Carswell's print *Canadian Abridgment* (3d ed.) (Constitutional Law XI.3.e.i)

to pay dues not infringing non-member's right not to associate with union or professional association.

Merry v. Manitoba (1989), [1989] 2 W.W.R. 526, 1989 CarswellMan 145 (Man. Q.B.); affirmed (1989), [1989] 6 W.W.R. 665, 1989 CarswellMan 187 (Man. C.A.).

e. *Mobility rights*

i. *General principles*

1913.   (XI.3.e.i)
Charter of Rights and Freedoms — Nature of rights and freedoms — Mobility rights — General principles —— Accused was involved in heroin smuggling — Australian police arrested accused after seizing large amounts of heroin — Accused escaped custody and was arrested in Canada — During rendition hearing, accused's motion for voir dire to determine admissibility of recorded statements made to Australian police was dismissed — Accused's application to British Columbia Supreme Court for habeas corpus with certiorari in aid was dismissed — Appeal dismissed — Lower courts did not err by concluding that no grounds existed to hold voir dire — Fact that accused was willing to plead guilty in Canada to lesser offence was irrelevant and did not affect his right to enter, leave and remain in Canada — Accused's mobility rights under Charter could only be violated by Governor General's order to surrender accused to demanding country — Current proceedings were incapable of violating accused's mobility rights under Charter — Cases stating that proceedings under Extradition Act do not violate Charter were directly applicable to current case — Possibility of serving life sentence did not violate accused's Charter rights — Canadian Charter of Rights and Freedoms — Extradition Act, R.S.C. 1985, c. E-23.

Australia v. Lau (2001), *(sub nom. Lau v. Australia (State))* 244 W.A.C. 171, 149 B.C.A.C. 171, 2001 CarswellBC 263, 2001 BCCA 40 (B.C. C.A.); affirming (1999), 1999 CarswellBC 2908 (B.C. S.C.); affirming (1998), [1998] B.C.J. No. 2427, 1998 CarswellBC 3136 (B.C. Prov. Ct.).

1914.   (XI.3.e.i)
Charter of Rights and Freedoms — Nature of rights and freedoms — Mobility rights — General principles —— Taxpayer accepted one-year teaching contract, which required him to move to remote location — During term of contract, taxpayer resided in furnished accommodation provided by college — Taxpayer's wife remained at their permanent residence, his mail was addressed

there, and he did not change his bank account, but did forward change of address notifications to some parties — Following expiry of contract, taxpayer returned to permanent residence — Taxpayer claimed deductions for costs of both moves — Minister disallowed deductions — Taxpayer appealed — Appeal allowed on other grounds — Argument that Minister's interpretation of s. 6(2) of Charter violated taxpayer's ss. 6 and 15 Charter rights was rejected — Even generous interpretation of s. 6(2) of Charter does not give rise to right to have citizen's mobility subsidized by public purse through deduction from taxable income — Contention that Minister's interpretation breached s. 15 of Charter, by discriminating among individuals on basis of length of contract of employment by which they earn living, was untenable — Basis of length of employment contracts was not personal characteristic, or in any way analogous to enumerated grounds of discrimination in s. 15 — Canadian Charter of Rights and Freedoms, ss. 6, 15 — Income Tax Act, R.S.C. 1985, c. 1 (5th Supp.), s. 62.

Cavalier v. R. (2001), [2002] 1 C.T.C. 2001, 2001 CarswellNat 2374 (T.C.C. [Informal Procedure]).

1915.   (XI.3.e.i)
Charter of Rights and Freedoms — Nature of rights and freedoms — Mobility rights — General principles —— Parties were citizens of South Africa — Parties moved to Pennsylvania and had one child — Mother took child to visit brother in Canada and did not wish to return to Pennsylvania — Father brought application for return of child under International Child Abduction Act — Application allowed — Child was habitually resident in Pennsylvania and Pennsylvania was appropriate forum for dispute — Order to return to Pennsylvania did not violate child's mobility rights under Charter — Right to enter and leave Canada rested with child and mother did not have standing to pursue issue — Canadian Charter of Rights and Freedoms — International Child Abduction Act, 1996, S.S. 1996, c. I-10.11.

Struweg v. Struweg (2001), [2001] S.J. No. 380, [2001] 9 W.W.R. 581, 208 Sask. R. 243, 2001 CarswellSask 420, 2001 SKQB 283 (Sask. Q.B.); additional reasons at (2001), 212 Sask. R. 290, [2002] 2 W.W.R. 508, 2001 CarswellSask 716, 2001 SKQB 503 (Sask. Q.B.).

1916.   (XI.3.e.i)
Charter of Rights and Freedoms — Nature of rights and freedoms — Mobility rights — General principles —— Doctor making 5-year commitment to practise in certain area in return for temporary permit — Doctor requesting release from commitment to move to other province —

Reprinted by permission of Carswell, a division of Thomson Canada Limited.

Figure 2.4

Sample Entry from Carswell's *Canadian Abridgment* on WestlaweCAR-SWELL (Education Law VI.5.a)

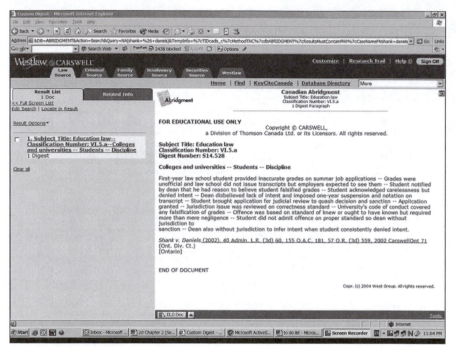

Reprinted by permission of Carswell, a division of Thomson Canada Limited.

A major British case law digest is *The Digest* (Butterworths), formerly the *English and Empire Digest*, which provides coverage of Commonwealth cases, with an emphasis on English cases, but includes limited coverage of Canadian cases. It is accessible by reference to a legal topic or case name in the main volume. Research is then updated by an annual cumulative update and then quarterly softcover updates (*The Digest Quarterly Survey*). Cross references are given to the relevant sections of *Halsbury's Laws of England*. Another important British case law digest is *Current Law* (Sweet & Maxwell), that appears as a monthly issue which is then consolidated annually and thereafter periodically. Cases can be found using either the current Cumulative Index (for the current year) or the Cumulative Index in the *Current Law Yearbook* (covering 1947 to the year previous to the current year). *Current Law* also includes a case law and legislative citator component to note up British case law and legislation.

The main American case law digest is found as part of *West's Digest System*, which is comprised of the *Decennial Digest* and the *General Digest*.

The *Decennial Digest* is a series now published in increments of five-year periods, with the most recent series being 1991–1996. Cases are organized alphabetically by topic and are classified by West's detailed "key-numbering" system, which assigns a unique key number to ever discrete sub-topics for each major legal topic. Cases in the *Decennial Digest* are then updated by using the *General Digest* of which every tenth volume consolidates cases from the previous nine volumes; once the topic and key number have been determined using the general index to the *Decennial Digest*, the updating in the *General Digest* can best be done by merely checking to see if the key number for that topic has any updates for that particular volume or volumes of the *General Digest*. The *General Digests* also contain a table of cases appealed, affirmed, or reversed.

In Australia, the case law digest system parallels the situation in Canada with Lawbook (Thomson) publishing the *Australian Digest*, currently in a second edition and in the process, like the *Canadian Abridgment*, of being reconsolidated into a new third edition. It is available in print and via online subscription. In addition, Butterworths Australia publishes a competitive case law digest service called *Australian Current Law*, also available in print and online.

Case law digests are an effective finding tool to locate cases by topic within a particular jurisdiction. Print case law digests often require checking multiple volumes (an index, the main volume, and supplemental "updater" volumes) but are generally easy to use. Online case law digests, such as WestlaweCARSWELL's "LawSource" (the online equivalent of the *Canadian Abidgment*) or Quicklaw's CCS database, provide a focused set of data that can effectively be searched by keyword, resulting in relatively precise search results.

E. GENERAL LEGAL REFERENCE RESOURCES

In addition to textbooks, law journals, encyclopedias, and case law digests, there are a number of general legal reference resources that are useful for legal research:

1) Legal Dictionaries

For first-time legal researchers, the use of reference tools such as legal dictionaries can help explain legal terms and provide useful information. Legal dictionaries usually define legal terms by citing how courts or legislatures have defined them. Some major legal dictionaries include

- Dukelow, Daphne A. and Betsy Nuse. *The Dictionary of Canadian Law*. 2d ed. Scarborough, ON: Carswell, 1994.
- Penner, James E. *Mozley & Whiteley's Law Dictionary*. 12th ed. London: Butterworths, 2001.
- Garner, Bryan A., ed. *Black's Law Dictionary*. 8th ed. St. Paul, MN: West Pub. Co., 2004.

Law students or other researchers on a budget may wish to consider buying any of the following "abridged" dictionaries which are condensed and cheaper (all are generally under $25.00) but which still provide definitions and explanations of key legal terms and Latin phrases:

- Dukelow, Daphne A. and Betsy Nuse. *Pocket Dictionary of Canadian Law*. 3d ed. Scarborough, ON: Carswell, 2002.
- Peter Collin Publishing. *Dictionary of Law*. 3d ed. London: Peter Collin Publishing, 2001.
- Yogis, John A. *Canadian Law Dictionary*. 5th ed. New York: Barrons Educational Series, 2003.

Word and phrases dictionaries also define legal terms but differ from legal dictionaries by attempting to provide a fairly exhaustive list of how a particular term has been defined by every court within a jurisdiction. Major words and phrases services include the following:

- *The Canadian Abridgment: Words and Phrases*. 2d ed. Toronto: Carswell, 1984 [updated regularly].
- Gardner, John D. *The Encyclopedia of Words and Phrases, Legal Maxims, Canada*. 4th ed. Looseleaf. Toronto: Carswell, 1990.
- Stroud, Frederick. *Judicial Dictionary of Words and Phrases*. 5th ed. Looseleaf. London: Sweet & Maxwell, 1986.
- *Words and Phrases*. Permanent edition. St. Paul, MN: West Publishing, 1940 [updated regularly].

Abbreviation dictionaries, on the other hand, explain the meaning of acronyms often used in the legal profession for legal resources, such as the abbreviation "C.C.L.T.," which stands for the *"Canadian Cases on the Law of Torts."* Many law-related publications, such as the *Canadian Abridgment*, contain their own "List of Abbreviations" at the front or back of the publication. Alternatively, there are a number of other sources for abbreviations:

- Price, Mary Miles, ed. *Bieber's Dictionary of Legal Abbreviations: Reference Guide for Attorneys, Legal Secretaries, Paralegals and Law Students*. 4th ed. Buffalo, NY: Hein, 1993.
- Noble, Scott. *Noble's Revised International Guide to the Law Reports*. Etobicoke, ON: Nicol Island Publishing, 1998.

- Raistrick, Donald. *Index to Legal Citations and Abbreviations*. 2d ed. London: Bowker-Saur, 1993.
- Kavass, Igor and Mary Price, eds. *World Dictionary of Legal Abbreviations*. Buffalo, NY: Hein, 1991.

2) Legal Citation Guides

Legal citation guides are also indispensable for legal research and writing since they explain the formats for how to cite case law, legislation, and secondary legal resources. In Canada, the leading style guide is the *Canadian Guide to Uniform Legal Citation* (5th ed.) (the "McGill Guide") (see Figure 2.5 for a sample entry from the McGill Guide), which was discussed in more detail in Chapter 1, section C. Some of the basic citation patterns are relatively easy to learn, such as how to cite a typical Canadian case by italicizing the parties' names, followed by the date, the volume, case reporter, page number information, and level of court: *Masson v. Kelly* (1991), 85 D.L.R. (4th) 214 (Ont. C.A.). Other citation formats are more technical, hence the advantage of having your own copy of the McGill Guide if you can afford the cost.

3) Legal Directories

There are a number of "competitive" Canadian legal directories that provide listings of addresses and other contact information for lawyers, courthouses, and other law-related organizations. The difference between these various directories is often one of preference or cost. Some of the major legal directories include the following:

- *Canada Legal Directory*. Toronto: Carswell [annual].
- *Canadian Law List*. Aurora: Canada Law Book [annual]. Modified form available online at <http://www.canadianlawlist.com>. Also available on CD-ROM.
- *Martindale-Hubbell International Law Directory*[annual]. Modified form available online at <http://www.martindale.com/locator/home.html>. The print multi-volume version also has a useful two-volume digest of the laws of countries throughout the world which provides a simplified overview of the laws of selected countries.
- *Ontario Legal Directory*. Toronto: Distributed by University of Toronto Press. Published Annually. [Commonly referred to as the "orange book."]
- *The Ontario Legal Desk Book*. Toronto: Carswell [annual]. This publication advertises itself as more than just a legal directory since it contains substantive information on various areas of law, a section

on limitation periods, a listing of Internet legal resources, a section on legal research, and a section on various court and real estate fees.

Figure 2.5
Sample Entry from Rule 6.2.1 (Books — General Form) of Carswell's *Canadian Guide to Uniform Legal Citation* (5th ed.) ("McGill Guide")

E-172 SECONDARY SOURCES AND OTHER MATERIALS

6.2 BOOKS

6.2.1 General Form

Examples

Author	title	edition	other elements	(place of publica-tion:	publisher,	year of publica-tion)	pin-point	(elec-tronic service) of applic-able).
Peter W. Hogg,	Constitu-tional Law of Canada,	5th ed.		(Toronto:	Carswell,	1998)	at 20.	
Margaret Somerville,	Death Talk: The Case against Euthanasia and Physician-Assisted Suicide			(Montreal and Kingston:	McGill-Queen's University Press,	2001)	at 78.	
J. Anthony VanDuzer,	The Law of Partnerships and Corporations			(Toronto:	Irwin Law,	1997)	c. 2 (B) (3)	(QL).

- Other elements should be provided as necessary following the format given below. Their order is: name of editor or compiler; name of translator; total number of volumes or number of cited volume; volume title; series title and volume number within series (if necessary); looseleaf.

Reprinted by permission of Carswell, a division of Thomson Canada Limited.

4) Forms and Precedents

Most lawyers learn quickly in their career to take advantage of a number of publications known as "forms and precedents" that provide sample wording for legal agreements, court pleadings, and other legal documents. There are a number of commercially available sources of these forms and precedents:

- *Canadian Forms & Precedents*. Looseleaf. Toronto: Butterworths Canada. This is a multi-volume (blue and red) set available from Butterworths in print and on CD-ROM that provides high-quality forms and precedents in a number of areas of law, including wills, land development, debtor/creditor, estates administration, commercial real estate financing, banking and finance, and commercial transactions.
- *O'Brien's Encyclopedia of Forms*. 11th ed. Looseleaf. Aurora, ON: Canada Law Book, 1987. This is a multi-volume burgundy set from Canada Law Book, also available on disk and now through an Internet subscription (called *O'Brien's Internet*[10]). The volumes, divided into "Divisions," cover a wide range of topics, including: Commercial and General, Corporations, Conveyancing and Mortgage, Leases, Wills and Trusts, Ontario — Family Law, Labour Relations and Employment, Ontario — Court Forms, Municipal Corporations, Computers and Information Technology.

In addition, many lawyers and law firms start to compile their own internal sample forms and precedents and make them available within the firm through an Intranet or networked database. Chapter 11, section G talks more about drafting agreements and court documents using forms and precedents.

5) Court Rules

Court rules govern procedure in lawsuits. Litigation lawyers will ordinarily have "rules of court" publications for their jurisdiction. These publications are usually published annually, may be kept current with pocket parts, and are generally annotated, providing commentary, digests of cases interpreting particular provisions of the court rules, and setting out other information relevant for litigators, such as practice directions from the court. There are several publications that explain these court rules and discuss how the rules have been interpreted by the courts: For matters in the Ontario Superior Court, for example, consult the current copy of *Ontario Civil Practice*[11] or *Ontario Annual Practice*.[12] For matters in Ontario Small Claims Court, consult

---

10   Online: O'Brien's Internet <http://www.obriensforms.com>.
11   Garry D. Watson & Michael McGowan, *Ontario Civil Practice* (Toronto: Carswell) [annual]. There is also an extended 5-volume version, Garry D. Watson & Craig Perkins, *Holmested and Watson: Ontario Civil Procedure*, looseleaf (Toronto: Carswell).
12   (Aurora, ON: Canada Law Book) [annual].

the current copy of the *Small Claims Court Practice*.[13] For matters in Federal Court, consult the current copy of *Federal Court Practice*[14] or the *Annotated Federal Court Act and Rules*.[15] For Supreme Court of Canada practice, consult *Supreme Court of Canada Practice*.[16] Chapter 8, section G sets out a more detailed list of resources relating to civil procedure, including several CD-ROM products.

6) Current Awareness Tools

There are a number of current awareness tools that are useful for legal research. One of the purposes of these resources is to provide current information on law-related topics. Current awareness tools tend to fall into the following categories:

*   **Newspapers**: There are two major, national law-related newspapers in Canada: *The Lawyer's Weekly*[17] and the *Law Times*.[18] Both papers provide good coverage of current legal issues, important court cases, trends in the legal industry, and special topical columns.
*   **Magazines**: There are a number of magazines that are more current and topical than the academic journals discussed above in Chapter 2, section B. One of the more popular "glossy" magazines is *Canadian Lawyer*.[19] The Canadian Bar Association also sends to its members its *National* magazine. The Vancouver Bar Association publishes *The Advocate*, a journal that combines scholarly articles with current awareness information.
*   **Netletters**: Quicklaw provides a number of excellent online "netletters" by topic that are written by experts in their field and that provide regular updates (usually weekly) on developments for that area of the law. One of the more popular netletters for criminal law lawyers is Alan Gold's Criminal Law Netletter. Netletters on Quicklaw are also provided for the following topics: aboriginal law, administrative law, advocacy and practice, bankruptcy and insolvency, civil

---

13   Marvin A. Zuker, *Ontario Small Claims Court Practice* (Toronto: Carswell) [annual].

14   David Sgayias, *Federal Court Practice* (Toronto: Carswell) [annual].

15   Roger T. Hughes, *Annotated Federal Court Act and Rules* (Toronto: Butterworths) [annual].

16   Brian A. Crane & Henry S. Brown, *Supreme Court of Canada Practice* (Toronto: Carswell) [annual].

17   (Toronto: Butterworths Canada).

18   (Aurora, ON: Canada Law Book).

19   (Aurora, ON Canada Law Book). Information is available online at <http://www.canadianlawyermag.com>.

procedure, commercial law, construction law, education law, environmental law, family law, health law, human rights, immigration law, insurance law, intellectual property law, labour and employment law, municipal law, natural resources, personal injury, professional responsibility, real property law, securities law, taxation, and transportation law. Carswell also provides online newsletters for its four subject-based Internet subscriptions (*CriminalSource*, *Securities-Source*, *InsolvencySource*, and *FamilySource*).

- **Ontario Reports**: Members of the Law Society of Upper Canada receive as part of their membership a weekly softcover copy of the *Ontario Reports*, which contains recent decisions of Ontario courts. Also included with these weekly softcover editions is a series of preliminary pages that include notices to the profession, upcoming legal conferences or seminars, new law-related publications, and job advertisements for law-related positions.
- **Law Society Web Sites**: Most of the Canadian law societies have Web sites that provide a variety of information to their members (and to the public), including "what's new?"-type information. Set out below in Table 2.2 is a list of those Canadian law societies that have Web sites, along with the Web site of the Canadian Bar Association and other lawyers' groups.

Table 2.2
Law Society Web Sites

Law Society	Web Site Address
Barreau du Québec	<http://www.barreau.qc.ca>
Canadian Bar Association	<http://www.cba.org>
Chambre des notaires du Québec	<http://www.cdnq.org>
Federation of Law Societies of Canada	<http://www.flsc.ca>
Law Society of Alberta	<http://www.lawsocietyalberta.com>
Law Society of British Columbia	<http://www.lawsociety.bc.ca>
Law Society of Manitoba	<http://www.lawsociety.mb.ca>
Law Society of New Brunswick	<http://www.lawsociety-barreau.nb.ca>
Law Society of Newfoundland	<http://www.lawsociety.nf.ca>
Law Society of Northwest Territories	<http://www.lawsociety.nt.ca>
Law Society of Nunavut	<http://lawsociety.nu.ca>
Law Society of Prince Edward Island	<http://www.lspei.pe.ca>
Law Society of Saskatchewan	<http://www.lawsociety.sk.ca>
Law Society of Upper Canada (Ontario)	<http://www.lsuc.on.ca>
Law Society of Yukon	<http://www.lawsocietyyukon.com>
Nova Scotia Barristers Society	<http://www.nsbs.ns.ca>

Law Society	Web Site Address
Advocates Society	<http://www.advsoc.on.ca>
Alberta Civil Trial Lawyers Association	<http://www.actla.com>
Ontario Trial Lawyers Association	<http://www.criminallawyers.ca>
Trial Lawyers Association of B.C.	<http://www.tlabc.org>

- **Online discussion groups**: Listservs — or online discussion groups — are an excellent way to share information and keep current on legal issues. Simply put, one can subscribe (usually for free) to any number of law-related online discussion groups. Any person subscribing to the group can send and receive messages to the group. One of the best listservs in Canada for legal research information is CALL-L, the listserv of the Canadian Association of Law Libraries. More details on online discussion groups are provided in Chapter 5, section K.

7) Web Guides

Increasingly, law schools, public interest organizations, law firms, and other organizations are publishing useful online Web guides that provide information or tips on finding law-related information by topic. Research on the Internet is discussed in more detail in Chapter 5. Set out below, though, are a few of the better online research guides for conducting Canadian legal research.

- **Access to Justice Network (ACJNet)**
  <http://www.acjnet.org>

  The Access to Justice Network is a Web site sponsored by the federal Department of Justice and other partners. The site provides topical access to a wide variety of Web sites useful for Canadian legal research.

- **Ted Tjaden's Guide to Doing Legal Research in Canada**
  <http://www.llrx.com/features/ca.htm>

  This online guide is aimed primarily at American researchers wishing to research Canadian law. The guide provides information and links on researching Canadian law. The host of this guide — LLRX (Law Library Resource Xchange) — has a number of other online guides to conducting legal research for various countries throughout the world.

- **Bora Laskin Law Library Links to Legal Resources**
  <http://www.law-lib.utoronto.ca/resources/>

  The Bora Laskin Law Library at the University of Toronto provides extensive links to Canadian legal topics.

- **LegalLine Online**
  <http://www.LegalLine.ca>

  Sponsored by Legal Information Ontario, a non-profit organization created in 1994, LegalLine is a Web site with legal information for people with legal problems and questions about legal matters. The site provides answers to over 800 typical legal problems divided into 28 areas of law. The organization also provides the same information over the telephone.

- **Jurist Canada**
  <http://jurist.law.utoronto.ca>

  This is the site of Jurist Canada, "The Legal Education Network." It is hosted by the University of Toronto Faculty of Law and has sister sites in the States (Jurist), England (Jurist UK), Australia (Jurist Australia), and most recently, Europe (Jurist EU) and Portugal (Jurist Portugal). The site's strength is in its organization of law-related material for legal academics, law students, and other legal researchers. There are links to legal news, legal materials by topic, and online articles. The site is also searchable.

- **Lexum**
  <http://www.lexum.umontreal.ca/index_en.html>

  This is an excellent site compiled by the University of Montreal Faculty of Law's Centre de recherche en droit public. The site includes links on Law Resources of Canada, Quebec, and International Law Resources, among other materials. Lexum also hosts the site containing decisions of the Supreme Court of Canada, in addition to hosting an online version of the *Civil Code of Québec*.

F. CONCLUSIONS

Secondary legal resources such as textbooks, journal articles, and encyclopedias should be relatively familiar and comfortable to use for most legal researchers. With competition in the legal publishing industry, the quality and currency of most secondary legal resources is excellent and makes them a useful way to find primary sources of law such as legislation (discussed next in Chapter 3) and case law (discussed in Chapter 4).

RESEARCHING LEGISLATION

A. INTRODUCTION

Legislative materials, in the form of statutes, regulations, and statutory instruments, are an important source of law. While some citizens may not realize the power of judge-made case law to affect their rights, most citizens do realize that statutes and regulations have the power to legally affect them. Created by or through elected politicians, legislation consists of written rules that govern or prescribe the conduct of the citizens who elected the government officials. Despite the importance of legislation to our legal system and to legal research, very few people enjoy conducting legislative research.

There are several reasons why legislative research can be a challenge:

- Legislation continues to be mired in 19th century print technology, replete with publishing delays, poor consolidation of amended provisions, and awkward "Tables" for updating changes to legislative text.
- The legislative process is still somewhat mysterious to most people, involving a sense of back-room lobbying and various technical legislative rules, such as the need for draft legislation to pass three readings.
- Legislation involves a fairly obscure vocabulary and literature unfamiliar to the uninitiated, including such concepts or terms as proroguement, Royal Assent, proclamations, and Orders-in-Council (these terms are explained later in this chapter).

Fortunately, legislators and commercial publishers are improving access to legislation with the advent of computer and Internet technology. Online legislative databases allow for keyword searching and can be kept fairly current. Quicklaw, WestlaweCARSWELL, and LexisNexis, for example, have legislation databases for both federal and provincial legislation (British Columbia, Alberta, Ontario, and other provinces) that are usually current and consolidated to within a few days. Increasingly, Canadian federal and provincial legislators are looking to make electronic versions of their legislation "official versions" for the purpose of being accepted in court (ordinarily, courts have traditionally accepted as evidence in court only official Queen's Printer versions of legislation as official versions). The federal government, for example, in the *Personal Information Protection and Electronic Documents Act*[1] amended sections 19 to 22 of the *Canada Evidence Act*[2] and added provisions after section 31 of that Act to provide that the electronic versions of legislation published by the federal Queen's Printer be deemed to be official versions of legislation for the purpose of court proceedings. Another development has been the announcement by the Ontario government of its ambitious e-Laws project in which it proposes to publish free Internet access to Ontario laws that will eventually be current to within 24 hours and that will allow "point-in-time" historical research.[3]

Given this improvement in online access to legislation, is it still necessary to learn print legislative research? Unfortunately, since online legislative databases tend to provide only current, consolidated "snapshots" of the law, it will still be necessary to conduct print legislative research for historical research, such as needing to confirm the state of the law at a period of time in the past. In addition, not all Canadian provincial jurisdictions have moved as quickly in making their legislation available online, and for these jurisdictions, it is still necessary to do most legislative research using print resources. Finally, learning how to conduct legislative research in print can provide valuable context for understanding what is being viewed online.

This chapter proposes that most legislative research can be successfully, and somewhat enjoyably, undertaken by following the steps in the legislative research checklist set out below:

---

1   S.C. 2000, c. 5.
2   R.S.C. 1985, c. C-5.
3   See online: E-Laws <http://www.e-laws.gov.on.ca>.

Legislative Research Checklist

Step 1: Identify which level of government has jurisdiction over the subject matter of your research.

Step 2: Identify and consult relevant statutes. If conducting historical research, use print resources. If researching current law, prefer online to print resources.

Step 3: Check to ensure there are no amendments to the provisions by consulting recent bills and "noter uppers."

Step 4: Check for relevant regulations, if any.

Step 5: Check for court decisions that have considered your legislation or check for statutory interpretation materials if the legislation is ambiguous.

B. STEP 1: IDENTIFYING THE RELEVANT JURISDICTION

Step 1 in the legislative research checklist is to identify the level of government that has jurisdiction to legislate on the topic being researched. In Canada, there is a division of power between the federal and provincial governments. Another level of government and legislation in the form of bylaws exist at the municipal level. When researching a particular topic, it is important to know which level of government has power to enact laws for that subject or whether power to legislate may be shared by more than one level of government.

Under section 91 of the *Constitution Act, 1867 (U.K.),*[4] for example, the federal government of Canada is given exclusive power to "make Laws for the Peace, Order, and good Government of Canada, in relation to all Matters not coming within the Classes of Subjects by this Act assigned exclusively to the Legislatures of the Provinces." Some of these federal powers to legislate include such topics as the regulation of trade and commerce, unemployment insurance, the postal service, militia, military and naval service, defence, banking, and patents and copyright. Federal statutes were last published as an up-to-date consolidated set in the mid 1980s as the *Revised Statutes of Canada* (1985), a multi-volume bilingual set that was published over approximately four years that includes a number of supplemental volumes and an index.[5]

---

4   30 & 31 Vict., c. 3, reprinted in R.S.C. 1985, App. II, No. 5.

5   Canadian federal statutes have been revised as a "set" in the following years: 1886, 1906, 1927, 1952, 1970, and 1985.

Under section 92 of the *Constitution Act, 1867*, the provincial governments have exclusive power over such areas as direct taxation within the province to raise revenue for provincial purposes, prisons (but not penitentiaries), the incorporation of companies with provincial objects, the solemnization of marriage in the province, property and civil rights in the province, and generally all matters of a merely local or private nature in the province. Ontario, for example, has recently published its statutes as up-to-date consolidated bilingual sets every decade, with the most recent set being the *Revised Statutes of Ontario* (1990).[6]

Power is shared between the federal Parliament and the provincial legislatures over agriculture, immigration, and over certain aspects of natural resources; but federal laws would prevail in the event of any conflict between federal and provincial laws over these subject areas.[7] Parliament and the provincial legislatures also have power over old age, disability, and survivors' pensions; but provincial laws would prevail if there were conflicts between federal and provincial laws over these subject areas.[8] Aside from these areas, there is a general rule that everything not listed in the *Constitution Act, 1867* as belonging to the provincial legislatures comes under the powers of Parliament.[9]

Municipal governments are generally given power by provincial legislation (typically called the *Municipal Act*) to enact bylaws to provide rules to govern on matters of a local nature including such things as school taxes, local roads and highways, and rules governing building permits.

Knowing which level of government has jurisdiction over a particular matter is often a matter of experience. Alternatively, one can check the legislative index of the revised statutes for the jurisdiction in question to see if the index covers the topic. In addition, one can consult the listing of the division of powers in sections 91 and 92 of the *Constitution Act, 1867*. For those researchers in Ontario, one can consult the *Index to Federal and Ontario Statutes Online*.[10] One of the easiest ways to identify relevant legislation, however, is to consult a good book on the topic since most authors of law-related textbooks will identify relevant legislation and will include a "Table of Legislation" at the start or end of the book identifying the legislation discussed in the book. See

---

6   Ontario statutes have been revised as a "set" in the following years: 1877, 1887, 1897, 1914, 1927, 1937, 1950, 1960, 1970, 1980, and 1990.

7   Above note 4, ss. 92A, 95.

8   *Ibid.*, s. 94A.

9   *Ibid.*, s. 91.

10   Mary K. McLean (Toronto: Captus Press), online: Captus Press <http:/www.captus.com> [paid subscription required].

Chapter 8 for an extensive listing of Canadian law-related textbooks, set out by various legal topics.

Ultimately, there will be a definite trend towards conducting legislative research using online resources where one can simply search applicable legislative databases by keyword or concept to determine if any legislative provisions deal with the keyword or concept.

C. STEP 2: ACCESSING STATUTES (PRINT AND ONLINE)

Step 2 of the legislative research checklist, once the correct jurisdiction has been chosen from Step 1, is to identify and then consult the relevant legislative provisions from that jurisdiction using either print or online sources. As mentioned above, researchers will sometimes have a choice between print and online resources for conducting legislative research. If the research being done is historical, there is often no choice but to follow the traditional print method of finding statutes, discussed below. If what is wanted is confirmation of the current law, then use of online resources (CD-ROM, Internet or commercial online database) — where available — can save time and avoid some of the multiple steps involved in using the traditional print method.

1) The Traditional Print Method for Identifying and Consulting Statutes

The way statutes in print are published and indexed varies across the Canadian federal and provincial jurisdictions; thus, the descriptions that follow are quite general. Researchers with specific questions for particular jurisdictions outside of Ontario and federally should consult *Updating Statutes and Regulations*,[11] a useful but now slightly dated resource, that provides details on conducting legislative research across all Canadian jurisdictions.

There is a three-step approach to identifying and consulting statutes in print:

1. Consult Index: Consult the print Index to the most recent consolidated set for the jurisdiction, look up the topic by keyword, and consult the statute and section indicated in the Index (see Figure 3.1 for a sample of the Index to the *Revised Statutes of Canada* (1985) show-

---

11   Mary Jane T. Sinclair, 4th ed. (Toronto: Carswell, 1995).

ing an entry under the heading "Indians," with one of the entries being "seizure, exemptions, c. I-5, s. 29") on the assumption you were researching whether Indian land could be seized by a creditor.

Figure 3.1
Index to the *Revised Statutes of Canada* (1985)

Index

INDIANS

- grave houses
  destruction, defacement or removal, unauthorized, c. I-5, s. 91(3)
  transactions, restrictions, c. I-5, s. 91
- grave poles
  destruction, defacement or removal, unauthorized, c. I-5, s. 91(3)
  transactions, restrictions, c. I-5, s. 91
- house posts, carved
  destruction, defacement or removal, c. I-5, s. 91(3)
  transactions, restrictions, c. I-5, s. 91
- Indian Act, application, c. I-5, s. 4
- intoxicants
  by-laws, procedure, c. I-5, s. 85.1
  defined, c. I-5, s. 2(1)
  goods and chattels, seizure, detention and forfeiture, circumstances, c. I-5, s. 103
- land
  Certificates of Occupation, cancellations or corrections, c. I-5, ss. 26, 27
  Certificates of Occupation, effect, c. I-5, ss. 20(5), (6)
  Certificates of Possession, cancellations or corrections, c. I-5, ss. 26, 27
  Certificates of Possession, effect, c. I-5, s. 20(2)
  control and management, c. I-5, s. 60
  electricity, international power lines, use, restrictions, c. N-7, s. 78
  estates and intestacies, court orders, restrictions, c. I-5, s. 44(3)
  expropriation, procedure, c. E-21, s. 4; c. I-5, ss. 18(2), 35
  gas pipeline companies, use, restrictions, c. N-7, s. 78
  gas, regulations, c. I-7, s. 3
  gas, royalties, requirements, c. I-7, s. 4
  improvements, compensation, c. I-5, s. 23
  improvements, effect, c. I-5, s. 22
  Indian bands, new bands, rights, c. I-5, s. 17(2)
  Indian land, defined, c. I-7, s. 2
  leases and other dispositions, amount payable and interest rates, reductions, c. I-5, s. 59(a)
  leases and other dispositions, restrictions, c. I-5, s. 37
  Location Tickets, effect, c. I-5, s. 20(3)
  oil pipeline companies, use, restrictions, c. N-7, s. 78
  oil, regulations, c. I-7, s. 3
  oil, royalties, requirements, c. I-7, s. 4
  Reserve Land Register, c. I-5, s. 21
  sales, restrictions, c. I-5, s. 37
  taxation, exemptions, c. I-5, s. 87
  title not vested in Crown, effect, c. I-5, s. 36
  uses, restrictions, c. I-5, s. 18
- land, possessory rights
  devisees and descendants, restrictions, c. I-5, ss. 49, 50
  lawful possession, deemed, circumstances, c. I-5, ss. 20(3), 22

possession, allotment, c. I-5, ss. 20(1), (4), (6)
possession, requirements, c. I-5, s. 20(1)
reversion to band, circumstances, c. I-5, s. 25(2)
sales, circumstances and procedure, c. I-5, s. 50
temporary possession, circumstances, c. I-5, s. 20(4)
transfers, restrictions, c. I-5, ss. 24, 25
- land, uncultivated or unused
  agricultural or grazing leases, c. I-5, s. 58(1)
  improvement and cultivation, c. I-5, s. 58(1)
- leases
  agricultural or grazing leases, rent, c. I-5, s. 58(2)
  amount payable, reduction, c. I-5, s. 59(a)
  effect, c. I-5, s. 58(3)
  interest rates, reduction, c. I-5, s. 59(a)
  restrictions, c. I-5, s. 37
- maintenance
  cost, liability, c. I-5, s. 34(2)
  roads, bridges, ditches and fences, c. I-5, s. 34
- mines and minerals, surrendered, regulations, c. I-5, s. 57(c)
- natural resources, transactions
  restrictions, c. I-5, s. 39
  unauthorized, c. I-5, s. 33
- occupation and use
  agreements, restrictions, c. I-5, s. 28
  authorization, c. I-5, s. 89(1)
  unauthorized, c. I-5, s. 31
- oil pipeline companies, use, requirements, c. N-7, s. 78
- personal property situated on a reserve
  conditional sales, effect, c. I-5, s. 89(2)
  distress, exemptions, c. I-5, s. 89(1)
  executions, attachments or levies, exemptions, c. I-5, s. 89(1)
  mortgages, charges or pledges, exemptions, c. I-5, s. 89(1)
  seizure, exemptions, c. I-5, s. 89(1)
- personal property situated on a reserve, deemed
  description, c. I-5, s. 90(1)
  destruction, unauthorized, c. I-5, s. 90(3)
  taxation, exemptions, c. I-5, s. 87
  transactions, restrictions, c. I-5, s. 90(2)
- property taxes, federal property, exclusions, circumstances, c. M-13, s. 2(3)
- reserves, defined, c. C-1, s. 10; c. I-5, s. 2(1); c. N-11, s. 2
- roads
  location and direction, c. I-5, s. 19(c)
  maintenance, c. I-5, s. 34
- rocks, painted or carved
  destruction, defacement or removal, c. I-5, s. 91(3)
  transactions, restrictions, c. I-5, s. 91
- searches, circumstances, c. I-5, s. 103(4)
- seizure

exemptions, c. I-5, s. 29
goods and chattels, circumstances, c. I-5, s. 103(1)
- subdivisions, c. I-5, s. 19(b)
- surrendered land
  assignments, certificates of registration, c. I-5, s. 56
  assignments, registration, requirements and effect, c. I-5, s. 55
  defined, c. I-5, s. 2(1)
  designated lands, defined, c. I-5, s. 2(1)
  devisees, descendants or assignees, applications for grants, requirements, c. I-5, s. 53(2)
  Indian Act, application, c. I-5, s. 4(2)
  leases, assignments, requirements, c. I-5, s. 54
  leases, requirements, c. I-5, s. 53
  leases, Surrendered and Designated Lands Register, inclusion, c. I-5, s. 55(1)
  management, c. I-5, s. 53
  maps, Territories land titles, effect, c. L-5, s. 87
  railway companies, powers, c. R-3, s. 137
- surrendered land, sales and dispositions
  amounts payable and interest rates, reduction, c. I-5, s. 59(a)
  assignments, requirements, c. I-5, s. 54
  requirements, c. I-5, s. 53
  Surrendered and Designated Lands Register, inclusion, c. I-5, s. 55(1)
  taxation, exemptions, c. I-5, s. 87
  timber licences, c. I-5, s. 57
- surrenders
  certification, c. I-5, s. 40
  effect, c. I-5, ss. 37, 41
  Indian bands, powers, c. I-5, s. 38
  procedure, c. I-5, s. 39
- surveys, c. I-5, s. 19(a)
- timber
  fallen or dead, dispositions, proceeds, c. I-5, ss. 58(4)(a), (5)
  restrictions, c. I-5, s. 57
- title, c. I-5, s. 18(1)
- totem poles
  destruction, defacement or removal, c. I-5, s. 91(3)
  transactions, restrictions, c. I-5, s. 91
- trespass, c. I-5, ss. 30, 31
- wild grass, dispositions, proceeds, c. I-5, ss. 58(4)(a), (5)

INDIANS
see also ABORIGINAL CANADIANS
- Acts (provinces), application, c. I-5, s. 88
- band councils
  gas royalties, agreements, approval, c. I-7, s. 4(2)
  inclusion in definition of agencies, c. F-24, s. 2
  Indian Oil and Gas Act, administration, consultation, c. I-7, s. 6(1)
  oil royalties, agreements, approval, c. I-7, s. 4(2)

451

Unfortunately, print indices to statutes and regulations are generally not very good or detailed. Some of the smaller provinces do not have indices to their statutes, due to the cost of preparation. To a certain extent, the advent of full-text electronic searching has minimized the problem caused by print indices. Some commercial publishers publish consolidated or annotated versions of legislation,[12] sometimes for one particular statute and other times on a group of statutes that affect a particular topic. Such publications often contain good quality indices that can provide another means of accessing statutes by topic. If you cannot identify relevant access points from the Index, it may be that you made a mistake in Step 1 and you should try consulting legislation from a different jurisdiction in case the matter is one of federal (or provincial) jurisdiction, as the case may be.

2. Consult applicable statute: Once you have identified relevant entries using the Index to the statutes, consult the applicable provisions by section and chapter number to determine if the statute identified in the Index is relevant for your research (see Figure 3.2 for a sample section of the *Revised Statutes of Canada* (1985) that matches the Index entry from Figure 3.1). If it is not relevant, re-consult the Index and try looking for additional terms. Make note of the format of the type of print statute you are consulting: Is it part of a bound, revised set, such as the 1985 *Revised Statutes of Canada*? Or is it part of a looseleaf set (such as is available for the *Continuing Consolidated Statutes of Manitoba*)? This consideration is relevant in order to determine how current (or how out-of-date) the print resource is.

3. Note up the statute: It is important when using print resources to be aware of the publishing delay for the particular resource. If one is consulting one of the blue volumes of the 1985 *Revised Statutes of Canada*, for example, the text may be close to twenty years or more out-of-date. It is therefore critical to note up any print-based legislative research to check for any possible amendments to or repeals of the legislation. Noting up is discussed in the next section of this chapter as Step 3 of the Legislative Research Checklist.

Another traditional technique for print-based "historical" legislative research is to follow Steps 1 and 2 above and then to trace the statutory section in question backwards (not forwards) to see predecessor

---

12   Consolidated statutes bring all relevant laws together in one publication, whereas annotated statutes provide summaries of cases that have considered particular sections of the legislation.

Figure 3.2

Sample Page from the *Revised Statutes of Canada* (1985)
(Showing s. 29 of the *Indian Act*, R.S.C. 1985, c. I-5)

14	Chap. I-5		*Indian*

Minister may issue permits

(2) The Minister may by permit in writing authorize any person for a period not exceeding one year, or with the consent of the council of the band for any longer period, to occupy or use a reserve or to reside or otherwise exercise rights on a reserve. R.S., c. I-6, s. 28.

(2) Le ministre peut, au moyen d'un permis par écrit, autoriser toute personne, pour une période maximale d'un an, ou, avec le consentement du conseil de la bande, pour toute période plus longue, à occuper ou utiliser une réserve, ou à résider ou autrement exercer des droits sur une réserve. S.R., ch. I-6, art. 28.

Le ministre peut émettre des permis

Exemption from seizure

29. Reserve lands are not subject to seizure under legal process. R.S., c. I-6, s. 29.

29. Les terres des réserves ne sont assujetties à aucune saisie sous le régime d'un acte judiciaire. S.R., ch. I-6, art. 29.

Insaisissabilité

TRESPASS ON RESERVES

VIOLATION DU DROIT DE PROPRIÉTÉ DANS LES RÉSERVES

Penalty for trespass

30. A person who trespasses on a reserve is guilty of an offence and liable on summary conviction to a fine not exceeding fifty dollars or to imprisonment for a term not exceeding one month or to both. R.S., c. I-6, s. 30.

30. Quiconque pénètre, sans droit ni autorisation, dans une réserve commet une infraction et encourt, sur déclaration de culpabilité par procédure sommaire, une amende maximale de cinquante dollars et un emprisonnement maximal d'un mois, ou l'une de ces peines. S.R., ch. I-6, art. 30.

Peine

Information by Attorney General

31. (1) Without prejudice to section 30, where an Indian or a band alleges that persons other than Indians are or have been

(*a*) unlawfully in occupation or possession of,

(*b*) claiming adversely the right to occupation or possession of, or

(*c*) trespassing on

a reserve or part of a reserve, the Attorney General of Canada may exhibit an information in the Federal Court claiming, on behalf of the Indian or band, the relief or remedy sought.

31. (1) Sans préjudice de l'article 30, lorsqu'un Indien ou une bande prétend que des personnes autres que des Indiens, selon le cas :

a) occupent ou possèdent illégalement, ou ont occupé ou possédé illégalement, une réserve ou une partie de réserve;

b) réclament ou ont réclamé sous forme d'opposition le droit d'occuper ou de posséder une réserve ou une partie de réserve;

c) pénètrent ou ont pénétré, sans droit ni autorisation, dans une réserve ou une partie de réserve,

le procureur général du Canada peut produire à la Cour fédérale une dénonciation réclamant, au nom de l'Indien ou de la bande, les mesures de redressement désirées.

Dénonciation par le procureur général

Information deemed action by Crown

(2) An information exhibited under subsection (1) shall, for all purposes of the *Federal Court Act*, be deemed to be a proceeding by the Crown within the meaning of that Act.

(2) Une dénonciation produite sous le régime du paragraphe (1) est réputée, pour l'application de la *Loi sur la Cour fédérale*, une procédure engagée par la Couronne, au sens de cette loi.

La dénonciation est réputée une action par la Couronne

Existing remedies preserved

(3) Nothing in this section shall be construed to impair, abridge or otherwise affect any right or remedy that, but for this section, would be available to Her Majesty or to an Indian or a band. R.S., c. I-6, s. 31; R.S., c. 10(2nd Supp.), ss. 64, 65.

(3) Le présent article n'a pas pour effet de porter atteinte aux droits ou recours que, en son absence, Sa Majesté, un Indien ou une bande pourrait exercer. S.R., ch. I-6, art. 31; S.R., ch. 10(2ᵉ suppl.), art. 64 et 65.

Les recours existants subsistent

SALE OR BARTER OF PRODUCE

VENTE OU TROC DE PRODUITS

Sale or barter of produce

32. (1) A transaction of any kind whereby a band or a member thereof purports to sell,

32. (1) Est nulle, à moins que le surintendant ne l'approuve par écrit, toute opération

La vente ou le troc de produits

versions of the section. One does this to trace the legislative history of the section, often with the goal of (i) tracing the section back to its origin or introduction or to look for any significant amendments to the section; or (ii) identifying previous section numbers of the section in question in order to find older cases that may have considered predecessor versions of the section (to do this, you need to know what the old section numbers are in order to use the "statutes judicially considered" type services discussed in section F below). To trace statutory sections, one can take advantage of the historical notes placed at the end of each section of the statute by the Queen's Printer by using the information in the historical note to trace the section backwards (see Figure 3.3 for an example of a historical note from the *Revised Statutes of Ontario*, 1990 showing, for example, that section 2(1) of the 1990 *Creditors' Relief Act*[13] was amended in 1985 while section 3(1) was amended in 1980). This sort of legislative history research is often used to help identify the date when the section in question was introduced by the legislature to then allow the researcher to check the Hansard debates for any relevant debate or discussion about the statutory provisions (see section F below on statutory interpretation for more on researching Hansard debates).

2) The Modern Online Method for Identifying and Consulting Statutes

Increasingly, legislative research is conducted using "electronic" sources of law (CD-ROMs, the Internet, Quicklaw, WestlaweCAR-SWELL or LexisNexis). These electronic sources of legislation tend to provide only current snapshots of the legislation,[14] the advantage of which is that the information is relatively current, especially with online databases like Quicklaw, WestlaweCARSWELL, and LexisNexis, which keep their legislative databases current to within a few days. Internet sources of Canadian legislation are discussed in Chapter 5 and commercial online databases and CD-ROMs are discussed in more detail in Chapter 6; the discussion that follows will use the legislative databases on Quicklaw as an example of using online resources for legislative research.

The typical three-step process for traditional print-based legislative research (checking index — consulting main volume — noting up) is collapsed in an online environment into one step — searching — since the data being searched upon is current and will produce current information in one search.

---

13   R.S.O. 1990, c. C.45, as am. by S.O. 1994, c. 27, s. 44; S.O. 1996, c. 31, s. 67.

14   One exception to there being only recent legislation online is the Alberta Heritage Digitization Project's Retrospective Law Collection available at <http://www.ourfutureourpast.ca/law/law_home.asp> where Alberta statutes have been digitized from 1906 to 1990 and made available online at this site for free, with plans to digitize retrospective bills and *Gazettes*.

Figure 3.3
Sample Page from the *Revised Statutes of Ontario* (1990)
(Showing Historical Notes at the End of Each Section)

CHAPTER C.45	CHAPITRE C.45
Creditors' Relief Act	**Loi sur le désintéressement des créanciers**

Definitions

1. In this Act,

"county" includes a district and a regional, district or metropolitan municipality; ("comté")

"execution" includes a writ of seizure and sale and every subsequent writ for giving effect thereto; ("saisie-exécution")

"judge" means a judge of the Ontario Court (General Division) sitting in the county the sheriff for which is required to take the proceedings directed by this Act; ("juge")

"sheriff" includes any officer to whom an execution is directed. ("shérif") R.S.O. 1980, c. 103, s. 1, *revised.*

No priority among execution or garnishment creditors

2.—(1) Subject to this Act, there is no priority among creditors by execution or garnishment issued by the Ontario Court (General Division), the Unified Family Court and the Ontario Court (Provincial Division). 1985, c. 1, s. 1, *revised.*

Exemption

(2) Subsection (1) does not affect the priority of a creditor by execution or garnishment issued by the Small Claims Court. 1989, c. 56, s. 9 (1).

Attachment to be for benefit of all creditors

3.—(1) A creditor who attaches a debt shall be deemed to do so for the benefit of all creditors of the debtor as well as for the creditor's own benefit. R.S.O. 1980, c. 103, s. 4 (1).

To whom to be paid

(2) Payment of the debt shall be made to the sheriff for the county in which the debtor resides or, if the debtor resides outside the Province, to the sheriff for the county in which the proceeding that gave rise to the judgment was commenced. 1985, c. 1, s. 2 (1).

Garnishment in courts and specified

(3) This section does not apply to a debt attached by garnishment in the Small Claims Court, the Ontario Court (Provincial Division) or the Unified Family Court unless, before the amount recovered by garnishment

Définitions

1 Les définitions qui suivent s'appliquent à la présente loi.

«comté» S'entend notamment d'un district et d'une municipalité régionale, de district ou de communauté urbaine. («county»)

«juge» Un juge de la Cour de l'Ontario (Division générale) siégeant dans le comté où le shérif est tenu d'introduire l'instance ordonnée par la présente loi. («judge»)

«saisie-exécution» S'entend notamment d'un bref de saisie-exécution et de tout bref subséquent destiné à lui donner suite. («execution»)

«shérif» S'entend notamment de l'officier de justice à qui est confiée une saisie-exécution. («sheriff») L.R.O. 1980, chap. 103, art. 1, *révisé.*

Aucun droit de priorité entre les créanciers saisissants

2 (1) Sous réserve de la présente loi, il n'existe aucun ordre de priorité à l'égard des créanciers aux termes d'une saisie-exécution ou d'une saisie-arrêt émanant de la Cour de l'Ontario (Division générale), de la Cour unifiée de la famille ou de la Cour de l'Ontario (Division provinciale). 1985, chap. 1, art. 1, *révisé.*

Exception

(2) Le paragraphe (1) n'a pas d'incidence sur le droit de priorité d'un créancier aux termes d'une saisie-exécution ou d'une saisie-arrêt émanant de la Cour des petites créances. 1989, chap. 56, par. 9 (1).

Saisie au profit de tous les créanciers

3 (1) Le créancier saisissant est réputé effectuer la saisie tant au profit de tous les créanciers du débiteur qu'à son propre profit. L.R.O. 1980, chap. 103, par. 4 (1).

Paiement

(2) Le paiement de la créance est fait au shérif du comté où réside le débiteur ou, si le débiteur réside en dehors de la province, au shérif du comté où a été introduite l'instance qui a donné lieu au jugement. 1985, chap. 1, par. 2 (1).

Saisies-arrêts émanant des cours spécifiées

(3) Le présent article ne s'applique pas aux saisies-arrêts émanant de la Cour des petites créances, de la Cour de l'Ontario (Division provinciale) ou de la Cour unifiée de la famille, sauf si un bref de saisie-exécu-

Quicklaw provides extremely current legislative databases for federal legislation and for Alberta, British Columbia, and Ontario (Quicklaw also provides legislative databases for other Canadian provinces but they are often not necessarily as current). Some of the more popular types of legislative databases on Quicklaw are as follows:

- **Full-text "entire" act databases:** These databases contain the full text of entire, current Acts for the jurisdiction being researched. One can browse through an alphabetical list of these statutes by title or by searching by keyword the entire text of all statutes for the jurisdiction. The full text of the entire Act is then displayed on the screen and can be downloaded or printed out (subject to the licence terms).
- **Full-text "section" act databases:** These databases allow the researcher to search the full text of all statutes or a particular statute for the jurisdiction but, instead of results being displayed by showing the entire full text of the Act, results are displayed only by sections where the keywords appear.

D. STEP 3: NOTING UP LEGISLATION (CITATORS AND BILLS)

Once one has identified the correct jurisdiction (Step 1) and then identified and consulted the relevant statute (Step 2), it is essential that one note up the statute to ensure that the section in question has not been amended or repealed (Step 3). There are two basic methods to note up statutory provisions: (i) the "official" print method; and (ii) "unofficial" print and online methods. Before these methods are discussed, it is important to understand the legislative process and the way in which legislation is amended or repealed.

1) The Legislative Process

There is much written in the legal literature about how laws are made in Canada. In order to properly note up statutes, it helps to understand the legislative process since it is often necessary to consult legislation when it is in its draft or "bill" form.

As a starting point, the political party holding the most number of seats controls the legislative process through its majority control of the legislature. As such, the party in power will introduce legislation that supports its political policies. Quite often, legislation and policies will be discussed by Cabinet and then the details of the legislation will be worked upon by the deputy minister and his or her staff for the relevant ministry most closely associated with the subject matter of the legislation.

Once the draft legislation has been prepared, it will be introduced into the legislature as a bill and must pass through three stages or "readings" before it can become law. The procedure below describes the process for Ontario legislation:

First reading: The bill is introduced by the Minister responsible, who also explains its objectives and makes a motion for its formal introduction. If the members vote in favour of the bill, it is assigned a number, printed, given to each member of the legislative assembly, and scheduled for future debate.

Second reading: The bill is debated in the House of Commons. There is then a vote whether the bill will proceed to the committee stage (or directly to third reading stage, in some cases).

If the bill was "sent to committee" this means it will be examined in detail by the committee for that subject matter or ministry (one of eleven standing committees) or by a specially created committee (a select committee). The committee will usually be made up of members from all political parties but controlled by the party with majority power. The bill is discussed section by section. This is the stage where changes are made, sometimes as a result of political compromise, sometimes because of a change in policy by the majority, and sometimes simply to improve clarity.

The committee process may last a few days or a few months, depending on the bill. The committee will then debate whether to send the bill to the Committee of the whole House (for more study by the entire legislature) or directly into final debate.

Third reading: This is the final debate on the bill. If the vote carries, the bill is sent to the Lieutenant Governor for approval (called "Royal Assent"). The bill is also given a chapter number at this time.

Federally, a bill must also pass through three readings in the House of Commons but it then must also pass through three readings in the Senate. Alternatively, the Senate itself can introduce legislation (usually only so long as it does not relate to taxes or financial expenditures). In this case, the bill must pass three readings in the Senate and then pass three readings in the House of Commons. Federal bills must be published in the *Canada Gazette, Part III* before they are official.

Most bills are public bills — these are typically introduced by a member of Cabinet and relate to laws of general application throughout the jurisdiction. There are also private member bills — these can be introduced by any member and are often introduced by members of the opposition party. If they are too controversial, they often do not pass third reading. In addition, there are private bills — these can be introduced by any member and are not of general application but typically relate to a particular organization or individual.

When is a statute in force? Once a bill has received Royal Assent, it may not yet be in force. A statute may come into force in one of three ways:

* The statute will state when it comes into force (usually at the end of the statute).
* The statute will state it comes into force upon Royal Assent.
* The statute will state it comes into force upon "proclamation."

The date of proclamation is usually given in the *Gazette*, a publication used by the government to publish regulations and other notices. The advantage to the government for having a law come into force upon "proclamation" is that it may not know at the time the bill passes third reading when it and the relevant ministry will be ready for the new legislation. Brochures may need to be printed, staff may need training, and so on. A proclamation date therefore provides flexibility since the government can cause the Lieutenant Governor (or Governor General, federally) to announce the proclamation date whenever it suits the needs of the government. Sections 5 and 6 of the federal *Interpretation Act*[15] provide special rules when federal legislation shall be deemed to come into force when the legislation does not specify a particular day.

If a legislative session ends (when it is "prorogued"), any bills not specifically brought forward to the next session of the legislative assembly are said to have "died on the Order paper" and will not come into force.

Federal proclamation dates can be found in a number of sources, including the "Proclamations of Canada" tables in the annual statute volumes, in *Canada Gazette Part III*, the *Canada Statute Citator* (Canada Law Book on CD-ROM or by Internet subscription), the *Canada Legislative Index* (B.C. Courthouse Library Society), and Quicklaw (database: CB).

Ontario proclamation dates can also be found in a number of sources including the *Ontario Gazette*, online on the Proclamations page of the Ontario Legislative Assembly Web site, the *Ontario Statute Citator* (Canada Law Book on CD-ROM or by Internet subscription), and Quicklaw (database: OB).

Provincial bills are assigned a (consecutive) number depending whether they are public bills (Bill 76) or private bills (Bill Pr 7). Feder-

---

15   R.S.C. 1985, c. I-21.

al bills are also assigned numbers in addition to a letter (C or S) signifying where the bill originated: Bill C-5 signifies the bill originated in the House of Commons; Bill S-11 signifies the bill originated in the Senate.

Statutes and regulations are ordinarily given a short title, the name by which you may refer to the statute. Use the short title plus the balance of the citation (year, chapter number, and source) when citing statutes or regulations. Refer to Chapter 2 of the McGill Guide for more information on citing legislation.

2) The Official Print Method of Noting Up Legislation

The official method of noting up statutes using print resources involves consulting the most recent Table of Public Statutes for the jurisdiction in question. Tables of Public Statutes are official alphabetical lists of statutes published by the Queen's Printer for the jurisdiction that show any amendments or repeals to specific statutory provisions or entire Acts up to the date indicated in the start of the Table (see Figure 3.4 for a sample of the Table of Public Statutes current to 31 December 2003 for the *Revised Statutes of Canada* (1985), which shows, for example, that there were no amendments to section 29 of the *Indian Act* shown above in Figure 3.2). To check for amendments or repeals since the date indicated in the start of the Table of Public Statutes it is necessary to check the Web site for the legislature for the applicable jurisdiction for any recent bills that may have amended the statute in question, checking for both specific amendment bills (relating to only the Act you are researching) and omnibus bills (which may affect more than one piece of legislation). Finally, you must check to see if the amending bill has been proclaimed in force. Alternatively, one can phone the legislative counsel or Clerk of the House for the jurisdiction in question to confirm such information.

3) Unofficial Methods of Noting Up Statutes (Print and Online)

The unofficial method of noting up statutes using print resources involves consulting commercial citator services, such as Canada Law Book's Internet and CD-ROM services for federal legislation and for Ontario and British Columbia.[16] These citator services contain alpha-

---

16   Including the *Canada Statute Citator*, the *British Columbia Statute Citator*, and the *Ontario Statute Citator*.

Figure 3.4
Table of Public Statutes, *Revised Statutes of Canada* (Current to 31 December 2003) (Showing No Amendments to section 29 of the *Indian Act*)

I

CIF, 2000, c. 12, s. 147 in force 31.07.2000 *see* SI/2000-76 *see also* s. 147(2) and (3) *re* application
CIF, 2001, c. 17, ss. 232 and 249 in force on assent 14.06.2001 *see also* s. 249(2) *re* application

Income Tax Agreements (or Conventions) (*see* **Agreements — Income Tax, etc.**)

Income Tax Conventions Interpretation Act — R.S., 1985, c. I-4
(*Interprétation des conventions en matière d'impôts sur le revenu, Loi sur l'*)

Minister of Finance

s. 5, 1993, c. 24, s. 147; 1998, c. 19, s. 286; 1999, c. 22, s. 84
s. 5.1, added, 1993, c. 24, s. 148; 1998, c. 19, s. 287; 1999, c. 22, s. 85
s. 6.1, added, R.S., c. 48 (1st Supp.), s. 2
s. 6.2, added, 1991, c. 49, s. 220
s. 6.3, added, 1999, c. 22, s. 86
CIF, R.S., c. 48 (1st Supp.) in force 29.10.85 *see also* ss. 2(1)
CIF, 1991, c. 49, s. 220 in force on assent 17.12.91
CIF, 1993, c. 24, ss. 147 and 148 in force on assent 10.06.93
CIF, 1998, c. 19, ss. 286 and 287 in force on assent 18.06.96 *see also* ss. 286(2) and 287(2) *re* application
CIF, 1999, c. 22, ss. 84 to 86 in force on assent 17.06.99

Indian Act — R.S., 1985, c. I-5
(*Indiens, Loi sur les*)

Minister of Indian Affairs and Northern Development; Minister of Health (Indian Health Regulations)

s. 2, R.S., c. 32 (1st Supp.), s. 1; R.S., c. 17 (4th Supp.), s. 1; 2000, c. 12, s. 148
s. 4, R.S., c. 32 (1st Supp.), s. 2
s. 4.1, added, R.S., c. 32 (1st Supp.), s. 3; R.S., c. 48 (4th Supp.), s. 1
s. 5, R.S., c. 32 (1st Supp.), s. 4
s. 6, R.S., c. 32 (1st Supp.), s. 4; R.S., c. 43 (4th Supp.), s. 1
s. 7, R.S., c. 32 (1st Supp.), s. 4
s. 8, R.S., c. 32 (1st Supp.), s. 4
s. 9, R.S., c. 32 (1st Supp.), s. 4
s. 10, R.S., c. 32 (1st Supp.), s. 4
s. 11, R.S., c. 32 (1st Supp.), s. 4; R.S., c. 43 (4th Supp.), s. 2
s. 12, R.S., c. 32 (1st Supp.), s. 4
s. 13, R.S., c. 32 (1st Supp.), s. 4
s. 13.1, added, R.S., c. 32 (1st Supp.), s. 4
s. 13.2, added, R.S., c. 32 (1st Supp.), s. 4
s. 13.3, added, R.S., c. 32 (1st Supp.), s. 4
s. 14, R.S., c. 32 (1st Supp.), s. 4

s. 14.1, added, R.S., c. 32 (1st Supp.), s. 4
s. 14.2, added, R.S., c. 32 (1st Supp.), s. 4
s. 14.3, added, R.S., c. 32 (1st Supp.), s. 4; R.S., c. 27 (2nd Supp.), s. 10 (Sch., item 13); 1990, c. 16, s. 14, c. 17, s. 25; 1992, c. 51, s. 54; 1993, c. 28, s. 78 (Sch. III, item 73), this amendment was repealed before it came into force by 1999, c. 3, s. 12 (Sch., item 16); 1998, c. 30, par. 14(*j*); 1999, c. 3, s. 69; 2002, c. 7, s. 183
s. 15, R.S., c. 32 (1st Supp.), s. 5
s. 16, R.S., c. 32 (1st Supp.), s. 6
s. 17, R.S., c. 32 (1st Supp.), s. 7
s. 18.1, added, R.S., c. 32 (1st Supp.), s. 8
s. 31, 2002, c. 8, par. 182(1)(*u*)
s. 37, R.S., c. 17 (4th Supp.), s. 2
s. 38, R.S., c. 17 (4th Supp.), s. 2
s. 39, R.S., c. 17 (4th Supp.), s. 3
s. 40, R.S., c. 17 (4th Supp.), s. 4
s. 41, R.S., c. 17 (4th Supp.), s. 4
s. 48, R.S., c. 32 (1st Supp.), s. 9; R.S., c. 48 (4th Supp.), s. 2; 2000, c. 12, ss 149, 151
s. 50.1, added, 2000, c. 12, s. 150
s. 52.1, added, R.S., c. 48 (4th Supp.), s. 3
s. 52.2, added, R.S., c. 48 (4th Supp.), s. 3
s. 52.3, added, R.S., c. 48 (4th Supp.), s. 3
s. 52.4, added, R.S., c. 48 (4th Supp.), s. 3; 1992, c. 1, s. 144 (Sch. VII, item 35)(F)
s. 52.5, added, R.S., c. 48 (4th Supp.), s. 3
s. 53, R.S., c. 17 (4th Supp.), s. 5
s. 54, R.S., c. 17 (4th Supp.), s. 6
s. 55, R.S., c. 17 (4th Supp.), s. 7
s. 58, R.S., c. 17 (4th Supp.), s. 8
s. 59, R.S., c. 17 (4th Supp.), s. 9
s. 64, R.S., c. 32 (1st Supp.), s. 10
s. 64.1, added, R.S., c. 32 (1st Supp.), s. 11
s. 66, R.S., c. 32 (1st Supp.), s. 12; 1996, c. 23, s. 187(*e*)
s. 68, R.S., c. 32 (1st Supp.), s. 13; 2000, c. 12, par. 152(*a*)
s. 77, R.S., c. 32 (1st Supp.), s. 14 (*see* SOR/86-925)
s. 81, R.S., c. 32 (1st Supp.), s. 15; 2000, c. 12, par. 152(*b*)
s. 83, R.S., c. 17 (4th Supp.), s. 10
s. 85, repealed, R.S., c. 17 (4th Supp.), s. 11
s. 85.1, added, R.S., c. 32 (1st Supp.), s. 16
s. 89, R.S., c. 17 (4th Supp.), s. 12
s. 94, repealed, R.S., c. 32 (1st Supp.), s. 17
s. 95, repealed, R.S., c. 32 (1st Supp.), s. 17
s. 96, repealed, R.S., c. 32 (1st Supp.), s. 17
s. 97, repealed, R.S., c. 32 (1st Supp.), s. 17
s. 98, repealed, R.S., c. 32 (1st Supp.), s. 17
s. 99, repealed, R.S., c. 32 (1st Supp.), s. 17
s. 100, repealed, R.S., c. 32 (1st Supp.), s. 17
s. 103, R.S., c. 32 (1st Supp.), s. 19
s. 106, R.S., c. 27 (1st Supp.), s. 203
s. 109, repealed, R.S., c. 32 (1st Supp.), s. 20
s. 110, repealed, R.S., c. 32 (1st Supp.), s. 20
s. 111, repealed, R.S., c. 32 (1st Supp.), s. 20
s. 112, repealed, R.S., c. 32 (1st Supp.), s. 20
s. 113, repealed, R.S., c. 32 (1st Supp.), s. 20
s. 114, 1993, c. 28, s. 78 (Sch. III, item 74); 2002, c. 7, s. 184

betical lists of statutes showing any amendments to each statute. They are kept current by the publisher and recent amendments can be ascertained by checking the "Weekly Bulletin Service" pages for the status of bills or table of proclamations that may affect the Act being researched. Since these print "Weekly Bulletin Service" pages ordinarily suffer a publishing lag time of a few weeks, it is sometimes necessary either to telephone the Clerk of the House or legislative counsel in order to completely update legislative research where only print sources are being used.

The *Canadian Abridgment* has a legislative component called *Canadian Current Law: Legislation* that provides the status of current bills. The British Columbia Courthouse Library Society also provides a federal citator service called *Canada Legislative Index* that provides information on federal bills that may amend or repeal federal statutes and an equivalent service for British Columbia (the *British Columbia Legislative Index*).

CCH Canadian has also launched its award-winning *Canadian Legislative Pulse* Internet subscription service at <http://pulse.cch.ca>. This database makes tracking of federal and provincial bills extremely easy (in addition to providing links to the full text of the bills). It is continuously updated and the system keeps track of changes since you last logged in. The database is searchable and allows legislation to be sorted by bill number, bill title, or chapter number.

Alternatively, as mentioned above, one can use unofficial sources of legislation provided by commercial publishers in the form of books of consolidated or annotated legislation by topic (Canada Law Book's *Ontario Landlord and Tenant Legislation*, for example), which are kept current on an annual basis. It is then possible to note up these unofficial sources of statutes by following the steps above.

Increasingly, current legislative research can be effectively conducted using online databases, which are often current to within a few days, thereby eliminating the noting up process. In addition, Quicklaw has two types of legislative databases that are useful for noting up the status of legislation:

- **Bills databases:** Quicklaw has full-text, searchable databases for federal, Alberta, British Columbia, and Ontario bills, the only source of such data in Canada as of the date of publication of this book. These databases are extremely useful to search by keywords to check for the introduction of any new legislative provisions for the jurisdiction in question based on the keywords being searched upon. For those jurisdictions such as Ontario that enact a large number of "omnibus" bills (such as its various *Miscellaneous Red Tape Reduction Acts*) that amend a number of existing statutory provisions, it is often very difficult to ascertain quickly what statutory provisions are being amended by the omnibus bill. Quicklaw's Ontario Bills database is often the only quick way to conclude definitively whether an existing statutory provision is being amended. To do this, search the full text of the Bills database by the name of the existing statutory enactment. Thus, if you want to know if there have been any amendments to Ontario's *Education Act* in the current legislative session, search on "education +1 act" in the Ontario Bills database.

- **Legislative tracking:** Quicklaw has useful databases for tracking the status of current federal bills and bills for Alberta, British Columbia, and Ontario. While this information can be found elsewhere, these databases are updated regularly and provide a nice snap-shot of a particular bill's legislative history. Figure 3.5 sets out an example of the Progress of Bills information that can be found on Quicklaw (the example shows part of the Quicklaw status of bills entry for the *Rate Stabilization Act, 2003*).

E. STEP 4: UNDERSTANDING AND RESEARCHING REGULATIONS

Once one has identified the correct jurisdiction (Step 1) and then identified and consulted the relevant statute (Step 2), and noted up the statute for amendments and repeals (Step 3), it is often prudent to check automatically for regulations enacted under the statute to determine if any regulations are relevant to the legal research problem. To start with, it is important to realize that statutes and regulations are both considered to be legislation since they regulate the conduct of people and have the impact of law. There are, however, several basic distinctions between statutes and regulations. Simply put:

- Statutes are enacted by the legislative assembly after debate and vote of the entire house. Regulations, on the other hand, do not endure the same public scrutiny but are instead promulgated by the appropriate government ministry bureaucrats or other bodies after varying degrees of public consultation and then most often enacted by the Lieutenant Governor or Governor General. As such, regulations are considered subordinate or delegated legislation.

Figure 3.5

Sample Entry from Quicklaw's Progress of Legislation Data from the Ontario Bills (OB) Database

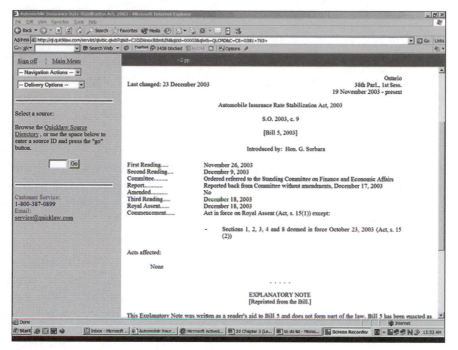

Reprinted by permission of Quicklaw Inc., a division of LexisNexis.

- The phrase "statutory instrument" is broader than the term "regulation" and is defined under the federal *Statutory Instruments Act*[17] to include "any rule, order, regulation, ordinance, direction, form, tariff of costs or fees, letters patent . . . made . . . under an Act of Parliament . . . or under the authority of the Governor-in-Council" (the Governor-in-Council is just a fancy way of saying the Governor General acting on behalf of the federal Cabinet — the same applies at the provincial level with a "Lieutenant Governor-in-Council"). Thus, an "Order-in-Council" is an order made by the Governor General (or Lieutenant Governor at the provincial level) on behalf of Cabinet, usually under statutory authority, although the power to issue these orders can arise under royal prerogative.
- The government may not legislate by regulation. What this means is that the contents of the regulation are prescribed by the governing statute — the regulations must not exceed the powers given for

---

17   R.S.C. 1985, c. S-22, s. 2.

making regulations in the main statute. This restriction prevents the government from attempting to do through regulation what would not have been allowed by statute. This is an important restriction since the regulatory process is often not subject to the same public scrutiny as the statutory process.

• Statutes tend to state broad principles or statements whereas regulations state the minute details that explain the broader principles or statements in the enacting statute. Thus, the *Highway Traffic Act*[18] provides that drivers must not speed and must yield to other drivers, while regulations to that Act will describe in very specific terms the size, shape, and colour of highway traffic signs, the safety features of school buses, and so on.

• One advantage of putting the details into regulations is that these details often change and it is — in theory — easier for the government to amend regulations than statutes since amendments to regulations are not debated in the legislative assembly.

The federal regulations were last consolidated in 1978 in the *Consolidated Regulations of Canada, 1978* (C.R.C. 1978). Amendments to these regulations and new amendments since are published in the *Canada Gazette Part II*.[19] The federal regulations are also available on CD-ROM (Canada Law Book or the Department of Justice), on Quicklaw, WestlaweCARSWELL, LexisNexis, and on the Internet.[20] Procedures for the publication of federal regulations are governed by the *Statutory Instruments Act*, R.S.C. 1985, c. S-22.

Ontario regulations were last consolidated in 1990 in the *Revised Regulations of Ontario* (1990). Amendments to these regulations and new amendments since then are published in the *Ontario Gazette*. The Ontario regulations are also available on CD-ROM (Canada Law Book), on Quicklaw, WestlaweCARSWELL, LexisNexis, and on the Internet.[21] Procedures for the publication of Ontario regulations are governed by the *Regulations Act*.[22]

Regarding regulations, there are no true subject indices to assist in finding relevant information in a regulation. Instead, indices to regula-

---

18   R.S.O. 1990, c. H.8.
19   The *Canada Gazette* is available online at <http://canada.gc.ca/gazette/main.html>.
20   Department of Justice Canada, "Consolidated Regulations," online: Department of Justice Canada <http://laws.justice.gc.ca/en/index.html>.
21   Above note 3.
22   R.S.O. 1990, c. R.21.

tions tend to be alphabetical lists of the enabling statute showing which regulations have been promulgated under each statute.

For federal regulations, use the "Consolidated Index of Statutory Instruments," a quarterly publication of the *Canada Gazette Part II*, which update the additions and revisions to the *Consolidated Regulations of Canada, 1978*. Commercial print sources for tracking federal regulations include Carswell's *Canadian Current Law Legislation* or the *Canada Regulations Index*.

For Ontario regulations, use the cumulative listings found in the *Ontario Gazette* or the "Table of Regulations" found in sessional statute volumes. Commercial print sources for tracking Ontario regulations include Carswell's *Canadian Current Law Legislation* or the *Ontario Regulations Service*. Better yet, search for current regulations by keyword using electronic resources (CD-ROM, the Internet, and Quicklaw, WestlaweCARSWELL, or LexisNexis).

For researching regulations from other provinces, and for more detail on researching regulations, consult *Updating Statutes and Regulations*[23] or the other legal research guides listed at the end of Chapter 1.

F. STEP 5: STATUTORY INTERPRETATION

Finding and updating legislation are important skills. Equally important is understanding what the legislation says, and knowing the rules and principles that courts use to interpret legislation. Some people take for granted that legislation means what it says and is the law. What is not always appreciated, however, is the interplay between legislatures and courts and the role that judges can play in interpreting legislation — legislation may not always mean what it says: if it is unconstitutional, it can be struck down, and if it is ambiguous, there are special rules to guide how the legislation should be interpreted. What follows next is a brief overview of Step 5 of the Legislative Research Checklist — understanding the basic principles of statutory interpretation and how these principles can affect legal research. Readers wanting more in-depth treatment should consult any of the leading textbooks on statutory interpretation set out at the end of this chapter.

---

23   Above note 11.

1) Statutes Judicially Considered

A useful starting point in legal research on statutory interpretation is to find cases in which courts have interpreted particular sections of statutes or regulations. There are two basic ways to find such cases:

- The traditional method is to use print-based services such as Carswell's *Canada Statute Citations* (also available on CD-ROM) or tables called "Statutes Judicially Considered" found in the back of indices to print case law reporters. These services list statutes (and sometimes regulations and court rules) alphabetically by jurisdiction providing citations to cases that have considered particular sections of the statute.

- A more modern technique is to use online databases. One unique feature of WestlaweCARSWELL is the ability to click on a "citing references" link on the left-hand side of the screen when viewing legislation. For example, if viewing section 16 of the *Criminal Code* on WestlaweCARSWELL, it is possible to click on the "citing references" link to generate a list of all of the cases that have cited, discussed, mentioned, or applied that section (as decided by Carswell's editors). This is in essence an Internet version of Carswell's *Canada Statute Citations* with the major advantage of being "clickable" and providing the full text of the cases that have considered the legislation being researched. Alternatively, for other databases such as Quicklaw or LexisNexis, one must search full-text case law databases by the name and section number of the statute. This technique will often retrieve more cases than the traditional print method, although the online technique can sometimes produce false hits, depending on how precisely the search terms are set out. An example of such a search on Quicklaw's Canadian Judgments (CJ) database is as follows:

  criminal /1 code /20 718.2 718.2(!

This searches for cases that have considered section 718.2 and any subsections of section 718.2 of the *Criminal Code*. Alternatively, instead of searching online by section number and the name of the Act, it is also possible to search on the keywords found in the section to see if any judicial decisions online have quoted that particular section of the statute.

As discussed above, it is important to remember when looking for cases that have considered a particular section of a statute that predecessor versions of the section may have had different section numbers in the past. It is therefore usually necessary, before looking for cases, to first trace the section historically to its origin.

2) Interpretation Statutes

Regular legal researchers will keep current copies of the federal and applicable provincial *Interpretation Act* on their desks for easy reference. The contents of these Acts are relatively uniform across all jurisdictions. Topics covered by this legislation include how legislation is to be interpreted, the effect of amendments and repeals, rules of construction, and the calculation of time. These interpretation statutes also define important terms that apply to all legislation across the jurisdiction, definitions such as the meaning of "holiday." An example regarding one of the calculations of time in section 27(2) of the federal *Interpretation Act*[24] is as follows:

> Where there is a reference to a number of days, not expressed to be clear days, between two events, in calculating that number of days the day on which the first event happens is excluded and the day on which the second event happens is included.

These are not rules that are necessarily easy to memorize, despite their importance and application to legislation across the applicable jurisdiction; hence the value in being aware of these Acts and keeping a copy close at hand for frequent consultation.

3) Hansard Debates

Legal researchers should also be familiar with Hansard debates and other legislative documents and the role that they can play in legal research and statutory interpretation. The name "Hansard" comes from the family of "reporters" who first began to officially transcribe the debates of the British Parliament in the 19th century and is used in Canada to describe the reports of legislative debates of the federal and provincial legislatures. The traditional method of researching Hansard debates is to use annual or sessional print volumes of the debates using a print index to access information by topic, speaker, or bill name, depending on the jurisdiction involved. The modern method of researching Hansard debates is through the Web sites of the applicable legislative assembly (see Table 5.11 for a list of these Web sites) and searching by keyword or by browsing through an online index. Another source of useful infor-

---

24   Above note 15.

mation can often be found in various legislative committee reports regarding questions raised by legislators when reviewing draft legislation. These are generally available in print and are increasingly available online through the various government Web sites. The reason to research Hansard debates or legislative committee reports is to gain a better understanding of the legislative purpose of a particular piece of legislation (discussed below under the "Purposive Analysis Rule").

4) Traditional Approaches to Statutory Interpretation

In researching legislation that has been judicially considered, it is important to have an understanding of the various approaches that courts take to interpret legislation. The danger in trying to simply list the various rules of statutory interpretation, however, is to trivialize what should ordinarily be a complex balancing act by judges that takes into account a number of cultural, legal, and social factors that affect how we use language.[25] Nonetheless, it is hoped that the brief overview that follows can provide an introduction to statutory interpretation that identifies some basic issues that legal researchers face when they conduct legislative research.

There are several broad approaches to statutory interpretation identified in the literature that have been used by the courts over time:

a) The Ordinary Meaning Rule
This rule, simply put, requires courts to interpret legislation using the ordinary meaning of its language unless there is a valid reason to reject the ordinary meaning in favour of another interpretation.[26] The ordinary meaning can be established by judicial notice or by reference to dictionary definitions, but is not always that simple a process since "ordinary meaning" usually would involve a textual analysis that requires looking at the words in their context. This analysis can be supported by other aids to statutory interpretation (such as looking to the purpose of the legislation).

b) The Purposive Analysis Rule
This rule requires the court to infer the legislative purpose when interpreting legislative text. As explained by Professor Sullivan, "an interpre-

---

25 See Ruth Sullivan, *Driedger on the Construction of Statutes*, 4th ed. (Toronto: Butterworths, 1994), "Foreword to the Third Edition."

26 Ruth Sullivan, *Statutory Interpretation* (Toronto: Irwin Law, 1997) at 41 (Available on Quicklaw: database identifier SULL). See also *Thomson v. Canada (Deputy Minister of Agriculture)*, [1992] 1 S.C.R. 385.

tation that promotes the purpose is preferred over one that does not, while interpretations that would tend to defeat the purpose are avoided."[27] Legislative purpose can be inferred from the language of the statute itself (often from a preamble to the Act) or from sources outside of the legislation, such as Hansard debates and legislative committee reports. Other methods used by courts are to look at the "mischief" to be cured by the legislation or to look at the evolution of the legislation through amendments as a means to aiding interpretation of the legislation.

c)   The Contextual Analysis Rule

This rule requires the court to interpret legislative text not just in its immediate context but the entire Act as a whole and even other legislation and the social conditions in which the legislation operates.[28]

d)   The Consequential Analysis or Absurdity Rule

This rule takes into account the fact that particular interpretations will result in particular consequences and that courts will take into account the likely outcome or effect of a particular interpretation:

> Consequences that are judged to be good are generally presumed to be intended and are regarded as part of the legislative purpose. Consequences that are judged to be absurd or otherwise unacceptable are presumed not to have been intended. As much as possible, interpretations that lead to unacceptable consequences are avoided.[29]

e)   The Plausible Meaning Rule

This rule is used by courts when they wish to depart from the "ordinary meaning" of a statute in order to give the statute a more plausible interpretation. This is only allowed, however, where the "plausible meaning" is reasonable given the language of the legislative text; courts usually cannot add or delete text to the legislation or otherwise change the intent of the legislators.

f)   The Original Meaning Rule

This is a special rule of statutory interpretation that most often applies to "ordinary" legislation as opposed to "constitutional" legislation (such as the *Charter of Rights and Freedoms*). The rule suggests that the meaning of words in ordinary legislation is relatively fixed at the time it was

---

27   Sullivan, *ibid.* at 135.
28   *Ibid.* at 108–9.
29   *Ibid.* at 149.

enacted and is hence imbued with its "original meaning," whereas constitutional text is "organic" and interpreted in light of changing times.

It can be seen that there is much overlap between the foregoing "rules" and there is no real sense of a hierarchy or systematic order by which a court will apply one rule over another. This will depend on individual circumstances before each court. In addition to these broad "rules," there are a number of presumptions in the literature of statutory interpretation that courts rely upon as aids, presumptions that are too numerous to list here but that include such things as a presumption that legislators exhibit linguistic and drafting competence, have encyclopedic knowledge, etc.[30] There are also special rules for interpreting bilingual legislation.[31]

There are also a number of Latin phrases or maxims that predominate in statutory interpretation with which every legal researcher should be familiar:

- *Ejusdem generis* ("of the same kind"): this "rule" presumes that a general term following a list of specific terms will be limited to the more specific type or class of things that proceed the general term.[32] Example: the phrase "other association" in the "list" of "a fraternal, trade, professional or other association" would be defined by the more specific terms "fraternal, trade, professional" and would not include, for example, the Consumers' Association of Canada.[33]
- *Expressio unius est exclusio alternius* ("to express one thing is to exclude another"): this maxim suggests that if the legislature left something out, it intended to do so since if it had wanted to include something, it would have expressly set it out. Professor Sullivan refers to this as the "implied exclusion rule."[34] Example: a bylaw that applies to owners of orange, blue, red, green, black, and yellow cars would not, it could be argued, apply to owners of brown cars.
- *Noscitur a sociis* ("one is known by one's associates"): this maxim suggests that courts should look to the common features of words linked by "and" or "or" and limit the interpretation of those words to fit within the scope of those terms.[35] Example: a petroleum stor-

---

30   *Ibid.* at 53–56.
31   *Ibid.*, c. 6.
32   See *National Bank of Greece (Canada) v. Katsikonouris* (1990), 74 D.L.R. (4th) 197 at 203 (S.C.C.). See also Sullivan, above note 25 at 203–13.
33   See *Consumers' Association of Canada v. Canada (Postmaster General)* (1975), 11 N.R. 181 (Fed. C.A.); Sullivan, *ibid.* at 203.
34   *Ibid.* at 168.
35   *Ibid.* at 200–2.

age tank will be considered an installation in the phrase "machinery, equipment, apparatus and installation" as part of a definition excluding items from a definition of real property for the purpose of assessment legislation.[36]

- *Generalia specialibus non derogant* ("the general does not detract from the specific"): this maxim suggests that a court prefer specific provisions over provisions of general application where the provisions are in conflict.[37]

Being aware of the general rules of statutory interpretation and the more detailed resources that discuss statutory interpretation is important for legal researchers since legislation is a key primary resource. Thus, finding and updating legislation is one thing; knowing how to interpret the legislation can be an equally important component of legal research.

G. CONCLUSIONS

Much has changed in the last decade regarding legislative research with the advent of current online legislative databases. To date, however, this has not meant the death of print-based legislative research as most historical legislative data and the legislation of the smaller provincial jurisdictions are not easily available in electronic format and may not be for some time. It is likely that both government and commercial publishers will continue to expand and improve upon electronic access to their legislation, so readers should monitor any developments regarding the publication and availability of legislative material in electronic format.

H. ADDITIONAL RESOURCES

Bale, Gordon. "Parliamentary Debates and Statutory Interpretation: Switching on the Light or Rummaging in the Ashcans of the Legislative Process" (1995) 74 Can. Bar Rev. 1.

Beaulac, Stéphane. "Parliamentary Debates in Statutory Interpretation: A Question of Admissibility or of Weight?" (1998) 43 McGill L.J. 287.

---

36   *New Brunswick (Minister of Municipal Affairs) v. Canaport Ltd.* (1976), 7 N.R. 367 (S.C.C.). See also Sullivan, *ibid.* at 201.
37   *Ibid.* at 186–88.

Beaulac, Stéphane. "Recent Developments at the Supreme Court of Canada on the Use of Parliamentary Debates" (2000) 63 Sask. L. Rev. 581.

Côté, Pierré-Andre. *The Interpretation of Legislation in Canada*. 3d ed. Toronto: Carswell, 2000.

Forsey, Eugene. *How Canadians Govern Themselves*. 5th ed. Available online: <http://www.parl.gc.ca/information/library/idb/forsey/index-e.asp>.

Graham, Randy N. *Statutory Interpretation: Cases, Text and Materials*. Toronto: E. Montgomery Publications, 2002.

Graham, Randy N. *Statutory Interpretation: Theory and Practice*. Toronto: E. Montgomery Publications, 2001.

Hall, Geoff R. "Statutory Interpretation in the Supreme Court of Canada: The Triumph of a Common Law Methodology" (1998) 21 Advocates Q. 38.

Jeffery, Michael I., Kenneth Harril Gifford and Donal James Gifford. *How to Understand Statutes and By-Laws*. Toronto: Carswell, 1995.

Keeshan, M. David and Valerie M. Steeves. *The Annotated Federal and Ontario Interpretation Acts*. Scarborough, ON: Carswell, 1996.

Larsen, Norman. "Statute Revision and Consolidation: History, Process and Problems" (1987) 19 Ottawa L. Rev. 321.

Ontario Legislative Library. Available online: <http://www.ontla.on.ca/library/libraryindex.htm>.

Rhone, Christopher. "Accepting the Words of Parliament: Parliamentary History as a Means to Interpret Legislation" (2001) 59 Advocate 697.

Risk, Richard. "Here Be Cold and Tygers: A Map of Statutory Interpretation in Canada in the 1920s and 1930s" (2000) 63 Sask. L. Rev. 195.

Roach, Kent. "The Uses and Audiences of Preambles in Legislation" (2001) 47 McGill L.J. 129.

Ross, Stephen F. "Statutory Interpretation in the Courtroom, the Classroom, and Canadian Legal Literature" (1999–2000) 31 Ottawa L. Rev. 39.

Sinclair, Mary Jane T., ed. *Updating Statutes and Regulations*. 4th ed. Toronto: Carswell, 1995.

Sullivan, Ruth. *Sullivan and Driedger on the Construction of Statutes*. 4th ed. Toronto: Butterworths, 2002.

Sullivan, Ruth. *Statutory Interpretation*. Toronto: Irwin Law, 1997. Available on Quicklaw, Database: SULL.

Sullivan, Ruth. "Statutory Interpretation in the Supreme Court of Canada" (1998–99) 30 Ottawa L. Rev. 175.

CHAPTER 4

RESEARCHING CASE LAW

A. INTRODUCTION

New law students and first-time legal researchers are sometimes surprised by how much judge-made law exists and how important it can be in determining legal rights. This judge-made law, made up of the decisions of judges and administrative tribunals, forms what is referred to as the "common law," a body of law that becomes the judicial precedents by which current judges are bound. Unfortunately, this body of law is not always well-organized or coherent, creating the challenge of researching case law to ensure that all relevant cases have been found and have not been over-ruled or questioned by subsequent court decisions. The goal of the lawyer or self-represented party in litigation in a common law system, therefore, is to find previous court decisions similar on the facts and favourable on the results so that the judge presently presiding over the current litigation will be obliged to follow the previous cases and rule in favour of the lawyer or self-represented litigant.

This chapter will discuss case law by first providing a brief overview of the judicial system, followed by an explanation of the role of "judicial precedent" (also known as *stare decisis*) and how case law is published. Techniques to find relevant cases will then be discussed, along with "noting up" case law, a technique to update or verify your research to ensure the cases you have found have not been overruled on appeal or negatively questioned by subsequent cases.[1]

B. THE JUDICIAL SYSTEM

There are a lot of similarities between the judicial systems in most common law countries, including but not limited to Canada, the United States, England, and Australia. Central to these systems is the rule of law, an idea that all persons are governed by a known set of rules and procedures that include agreed upon methods for parties to resolve their disputes. In reality, litigating disputes in the judicial systems of most modern countries can be unduly complex, time-consuming, and expensive. Fortunately, for the purpose of putting legal research in context, it is generally sufficient to have only a broad understanding of how the judicial system operates, an understanding that can be simplified to explain how legal research relates to the judicial process.

Judges are appointed by the state to resolve criminal and civil disputes, given power to enforce laws, and punish wrongdoers through the threat of imprisonment and fines, enforceable by the state or parties to the dispute. The independence of judges is ensured in most modern countries through various means, including appointment procedures, security of tenure, high salaries, and institutional independence of the courts.[2] A recent "hot" issue in the legal literature has been judicial activism, a notion held by some commentators that judges, as unelected officials, wield too much (political) power in their decision-making, deciding matters that are more properly decided by elected politicians.[3]

---

1   Readers needing specific information on researching Quebec legal materials should consult any of the following resources: Denis LeMay, *La recherche documentaire en droit*, 5th ed. (Montreal: Wilson & Lafleur, 2002); Denis LeMay, "Researching Quebec Law" in Douglass T. MacEllven et al., eds., *Legal Research Handbook*, 5th ed. (Toronto: Butterworths, 2003), c. 12; or the research Web pages of the University of Montreal Law School <http://www.droit.umontreal.ca> and the University of Laval Law School <http://www.fd.ulaval.ca/index.html >.

2   W.R. Lederman, "The Independence of the Judiciary" (1956) 34 Can. Bar Rev. 769; *Valente v. R.*, [1985] 2 S.C.R. 673.

3   Robert Martin, *The Most Dangerous Branch: How the Supreme Court of Canada has Undermined Our Law and Our Democracy* (Montreal: McGill-Queen's University Press, 2003); F.L. Morton, ed., *Law, Politics and the Judicial Process in Canada*, 3d ed. (Calgary: University of Calgary Press, 2002); Kent Roach, *The Supreme Court on Trial: Judicial Activism or Democratic Dialogue* (Toronto: Irwin Law, 2001); F.L. Morton & Rainer Knopff, eds., *The Charter Revolution and the Court Party* (Peterborough, ON Broadview Press, 2000); Christopher P. Manfredi & James B. Kelly, "Six Degrees of Dialogue: A Response to Hogg and Bushell" (1999) 37 Osgoode Hall L.J. 513; Peter W. Hogg & Allison A. Bushell, "The Charter Dialogue Between Courts and Legislatures" (1997) 35 Osgoode Hall L.J. 75.

When conducting case law research, it helps to have a basic understanding of the judicial process, the ways in which disputes begin in
the legal system and proceed through to the appeal level. The chart set
out in Table 4.1, albeit overly simplistic, represents a broad description
of the three levels that represent the judicial system in most common
law jurisdictions.

In reality, the structure of the court system is much more complicated than what is presented in Table 4.1. Many jurisdictions, for
example, have several different trial courts, including a small claims
court (for matters involving smaller amounts of money), a family
court, and a provincial criminal court. Some jurisdictions may also
have an intermediate appeal court between the trial court and the
Court of Appeal to screen appeals and to decide other matters (in
Ontario, such a court is called the Divisional Court).

In Canada, the power of the legislature over courts is set out in the
Constitution Act, 1867[4] and is shared between the federal and provincial
governments. Simply put, the federal government has power to appoint
and pay for judges in the superior courts of the provinces and to establish a federal court system (sections 96–105). The provinces have
power under section 92, paragraph 14 for the "Administration of Justice in the Province, including the Constitution, Maintenance, and
Organization of Provincial Courts, both of Civil and Criminal Jurisdiction, and including Procedure in Civil Matters in those Courts."

For most Canadian provinces, there is in essence only the first-
level and second-level of courts described above, being a trial court and
a provincial Court of Appeal. The third level of courts for the provinces
is the national Supreme Court of Canada in Ottawa, where it is possible to appeal (in very limited circumstances) from a provincial Court
of Appeal. In addition to the provincial system, there is the separate
federal court system established by the federal government. The federal court system consists of a trial division and a Court of Appeal (with
the third level also being the Supreme Court of Canada in Ottawa). The
federal courts have offices in all major cities across the country. The
majority of lawyers do not regularly appear in federal court since its
jurisdiction is for special matters falling under federal jurisdiction,
such as copyright actions, immigration, maritime law matters, and
actions against the Crown.

---

4   30 & 31 Vict., c. 3, reprinted in R.S.C. 1985, App. II, No. 5.

Table 4.1
Simplified Overview of the Court System

First Level: Trial Court
• A single judge who usually hears "live" witnesses (or affidavit evidence) in court
• The judge's decisions are often unreported, available only in the court file or on commercial online legal databases
• It can be a superior court (with federally appointed judges), a provincial court (with provincially appointed judges), or a federal court.
• Typical abbreviations for trial level courts in Canada: Supreme Court (S.C.), Trial Division (T.D.), Queen's Bench (Q.B.), Superior Court of Justice (S.C.J.)
Second Level: Provincial/Federal Court of Appeal
• Usually 3 judges (sometimes 5) sit as a panel; "majority" rules in the case of a split decision
• There are usually no "live" witnesses; appeal based on a written appeal record
• Decisions are more likely reported in print case reporters
• Court abbreviation: C.A.
Third Level National Supreme Court
• Seven or nine judges sit as a panel in Ottawa
• The Court screens appeals by requiring that "leave to appeal" be obtained for most cases
• Because of the volume of appeals, the Court hears only the most important appeals, usually those involving national or constitutional issues, or those limited number of appeals — usually serious criminal charges — where leave to appeal is a right
• Decisions are reported in English and French, both through its Web site, in the *Supreme Court Reports* and in various commercial print case reporters and commercial online databases

Viewed in its most basic structure, it can be said that the British and American legal systems follow the same three-level structure with a single trial judge, an intermediate court of appeal, and a national court of final appeal, but as in the Canadian system, there is much complexity involved in the British and American legal systems. In particular, the American federal court system is much more "active" than the relatively "sleepy" Canadian federal court system, whereas Britain, as a unitary jurisdiction, has no direct equivalent of a federal court system.

Unlike the legislative process, which involves a systematic, formalized method of rule-making, case law develops organically. At the court of first instance, legal issues are framed by the parties themselves (the plaintiff and the defendant), with the judge being a neutral arbitrator (unlike civil code jurisdictions, such as France, where the judge often takes a much more active role in the process). A trial judge in Canada is charged with hearing the evidence of the witnesses and then deciding the matter before him or her. Juries are in decreasing use in Canada, but where a jury is involved, it becomes the decider of fact and there is therefore often less need or reason for a judge to issue written reasons.

Case law usually develops in one of two ways:

- One way case law develops is when a judge issues a written ruling based on an interlocutory or pre-trial dispute between the parties. These types of decisions are based largely on procedural disputes between the parties, such as whether a party is properly named, whether the pleadings (the court papers) disclose a proper cause of action, or whether a party must disclose certain documents to the other side. *Carswell's Practice Cases* (C.P.C.) is a good example of a case reporter series that publishes these types of decisions.

- Another way case law develops is when a judge issues a written ruling after a trial (or an appeal) has finished. In these types of cases, the judge is deciding issues on their merits, and the judge's ruling — subject to an appeal — is binding on the parties and may affect their legal rights (such as whether they can collect damages, whether they must go to jail, and so on). The judge's reasons, once again subject to being appealed, can act as a precedent and affect the rights of subsequent litigants.

C. *STARE DECISIS* AND THE ROLE OF PRECEDENT

The doctrine of *stare decisis* ordinarily requires a judge to follow past court decisions from higher courts within that judge's jurisdiction. This requirement provides certainty and stability in the way in which the common law develops since it restricts a judge from making completely ad hoc rulings depending on how he or she was feeling that day.

Because of this doctrine, which is also known as judicial precedent, it becomes important for lawyers and law librarians to find "like" cases, that is, cases from the past dealing with the client's issue that are similar on the facts and which result in a favourable ruling for the lawyer's client. Much of the lawyer's advocacy skills will be in convincing the judge that the cases that the lawyer is relying upon in support of his or her arguments are more similar and therefore more relevant than those of his or her opponent. In doing so, the lawyer "distinguishes" the cases of his or her opponent.

Because of *stare decisis*, an Ontario lawyer, for example, is less interested in a previous trial decision of a judge in Prince Edward

Island than a previous decision of the Ontario Court of Appeal or the Supreme Court of Canada on the same facts and issues. This is because the decision of the judge in Prince Edward Island is of less precedential value and not necessarily binding on the Ontario judge, whereas the past decisions of the Ontario Court of Appeal or the Supreme Court of Canada on the same facts and issues are binding on the Ontario judge.

Thus, when researching case law, the researcher must always be sensitive to the desirability of finding court decisions from the appeal courts of his or her province or of the Supreme Court of Canada. Having said that, however, since some provincial laws do not differ much from province to province (such as securities legislation), decisions from other provinces may have relatively strong persuasive value (especially if the issue involved stems from federal statutes, such as the *Criminal Code*, where the statute applies across the entire country). Occasionally, it is not possible to find any relevant case law from the courts of the jurisdiction in which the matter is being tried. In such cases, it may be necessary to resort to case law from other provinces (or other countries — decisions of the U.S. Supreme Court or the English Court of Appeal and House of Lords, for example, are generally treated with much respect by Canadian courts).

D. HOW CASE LAW IS PUBLISHED

A judge usually keeps notes during the trial of the argument and evidence he or she has heard. In most cases, the judge simply makes a decision at the end of the trial or hearing without giving detailed reasons or judgment (there is simply a notation in the court file called an endorsement in which the trial judge might say "case dismissed" and provide one or two handwritten lines of "reasons"). In other cases, the judge will "reserve" his or her reasons, which means that the judge is going to think about how he or she will rule. In some cases, these reasons will be oral, a simple explanation in open court of how the judge has ruled. In other cases, however, where the reasons may be of interest to other parties (such as where there has been a complicated point of law argued) or where the case may likely be appealed, the judge will issue written reasons. Ordinarily, a judge will dictate his or her reasons or type them up. Sometimes, if the judge gives oral reasons in court, a court reporter will transcribe the judgment and the judge will later re-edit the reasons, if necessary.

1) Published Print Case Law Reporters

Cases or judicial decisions can be found in print in books called "case reports" or "case reporters." Decisions are typically available in full text, with most publishers providing a "headnote" or summary of the case. It is important to remember, however, that not all written reasons of judges get reported in print. Editors of print case reporters will ordinarily choose only cases of interest or significance, not merely "run-of-the-mill" type decisions of interest only to the parties involved in the dispute. Electronically, cases can be found in a variety of online legal databases, including the more ordinary sorts of cases. Quicklaw editors, for example, do not apply the same selection criteria as editors of print case law reporters, hence more cases tend to get published on Quicklaw than in print-based case law reporters (in other words, online commercial databases will publish all cases provided to them by the courts, regardless of their precedential value). In the old days, it would usually be one of the lawyers who would submit the reasons to a traditional print-based publisher of case law reporters for publication (presumably, some judges would also do the same). If the judgment raised an important point, the publisher would then publish the judgment, either in a topical reporter (such as the *Municipal & Planning Law Reports*, if the case involved an issue of municipal law) or a national reporter (such as the *Dominion Law Reports*). All of the decisions of the Supreme Court of Canada are published in the *Supreme Court Reports*. There is usually a publishing lag of at least several months for a full-text case to appear in a print case law reporter from the time the decision has been released by the court (on Quicklaw and other online databases, this publishing lag is reduced for important cases to a matter of a few days or less, slightly longer for "run-of-the-mill" cases).

In Canada, some of the well-known, national coverage, print case reporters include the following:

• *Supreme Court Reports* (S.C.R.)
• *Federal Court Reports* (F.C.)
• *Dominion Law Reports* (D.L.R.)
• *Western Weekly Reports* (W.W.R.)

Other reports can be found by region. There are, for example, case law reporters for each of the Canadian provinces, ranging from the *British Columbia Law Reports* (Carswell) on the West coast to the *Newfoundland and Prince Edward Island Reports* (Maritime Law Book) on the East coast. To the extent that the rule of *stare decisis* or judicial precedence encourages lawyers to first look for decisions from within their own jurisdiction, these provincial case law reporters are an important (albeit not complete) source of case law for lawyers. There are also regional case law reporters that report cases from a number of provinces. These regional case law reporters include, but are not limited to, the *Western Weekly Reports* (Carswell) and the *Atlantic Provinces Reports* (Maritime Law Book). As discussed in the section below on unreported case law, one of the ways in which vendors such as Quicklaw provide access to their online cases is by jurisdiction, allowing the researcher to search for cases across all jurisdictions in "global" databases or only within a single jurisdiction.

Decisions of administrative tribunals are reported in print by both commercial legal publishers, such as the *Administrative Law Reports* (Carswell), and directly by individual administrative tribunals, such as the decisions of the Canadian Radio-Television and Telecommunications Commission (CRTC).

In the United Kingdom, the leading case reporters are *The Law Reports*, the *All England Law Reports* (All E.R.), and the *Weekly Law Reports* (W.L.R.). There are also numerous print-based topical reporters for U.K. case law.

In Australia, there are a number of privately published case law reporters in print, ranging from jurisdictional, type of court, or topic. The Australian *Commonwealth Law Reports*, for example, only publishes decisions of the Australian High Court. The Australian *Federal Law Reports*, on the other hand, publish selected decisions of various Australian courts that exercise federal jurisdiction. There are also various "state" reporters and a number of topical reporters. The two major commercial database providers in Australia (Lawbook Online — Thomson and LexisNexis Butterworths Australia) both have good databases of Australian case law. Finally, as discussed in Chapter 5 (Legal Research on the Internet), the Australasian Legal Information Institute — AustLII — has an extensive, free Web site of Australian case law at <http://www.austlii.org>.

In the United States, West Publishing is the dominant case reporter publisher with its National Reporter System, which includes full-text American court decisions organized into the following geographic areas:

- *Atlantic Reporter* (A. and A. 2d): Connecticut, Delaware, District of Columbia, Maine, Maryland, New Hampshire, New Jersey, Pennsylvania, Rhode Island, and Vermont.
- *California Reporter* (Cal. Rptr. and Cal. Rptr. 2d): California supreme and intermediate appellate courts.

- *New York Supplement* (N.Y.S.): New York supreme and intermediate appellate courts.
- *Northeastern Reporter* (N.E. and N.E. 2d): Illinois, Indiana, Massachusetts, New York (Court of Appeals), and Ohio.
- *Northwestern Reporter* (N.W. and N.W. 2d): Iowa, Michigan, Minnesota, Nebraska, North Dakota, South Dakota, and Wisconsin.
- *Pacific Reporter* (P. and P. 2d): Alaska, Arizona, California (limited), Colorado, Hawaii, Idaho, Kansas, Montana, Nevada, New Mexico, Oklahoma, Oregon, Utah, Washington, and Wyoming.
- *Southeastern Reporter* (S.E. and S.E. 2d): Georgia, North Carolina, South Carolina, Virginia, and West Virginia.
- *Southern Reporter* (So. and So. 2d): Alabama, Florida, Louisiana, and Mississippi.
- *Southwestern Reporter* (S.W. and S.W. 2d): Arkansas, Kentucky, Missouri, Tennessee, and Texas.

West publishes selected federal U.S. District court cases in the *Federal Supplement* (F. Supp.) or the *Federal Rules Decisions* (F.R.D.), and U.S. Court of Appeals decisions are published by West in the *Federal Reporter* (F. and F. 2d).

2) Unpublished Cases

In Canada, aside from Supreme Court of Canada decisions, not all decisions of judges are published. Hence, there are a large number of judicial decisions being handed down every day that are unpublished. Access to some of these unpublished cases can be provided through digest services, such as the *All Canada Weekly Summaries*, which provide a basic digest of the case and offer to provide the full text of the decision for a fee. Another way unpublished judgments may be accessed is through online databases, such as Quicklaw, LexisNexis, and WestlaweCARSWELL.

Quicklaw, for example, has agreements with all Canadian courts for the courts to release to them all court judgments in digital (and print) form for publication on Quicklaw. There is usually little post-editing done to these electronic judgments, except for the formatting of selected fields and other matters, including the addition by Quicklaw of case summaries used in their Canadian Case Summaries (CCS) database. Quicklaw also has agreements with other publishers to post their publications and published case reports online (including their headnotes). It is important to note, however, that Quicklaw contains not only unpublished decisions but also decisions that get published in print-based case law reporters. Stated differently, Quicklaw contains both published and unpublished decisions. One can easily determine within Quicklaw whether a decision is published or unpublished by "noting up" the decision (discussed below in more detail in section F) to see where, if it all, the case has been reported. For example, when noting up the decision *Bank of Montreal v. Unified Homes Ltd.*, [1990] O.J. No. 875 (Gen. Div.) on Quicklaw, one learns from the "Reported at" field near the top of the screen that the decision is reported only at [1990] O.J. No. 875, meaning that it is only available on Quicklaw (or possibly other commercial online databases). On the other hand, when noting up *Nijjer v. Hildebrant*, [2000] B.C.J. No. 727 (C.A.), one learns from the "Reported at" field that the decision has also been reported at (2000) B.C.L.R. (3d) 322 (in addition to other print-based reporters).

On Quicklaw, the largest global database of Canadian case law is the Canadian Judgments database, which has the acronym "CJ." Thus, to conduct the most exhaustive search of Canadian case law, one should choose the CJ database. Alternatively, one can limit a search to cases within a particular jurisdiction, such as the Alberta Judgments database (database identifier: AJ).

Quicklaw also has a large number of databases providing access to decisions of administrative tribunals which are otherwise difficult or impossible to find using only print resources. Examples of these online databases include British Columbia Commercial Appeals Commission decisions (1975 to date) (database identifier: BCCO) and Nova Scotia Labour Arbitration Awards (1980s to date) (database identifier: NSLA), to name two of many such databases on Quicklaw. In addition, some tribunals are starting to publish their decisions on the Internet, such as the CRTC.[5]

LexisNexis Canada recently acquired Quicklaw, and at the time of the publication of this edition, both Quicklaw and LexisNexis Canada remain separate databases, although they share a lot of data. It is still unclear to what extent, if at all, Quicklaw's databases will be completely submerged into LexisNexis Canada, but readers should closely monitor any developments in this regard. In the meantime, LexisNexis Canada is well known for its easy-to-use interface, its excellent coverage of Canadian case law and other materials (as well as strong American coverage), and its noter upper or citator, called *Shepards*.

---

5   See Canadian Radio-Television and Telecommunications Commission, *Indexes of CRTC Official Documents*, online: <http://www.crtc.gc.ca/eng/public/Index.htm>.

WestlaweCARSWELL — discussed in more detail in Chapter 6 — is the other major, comprehensive legal database in Canada providing not only full-text Canadian court cases but also its *Canadian Abridgment* case law digests (organizing summaries of Canadian cases by topic) and its encyclopedia of law for Canada, the *Canadian Encyclopedic Digest* (both products are discussed in more detail in Chapter 2). WestlaweCARSWELL also has extensive legal materials for the United States, the United Kingdom, and other jurisdictions.

One final development to mention is the Canadian Legal Information Institute (CanLII), a free Web site of Canadian case law at <http://www.canlii.org>, a site discussed in more detail in Chapter 5 (Legal Research on the Internet). Although CanLII's database does not have the depth or scope of the commercial services, it is an excellent source of recent Canadian cases; the editors of CanLII are also experimenting with a "noter upper."

Case law is increasingly being published in electronic format, which brings with it the advantage of keyword searching, avoidance of publication delays, and savings in the space required by print materials. Since the market in Canada for legal materials is so small and the cost of publishing small runs of print case law reports is so great, one can easily imagine that the publication of print case law reporters will diminish and the publication of case law in electronic format will continue to expand.

E. FINDING CASE LAW

There are several legal resources that can be used to find case law by topic:

- **Case law digests:** Simply put, a digest in the context of legal literature is a summary (or digest) of case law, arranged by topic and by case name. In Canada, the leading print-based case law digest is the *Canadian Abridgment*, discussed in more detail in Chapter 2, section D. Another well known case digest system in Canada is the *All Canada Weekly Summaries* from Canada Law Book.

- **Legal encyclopedias:** Legal encyclopedias are also a good way of finding cases, especially by topic, since the various articles or paragraphs in the encyclopedia on a particular topic are usually supported in the footnotes by citations to the cases that support the principles discussed in the main text. In Canada, a leading legal encyclopedia is Carswell's *Canadian Encyclopedic Digest*, discussed in more detail in Chapter 2, section C.

- **Online legal databases:** Online legal resources are an excellent way to find case law, using keyword searches by subject or by case name. Each of the major commercial online databases allows searches across full-text case law databases that can retrieve cases based on quite discrete criteria, such as individual keywords or combinations thereof.
- **Print indices to case reporters:** Print publishers of case reporters provide indices to their publications that allow access by subject and by case name. Thus, to find cases dealing with insurance law, one could search the indices to the *Canadian Cases on the Law of Insurance* (C.C.L.I.) to get a relatively good overview of a limited number of cases on topic.
- **Legal textbooks:** Legal textbooks also provide some access to case law since most authors provide footnoted citations to important cases that support the points they are making in the textbook. Textbooks are discussed in more detail in Chapter 2, section A.
- **Law journals:** Articles written by law students or law professors will often discuss important or leading cases and can be used to identify relevant cases. Law journals are discussed in more detail in Chapter 2, section B.

F. NOTING UP CASE LAW

Once a case is published — whether in print or on an electronic database — it is important to realize that two things could happen: (i) the case could be appealed and possibly overturned; and (ii) the case could be used as a precedent or instead criticized in other subsequent court decisions. To speak of whether a case has been reversed or affirmed on appeal is to speak of its judicial history. To speak of how a case has been followed by subsequent courts is to speak of its judicial treatment.

The *judicial history* of a case is important since, if a case has been overturned on appeal, the lower court decision that has been overturned will be of little or no precedential value and a lawyer relying upon a case that is overturned stands to be greatly embarrassed in court. The *judicial treatment* of a case is equally important since the number of times a case may have been considered may indicate the strength of the case: if the case you are interested in has been mentioned and considered by a large number of subsequent judges in other cases, it may likely be important. There is also the other possibility, however, that other subsequent courts may now look upon your case with disfavour, due to changes in the law (this is one way in which the common law evolves). Hence, it is extremely important to know the judicial treatment of a particular case (even if the case you are interested in has no judicial treatment, this does not mean your case is unimportant or of questionable precedential value — many relevant cases have no judicial treatment). Learning the judicial treatment of your case is also important since it may lead you to other, more recent relevant cases on the topic of your research. To this extent, noting up for judicial treatment is a way of creating a "chain" of related cases. In this way, it is often possible to see how a particular legal principle has evolved over time through subsequent cases that have considered cases on point. The techniques to note up case law are relatively similar across Canada, the United States, Australia, and the United Kingdom.

Generally, there are several methods for noting up case law:

- **Tables of cases judicially considered**: Most print publishers of case law reporters have a section in the indices to their reporters called "Table of Cases Judicially Considered," which is an alphabetical list of cases published in their reporters that have judicial histories or treatment.

- **Print citators**: There are print publications available in Canada (Carswell's *Canadian Case Citations*) and the U.S. (*Shepards*) whose sole purpose is to provide the judicial history and judicial treatment of case law (there is no equivalent British publication that provides exhaustive treatment; both *The Digest* and *Current Law* provide some print-based noting up of U.K. case law, as do Tables in the indices to the *All England Law Reports*). In Australia, there are two competing print products: the *Australian Case Law Citator* (Lawbook) and the *Australian Current Law Reporter* (Butterworths Australia).

- **Online citators**: There is a definite move towards noting up case law using online noter uppers. Quicklaw has an extensive online citator in its Quickcite database (QC). LexisNexis Canada has *Shepard's Canada* for its online noter upper of Canadian cases. WestlaweCAR-SWELL provides *KeyCite Canada* as its online citator. Westlawe-CARSWELL also provides an online citator for United Kingdom caselaw (database: UK-CASELOC). For Australia, there are online equivalents of the Australian print citators: on Lawbook Online (Thomson) there is the *Australian Case Law Citator* PLUS and on LexisNexis Butterworths Online (Australia) there is *CaseBase* (both by subscription).

A key feature of these online databases is the ability to click on the appropriate "link" to note up the case to get a list of the case's judicial history (i.e., whether it has been appealed or not) and a list of the case's judicial treatment (i.e., whether other courts have considered the case). When noting up cases with a lot of judicial treatment, these online citators have various features that allow you to "limit" the list of treating cases by jurisdiction or level of court, for example.

For additional resources on noting up, see the following:

- Dabney, Dan. "Another Response to Taylor's Comparison of KeyCite and Shepard's" (2000) 92 Law Libr. J. 381.
- Gannage, Mark. "Noting-up Cases" (1999) 21 Advocates' Q. 489.
- McKenzie, Elizabeth M. "Comparing KeyCite with Shepard's Online" (1999) 17:3 Legal Ref. Serv. Q. 85.
- Morris, Jane W. "A Response to Taylor's Comparison of Shepard's and KeyCite" (2000) 92 Law Libr. J. 143.
- Rintoul, Ruth, with contributions from Rosalie Fox. "Case Law in Canada" (2003) 28 Can. L. Libraries Rev. 166.
- Taylor, William L. "Comparing KeyCite and Shepard's for Completeness, Currency, and Accuracy (2000) 92 Law Libr. J. 127.
- Wurzer, Greg, Aleksandra Zivanovic, and Rhonda O'Neill. "Canadian Electronic Citators: An Evaluation of their Accuracy and Efficiency" (2004) 29 Can. L. Libraries Rev. 68.

G. CONCLUSIONS

Expect to see an ongoing increase in the availability of case law in electronic format. The advantages of being able to search full text by keyword, the ability to store large amounts of data, and the ability to provide access to recent material are all reasons why case law in electronic format will flourish.

CHAPTER 5

LEGAL RESEARCH ON THE INTERNET

A. INTRODUCTION

Legal research has changed drastically over the last five to ten years due to the Internet. Traditionally, legal researchers used print materials in law libraries to find law-related information. This meant that one was limited to the amount of space and materials the print-based law library could afford, a limitation that often meant that the law library had a finite collection focusing on materials from within its own jurisdiction. While CD-ROMs and online commercial databases (Chapter 6) have brought legal research to the researcher's desktop (especially over the last ten to fifteen years), it has been recent Internet technology that promises to revolutionize the way legal research is conducted. This chapter will focus on freely available Internet resources, which have several applications for legal research:

- as a source of information (searching the World Wide Web)
- as a means of communication (using e-mail)
- as a virtual community (using law-related discussion groups)

The usefulness of the Internet for legal research is reinforced by its wide availability throughout most jurisdictions in the world and its relative ease-of-use.[1] A particularly nice feature of the Internet is the abil-

---

1   This chapter assumes the reader has some experience in "surfing the Net" and is
    comfortable with using Web browsers to navigate "back" and "forward" through

ity to expand legal resources beyond the walls of one's own print law library to online international and foreign legal resources that would not have been easily accessible to most researchers through traditional means. While the Internet has a number of useful features, it is always necessary for the researcher to evaluate the quality of information that is being found, especially since not all material on the Internet has been subject to the same level of editorial control as most print or fee-based publications.

B. EVALUATING WORLD WIDE WEB INFORMATION

There are standard criteria by which free Web sites should be evaluated.[2] These criteria include a number of things that evaluate the quality and reliability of the information to be found on the site:

- **Authorship:** Who authored the material? Is it clear who owns the Web site? Is the site affiliated with a reliable or known publisher or organization? Does the site provide a mailing address, phone number, and e-mail address? It is always important to consider authorship when using freely available Web sites — anyone can publish a Web site with relative ease with no objective editorial policies or control.
- **Accuracy and quality:** Is the site free of spelling and grammatical errors? Does the site contain broken links? Well-maintained Web

---

Web pages, to "bookmark" favourite Web pages, and in downloading or saving information. If readers are not familiar with these sorts of things, they should first consult introductory books on the topic, including such works as Lewis S. Eisen's *Canadian Lawyer's Internet Guide*, 3d ed. (Thornhill, ON: Amicus Legal Publishing, 1997) (also available on Quicklaw, database identifier: CLIG); or Drew Jackson & Timothy L. Taylor, *The Internet Handbook for Canadian Lawyers*, 3d ed. (Toronto: Carswell, 2000), both of which are listed at the end of this chapter.

2   See, e.g., Hope N. Tillman, "Evaluating Quality on the Net" (March 2003), online: Hope's Happy Home Page <http://www.hopetillman.com/findqual.html>; Sabrina I. Pacific, "Getting it Right: Verifying Sources on the Net" (1 March 2002), online: LLRX.com <http://www.llrx.com/features/verifying.htm>; Mirela Roznovschi, "Evaluating Foreign and International Legal Databases on the Internet," online: LLRX.com <http://www.llrx.com/features/evaluating.htm>; Brian Jones, "Evaluating Internet Legal Resources" (1997) 22 Can. L. Libraries 8; Gene Tybursky, "Publishers Wanted, No Experience Necessary: Information Quality on the Web" (24 June 1997), online: LLRX.com <http://www.llrx.com/columns/quality.htm>.

sites tend to mean that the owner of the site is taking the time to keep the information current and accurate.

- **Purpose**: Why does the Web site exist? Is it trying to sell a product or advocate a particular viewpoint? Print publications, like Web sites, can contain biased points of view. The one difference between print publications and Web sites, however, may be the ease with which one can access Web pages and the speed by which one may scan the information without appreciating that the information may contain subtle biases.
- **Scope**: What is the scope or date range of the material on the Web site? How often is the site updated? Good Web sites will show when the page was last updated. This information is often on the bottom of the page (hold down the "Ctrl" key on your keyboard and then press the "End" or the "PgDn" key to get quickly to the bottom of the Web site page to check this information).

When evaluating Web sites, it helps to consider the different categories of Web sites that exist, including personal Web sites, business/marketing Web sites, advocacy Web sites, university, and government Web sites. Each of these different types of Web sites has a different reason for existing with differing goals and motivations that can affect the quality of information to be found on them. One major difference between free Internet sites and commercial online databases is often the amount of editorial and quality control (in addition to value-added features). Thus, when using free Web sites, it is important to constantly evaluate the quality of information being found.

C. SEARCH ENGINES

A basic technique for finding information on the Internet is to search for material by keyword using search engines (see Table 5.1 for a list of popular search engines). Simply put, search engine companies, such as Google (listed below), regularly have "robots" or "spiders" that periodically mine through or "scrape" the full text of Web pages on the Internet to index or "catalogue" words and other information found on Web pages. The company then stores this information in its databases. When the researcher types in keywords in the search engine, a search is done against the site's database to look for appropriate matches.

Not all search engines are the same — differences between search engines usually relate to any or all of the following three major factors: (i) the number of pages "catalogued"; (ii) the frequency by which the search engine updates its database; and (iii) the level of sophistication of the different types of searches that can be run on the search engine. There are a number of useful Web sites that compare or rank search engines.[3] There are, fortunately, several basic techniques that apply to most search engines:[4]

- Know your search engine — get to know one or two search engines well and do not be afraid to click on the "help" or "advanced find" link of the search engine to learn more about the search engine, such as whether it allows Boolean searching, truncation of terms, or nested searches.
- If you are getting too many results for your search ("4,045,720 pages found"), consider having at least four or five search terms in your search using the "AND" format (an "and" search is now the default form of search in most Internet search engines so you usually do not need to add the word "and"). Also try to use unique terms whenever possible.
- Use phrases — most search engines allow phrase searches ("To Kill a Mockingbird"); this will usually provide more precise results.

Google appears to be one of the dominant search engines (for now). A Google "advanced search" has a number of useful advantages to make your Internet searches more precise. Some of the Google advanced search techniques include but are not limited to the following:

- You can easily change the default results from "10 results" to "100 results" (this allows you to quickly scan more results on a single page).
- There are useful search templates for phrase searches or to exclude words from your search.
- Under the "Domain" field, you can use Google to limit your search to a particular Web site (www.un.org, for example).
- Under the "Occurrences" field, you can limit your search to where the terms only appear in the title of the Web page (this often results in more focused search results on the theory that the "title" of a Web page likely means that the Web page is about that topic).

---

3   See, e.g., Diana Botluk, "Update to Search Engines Compared" (15 July 2000), online: LLRX.com <http://www.llrx.com/features/engine3.htm>. In addition the University at Albany has a useful page on search engines — see <http://library.albany.edu/internet/engines.html>. Search Engine Watch at <http://www.searchenginewatch.com> provides information on Internet search engine developments.

4   See also Librarians' Guide to the Internet, "Internet Guides, Search Tools, & Web Design," online: LLRX.com <http://lii.org/search/file/netsearch>.

Table 5.1
Common Search Engines

Search Engine	Web Site Address
Alta Vista	<http://www.altavista.com>
Alta Vista Canada	<http://ca.altavista.com>
Ask Jeeves	<http://www.ask.com>
Google	<http://www.google.com>
HotBot	<http://hotbot.lycos.com>
Mooter	<http://www.mooter.com>
Teoma	<http://www.teoma.com>
WiseNut	<http://www.wisenut.com>

Another type of search engine is a subject guide or "directory" that provides a means of browsing through a clickable directory of topics (see Table 5.2 for a list of subject directories). The most popular of these types of Web directory search engines is Yahoo! <http://www.yahoo.com> or Yahoo! Canada <http://ca.yahoo.com>, whose editors have organized categories of information on the Internet by a hierarchical directory of topics. By way of example, Yahoo!'s directory for legal research can be found by clicking through Government — Law — Legal Research <http://ca.yahoo.com/Government/Law/Legal_Research/>. There are a number of law-related Internet subject directories, such as Findlaw/Law-Crawler and Hieros Gamos (listed in table 5.2 below), that organize links to online material by law-related topics.

Table 5.2
Popular Internet Subject Guides

Search Engine	Web Site Address
BAR-eX	<http://www.bar-ex.com>
Findlaw/LawCrawler	<http://www.findlaw.com>
Hieros Gamos	<http://www.hg.org>
Law Library Resource XChange	<http://www.llrx.com>
Yahoo!	<http://www.yahoo.com>
Yahoo! Canada	<http://ca.yahoo.com>

Another variation of Internet search engines is the so-called "meta" or "all-in-one" search engine (see Table 5.3 for a list of meta search engines). Meta search engines run searches over more than one search engine and then organize the search results usually by search engine.

Table 5.3
Popular "Meta" Search Engines

Search Engine	Web Site Address
Dogpile	<http://www.dogpile.com>
FastSeeks	<http://www.fastseeks.com>
KillerInfo	<http://www.killerinfo.com>
Mamma	<http://www.mamma.com>
Metacrawler	<http://www.metacrawler.com>
Search.com	<http://www.search.com>
SurfWax	<http://www.surfwax.com>

A more recent phenomenon in Internet searching has been the development of search engine sites to search the so-called "deep web" or "invisible web."[5] Statistics suggest that normal search engines (discussed above) catalogue only a small percentage of World Wide Web pages and that there is a large amount of information resident on proprietary servers or unindexed pages that form the "deep web."[6] There are several search engines that identify the "deep web" and Web sites that contain their own databases of pages, pages that would not otherwise be found using normal search engines (see Table 5.4 for a list of deep web search engines). For example, Completeplanet.com, listed below, is a directory of over 10,000 of these otherwise invisible databases on the Internet.

Table 5.4
Deep or Invisible Web Search Engines

Search Engine	Web Site Address
Completeplanet.com	<http://www.completeplanet.com>
Copernic	<http://www.copernic.com>
Invisible-web.net	<http://www.invisible-web.net>
Search.com	<http://www.search.com>

---

5   Marcus P. Zillman, "Deep Web Research" (23 February 2003), online: LLRX.com <http://www.llrx.com/features/deepweb.htm>; Diana Botluk, "Mining Deeper into the Invisible Web" (15 November 2000), online: LLRX.com <http://www.llrx.com/features/mining.htm>.

6   Botluk, *ibid.*, citing e.g., Steve Lawrence & C. Lee Giles, "Accessibility of Information on the Web" (1999) 400 Nature 107.

D. FINDING PEOPLE

Although not directly related to pure legal research, finding information about people is an important part of lawyering, whether it be tracking down the phone number or address of a potential witness or party to a lawsuit, trying to find an expert, or another lawyer.[7] The Internet is extremely useful for this purpose given the large number of directories and phone books available online. Set out below in Table 5.5 is a list of some of the more useful Internet tools for finding information about people. Some of the sites, such as InfoSpace (listed below), provide such added-value features as the ability to look up people by phone number or mailing address in addition to looking up people by name. Legal directories are listed below in Table 5.6 and sites for finding experts are listed in Table 5.7.

Table 5.5
Online Directories and Phone Books

Web Sites	Address
Canada 411	<http://canada411.com>
Canada Yellow Pages	<http://www.canadayellowpages.com>
InfoSpace	<http://www.infospace.com>
Infobel.com	<http://www.infobel.com>
555-1212.com	<http://www.555-1212.com>

Table 5.6
Online Legal Directories

Web Sites	Address
Canadian Law List	<http://www.canadianlawlist.com>
Lexpert.ca	<http://www.lexpert.ca>
Martindale-Hubbell	<http://lawyers.martindale.com>
FindLaw / West Legal Directory	<http://lawyers.findlaw.com>

---

7   For finding legal experts, see Jim Robinson, "Finding and Researching Expert Witnesses on the Web" (1 October 2002), online: LLRX.com <http://www.llrx.com/features/findingexperts.htm>.

Table 5.7
Sites for Finding Experts

Web Sites	Address
ExpertLaw	<http://www.expertlaw.com>
Expert Pages	<http://expertpages.com>
Findlaw: Market Center	<http://marketcenter.findlaw.com>
Internet Online Directory	<http://national-experts.com/online.html>
University of Toronto Blue Book	<http://www.library.utoronto.ca/bluebook>

E. FINDING COMPANIES AND PRIVATE ORGANIZATIONS

The Internet is also an excellent place to find information on companies. Two obvious starting points for companies that publicly trade their shares are the SEDAR Web site for Canadian companies and the EDGAR Web site for American companies (both of these sites are listed below) since public disclosure rules in both countries require public companies to post their documents on these sites. Other sources of corporate information include company home pages, investor Web sites, and newswire Web sites, which will include news releases and other public statements by corporations. Finding information on privately-held corporations is much more difficult. A list of some of the more popular Web sites for finding information on corporations is set out in Table 5.8 below.

Table 5.8
Web Sites for Finding Corporation Information

Web Sites	Address
Canada NewsWire	<http://www.newswire.ca>
EDGAR (U.S.)	<http://www.sec.gov/edgar.shtml>
Ontario Securities Commission	<http://www.osc.gov.on.ca>
SEDAR (Canada)	<http://www.sedar.com>
Strategis (Industry Canada)	<http://strategis.ic.gc.ca>
Toronto Stock Exchange	<http://www.tse.com>

F. FINDING REFERENCE MATERIALS

In addition to the various directories already discussed above, there are a number of extremely useful reference materials freely available on the Internet that include dictionaries, encyclopedias, currency converters, translation services, and news sites. Table 5.9 sets out some general reference sites available on the Internet, along with several subject-specific reference sites.

Table 5.9
Online Reference Sites

Web Sites	Address
CIA World Factbook	<http://www.odci.gov/cia/publications/factbook>
Currency Converter (Yahoo!)	<http://finance.yahoo.com/m3?u>
Law Dictionary (Nolo Press)	<http://www.nolo.com/lawcenter/dictionary/wordindex.cfm>
Library Spot	<http://www.libraryspot.com>
Mapquest (maps)	<http://www.mapquest.com>
Refdesk.com	<http://www.refdesk.com>
Statistics Canada	<http://www.statcan.ca>
Translations	<http://www.foreignword.com>
Xrefer.com	<http://www.xrefer.com>
Your Dictionary	<http://www.yourdictionary.com>

G. FINDING GOVERNMENTS

In recent years, governments have taken advantage of Internet technology to publish useful information, forms, and pamphlets on the Internet that — in the past — would have only been published in print. Table 5.10 lists the home pages for the Canadian federal and provincial governments, along with a few "meta" sites that provide links to other government information.

Table 5.10
Online Government Web Sites

Web Sites	Address
Access to Justice Network	<http://www.acjnet.org>
Canadian Government Information	<http://cgii.gc.ca>

Web Sites	Address
Federal Government (Canada)	<http://canada.gc.ca>
Alberta	<http://www.gov.ab.ca>
British Columbia	<http://www.gov.bc.ca>
Manitoba	<http://www.gov.mb.ca>
New Brunswick	<http://www.gov.nb.ca>
Newfoundland	<http://www.gov.nf.ca>
Northwest Territories	<http://www.gov.nt.ca>
Nova Scotia	<http://www.gov.ns.ca>
Nunavut	<http://www.gov.nu.ca>
Ontario	<http://www.gov.on.ca>
Prince Edward Island	<http://www.gov.pe.ca>
Quebec	<http://www.gouv.qc.ca>
Saskatchewan	<http://www.gov.sk.ca>
Yukon Territory	<http://www.gov.yk.ca>

H. FINDING LEGISLATION

Until now, commercial services like Quicklaw, LexisNexis, or West-laweCARSWELL have provided the most current and complete legislative coverage, but only for certain major Canadian jurisdictions (typically federal, B.C., Alberta, and Ontario, although up-to-date coverage is now expanding to most provinces on these commercial databases). These commercial services have value-added annotations, legislative histories, and other information that is very useful for legal research. Canadian federal and provincial governments, however, have been much slower to publish their statutes, regulations, bills, Hansard debates, and other legislative documents freely available on the Internet (see Table 5.11 for a list of these Web sites). Most of the government Web sites have only the current or fairly recent versions of legislation, with little historical archive of older versions of statutes, regulations, or bills. One exception, however, is the Alberta Heritage Digitization Project's Retrospective Law Collection,[8] where Alberta statutes have been digitized from 1906 to 1990 and made available online at this site for free, with plans to digitize retrospective bills and *Gazettes*.

---

8   Online: The Alberta Heritage Digitization Project
     <http://www.ourfutureourpast.ca/law/law_home.asp>.

Table 5.11
Online Government Legislative Web Sites

Web Sites	Address
Federal Government (Canada)	\<http://laws.justice.gc.ca/en/index.html\>
Alberta	\<http://www.qp.gov.ab.ca\> \<http://www.assembly.ab.ca\>
British Columbia	\<http://www.legis.gov.bc.ca\>
Manitoba	\<http://www.gov.mb.ca/legislature/index.html\> \<http://www.gov.mb.ca/chc/statpub/\>
New Brunswick	\<http://www.gnb.ca/0062/acts/acts-e.asp\> \<http://www.gnb.ca/legis/index-e.asp\>
Newfoundland	\<http://www.gov.nf.ca/hoa/sr/\> \<http://www.gov.nf.ca/hoa/\>
Northwest Territories	\<http://www.justice.gov.nt.ca/Legislation/SearchLeg&Reg.htm\> \<http://www.assembly.gov.nt.ca\>
Nova Scotia	\<http://www.gov.ns.ca/legi/legc/acts.htm\> \<http://www.gov.ns.ca/legislature/\>
Nunavut	\<http://www.assembly.nu.ca\> \<http://www.nunavutcourtofjustice.ca/library/index.htm\>
Ontario	\<http://www.e-laws.gov.on.ca\> \<http://www.ontla.on.ca\>
Prince Edward Island	\<http://www.gov.pe.ca/law/statutes/index.php3\> \<http://www.assembly.pe.ca/index.php\>
Quebec	\<http://doc.gouv.qc.ca/home.php\> \<http://www.assnat.qc.ca/eng/publications/index.html\>
Saskatchewan	\<http://www.qp.gov.sk.ca\> \<http://www.legassembly.sk.ca\>
Yukon Territory	\<http://www.canlii.org/yk/sta/index.html\> \<http://www.gov.yk.ca/leg-assembly/\>

The ease-of-use and the currency of information on these freely available government Web sites varies from province to province, as does the range of legislative information that is available.

There has been a move in several jurisdictions, including Canada, to establish online "Legal Information Institutes," which allow the researcher to search for case law and legislation of the jurisdiction in question using a single search engine/interface, thereby eliminating the need to visit individual case law or legislative Web sites (see Table 5.12 for a list of these sites).

Table 5.12
Legal Information Institute Web Sites

Web Sites	Address
Canada — CanLII	<http://www.canlii.org>
Australia — AustLII	<http://www.austlii.edu.au>
U.S. — Cornell's LII	<http://www.law.cornell.edu/index.html>
U.K./Ireland — BAILII	<http://www.bailii.org>
International — WorldLII	<http://www.worldlii.org>

I. FINDING CASE LAW

Free World Wide Web sites are still not very good for trying to find Canadian court decisions by topic or keyword due to the relatively crude sophistication of the search engines on the various court Web sites. What these sites are good for is as an archive for relatively recent court decisions (usually from the late 1990s to current) where one is looking for a specific case by name or date. Table 5.13 sets out a list of the Web site addresses for those Canadian court Web sites that release their judgments for free on the Internet, along with the Canadian Legal Information Institute, already mentioned above, which acts as a clearinghouse for free Canadian court decisions on the Internet. In most cases, using the CanLII Web site will be the preferred method of accessing free Canadian case law, although in some situations you may need or want to visit the actual court Web site as well.

Table 5.13
Canadian Court Web Sites

Court	Web Site Address
Canadian LII	<http://www.canlii.org>
Supreme Court of Canada	<http://www.lexum.umontreal.ca/csc-scc/en/index.html>
Federal Court of Canada	<http://decisions.fct-cf.gc.ca/fct/index.html>
Tax Court of Canada	<http://www.tcc-cci.gc.ca>
British Columbia	<http://www.courts.gov.bc.ca>
Alberta	<http://www.albertacourts.ab.ca>
Saskatchewan	<http://www.lawsociety.sk.ca/NewLook/Library/database.htm>
Nova Scotia	<http://mail.nsbs.ns.ca/dbtw-wpd/qsets/LNQBE.HTM>
Ontario	<http://www.ontariocourts.on.ca>
Prince Edward Island	<http://www.gov.pe.ca/courts/supreme/index.php3>
Northwest Territories	<http://www.justice.gov.nt.ca/dbtw-wpd/nwtjqbe.htm>

Commercial online databases, such as Quicklaw, LexisNexis, and WestlaweCARSWELL, have a number of advantages over free worldwide court Web sites primarily as a result of their deeper scope of materials and their sophisticated search engines that allow one to search by judge's name, by party name, and by keywords using proximity connectors (searching on the name of a judge before whom one is arguing a case can be very strategic if you are able to find cases that can help you identify any particular viewpoints of that judge from cases he or she may have decided in the past). In addition, the commercial online databases have other valued-added features, such as extensive online citators that allow one to easily verify or note up a case's judicial history or treatment.

One place where free worldwide court Web sites are useful is for those jurisdictions outside of Canada that have developed extensive online collections, such as Cornell's Legal Information Institute or the Australasia Legal Information Institute, sites listed above in Table 5.12. Another useful link to worldwide court Web sites can be found online at <http://www.gksoft.com/govt/en/courts.html>.

J. FINDING INTERNATIONAL AND FOREIGN LAW MATERIALS

As mentioned at the start of this chapter, the Internet has brought the world to the desktop of the legal researcher. International or foreign law materials that were once only available in print through interlibrary loan are now available at the click of the mouse via the Internet. Material now widely available on the Internet includes such primary sources of international law as treaties, conventions, and decisions of international courts and tribunals. Increasingly, foreign jurisdictions are making their own legislation and court decisions available on the Internet. Fortunately, a number of good Web sites exist that provide links to international and foreign law sites. Table 5.14 below lists some of the more popular international and foreign law sites on the Internet, along with a list of some excellent guides to conducting international legal research on the Internet, many of which contain additional links. In addition, Chapter 7 provides detailed information on researching international and foreign law.

Table 5.14
International and Foreign Law Web Sites and Research Guides

Web Sites	Address
Canada Treaty Information	<http://www.treaty-accord.gc.ca>
Canado-American Treaties	<http://www.lexum.umontreal.ca/ca_us/index_en.hml>
Foreign Affairs Canada	<http://www.fac-aec.gc.ca>
International Trade Canada	<http://www.itcan-cican.gc.ca>
European Commission of Human Rights	<http://www.commissioner.coe.int>
European Court of Human Rights	<http://www.echr.coe.int>
Hague Conference on Private International Law	<http://www.hcch.net>
International Court of Justice	<http://www.icj-cij.org>
Project on International Courts and Tribunals	<http://www.pict-pcti.org>
UNCITRAL: United Nations Commission on International Trade Law	<http://www.uncitral.org>
UNIDROIT: International Institute for the Unification of Private Law	<http://www.unidroit.org>
United Nations	<http://www.un.org>
United Nations Treaty Collection	<http://untreaty.un.org>
World Trade Organization	<http://www.wto.org>
Guides	**Address**
ASIL Guide to Electronic Resources for International Law	<http://www.asil.org/resource/Home.htm>
International Constitutional Law	<http://www.oefre.unibe.ch/law/icl/>
Foreign Databases (Mirela Roznovschi, N.Y.U. Law School)	<http://www.law.nyu.edu/library/foreign_intl/country.html>
Lexadin World Law Guide	<http://www.lexadin.nl/wlg/index.htm>
Max Planck Institute for Comparative Public Law and International Law	<http://www.virtual-institute.de/eindex.cfm>
University of Toronto Bora Laskin Law Library List of International Resources	<http://www.law-lib.utoronto.ca/intmat.htm>
Women's Human Rights Resources	<http://www.law-lib.utoronto.ca/diana/mainpage.htm>

K. USING DISCUSSION GROUPS FOR LEGAL RESEARCH

Online discussion groups — also known as listservs — have been formed on almost any conceivable topic, from jazz music to figure-skating.[9] There are a huge number of law-related discussion groups that allow one to subscribe (usually for free) to be added to the group. When one subscribes to a discussion group, any e-mails sent to the group are sent to all subscribers. In many cases, what then happens is a discussion, or at least responses to the initial e-mail, that are sent to that discussion group by the subscribers. Every legal researcher should be aware of several things about discussion groups:[10]

- Some discussion groups are moderated, which means that questions to be posted to the group are first vetted by the moderator; most discussion groups are unmoderated, however, meaning that questions are not vetted in advance, which sometimes results in irrelevant or inappropriate questions being posted.
- The quality of the discussions or responses varies widely among various discussion groups. Fortunately, for law-related discussion groups, the quality of discussion is generally quite good, but as can be imagined, it is prudent for subscribers to avoid giving legal advice (or even the appearance of giving legal advice).
- Some discussion groups provide archives of the entire history of all questions and responses for that particular group. Many of these archives are searchable and can sometimes provide valuable information. An example of a searchable archive is the discussion group of the Canadian Association of Law Libraries (discussed below), the archive of which is available at <http://listserv.unb.ca/archives/call-l.html>.

The most exhaustive list of law-related discussion groups is provided by Lyonette Louis-Jacques, an international law librarian at the University of Chicago Law School, whose *Law Lists* site is available at <http://www.lib.uchicago.edu/~llou/lawlists/info.html>. While a large number of the listservs mentioned at this site are American-based and

---

9   See online: CataList <http://www.lsoft.com/lists/listref.html> for a searchable and browsable list of over 70,000 publicly available online discussion groups.

10   See also *Canadian Lawyer's Internet Guide*, 3d ed. (Thornhill, ON: Amicus Legal Publishing, 1997) at c. 8 entitled "Mailing Lists"; Catherine J. Lanctot, "Attorney-Client Relationships in Cyberspace: The Peril and the Promise" (1999–2000) 49 Duke L.J. 147 for a useful overview of online discussion groups and listservs.

geared towards those in the academic community, there are a number of specifically Canadian sites and sites geared towards practitioners.

One of the better sites in Canada for getting information on legal research or issues affecting the world of legal researchers is the discussion group of the Canadian Association of Law Libraries (CALL-L) — see: <http://www.callacbd.ca> and click on the appropriate link for its listserv. There are also a number of American-based law library listservs, such as the Law-Lib discussion group hosted by the Law Library of the University of California, Davis. Information on some of the major law library discussion groups is available through *Law Lists* (mentioned above) or through the following page of the American Association of Law Libraries: <http://www.aallnet.org/discuss/list_other.asp>.

L. THE BEST SITES FOR LEGAL RESEARCH

There are a number of excellent "meta" Web sites that provide an overview of legal research resources on the Internet. Some of the more popular Canadian sites include the following:

- **Access to Justice Network (ACJNet)**
  <http://www.acjnet.org>

- **Jurist Canada**
  <http://jurist.law.utoronto.ca>

- **Catherine P. Best's "Best Guide to Canadian Legal Research"**
  <http://legalresearch.org>

- **University of Montreal, Faculty of Law, Centre de recherche en droit public**
  <http://www.lexum.umontreal.ca/index_en.html>

- **Ted Tjaden's Doing Legal Research in Canada**
  <http://www.llrx.com/features/ca.htm>

- **The Bora Laskin Law Library Legal Resources Link**
  <http://www.law-lib.utoronto.ca/resources/intro.htm>

M. CITING MATERIAL FOUND ON THE INTERNET

Chapter 1, section C discusses citation of legal materials in depth, including the citation of online materials. Citing material on the World

Wide Web can be more of a challenge than citing to an unreported decision on Quicklaw, as Web sites are not always stable and often do not provide numbered paragraphs for pinpoint citations. There is no single, uniform method for citing material on the Internet. The 5th edition of the McGill Guide provides several examples in different contexts of how to cite material found on the Internet: Rule 2.9 (legislation), Rule 3.11 (case law), Rule 4.8 (government documents), Rule 5.3 (international materials), and Rule 6.17 (secondary sources). The recommended citation practice — generally speaking — is to cite the material as if it were from a traditional print source followed then by the designation "online," the name of the organization or Web site, and the URL in angle brackets. Set out below are some additional examples that attempt to follow the McGill Guide style. Other style books are available and since there is not yet a universal standard for citing Internet material, researchers should apply a consistent standard that provides the most helpful information to the user:[11]

- The Law Society of Upper Canada, "Home page," online: The Law Society of Upper Canada <http://www.lsuc.on.ca>.
- Canadian Judicial Council, "Members and Staff of Council" (June 2000), online: Canadian Judicial Council <http://www.cjc-ccm.gc.ca/english/members.htm>.
- Christine Hart, "Online Dispute Resolution and Avoidance in Electronic Commerce" *Uniform Law Conference of Canada* (August 1999), online: Faculty of Law, University of Alberta <http://www.law.ualberta.ca/alri/ulc/current/hart.htm>.

As discussed in Chapter 1, section C, the Canadian Citation Committee has developed neutral citation formats, which are being adopted by Canadian courts. These formats are expected to be more widely seen over the next few years and will greatly simplify the citation of online cases.[12] In addition, the Supreme Court of Canada has special rules governing the citation of electronic versions of decisions of the Supreme Court of Canada and other courts.[13]

---

11   For citing general information from the Internet, see Janice R. Walker & Todd Taylor, *The Columbia Guide to Online Style* (New York: Columbia University Press, 1998); Kate L. Turabian, *A Manual for Writers of Terms Papers, Theses, and Dissertations*, 6th ed. (Chicago: Chicago University Press, 1996) at 158–59.

12   See the Web page of the Canadian Citation Committee <http://www.lexum.umontreal.ca/ccc-ccr/neutr/index_en.html>.

13   Supreme Court of Canada, *Bulletin* (6 October 2000), online: University of Montreal <http://www.lexum.umontreal.ca/csc-scc/en/bul/2000/html/00-10-06.bul.html>.

N. USING E-MAIL AND SOLICITOR-CLIENT PRIVILEGE

Although e-mail has no direct application for hands-on legal research, it has revolutionized the ways in which lawyers communicate with each other and with clients. The advantages of e-mail are obvious: e-mail is inexpensive, easy to use, widely available, and instantaneous. E-mail also allows the sender to attach documents that can then be sent around the world to be retrieved, opened by the recipient, and sent back to the original sender with comments or amendments.

With these advantages comes a potential disadvantage: the very speed of e-mail raises the risk of the lawyer inadvertently (i) disclosing confidential information by accidentally sending the e-mail to an unintended recipient; or (ii) sending a message in haste that, if written in print, may have brought more thought and deliberation. Clearly, the risk exists that a lawyer could inadvertently waive a client's right to privilege by sending an e-mail message to an unintended recipient.[14] This may explain the increase in the use of standard "privileged and confidential" notices that are inserted in e-mails being sent by law firms (just in the same way that law firms include "privileged and confidential" notices as part of their fax cover sheets when sending faxes). In addition to using such notices, lawyers can consider using encryption software for e-mail communications or establishing office training and policies (including a policy not to use e-mail for highly sensitive matters).

O. CONFIDENTIALITY: AVOIDING ELECTRONIC FOOTPRINTS

Another potential risk of disclosure on the Internet is in inadvertently identifying one's self or a client's interest by leaving "electronic footprints" on various Web sites being visited on behalf of a client. When you use a Web browser to find information on a Web site, your Internet Service Provider (ISP) has the technical capability of tracking the details of your visits (due to the volume of traffic, it is unlikely it would have the time to do this on a regular basis). In addition, the Web site

---

14   See Paul Dodd & Daniel R. Bennett, "Waiver of Privilege and the Internet" (1995) 53 Advocate 365; Jane Bailey, "Email's Impact on Lawyers and Litigation: Recent Developments in Ontario" (2002) 3 Internet & E-Com. L. Can. 9 for a discussion of this issue.

you are visiting can gather basic information about you, including the time you visited the site, the identity of your ISP, and even your e-mail address (if you have provided this information). In addition, your browser has "cookie" technology, which — if enabled — leaves information in a "cookie" text file on your computer that provides information about you the next time you visit the same Web site. In addition, although the risk is likely extremely low, there is a potential opportunity for hackers to eavesdrop on your Internet activity. Since lawyers have strict professional obligations to protect a client's confidentiality, and although the risk of disclosure is likely extremely low, some legal researchers or law firms may wish to implement confidentiality policies to minimize these risks further. One thing to consider is the need to clear the "history" button of your Web browser (especially on public or shared computers). If this is not done, the next user can identify Web sites you have visited or even e-mails that you have sent (assuming you use Web-browser based e-mail software). Another solution is to obviously "disable" cookies in your Web browser by turning off this feature in the browser's "preferences."[15] Alternatively, you may wish to conduct highly confidential Web searches (such as "due diligence" searches on possible target companies in a merger and acquisition) on a secure line or through an Internet service provider not connected with the law firm.

P. CONCLUSIONS

The Internet will continue to dramatically impact the way lawyers practise law and conduct legal research. Governments, courts, universities, and other institutions will continue to publish an increasing amount of law-related information on the Internet. New technologies will increase the speed and ease-of-use of the Internet and new applications of the Internet will flourish, such as the delivery of continuing legal education programs to lawyers and legal researchers. It is also reasonable to expect that governments will take steps in the future to publish historical legal materials on the Internet (older statutes, for example) as scanning technology improves.

---

15   To change cookie preferences in Netscape browsers, go to the "Edit" toolbar at the top of the screen and choose "Preferences" and then the "Advanced" option and select your desired cookie choice. To change cookie preferences in Microsoft Internet Explorer browsers, go to the "Tools" toolbar at the top of the screen and choose "Internet Options" and then the "Security" tab and adjust your level of security as desired.

Q. ADDITIONAL RESOURCES

There is plenty of print and online information available on legal research and the Internet. Set out below is a list of some of the more popular print publications that discuss the Internet and legal research:

Ambrogi, Robert J. *The Essential Guide to the Best (and Worst) of Legal Sites on the Web*. New York: ALM Publishing, 2001.

Biehl, Kathy and Tara Calashain. *The Lawyer's Guide to Internet Legal Research*. Lanahan, MD: Scarecrow Press, 2000.

Botluk, Diana. *The Legal List: Research on the Internet*. Danvers, MA: West Group [annual].

Chandler, Yvonne J. *Neal-Schuman Guide to Finding Legal and Regulatory Information on the Internet*. New York: Neal-Schuman, 1998.

Eisen, Lewis S. *Canadian Lawyer's Internet Guide*. 3d ed. Thornhill, ON: Amicus Legal Publishing, 1997. Available on Quicklaw (database identifier: CLIG).

Gordon, Stacey L. *Online Legal Research: A Guide to Legal Research Services and Other Internet Tools*. Buffalo, NY: W.S. Hein, 2003.

Halvorson, T.R. *Law of the Super Searchers: The Online Secrets of Top Legal Researchers*. Medford, NJ: CyberAge Books, 2000.

The Internet Lawyer: Navigating the Internet . . . For the Legal Profession. Gainesville, FL: GoAhead Productions [monthly].

Jackson, Drew and Timothy L. Taylor. *The Internet Handbook for Canadian Lawyers*. 3d ed. Toronto: Carswell, 2000.

Kozlowski, Ken. *The Internet Guide for the Legal Researcher*. 3d ed. Teaneck, NJ: Infosources Pub., 2001.

Mintz, Anne P., ed. *Web of Deception: Misinformation on the Internet*. Medford, NJ: CyberAge Books, 2002.

Tjaden, Ted. "The Impact of Web Technology on Law Librarianship" (2002) 27 Can. L. Libraries 8.

Tjaden, Ted. "Legal Issues in Using the Internet for Law-Related Work and Research" (1996) 21 Can. L. Libraries 180.

CHAPTER 6

LEGAL RESEARCH DATABASES AND CD-ROMS

A. INTRODUCTION

The impact of computer technology on the practice of law has been huge. Its impact on legal research has been no less. With computers comes the capacity to store and search a large body of textual information, which has given researchers the ability to locate specific terms within that body of information. There are now a growing number of high quality, easy-to-use commercial databases for conducting online legal research. These databases usually contain one or more of the following features: they have sophisticated search engines that allow a number of different ways of finding information; they contain a variety of law-related information, in most cases including case law, legislation, journal literature, and news; they are available only by subscription for a fee; they are increasingly made available to subscribers via the Internet; and their publishers are constantly making value-added improvements to these databases, including extra content and easier-to-use interfaces.

For law students, your law school has or can likely obtain passwords for you to use some of these databases for academic research. For lawyers and other professionals, the vendors of these online databases will negotiate access to their databases through one of several methods (usually hourly rates, flat-rate fees, or transactional fees, discussed below in more detail). For members of the public, short-term access to these databases is more difficult, and it may be necessary to instead either hire a lawyer or other legal researcher to conduct research on these databases on your behalf or conduct your own legal research using other resources discussed in this book.

This chapter will discuss the advantages and disadvantages of conducting legal research using online law-related commercial databases, followed by a brief review of some of the leading Canadian and American services, including those provided by Quicklaw, LexisNexis, WestlaweCARSWELL, CCH Online, Canada Law Book, Maritime Law Book, and SOQUIJ. At the end of this chapter will be a review of law-related CD-ROMs, their advantages and disadvantages, search tips for searching CD-ROMs, and a list of law-related CD-ROMs.

B. ADVANTAGES AND DISADVANTAGES OF ONLINE COMMERCIAL DATABASES

There are a number of fairly obvious advantages to using online law-related databases for legal research compared to using print resources:

- **Current information:** The delay that occurs in publishing law-related material in print or CD-ROM is ordinarily eliminated with online databases, which can be updated instantaneously. Supreme Court of Canada decisions, for example, are now made available on many databases within an hour of being released. Rather than publishing annual or monthly cumulative supplements in print for updates to legislation, commercial publishers such as Quicklaw, LexisNexis, and WestlaweCARSWELL can update their legislative databases very quickly, providing the researcher with current, cumulative versions of legislation.
- **Scope of coverage:** Publishers of online legal databases are increasingly broadening the scope of the databases by adding more judgments and a wider variety of material to their databases, including full-text legal textbooks (Quicklaw), full-text legislation (Quicklaw, LexisNexis, WestlaweCARSWELL, and Canada Law Book), the *Canadian Encyclopedic Digest,* and the *Canadian Abridgment* (both WestlaweCARSWELL). Since most court judgments in Canada are not published in print, these online databases can often be the only convenient source of obtaining unreported judgments.
- **Full-text searching:** Historically, print law-related material in Canada has not been well indexed, sometimes making it more difficult than it should be to find relevant material. Online legal research,

however, allows the researcher to search for the single or multiple occurrence of a particular word or phrase within a case or statute, something that cannot be done using print resources. Since most information in online databases is in full text, and since most of these databases have relatively sophisticated search engines, it is possible to conduct fairly exhaustive research.

- **Noting up:** Online legal databases provide online citators that allow a legal researcher to note up cases quickly and accurately for judicial history and judicial treatment. Due to the volume of case law, it is becoming difficult, if not impossible, for legal publishers to publish their citators in print format. As such, expect to see a movement towards case law citators being available only in electronic format.

- **Reliability:** The vendors of online legal databases and sources of law-related information in electronic format retain very high levels of quality and editorial control, thereby making the content of their databases very reliable. This gives online legal databases an advantage over other material found on the Internet, although the trade-off in favour of reliability is the cost of online commercial databases, a problem not generally associated with information on the Internet.

- **Availability/remote access/space savings:** The information in these online law-related databases is generally available twenty-four hours per day and can be accessed by multiple users, unlike a single copy of a volume of a print case law reporter. In addition, these online databases save large amounts of space by avoiding the need to store print materials in a library.

- **Time tracking:** For law libraries in the private sector, online legal databases are an excellent value for their cost since most of the cost of online searches is passed on to the client as a disbursement. As such, a law firm law library could in theory not subscribe to any print publications yet still operate a high level of research service at a very low overhead, if the costs of online searches can be billed back to the firm's clients.

Although there are a number of advantages to electronic legal resources, there are a number of potential disadvantages:

- **Cost:** Some people find the cost of online legal databases or Internet subscription services to be prohibitive, usually in the range of $100 to over $200 per hour, depending on the vendor. To the casual researcher who cannot bill back this cost to a client, the cost may well be prohibitive. Many firms, however, are moving to a fixed monthly fee price arrangement or a transactional charge arrangement with the online vendors, thereby stabilizing part of the cost of online searches. In addition, the fees paid to online vendors by the private sector help to subsidize the free access that most online vendors provide to academics, law students, and law librarians.

- **Difficulty in use:** To an untrained user, some online legal databases may be difficult to use. These difficulties include vendor-specific search commands and knowing which databases within a particular vendor's database to choose. When these difficulties are combined with the hourly cost of online charges, the average person may find it difficult to use online legal databases for legal research. Fortunately, improvements, such as online help guides and search templates, are constantly being made by publishers for their databases making it easier and more intuitive to use their products.
- **Limited material:** Most online legal databases emphasize current information, thereby making online access to older, historical, or archival material less available. To a certain extent, this problem is lessened with the court judgments of the higher courts for which online vendors usually carry a complete online set, but for lower courts and for older volumes of legal journals, there is no consistently good online historical coverage.
- **Lack of ownership:** One usually owns the books and other print materials in one's library, whereas a subscription to online commercial databases only provides access and use of data — there is no ownership. Thus, when one stops paying for or subscribing to an online service, one is left with no tangible materials with which to research.

Since technology is changing so quickly and since there appears to be a relatively healthy amount of competition among the vendors of online commercial law-related databases, it may well be that most of the disadvantages of these databases listed above will diminish or disappear over time.

What follows for the next few sections is a review of some of the major Canadian commercial online law-related databases.

C. QUICKLAW <http://www.quicklaw.com>

Quicklaw started in 1967 at Queen's University Faculty of Law by Professor Hugh Lawford as a joint research project between IBM and the University. In 1972, IBM was forced to withdraw from the project due to the policies of the Canadian federal government that require Canadian companies to control information systems. Since the government did not continue to fund the database, Professor Lawford and Richard vonBriesen founded QL Systems Ltd. as a private company and took over the database.[1]

Since that time, Quicklaw has continued to grow in size and has improved its search capabilities. One of the key features is "relevance ranking," which allows less common terms to be given more weight in the search, thereby improving relevancy of the search results. Searches can also be ranked in chronological or reverse chronological order. Its interface has evolved from a simple DOS-based, command-line driven interface to a much more user-friendly Windows-based GUI interface that still allows most of the older keyboard commands, and most recently to a Web-based interface. With the Web-based interface, Quicklaw has added user-friendly search templates and online help. Quicklaw offers free training to students and lawyers and provides telephone support at 1-800-387-0899 or e-mail support at *service@quicklaw.com*.

Quicklaw has over 2,500 databases of legislation, case law, decisions of administrative tribunals, newsletters, textbooks, and full-text legal journal articles. The strength of its online collection is with its Canadian material, but Quicklaw is developing strong databases in a number of other jurisdictions, including the United States, the United Kingdom, Australia, Africa, and the East Caribbean.

In July 2002, LexisNexis Butterworths Canada acquired Quicklaw but still maintains Quicklaw as a separate database with its own login and some unique content not yet found on LexisNexis (although some sharing of data has taken place). Since the takeover, in fact, Quicklaw has taken on several LexisNexis features and its "look and feel" (in part). At the time of publication of this book, both databases remain separate; however, over time, expect to see the two databases completely merged. For the comments that remain on Quicklaw, it will be assumed that Quicklaw is (and has remained) a separate database.

Although it is impossible to discuss all 2,500 databases on Quicklaw, it may be useful to highlight some of the company's more popular databases. In all situations of doubt or uncertainty, however, the researcher can consult the Quicklaw online database directory to help identify relevant databases on which to search, ranging from court or administrative tribunal databases by jurisdiction or topic, legislation, journals or journal indices, full-text books, and news. Table 6.1 sets out a chart of some of the more popular databases on Quicklaw.

---

1   See Bill Rogers, "QuickLaw Founder a Trailblazer in Online Legal Research" (1998) 18:24 Lawyers Wkly. 18.

Table 6.1
Popular Quicklaw Databases

Database	Identifier	Description
Canadian Judgments	CJ	A global database that contains full-text cases from all Canadian jurisdictions, including the Supreme Court of Canada, Federal Court of Canada, and all provincial courts.
Canadian Case Summaries	CCS	Contains over 360,000 summaries of Canadian (and some English) cases, from 1574 to the present.
Revised Statutes of Canada	RSC	A database of the Revised Statutes of Canada that includes the full text of federal legislation (current usually to within a few days), along with links to other Canadian legislative databases (including federal regulations and bills).
Canada Bills Service	CB	Contains the full text of current federal bills, including progress tables for each bill, and government news releases regarding each bill.
Law Journals	JOUR	Searches a number of full-text Canadian law journals, ranging in start coverage from the mid 1990s to date.
Index to Canadian Legal Literature	ICLL	The Index to Canadian Legal Literature indexes Canadian law journal articles and other legal literature (from 1987 to current).
Canadian Law Symposia Index	CLSI	The Canadian Law Symposia Index is an index to papers presented at seminars and conferences since 1986.
Irwin Law Textbooks	TEXT	Under the Canada Legal Databases link there is a link to legal texts. Here, Irwin Law has published over 35 full-text books that are both fully searchable by keyword on various fields and browsable through clickable Table of Contents.
United States Legal Databases	N/A	In addition to Canadian content, and content from England, Australia, Africa, and the Caribbean, Quicklaw has recently added a large number of American databases, including case law and legislation.

In order to use Quicklaw, subscribers in the past have had to download free QuickLink software from its Web site. Quicklaw has now made its databases available to subscribers through the Internet at <http://ql.quicklaw.com> without the need to download additional software. For practitioners, Quicklaw provides an hourly-rate option or will ordinarily negotiate flat-rate monthly fees depending on the number of lawyers or researchers in the organization. Quicklaw provides a special student password to law and library science students for academic use only.

D. LEXISNEXIS CANADA <http://www.lexis.com>

LexisNexis Canada is part of the LexisNexis group of companies owned by Reed Elsevier, one of the world's largest publishers. Lexis-Nexis began in 1973 in Dayton, Ohio as an American-based provider of online legal resources that emphasizes American legal materials but also includes news databases and law-related information from around the world, including Canada and the United Kingdom. LexisNexis has a common parent with other well-known legal publishers such as Matthew Bender, Martindale-Hubbell, and Butterworths. LexisNexis is well known for its online citator for U.S. law called *Shepards*, which has been adapted to its Canadian case law database in the form of *Shepards Canada*. As mentioned above, LexisNexis recently acquired Quicklaw and has started to merge data and greatly expand its Canadian content on LexisNexis Canada.

E. WESTLAWECARSWELL
  <http://www.westlawecarswell.com>

WestlaweCARSWELL is a new Internet-based subscription service provided by Carswell, a sister company of Westlaw, and part of the Thomson Group. The WestlaweCARSWELL databases extend over several practice areas, as set out below, and offer a variety of information including relevant legislation, case law, commentary, and newsletters from Carswell-published authors, in addition to the full text of the *Canadian Encyclopedic Digest* and the *Canadian Abridgment*. Tables of concordance are also provided that concord legislation across the provinces on selected topics. Each database provides full-text information, including the ability to note up cases using Carswell's *Canadian Case Citations* data. In addition, searches can be programmed to run on a regular basis. One advantage WestlaweCARSWELL has over other commercial databases is in fact its ownership of the *Canadian Encyclopedic Digest* and the *Canadian Abridgment*, making this unique content on WestlaweCARSWELL. WestlaweCARSWELL also has "browsability" in addition to "searchability." What this means is that it is possible to browse online alphabetically certain databases on WestlaweCAR-SWELL, including the *Canadian Encyclopedic Digest*, the *Canadian Abridgment* case digests, legislation, and textbooks.

   There are currently five components to the service (and Westlawe-CARSWELL has announced plans to add more services):

- **LawSource:** an online version of the *Canadian Abridgment* case law summaries with links to full-text versions of most decisions; includes an online citator to note up case law.
- **FamilySource:** a database of family law materials that includes relevant legislation, case law, newsletters, and family law textbooks.
- **SecuritiesSource:** a database of securities law materials that includes relevant legislation, case law, precedents, newsletters, and securities law textbooks.
- **InsolvencySource:** a database of bankruptcy and insolvency law materials that includes relevant legislation, case law, newsletters, and insolvency law textbooks.
- **CriminalSource:** a database of criminal law materials that includes relevant legislation, case law, newsletters, and criminal law textbooks.

These Internet products offer several advantages over the equivalent subject CD-ROMs published by Carswell, including more current updates, added content, the ability to note up cases, and an improved search engine.

WestlaweCARSWELL also provides access to the purely "American" Westlaw database that emphasizes U.S. case law, statutes and regulations, legal texts, news, and other information. Westlaw is part of the West Group, which traces its roots to the very beginning of the American legal publishing industry with the publication of a systematic case reporter series for American case law. The West Group is also known for the development of its "key number" system for identifying legal concepts or issues within the headnotes of the cases it published. West shares a common parent with Carswell (Canada) and Sweet & Maxwell (U.K.). Westlaw has extensive online U.K. case law databases, a U.K. case law citator, and the *Legal Journals Index* (for finding British and E.U. law journal articles).

F. CCH ONLINE <http://online.cch.ca>

CCH Online is an Internet-based subscription service provided by CCH for many types of information, including tax, law, and human resources. The family of law-related products are called LegalWorks Online and include databases that cover alternative dispute resolution (ADR), business law, environmental law, family law, health law, estate law, insurance law, real estate law, securities law, and international law. The TaxWorks library provides various databases regarding federal and provincial income tax and the GST. The BusinessWorks library covers employment and labour law, health and safety law, and pension benefits. The online content mirrors the multi-volume CCH "black binders" for which the company is well known. Coverage includes legislation, case law, and commentary.

CCH also provides excellent legislative and "bill-tracking" options for Canadian federal and provincial legislation through a separate CCH LegislativePulse database (which requires a subscription) at <http://pulse.cch.ca>.

G. CANADA LAW BOOK
<http://www.canadalawbook.ca>

Canada Law Book currently offers Internet-based subscriptions to a number of its print-based products that contain some value-added features. Its Internet subscriptions include such products as the *Dominion Law Reports*, Ontario and federal legislation, and access to its criminal law, patent law, and labour law libraries.

H. MARITIME LAW BOOK <http://www.mlb.nb.ca>

Maritime Law Book, founded in 1969, is a publisher of Canadian case law and publishes the following case law reporters in print and now through an online Internet subscription: *Alberta Reports* (A.R.), *Atlantic Provinces Reports* (A.P.R.), *British Columbia Appeal Cases* (B.C.A.C.), *British Columbia Trial Cases* (B.C.T.C.), *Federal Trial Reports* (F.T.R.), *Manitoba Reports* (2d) (Man. R.(2d)), *National Reporter* (N.R.), *New Brunswick Reports* (2d) (N.B.R.(2d)), *Newfoundland and Prince Edward Island Reports* (Nfld. & P.E.I.R.), *Nova Scotia Reports* (2d) (N.S.R.(2d)), *Ontario Appeal Cases* (O.A.C.), *Ontario Trial Cases* (O.T.C.), *Saskatchewan Reports* (S.R.), and *Western Appeal Cases* (W.A.C.).

I. SOQUIJ <http://www.soquij.qc.ca>

La Société québécoise d'information juridique (SOQUIJ) was founded in 1976 and is a legal information society created for the purpose of making Quebec law available and for promoting legal research in Quebec. It publishes various sources of primary law in Quebec, including legislation, the reports of the Quebec courts, and various administrative tribunals within Quebec. Decisions are available in summaries and full text.

J. INTRODUCTION TO CD-ROMS

In the last decade, CD-ROMs have been an important storage medium for electronic information, used by software publishers for storing and publishing various forms of data. In the legal field, CD-ROMs have been popular because of the large amount of textual information they can contain. With the advent of the Internet, some have started to question whether CD-ROMs will face extinction since large amounts of information can be easily stored and distributed via servers on the Internet.[2] For now, CD-ROMs have one main advantage over the Internet — portability. Until wireless remote access to the Internet becomes more widely available, a market for CD-ROMs will likely remain for some time for those researchers who need and appreciate the storage capacity and portability of CD-ROMs.

K. ADVANTAGES AND DISADVANTAGES OF CD-ROMS

Law-related CD-ROMs have a number of obvious advantages:

- **Space savings:** They store lots of information and do not require extensive shelf space.
- **Portability:** They are portable, allowing the individual legal researcher to carry in his or her laptop a wide variety of legal material, including case law and legislation.
- **Searching:** They are searchable by keyword.
- **Replace looseleaf:** CD-ROMs that replace print looseleaf equivalents (such as the *Canadian Encyclopedic Digest*) avoid the hassle of looseleaf filing of the print publication and missing or stolen pages.

---

2   See, e.g., Elizabeth H. Klampert, "CD-ROM: An Interim Technology?" (1997) 466 PLI/Pat 67. See also Mary A. Sharaf, "Taking the Plunge: The Switch from Books to CD-ROMs — A Pessimist's View" (1997) 444 PLI/Pat 81; Barbara A. Bintliff, "Introducing CD-ROMs into a Law Library: Administrative Issues and Concerns" (1992) 84 Law Libr. J. 725.

- **Low manufacturing costs:** Their manufacturing cost is cheap, making it inexpensive for publishers to provide updated information monthly or quarterly.
- **Sharing:** Information can be shared by more than one person at a time.
- **Familiar:** They are becoming a "comfortable" medium in the computer world, with a number of software titles and products being available on CD-ROM.

There are, however, a number of disadvantages to law-related CD-ROMs:

- **Maintenance:** When CD-ROMs have been licensed to be distributed to multiple users over a computer network, it can be very time-consuming (and sometimes difficult) for technical staff to be constantly re-installing updated CD-ROMs (some CD-ROM products do not network very well).
- **Lack of ownership:** Some people are surprised when they are reminded that they generally do not own the CD-ROM or the information on it when they pay for it. What one is paying for is merely a license to access the information on the CD-ROM. In addition, most law-related CD-ROMs published in Canada are "time-bombed," meaning that built into the software is a mechanism that denies access to the information on the CD-ROM once the licence period for which access has been paid for has expired.
- **Difficulty in use:** Many law-related CD-ROMs in Canada (including those from Carswell and Canada Law Book) use Folio software[3] for the organization and searching of the information on the CD-ROM. Unfortunately, this software has a bit of a learning curve for first-time users. Other CD-ROMs may have their own search engine, which then requires users to learn multiple search engines.
- **Limited coverage:** Law-related CD-ROMs are great as portable, electronic versions of a print equivalent publication, but they cannot and should not act as the only source of research for particular legal problems.
- **Expense:** Licensing CD-ROMs can be expensive, especially when multiple user access is negotiated. In addition, since many libraries are not yet automatically cancelling print in favour of a CD-ROM alternative, licensing CD-ROMs is often an added cost to a library's budget, although many legal publishers will soften the blow by

---

3   See online: Nextpage <http://www.nextpage.com/folio/products/>.

offering a discount to libraries who subscribe to both print and CD-ROM equivalents.

Whether the advantages of CD-ROMs outweigh the disadvantages depends on the needs of the individual legal researcher. CD-ROMs are ideal for lawyers who practise in a fairly narrow subject specialty (such as criminal law) who want to carry a wide body of relevant law in their laptop. CD-ROMs are also good for those law libraries willing to cancel print publications in favour of the CD-ROM equivalent as a space-saving measure (remembering, however, that this would result in a loss of ownership of the material).

L. EFFECTIVE SEARCHING ON CD-ROMS

There are a number of basic tips and strategies for searching CD-ROMs. Since many law-related CD-ROMs in Canada use Folio software, once one has learned a few things about the Folio interface, it is relatively easy to use any law-related CD-ROM, regardless of publisher. One feature of Folio software includes the plus (+) and minus (-) symbols next to major headings that allow the researcher to click on them to expand or shrink the level of detail. While plus signs remain, one can keep clicking on the plus sign to expand the level of detail until there are no more plus signs. Clicking on a minus sign shrinks the text to its previous level.

Here are a few basic things to consider when searching CD-ROMs that use Folio software as their operating system:

- **Table of Contents**: For first-time users, browsing through the CD-ROM via the clickable Table of Contents is a very comfortable way to find information on the CD-ROM since this mirrors the print experience quite closely. Typically, there is a Table of Contents button on the toolbar (either down the left hand side or along the top of the screen — if there is no Table of Contents button on the toolbar, you can add it to the Toolbar by choosing File — Preferences — Toolbelt from the drop-down menu or you can simply choose View — Table of Contents from the drop-down menu or press Ctrl-T to access the Table of Contents). The Table of Contents button acts as a "toggle," which means that clicking on it once will bring up the Table of Contents and clicking on it again will return you to your text. Clicking on the text in the Table of Contents (as opposed to clicking on a + or – sign) will link you to that part of the text on the CD-ROM.

- **Reference Window:** First-time users of Folio-based CD-ROMs sometimes find it difficult to know where they are on the CD-ROM. The Reference Window (under the View menu on the drop-down menu) provides a window pane at the top of the screen that can be shrunk or enlarged by placing the cursor on the bottom pane of the window. The Reference Window will provide a hierarchical menu of your location on the CD-ROM if you place the cursor on any text in the main window. The text in the Reference Window is also clickable if you wish to jump to another section in the hierarchy presented in the Reference Window.
- **Query search:** To search the entire CD-ROM, choose a Query search (by clicking on the Query button on the Toolbar or by choosing Search — Query from the drop-down menu or press the F2 function button). Type your search words in the "Query for" box and click on OK. The number of "hits" for each keyword will show in the upper right hand panel. If there is more than one word in your search, the number of hits for the combined sets of words will be displayed. You can then use the Next or Back button to navigate through the search. See Figure 6.1 for a sample Query search.

Figure 6.1
Query Template Search on Canada Law Book's *Ontario Citator Service* CD-ROM

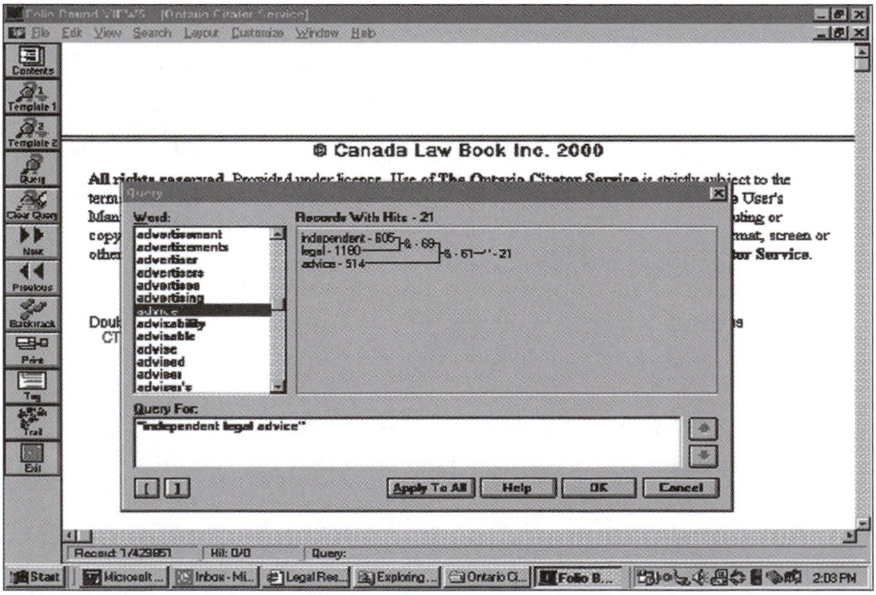

Reprinted by permission of Canada Law Book.

This search shows, for example, that the phrase "independent legal advice" is found 21 times in the legislation (whereas the single word "advice," for example, would have been found 514 times if it were searched alone).

- **Template searching:** Folio CD-ROMs also usually provide Template searches, which depending on the actual CD-ROM, will allow you to search specific segments or "folios" of the CD-ROM. In the Canada Law Book *Ontario Statute Citator* CD-ROM, for example, a Template 1 search allows you to limit your search to only the full text of a particular statute (the *Land Titles Act*, for example). Template 2 on the *Dominion Law Reports* CD-ROM, on the other hand, allows you to retrieve cases by case name. Thus, use template searching when you want to limit your search to particular material on the CD-ROM.
- **Connectors and other search tips:** Unfortunately, Folio software uses some fairly unique connectors for conducting more complicated searches. Set out in table 6.2 are some of the more basic search formulations:

Table 6.2
Basic Search Formulations

Search	Format	Result
Single word	liability	Will find any instance of the word "liability"
Combination	electoral district	Will find records that contain both words (not necessarily as a phrase)
Phrase search	"right to counsel"	Will find records that contain only this phrase
Ordered proximity	"ownership control corporation"/5	Will search for the words within 5 words of each other in the order in which they are typed
Unordered proximity	"municipal corporation"@7	Will search for both words within 7 words of each other, in either order
Expansion/truncation	swim*	Will search for truncations of swim present on the CD-ROM: swim, swims, swimmer, swimsuit
Wildcard	wom?n	Will search for women or woman

- **Modifying your search:** Unfortunately, Folio software does not automatically keep your previous search in the same text box you used. To retrieve your previous searches, you must use the black up and down "history" arrows to the right of the search text box (see Figure

6.1). By clicking the up arrow, you can scroll through your previous searches, choose an old search, and then modify it. Alternatively, you can simply re-type from scratch a modified version of your search in the search box.

- **Tagging your search results:** Use the F6 function key on your keyboard to tag relevant hits in your search. If there is a lot of text to be tagged, drag your mouse over the text to block the text and then click F6. This will place a red line down the left margin of the text, indicating which text has been tagged. When you choose the print or save command, the print or save options will default to printing or saving the tagged text. When you have finished printing or saving, it is important to clear your tagged text prior to conducting a new search — do this by choosing Edit — Clear All Tags from the drop-down menu.

When searching CD-ROMs, it is important to know how current the information is on the CD-ROM. This information will usually appear in the Reference Window at the very top; if it does not, you can usually check the currency information on CD-ROMs that use Folio software by clicking on the Table of Contents button and clicking on the top line of the reference window for currency information and looking for the "What's New" button.

M. LIST OF LAW-RELATED CD-ROMS

Chapter 8 provides a list of resources by topic, which includes some of the leading CD-ROMs by topic. Increasingly, as discussed above, there is a move by Canadian legal publishers to publish their CD-ROMs through Internet subscriptions. Set out in this section is a discussion by publisher of some of the more popular Canadian law-related CD-ROMs. More information on these and other law-related CD-ROMs can be found on the respective Web pages of these publishers or by consulting the *Directory of Law-Related CD-ROMs*.[4]

1) Canada Law Book <http://www.canadalawbook.ca>

Canada Law Book publishes a number of its print products on CD-ROM (and now via Internet subscription — see above). The following Canada Law Book CD-ROMs are particularly useful for lawyers:

---

4   (Teaneck, NJ: Infosources Publishing) [annual].

- *Dominion Law Reports*: contains the full text of the *Dominion Law Reports* (including pagination).
- *Ontario Citator Service*: contains the (English only) full-text *Revised Statutes of Ontario* and *Revised Regulations of Ontario*, as amended, along with selected interpretive case law for particular sections of the legislation.
- *Canada Statute Service*: contains the (English only) full-text *Revised Statutes of Canada* and *Consolidated Regulations of Canada*, as amended, along with selected interpretive case law for particular sections of the legislation.
- *Canadian Criminal Law Library*: contains *Martin's Annual Criminal Code*, *Martin's Annual Related Criminal Statutes*, and the *Canadian Criminal Cases*.
- *Canadian Labour Law Library*: contains the full text of Brown and Beatty's *Canadian Labour Arbitration* and the *Labour Arbitration Cases*.

2) Carswell <http://www.carswell.com>

Carswell publishes a number of CD-ROMs, perhaps the most success-ful of which have been ITS "Partner" CD-ROMs, which combine, by topic, relevant legislation, case law, and full-text textbooks. These are extremely useful products for practitioners who work in a particular area covered by the CD-ROM and can be a useful (albeit not necessar-ily exhaustive) resource for legal research. Some of the more popular Carswell "Partner" CD-ROMs include the following:

- *Corporate Law Partner (Federal and Ontario)*: Updated quarterly. Contains the *Business Law Reports*, relevant federal and Ontario leg-islation, commentary, and full-text books on corporate law from var-ious Carswell authors.
- *Bankruptcy Partner*: Updated quarterly. Contains the *Canadian Bank-ruptcy Reports*, relevant insolvency legislation, policy statements, forms, and commentary from Houlden and Morawetz's *Bankruptcy and Insolvency Law of Canada*.
- *Employment Law Partner*: Updated quarterly. Contains the *Canadian Cases on Employment Law*, relevant federal, Alberta, British Colum-bia and Ontario legislation, commentary, and full-text books on employment law from various Carswell authors.
- *Tax Partner*: Updated monthly. A very detailed product providing legislation, case law, and commentary on income tax law. Also avail-able in different "provincial" components that include relevant provincial income and sales tax materials.

- *Criminal Law Partner*: Updated quarterly. Contains relevant legislation, case law, commentary, and full-text books on criminal law from various Carswell authors.
- *Civil Practice Partner*: Updated quarterly. Contains Carswell's *Practice Cases, Ontario Civil Practice, Ontario Small Claims Court Practice, Ontario Civil Procedure, Federal Court Practice*, and *Supreme Court of Canada Practice*.

3) CCH Canadian <http://www.cch.ca>

CCH is well known in the legal field for its black three-ring binders on various topics of law. It has increasingly published CD-ROM equivalents of these print products (and is now moving towards Internet subscriptions — see above). CCH Canadian CD-ROMs cover a number of legal topics, including corporate law, real estate law, commercial law, family law, insurance law, estate administration, securities law, and tax law. A sample of some of the CCH Canadian law-related CD-ROMs include the following:

- *Corporations Law Guide*. Available for Alberta, British Columbia, Ontario, and federally, with monthly updates. Provides commentary, legislation, and forms and precedents.
- *Real Estate Law Guide*. Available for British Columbia and Ontario. Provides commentary and legislation for real estate transactions in the applicable jurisdiction.
- *Canadian Commercial Law Guide*: Updated monthly. Provides coverage of federal and provincial laws on sales contracts, personal property security, statutory liens, trusts, debt collection, consumer protection, competition law, and bankruptcy and insolvency.
- *Ontario Family Law*. Updated bi-monthly. Provides commentary, legislation, rules of court, and case digests on matters of Ontario family law.
- *Canadian Insurance Law Reporter*: Updated monthly. Provides full-text Canadian court decisions on insurance contracts in areas of health, life, accident, fire, disability, and automobile.
- *Canadian Estate Administration Guide*. Updated monthly. Provides commentary and legislation relating to the administration of estates for all Canadian jurisdictions.
- *Canadian Securities Law Reporter*: Updated monthly. Provides full text of relevant federal and provincial securities legislation, including policy statements, bylaws, and rules of Canadian stock exchanges.

- *Canada Income Tax Guide*. Updated monthly. One of many tax-related CD-ROMs that provides commentary, legislation, and case law digests.

N. CONCLUSIONS

It may well be that in several years CD-ROMs will become extinct with the information they contain instead being made available through Internet subscriptions by the publishers. Pending improvements in wireless Internet technology, however, it is reasonable to assume that CD-ROMs will remain a fairly important part of legal research and legal publishing, at least for the next few years. Regardless, learning how to search CD-ROMs using Folio software can be a useful exercise since Folio software is already being used on Internet Web sites; as a result, some of these search skills will be transferable to the Web.

Given the wide choices of legal resources — ranging from print, CD-ROM, Internet, and commercial online services — why or when does one choose commercial online services? There can usually be several possible answers to this question:

- **Scope of material:** Services like Quicklaw, WestlaweCARSWELL, and LexisNexis provide access to materials, such as unreported court decisions, that are otherwise unavailable or extremely difficult or expensive to acquire directly from the court file. Most lawyers and legal researchers will therefore want to access these databases to ensure the widest possible scope of their searches.
- **Precision of searching:** Commercial online databases have sophisticated search engines that allow the user to limit keyword searches precisely to specific fields (the name of a party to the lawsuit or the name of opposing counsel), a feature not usually available on free Web resources.
- **Online noting up:** These commercial services also have current, easy to use note up abilities that allow the researcher to verify whether the case being researched is still good law. While noting up can still be done in print, the speed, currency, and accuracy of noting up online is far superior to print resources.
- **Bill back:** While a potential disadvantage of these commercial online services is their cost, this can also be a potential advantage since, in theory and in practice, it is usually possible to bill back the cost of many online search charges to the client (and to the losing party in a lawsuit) where the research was necessary and reasonable (see the

cases discussed in Chapter 1, section A(2)). Thus, while many larger firms will maintain both a print and online law library collection, it may be that other firms can rationalize parts of their print collection (usually case law reporters and legislation) in favour of using online resources, especially where the firm has the resources of a larger academic, law society, or courthouse library nearby that can be relied upon for access to print materials not held by the firm. Advice on selecting and acquiring legal resources is found in Chapter 9.

CHAPTER 7

INTERNATIONAL AND FOREIGN LEGAL RESEARCH

In today's world, most Canadian lawyers will regularly be exposed to some aspect of international or foreign law. Despite its growing importance, however, many Canadian lawyers may lack the confidence to know that they are undertaking international or foreign law research competently and thoroughly. The goal of this chapter is to introduce international and foreign legal research and to provide a good overview of relevant print and online resources for effectively conducting international and foreign legal research.[1] Material in this chapter is divided into the following sections:

A. The importance of international and foreign law
B. Tips for conducting international and foreign legal research
C. Print and online *secondary* sources of international law
D. Print and online *primary* sources of international law
E. Researching the domestic laws of foreign countries
F. Sample problems and suggested approaches

---

1   This chapter incorporates, with permission, material from Ted Tjaden, "The Best Online Sources for International and Foreign Law" in Bonnie Fish, ed., *You've Got the Whole World in Your Hands: Using the Internet to Expand the Boundaries of Legal Research* (Toronto: Ontario Bar Association, 2004).

A. THE IMPORTANCE OF INTERNATIONAL AND FOREIGN LAW

Canadian courts are increasingly looking to international treaties and conventions as an indication of standards and norms that should be applied in interpreting and applying *Charter* standards in the Canadian context. There are numerous incidences of this occurring. In *Baker v. Canada (Minister of Citizenship and Immigration)*,[2] for example, Madam Justice L'Heureux-Dubé wrote that "the values reflected in international human rights law may help inform the contextual approach to statutory interpretation and judicial review,"[3] even where, as in that decision, the Canadian Parliament had not yet implemented the Convention being considered. Likewise, in *Suresh v. Canada (Minister of Citizenship and Immigration)*,[4] the Supreme Court of Canada looked to international treaties dealing with the prohibition of deporting persons to countries that allow torture in assessing whether the government was justified in deporting a Sri Lankan refugee to his home country where he might be tortured:

> International treaty norms are not, strictly speaking, binding in Canada unless they have been incorporated into Canadian law by enactment. However, in seeking the meaning of the Canadian Constitution, the courts may be informed by international law. Our concern is not with Canada's international obligations *qua* obligations; rather, our concern is with the principles of fundamental justice. We look to international law as evidence of these principles and not as controlling in itself.[5]

Likewise, with the increase in global business and trade, all lawyers will increasingly be required to have some familiarity with international and foreign law, regardless of their area of practice. This can range from international trade issues governed by the World Trade Organization (WTO) or the *North American Free Trade Agreement* (NAFTA), international intellectual property laws governed by World Intellectual Property Organization (WIPO) conventions, international environmental treaties, and international child abduction conventions, to name but a few examples. Recent literature in Canada and abroad is

---

2   [1999] 2 S.C.R. 817.
3   *Ibid.* ¶ 70.
4   [2002] 1 S.C.R. 3.
5   *Ibid.* ¶ 60.

rife with examples of the increasing domestic application of international and foreign law.[6]

There has also been a relatively strong tradition in Canada for our courts to rely on case law from individual countries outside of Canada, particularly from Commonwealth countries and the United States, depending on the issues or areas of law. A number of studies have been done to examine the extent to which the Supreme Court of Canada, for example, has relied on British and American precedents or decisions from other countries.[7] As might be expected, in Canada's early history there was a heavy reliance on British precedent, but over time, as Canadian courts developed their own bodies of decisions, dependence on British precedence has declined over time.[8] But given the similarities between our legal systems, Canadian judges still show a great deal of deference to the persuasive value of decisions from the House of Lords or the English Court of Appeal, especially in areas of common law or other areas of law where Canadian law has remained relatively consistent with English law, including such areas of law as contracts, torts,

---

6   See, e.g., Reem Bahdi, "Truth and Method in the Domestic Application of International Law" (2002) 15 Can. J.L. & Jur. 255; Robert K. Goldman et al., *The International Dimension of Human Rights: A Guide for Application in Domestic Law* (Washington, DC: Inter-American Development Bank: American University, 2001); Hugh M. Kindred et al., *International Law, Chiefly as Interpreted and Applied in Canada*, 6th ed. (Toronto: Emond Montgomery, 2000); Karen Knop, "Here and There: International Law in Domestic Courts" (2000) 32 N.Y.U.J. Int'l L. & Pol. 501; William A. Schabas, "Twenty-five Years of Public International Law at the Supreme Court of Canada" (2000) 79 Can. Bar Rev. 174; Stephen J. Toope, "The Uses of Metaphor: International Law and the Supreme Court of Canada" (2001) 80 Can. Bar Rev. 534; Gibran van Ert, *Using International Law in Canadian Courts* (The Hague: Kluwer Law International, 2002); Gérard V. La Forest, "The Expanding Role of the Supreme Court of Canada in International Law Issues" (1996) 34 Can. Y.B. Int'l. L. 89; Anne F. Bayefsky, *International Human Rights Law: Use in Canadian Charter of Rights and Freedoms Litigation* (Toronto: Butterworths, 1992).

7   See generally C.L. Ostberg, Matthew E. Wetstein, & Craig R. Ducat, "Attitudes, Precedents and Cultural Change: Explaining the Citation of Foreign Precedents by the Supreme Court of Canada" (2001) 34 Can. J. Pol. Sci. 377; Peter McCormick, "The Supreme Court of Canada and American Citations 1945–1994: A Statistical Overview" (1997) 8 Sup. Ct. L. Rev. (2d) 527; Peter McCormick, "What Supreme Court Cases Does the Supreme Court Cite? Follow-up Citations on the Supreme Court of Canada, 1989–1993" (1996) 7 Sup. Ct. L. Rev. (2d) 451; Christopher Manfredi, "The Use of United States Decisions by the Supreme Court of Canada Under the Charter of Rights and Freedoms" (1990) 23 Can. J. Pol. Sci. 499; Ian Bushnell, "The Use of American Cases" (1986) 35 U.N.B.L.J. 157.

8   McCormick, "The Supreme Court of Canada," *ibid.* at 533.

equity, partnership law, sale of goods, and land law.[9] With the introduction of the *Charter*, we have also seen an increase in the number of times the Supreme Court of Canada has relied upon American case law in helping it interpret constitutional provisions (and in other areas of private law as well), at least in the early days of the *Charter*.[10]

In addition to using international and foreign law materials as "tools of persuasion" to convince a Canadian judge to follow particular arguments or principles being espoused in international or foreign law, Canadian lawyers might also need to research international or foreign law to understand what the law actually is on a particular point in order to understand how a client may be affected by a particular international or foreign transaction (but lawyers must always be careful not to provide legal opinions on the law outside of the jurisdiction in which they are licensed to practice law).

Finally, international and comparative law is increasingly an important focus of scholarly research by legal academics on a variety of important and timely topics, ranging from terrorism to international environmental law to cross-border trade, to name but a few examples.

B. TIPS FOR CONDUCTING INTERNATIONAL AND FOREIGN LEGAL RESEARCH

Until recently, international and foreign law was a relatively isolated and specialized area of law practised by a select few; its literature was also highly specialized, organized, and taught by specialized international and foreign law librarians. In the last ten years, however, the World Wide Web has transformed the way in which legal researchers access international and foreign legal materials. Prior to the Internet, only major academic law libraries could afford to maintain print collections of major international legal resources with selected print coverage of the domestic laws of foreign countries. Very often these collections would be incomplete or out-of-date and not easily accessible by researchers who did not live in major cities that had large academic law libraries. With the Internet, however, we see an explosion of intergovernmental organizations and foreign countries publishing both primary and secondary legal resources online. The tips in this section

---

9   See, e.g., Simon Chester, "Is the Internet Ready for English Legal Research?" in Fish, ed., above note 1.

10   Ostberg, Wetstein & Ducat, above note 7 at 391–92; Manfredi, above note 7 at 505–6.

will discuss several ways to approach international and foreign legal research, many of which take advantage of the Internet.

Tip #1. *Start with secondary resources before primary resources.* For researchers who do not regularly conduct international and foreign legal research, it can be a challenge to start a research project if you do not have a good overview of the area of law or the issues. The simplest way to get over any fear of doing international or foreign legal research is to apply the same techniques discussed in Chapter 1 — start your international or foreign legal research project by using *secondary* resources (books, journals, or Web sites, for example) to help you identify, locate, and understand relevant *primary* resources (international case law, arbitral awards, treaties, foreign case law, or legislation). Secondary resources are usually written by experts in their field and provide a good overview or explanation of the law. The leading textbooks, journals, dictionaries, and Web sites for researching international law are discussed in section C below. Those for researching the domestic laws of foreign countries are discussed in section E below.

Tip #2. *Google it!* You can often easily locate international or foreign materials by simply typing in the name of a treaty, a UN Document Symbol (e.g., E/CN.4/Sub.2/1997/1) or the name of a case. Legal research on the Internet is discussed in detail in Chapter 5 and using the Internet specifically for international and foreign legal research is discussed below. As with any Internet research, care must be taken to evaluate the source of the information and preferring information found on the official Web sites of IGOs, NGOs, or foreign governments or on other reliable sources, such as reputable law schools and other public interest organizations. For one of the better sites on evaluating international and foreign law Internet sources, see the excellent guide prepared by Mirela Roznovschi entitled "Evaluating Foreign and International Legal Databases on the Internet"[11] in which she discusses the following fourteen criteria in evaluating online information: accuracy, archiving, author, publisher, completeness, cost over print format, coverage, currency, language, licensing, search quality, source of data stability, user interactivity, and workability.

Tip #3. *Know your definitions and acronyms.* With the increasing integration of international and foreign legal materials in general legal practice, legal researchers should become more familiar with some of the terminology of international and foreign law. Not too much rests on

---

11   Online: LLRX.com <http://www.llrx.com/features/evaluating.htm>.

the strict definitions of some of the terms discussed below — lines between categories of international and foreign law are blurring every day. Despite this, for the sake of clarity, here are a few key definitions:

- *Public international law*: "That division of international law that deals primarily with the rights and duties of states and intergovernmental organizations as between themselves."[12] Example: *United Nations Convention on the Law of the Sea.*[13]

- *IGO*: InterGovernmental Organization: A permanent organization set up by two or more states to carry on activities of common interest.[14] Example: United Nations[15] or the World Intellectual Property Organization (WIPO).[16]

- *NGO*: NonGovernmental Organization: "An international organization made up of persons other than states."[17] Example: International Chamber of Commerce.[18]

- *Private international law*: "That division of international law that deals primarily with the rights and duties of individuals and nongovernmental organizations in their international affairs."[19] Example: *Hague Convention on the Service Abroad of Judicial and Extrajudicial Documents in Civil or Commercial Matters.*[20]

- *Treaties, conventions*: For the most part, there is no major difference in the generic meaning of the term "treaty" or "convention." The 1969 *Vienna Convention* defines a treaty as "an international agreement concluded between States in written form and governed by international law, whether embodied in a single instrument or in two or more related instruments and whatever its particular designation." The 1986 *Vienna Convention* extends the definition of treaties

---

12 Ray August, *International Law Dictionary & Directory, s.v.* "Public international law," online: International Law Dictionary & Directory <http://www.august1.com/pubs/dict/index.shtml>.

13 *United Nations Convention on the Law of the Sea*, 10 December 1982, 21 I.L.M. 1245, online: United Nations <http://www.un.org/Depts/los/convention_agreements/convention_overview_convention.htm>.

14 Above note 12, *s.v.* "InterGovernmental Organization."

15 Online: United Nations <http://www.un.org>.

16 Online: World Intellectual Property Organization <http://www.wipo.int/>.

17 Above note 12, *s.v.* "NonGovernmental Organization."

18 Online: International Chamber of Commerce <http://www.iccwbo.org>.

19 Above note 12, *s.v.* "Private international law."

20 *Hague Convention on the Service Abroad of Judicial and Extrajudicial Documents in Civil or Commercial Matters* (15 November 1965), online: Hague Conference on Private International Law <http://www.hcch.net/e/conventions/menu14e.html>.

to include international agreements involving international organizations as parties.[21]

- *Foreign law*: For Canadian legal researchers, most would agree that "foreign law" represents the domestic law of countries outside of Canada. Some will debate, though, whether the laws of other Commonwealth countries are "foreign laws" or whether "foreign law" is limited to countries using civil or Islamic law, for example. Not much rests on the distinction, although these terms are sometimes used with some precision in the legal literature and you should be aware of the distinctions, when they matter.

While the traditional definition of public international law incorporates the notion of "state" to "state" action, we have seen a shift (particularly in recent years) in public international laws being used to prosecute individuals, such as in the various war crimes prosecutions taking place right now. Likewise, there are aspects of private international law involving a fair amount of state activity and coordination. And as more countries incorporate international law into their domestic laws in a variety of ways, the entire "globalization" phenomena is truly blurring the boundaries between the terms defined above.

For those conducting treaty research (discussed below in more detail in section D), it helps to be familiar with the following treaty-making terminology:[22]

- *adoption*: when the treaty was concluded or fixed
- *entry into force*: the date the treaty becomes effective
- *ratification*: indicates a country's consent to be bound by the treaty
- *accession*: where a state, not one of the original parties, later consents to be bound by the treaty
- *reservation*: where a state excludes part of the treaty

Abbreviations and acronyms are also common in international and foreign legal research. Be aware of the many abbreviation dictionaries available (discussed in more detail in Chapter 2) that can explain these terms. Often simply searching on the acronym or abbreviation in an Internet search engine will identify the term in the top ten search results

---

21 See United Nations, "Treaty Reference Guide," online: United Nations <http://untreaty.un.org/English/guide.asp>.

22 See, e.g., United Nations, "Treaty Reference Guide," *ibid*. These terms are also nicely explained in Jeanne Rehberg, "Finding Treaties and Other International Agreements" in Jeanne Rehberg & Radu Popa, eds., *Accidental Tourist on the New Frontier: An Introductory Guide to Global Legal Research* (Littleton, CO: F.B. Rothman, 1998) 123.

or provide a link to the organization if the acronym is the name of a well-known NGO or IGO (for example, a Google search on "UNCTAD" results in the first result providing a link to <http://www.unctad.org>, being the home page for the United Nations Conference on Trade and Development).

Tip #4. *Learn another language, understand civil law concepts.* Although English is one of several official languages of the United Nations, a lot of international and foreign legal material will be in languages other than English. Knowledge of other languages can therefore be useful, especially when the free online translation tools are somewhat limited and not a substitute for an official translation, preferably by a qualified translator with legal experience.[23] Equally important, especially for law students or lawyers trained in the common law tradition, is an understanding of civil law since most international law incorporates civil law concepts.

C. PRINT AND ONLINE SECONDARY SOURCES OF INTERNATIONAL LAW

This section will provide information on secondary sources of international law, focusing on the major books, journals, encyclopedias/dictionaries, and Web sites that provide commentary or overviews of international legal research. As mentioned above, the resources listed below should ordinarily be the first place you go to get an explanation or overview of a particular area of international law.

---

23   The University of Toronto Multilingual Translation Technology Centre has a useful Web site providing links to online translation tools and multilingual dictionaries and thesauri — online: University of Toronto Libraries <http://www.library.utoronto.ca/translation>. BabelFish <http://world.altavista.com> is a free Web site that provides basic translations across about 10 major languages, including Chinese, Japanese, and Korean. It allows translation of up to 150 words of text (and is therefore quite limited) or will allow the "pasting" of a Web address (URL) to translate a page. Likewise, Google also provides basic free translation at the site above, but limited to English, French, German, Spanish, Italian, and Portugese in addition to providing translation of Web pages in those same languages. Google search results usually also offer a "Translate this Page" link for search results of pages not in the default search language.

1) Books

You can safely assume that someone, somewhere, has written a book on an area of international law that you need to research. The titles below are only a selected list of fairly general titles on international law. If you need to find more specific or topical books, simply try a title keyword search in a major law library catalogue using the keywords "international" and "law" plus a keyword for the particular sub-topic, for example, "environmental," if you were looking for a book on international environmental law.

a) Selected Canadian Texts on Public International Law
- Alexandrowicz, George et al. *Dimensions of Law: Canadian and International Law in the 21st Century*. Toronto: Emond Montgomery, 2004.
- Currie, John H. *Public International Law*. Toronto: Irwin Law, 2001.
- Freeman, Mark and Gib van Ert. *International Human Rights Law*. Toronto: Irwin Law, 2004.
- Kindred, Hugh M. et al. *International Law, Chiefly as Interpreted and Applied in Canada*. 6th ed. Toronto: Emond Montgomery, 2000.
- Mulamba-Mbuyi, Benjamin. *Refugees and International Law*. Toronto: Carswell, 1993.
- Schabas, William A. *International Human Rights Law and the Canadian Charter*. 2d ed. Toronto: Carswell, 1996.
- van Ert, Gibran. *Using International Law in Canadian Courts*. The Hague: Kluwer Law International, 2002.

b) Selected Canadian Texts on Private International :aw
- Appleton, Barry. *Navigating NAFTA: A Concise User's Guide to the North American Free Trade Agreement*. Toronto: Carswell, 1994.
- Baer, Marvin. *Private International Law in Common Law Canada: Cases, Text, and Materials*. 2d ed. Toronto: Emond Montgomery, 2003.
- Baran, Babak. *Carswell's Handbook of International Dispute Resolution Rules*. Toronto: Carswell, 1999.
- Castel, J.-G. *Canadian Conflict of Laws*. 5th ed. Looseleaf. Toronto: Butterworths, 2002.
- Castel. J.-G. *Introduction to Conflict of Laws*. 4th ed. Toronto: Butterworths, 2002.
- Gold, Edgar et al. *Maritime Law*. Toronto: Irwin Law, 2004.
- Johnson, Jon R. *International Trade Law*. Toronto: Irwin Law, 1998.
- Krishna, Vern. *Canadian International Taxation*. Looseleaf. Toronto: Carswell, 1995.
- Lemieux, Denis and Ana Stuhec. *Review of Administrative Action under NAFTA*. Toronto: Carswell, 1998.

- Thomas, Jeffrey S. and Michael A. Meyer. *The New Rules of Global Trade: A Guide to the World Trade Organization*. Toronto: Carswell, 1997.

c) **Selected American and British Texts on Public and Private International law**

- Brownlie, Ian. *Principles of Public International Law*. 6th ed. Oxford: Oxford University Press, 2003.
- Brownlie, Ian. *Basic Documents in International Law*. 5th ed. Oxford: Oxford University Press, 2002.
- Buergenthal, Thomas. *Public International Law in a Nutshell*. 3d ed. St. Paul, MN: West Group, 2002.
- Cassese, Antonio. *International Law*. Oxford: Oxford University Press, 2001.
- Collins, Lawrence et al., eds. *Dicey and Morris on the Conflict of Laws*. 13th ed. London: Sweet & Maxwell, 2000.
- George Washington University Journal of International Law and Economics. *Guide to International Legal Research*. 4th ed. Newark, NJ: LexisNexis Matthew Bender, 2002.
- Janis, Mark W. *An Introduction to International Law*. 4th ed. New York: Aspen Publishers, 2003.
- Koskenniemi, Martti. *Sources of International Law*. Burlington, VT: Ashgate/Dartmouth, 2000.
- North, Peter, Sir and J.J. Fawcett. *Chesire and North's Private International Law*. 13th ed. London: Butterworths, 1999.
- Rehberg, Jeanne and Radu Popa, eds. *Accidental Tourist on the New Frontier: An Introductory Guide to Global Legal Research*. Littleton, CO: F.B. Rothman, 1998.
- Sands, Philippe and Pierre Klein. *Bowett: Law of International Institutions*. London: Sweet & Maxwell, 2001.
- Shaw, Malcolm N. *International Law*. 5th ed. New York: Cambridge University Press, 2003.

2) Journals

Increasingly, Canadian scholars and lawyers are writing on international legal issues. To find law journal articles dealing with international (or foreign) law, consider first checking any of the following print or online journal indices:

- *Index to Canadian Legal Literature*. 2d ed. Toronto: Carswell, 1985 [updated annually with more frequent updates in Canadian Current

Law — Canadian Legal Literature]. Also available online on West-laweCARSWELL and Quicklaw. Older print volumes covering pre-1985 are also available.

- *Index to Canadian Legal Periodical Literature.* Canadian Association of Law Libraries, 1961 [updated quarterly]. Available in print only.
- *Index to Foreign Legal Periodicals.* American Association of Law Libraries, 1985 [updated quarterly].

In addition, law journal articles on international or foreign legal topics are well indexed in the *Index to Legal Periodical and Books* and *Legal-Trac*, available online at most major academic law libraries.

The following is a list of the major Canadian law journals with an international focus:[24]

- *Asper Review of International Business and Trade Law.* Asper Program, Faculty of Law, University of Manitoba, 2001 [published annually]. Also available on Quicklaw (database: ASPR).
- *Bulletin.* Canadian Council on International Law, 1974 [published three times per year].
- *Canada-United States Law Journal.* Canada-United States Law Institute, 1978 [published annually]. Selected coverage also available on LexisNexis and WestlaweCARSWELL.
- *Canadian Foreign Policy.* The Norman Paterson School of International Affairs, Carleton University, Ottawa, 1992 [published three times per year].
- *Canadian International Lawyer.* Canadian Bar Association, International Law Section, 1994 [published irregularly].
- *The Canadian Yearbook of International Law.* International Law Association, Canadian Branch. University of British Columbia Press, 1963 [published annually].
- *International Insights: A Dalhousie Journal of International Affairs.* John E. Reed International Law Society, Dalhousie Law School, 1985 [published annually].
- *Journal of International Law and International Relations.* University of Toronto, Faculty of Law and Munk Centre for International Studies, 2004 [published annually].

---

24 There are too many American, British, and other international law journals to mention. The Bora Laskin Law Library has an extensive list of law journals available — online: Bora Laskin Law Library <http://www.law-lib.utoronto.ca/journals/search.asp>, where you can search on the keyword "international" to generate a list of all international law journals available online, regardless of country of publication.

3) Encyclopedias/Dictionaries

There are a number of useful international law encyclopedias and dictionaries:

- August, Ray. *International Law Dictionary & Directory*. Available online: <http://www.august1.com/pubs/dict/index.shtml>.
- Bernhardt, Rudolf, ed. *Encyclopedia of Public International Law*. Amsterdam: North-Holland Pub. Co., 1992 [Consolidated library edition].
- Fox, James R. Dictionary of International and Comparative Law. 3d ed. Dobbs Ferry, NY: Oceana Publications, 2003.
- Gibson, John S. *Dictionary of International Human Rights Law*. Lanham, MD: Scarecrow Press, 1996.
- Grant, John P. and J. Craig Barker. *Parry and Grant Encyclopaedic Dictionary of International Law*. 2d ed. New York: Oceana Publications, Inc., 2004.
- Lindbergh, Ernst. *Modern Dictionary of International Legal Terms: English-French-German*. Boston: Little, Brown, 1993.

Another useful reference source for international and foreign law is Chapter 5 of the *Canadian Guide to Uniform Legal Citation* (5th ed.) (the "McGill Guide"). This chapter discusses in detail how to properly cite treaties and international case law and has other useful information on international and foreign legal materials.

4) Web Sites

There are Web sites too numerous to list here that provide excellent overviews or explanation of international or foreign law. The main publishers of these Web sites are IGOs, NGOs, law schools, or universities and other public interest groups. The sites listed below — in no particular order — are included for their quality and comprehensiveness.

- **American Society for International Law (ASIL).** *ASIL Guide to Electronic Resources for International Law.*
  <http://www.asil.org/resource/ Home.htm>

  Founded in 1906, ASIL is described as "the premier membership organization in the United States dedicated to advancing the study and use of international law." The online guide listed above, which is also available in print book format, provides free, excellent information, commentary, and links on international legal topics ranging from human rights, international commercial arbitration, international criminal law, international economic law, international environmental law, international intellectual property law, international organizations, treaties, and the United Nations.

- **Law Library Resource Xchange (LLRX.com).** *International Law Guides.*
  <http://www.llrx.com/international_law.html>

  LLRX describes itself as "a free Web journal dedicated to providing legal, library, IT/IS, marketing and administrative professionals with the most up-to-date information on a wide range of Internet research and technology-related issues, applications, resources and tools, since 1996." The page above provides free links to over forty customized guides prepared by leading law librarians and lawyers on various international legal topics.

- **Library and Archives Canada.** *International Organizations and Related Information*
  <http://www.collectionscanada.ca/8/4/r4-240-e.html>

  This page provides links to international organizations, constitutions of the world, treaties, and international covenants.

- **University of Michigan Documents Center.** *International Agencies and Information on the Web.*
  <http://www.lib.umich.edu/govdocs/intl.html>

  This site provides extensive links to various IGOs, NGOs, and other international agencies and treaties.

- **Harvard Law School.** *Foreign & International Law Resources: An Annotated Guide to Web Sites Around the World.*
  <http://www.law.harvard.edu/library/services/research/guides/international/web_resources/index.php>

  This site has extensive links, with annotations.

- **Bora Laskin Law Library, University of Toronto, Faculty of Law.** *Women's Human Rights Resources.*
  <http://www.law-lib.utoronto.ca/diana/mainpage.htm>

  The main goal of the Women's Human Rights Resources site is to assist individuals and organizations in using international women's human rights law to promote women's rights. The material is organized into 26 subject areas that relate to women's human rights and within each subject area links are provided to scholarly literature, books, case law, and treaties, with full-text information being provided, wherever possible.

- **Arthur W. Diamond Law Library at Columbia Law School.** *Human Rights and Constitutional Rights.*
  <http://www.hrcr.org>

  This site provides excellent access to Web resources dealing with human rights and constitutional law, albeit from an American perspective. For direct access to constitutions of the world, see the "International Constitutional Law" Web page of the Institut für öffentliches Recht-Aktuell available online at <http://www.oefre.uni-be.ch/law/icl/>.

- **David A. Levy.** *Private International Law.*
  <http://www. asil.org/resource/pil1.htm>

  On the Web site of ASIL, this excellent online guide provides commentary on researching private international law on the Web, in addition to providing links to major sites, including UNCITRAL, UNIDROIT, and the Hague Conference on Private International Law, in addition to other topical sites relating to international trade and business.

- **Marci Hoffman, "Revised Guide to International Trade Law Sources on the Internet."**
  <http://www.llrx.com/features/trade3.htm>

  International and foreign law librarian Marci Hoffman provides excellent commentary on researching international trade law, including providing links for finding WTO, GATT, and NAFTA decisions and other information.

- **Jeanne Rehberg. "WTO/GATT Research."**
  <http://www.llrx.com/features/wto2.htm>

  This excellent online guide from LLRX by law librarian Jeanne Rehberg provides an excellent overview on researching World Trade Organization and GATT issues, including both print and online material.

- *INT-LAW: Foreign and International Law Librarians List.*
  <INT-LAW@listhost.ciesin.org>

  This is a fairly active listserv of foreign and international law librarians and other researchers interested in international and foreign legal research. To register for the listserv, send the following message to majordomo@listhost.ciesin.org: subscribe int-law. Archives of recent INT-LAW messages can be found online at <http://listhost.ciesin.org/lists/public/int-law/>.

- **Foreign Affairs Canada.**
  <http://www.fac-aec.gc.ca>

  As of December 2003, the Canadian federal government has separated "foreign affairs" and "international trade" (in what previously used to be combined units in the Department of Foreign Affairs and International Trade — DFAIT). The Web site of Foreign Affairs

Canada can provide useful background information on international law and Canada's role in international affairs.

- **International Trade Canada**
  <http://www.itcan-cican.gc.ca>

According to its Web site, International Trade Canada "works to position Canada as a business leader for the 21st century" and offers services in three key areas:
  - Services for Canadian businesses;
  - Services for non-Canadian businesses; and
  - Information on Canada's trade and economic policy.

D. PRINT AND ONLINE PRIMARY SOURCES OF INTERNATIONAL LAW

In the previous section, discussion focused on secondary sources of international law, such as leading books, law journals, dictionaries/encyclopedias, and Web sites that explain international law. In this section, the discussion will focus on print and online primary sources of international law in the form of treaties and international case law.

1) Treaties

Treaties — in their broad sense — are the means by which nation states enter into bilateral or multilateral agreements on subjects of mutual interest, ranging anywhere from postal services to the environment to extradition. In Canada, the Treaty Section of the Department of Foreign Affairs is responsible for the implementation and publication of treaties entered into by Canada. These treaties are officially published in the *Canada Treaty Series*, available at most major academic law libraries. Recently, the Canadian government is making access to Canadian treaties accessible through its Canada Treaty Information Web site at <http://www.treaty-accord.gc.ca>. This Web site provides access to lists of treaties Canada has entered into, along with the full-text of most treaties. Treaties are divided between bilateral and multilateral and "word wheels" are provided to allow the searcher, if desired, to choose a treaty by subject, country, or IGO. Another important source of Canadian-American treaties is the Canado-American Treaties Web site available online at <http://www.lexum.umontreal.ca/ca_us/index_en.html>. This site provides free access to the text of all bilateral treaties established between the United States of America and Canada from 1783 to 1997.

Treaties entered into by other countries are also published in print, but will not necessarily be widely held by law libraries in Canada. Fortunately, most countries now publish online versions of their treaty series. Here is a partial list of some of the international treaties of possible interest to most Canadian legal researchers:

- UK — Treaties: <http://www.fco.gov.uk>
- US — Treaties: <http://www.gpoaccess.gov/serialset/cdocuments/index.html>
- US — Treaties (via Tufts): <http://fletcher.tufts.edu/multilaterals.html>
- EU — Treaties: <http://europa.eu.int/abc/obj/treaties/en/entoc.htm>
- France — Treaties (Base Pacte): <http://www.doc.diplomatie.gouv.fr/pacte/index.html>
- Australia — Treaties: <http://www.austlii.edu.au/au/other/dfat>

However, one of the most prolific producers of international treaties and other primary sources of international law is the United Nations, available online at <http://www.un.org>, which was established on 24 October 1945, when fifty-one original member countries including France, the UK, and the USA ratified the *UN Charter*. Today, nearly every nation in the world belongs to the UN bringing its membership total to 191 countries. UN members are sovereign countries. The United Nations is not a world government, nor does it make laws. It does, however, provide the means to help resolve international conflict and formulate policies on matters affecting all of us. The United Nations has six main organs. Five of them — the General Assembly, the Security Council, the Economic and Social Council, the Trusteeship Council, and the Secretariat — are based at UN Headquarters in New York. The sixth main organ is the International Court of Justice, located in The Hague.

Because the UN Web site is so massive, it helps to be aware of some online guides available on its site to help with research:

- UN Documentations: Research Guide: <http://www.un.org/Depts/dhl/resguide/symbol.htm>. Among other things, this guide explains UN symbols (e.g., E/CN.4/Sub.2/AC.2/1987/WP.4/Add.1).
- Official Web Site Locator of the United Nations Systems of Organizations: <http://www.unsystem.org>
- UN Organization Chart: <http://www.un.org/aboutun/chart.html>

An excellent source of UN treaties is the UN Treaty Database, available online at <http://untreaty.un.org>, albeit on a subscription basis.

This database provides access to the full text of treaties from the United Nations Treaty Series as well as HTML versions of treaties deposited with the Secretary-General. The location and status of each treaty, and full text of all declarations and reservations of parties, are also included and kept current.

In addition, the United Nations Official Document System (UNODS), available online at <http://www.ods.un.org>, is a full-text, searchable subscription database of nearly all United Nations official documents from 1992 onwards. You can search by UN document number, keywords, and author, with date restrictions. Documents display in PDF or TIFF format.

One final important source of treaty information — although unofficial — is the highly cited *International Legal Materials* (cited I.L.M.), published by the American Society for International Law (ASIL) since 1962. It is published bi-monthly and includes the full text of new, important treaties in addition to other important legal materials, including selected international case law. This publication is also available as a full-text database on both LexisNexis (database: ILM) and WestlaweCARSWELL (database: ILM); it is also available by subscription on Hein Online.

Treaties or conventions relating to private international law are readily found online and will be the way most researchers access such materials. Set out below are some of the major primary sources of private international law available on the Internet:

- **Hague Conference on Private International Law**.
  <http://www.hcch.net/e/index.html>

  As stated on its Web site, The Hague Conference on Private International Law is an intergovernmental organization, the purpose of which is "to work for the progressive unification of the rules of private international law." There are sixty-four member States. There are over thirty-six Conventions entered into ranging in topics from civil procedure and the international sale of goods to child support, and enforcement of judgments, to name a few. The full text of conventions is provided, along with full status information.

- **UNCITRAL — United Nations Commission on International Trade Law**.
  <http://www.uncitral.org>

  The mandate of UNCITRAL is "the progressive harmonization and unification of the law of international trade." UNCITRAL has produced a number of texts on the international sale of goods, arbitration, insolvency, international payments, transport, and e-commerce in the form of conventions, model laws, guides to enactment, legislative guides, legislative recommendations, and model contract rules, all available on the Web site.

- **UNIDROIT — International Institute for the Unification of Private Law.**
  <http://www.unidroit.org>

UNIDROIT is an independent intergovernmental organization whose purpose is to study needs and methods for modernizing, harmonizing, and coordinating private and, in particular, commercial law as between States and groups of States. There are currently 59 member States, including Canada, the United Kingdom, and the United States. The Web site contains the full text of the UNIDROIT Conventions, including, for example, the *Convention Relating to a Uniform Law on the International Sale of Goods* (The Hague, 1964). The site also contains, among other things, UNILEX, a database of international case law and bibliography on the *United Nations Convention on Contracts for the International Sale of Goods* (CISG) and the *UNIDROIT Principles of International Commercial Contract*.

2) International Courts

There are a number of important international courts, the oldest continuing one being the International Court of Justice through the United Nations, whose decisions are available online at <http://www.icj-cij.org>. As explained on its Web site, the International Court of Justice has two main roles: (1) to settle in accordance with international law the legal disputes submitted to it by States; and (2) to give advisory opinions on legal questions referred to it by duly authorized international organs and agencies. The court only hears decisions by party States who are members of the United Nations.

Rather than individually listing the Web sites for the other major international courts, readers are encouraged to consult the excellent Project on International Courts and Tribunals Web site at <http://www.pict-pcti.org>. This project, established in 1997, is now undertaken by the Centre on International Courts and Tribunals at the Faculty of Laws, University College, London and the Center on International Cooperation at New York University. Its purpose, according to its Web site, is to couple "academic research with concrete action aimed at facilitating the work of international courts and tribunals at developing the lawyering skills of potential actors, in particular, in developing countries and economies-in-transition." This site, among other things, provides academic research, bibliographies, and links to the major international courts and tribunals, including the following courts:

- International Court of Justice (ICJ)
- International Tribunal for the Law of the Sea (ITLOS)
- Dispute Settlement System of the World Trade Organization (WTO)
- International Criminal Tribunal for the Former Yugoslavia (ICTY)
- International Criminal Tribunal for Rwanda (ICTR)
- International Criminal Court (ICC)
- Internationalized criminal tribunals in Sierra Leone, East Timor, Kosovo, and Cambodia
- European Court of Human Rights (ECHR)
- European Court of Justice and the Court of First Instance (ECJ/CFI)
- European Free Trade Association Court (EFTA)
- Benelux Court of Justice (BeneluxCJ)
- Inter-American Court of Human Rights (IACHR)
- Andean Court of Justice (TJAC)
- Central American Court of Justice (CACJ)
- Caribbean Court of Justice (CCJ)
- Common Court of Justice and Arbitration of the Organization for the Harmonization of Corporate Law in Africa (OHADA)
- Court of Justice of the Common Market for Eastern and Southern Africa (COMESA)
- African Commission and Court of Human and Peoples' Rights (ACHPR)
- Permanent Court of Arbitration (PCA)
- International Centre for Settlement of Investment Disputes (ICSID)
- Arbitral decisions under the North American Free Trade Agreement (NAFTA)

Each of the international courts or tribunals has fairly extensive information on itsindividual Web site that explains the procedures for that court or tribunal in addition to providing access to its decisions.

E. RESEARCHING THE DOMESTIC LAWS OF FOREIGN COUNTRIES

Governments around the world are increasingly publishing their legislation and case law for free on the Internet. The scope and depth of such material is variable from country to country. Equally important is the notion that it is rare for countries whose official languages are not English to publish their primary sources of law in English. Do not therefore expect to get Italian case law translated into English for free on the Internet. Most primary sources of law are published in the vernacular or "native" tongue. It also goes without saying that lawyers should not provide legal advice outside of the jurisdiction in which they are licensed to practise law. Nonetheless, access to foreign laws still plays an important role for lawyers in getting a sense of what foreign law might be with the goal of getting an understanding of the foreign law and assessing when it might be necessary to retain counsel from that foreign jurisdiction to provide a formal legal opinion.

There are a number of excellent print and online sources for finding the domestic laws of foreign countries (set out below in no particular order):[25]

- Reynolds, Thomas H. and Arturo A. Flores. *Foreign Law: Current Sources of Codes and Basic Legislation in Jurisdictions of the World.* Littleton, CO: F.B. Rothman, 1989 [updated regularly]. Also available online via subscription as the *Foreign Law Guide*: <http://www.foreignlawguide.com>

   As described in the online version of this product, the *Foreign Law Guide* "is designed for the practitioner, scholar, and researcher and provides essential information on primary and secondary sources of foreign law — what it is, where to find it, and how to use it. It contains information on nearly 200 jurisdictions from major nations to crown colonies, semi-independent states, and supra-national regional organizations. The work is comprehensive in content and global in scope and contains exhaustive links within the work and to many URLs on the world level."

- LexisNexis Martindale-Hubbell. *International Law Digest* (3 volumes). Also available online on LexisNexis by subscription.

   This three-volume set, often included in the multi-volume legal directory published by Martindale-Hubbell provides digests of the laws of the fifty states, the District of Columbia, Puerto Rico, and the US Virgin Islands and summaries of the laws of eighty countries, in addition to the complete texts of over fifty Uniform and Model Acts and International Conventions.

- Redden, Kenneth Robert, ed. *Modern Legal Systems Cyclopedia* (10 volumes). Buffalo, NY: W.S. Hein, 1984 [updated periodically].

   This multi-volume (red) set is organized by regions of the world and provides detailed information about the legal systems of individual countries within those regions.

---

25   In this section, I use the term "foreign law" to not necessarily include British, American, or Australian law. To conduct British, American, or Australian legal research, see the relevant sections of Chapters 2 and 3.

- **Germain, Claire M.** *Germain's Transnational Law Research: A Guide for Attorneys*. Ardsley-on-Hudson, NY: Transnational Juris Publications, Inc., 1991 [updated periodically].

This practical text by Cornell Law Librarian and Professor Claire Germain provides an excellent overview of cross-jurisdictional legal research, particularly from an American point-of-view.

- **Blanpain, Roger, ed.** *International Encyclopaedia of Laws*. Deventer, Netherlands: Kluwer Law and Taxation Publishers, 1994 [updated periodically].

This multi-volume encyclopedia is organized in the following broad topics: civil procedure, commercial and economic law, constitutional law, contracts, corporation and partnership law, criminal law, environmental law, family and succession law, insurance law, intellectual property law, intergovernmental organizations, medical law, social security law, and transport law. Within each topic, information is provided on primary and secondary sources of law for about sixty different countries.

- **Roznovschi, Mirela.** *NYU Foreign Databases — By Jurisdiction* Available online: <http://www.law.nyu.edu/library/foreign_intl/country.html>

This page is part of the excellent Web pages provided by the New York University Law Library. It currently provides links to the domestic laws of forty-eight countries (from Argentina to Venezuela). Some of the links found on the individual pages for countries may require passwords but the pages clearly indicate this and the editors of the site regularly update the information for each country and try to provide freely available links whenever possible.

- **Law Library Resource Xchange (LLRX.com).** *Comparative and Foreign Law Guides*. Available online: <http://www.llrx.com/comparative_and _foreign_law.html>

An excellent starting point when conducting research on the domestic laws of foreign countries. The goal of the LLRX editors is to eventually have a "Guide to Doing Legal Research in . . ." for every country of the world. There are currently over fifty countries or regions represented by these online guides.

- **GLIN — Nations of the World**
  <http://www.loc.gov/law/guide/ nations.html>

This page, from the Law Library of Congress Global Legal Information Network, provides an alphabetical list of links to countries of the world. At each country link are a series of well-organized, "standardized" links to the following sources of law for each country: constitution, executive, judicial, legislative, legal guides, and miscellaneous general sources.

• **AustLII's World Law**
  <http://www.worldlii.org>

  This page, from the Australasian Legal Information Institute, provides an alphabetical list of links for countries of the world. At each country link are further links to both primary sources of law (legislation and cases) and other background material for each country, where available.

• **Findlaw List of Countries**
  <http://www.findlaw.com/12international/countries/>

  This is Findlaw's alphabetical list of countries (currently around ninety countries, from Afghanistan to Zimbabwe). You will find the quality of information for each country is quite variable and often only contains links to other pages that provide links. The page for Turkey, for example, ranges from useful links to the Turkish Grand National Assembly to the Ankara University Faculty of Law.

• **Harvard Law School.** *European Union Legal Research.*
  <http://www.law.harvard.edu/library/services/research/guides/international/eu/index.php>

  A very thorough introduction and guide to doing EU legal research; some coverage includes commercial databases.

In addition to the print materials and Web sites listed above on foreign law, each of Quicklaw, LexisNexis, and WestlaweCARSWELL is substantially adding legal materials to its databases from jurisdictions outside of Canada (primarily being British, Australian, and European). Note that Quicklaw has some unique Caribbean and African content. There are also a number of other commercial online services that provide access to foreign laws; a few examples of these commercial databases include but are not limited to the following:[26]

---

26   For more sites, see the NYU Foreign Databases link mentioned above, where information is provided under each country's listing on the commercial database providers available for the particular country, where applicable.

- **Africa**: Jutastat <http://www.jutastat.com>. This commercial site provides Internet access (for a fee) to various African legislation and case law for various countries, including South Africa, Botswana, Zimbabwe, Namibia, and Tanzania (this site also has the *English Reports* online, by subscription).
- **Africa**: LawAfrica.com <http://www.lawafrica.com>. This commercial site provides limited free information on African legal matters but also provides an online (and print) subscription to the *East Africa Law Reports* and the *LawAfrica Law Reports*.
- **Caribbean**: CariLaw <http://carilaw.cavehill.uwi.edu>. This commercial database is provided by the University of West Indies Faculty of Law Library and provides online access (by subscription). The database has over 20,000 Caribbean decisions, some dating back to the 1950s, and there are plans to add selected legislation.
- **China**: LawInfo China <http://www.lawinfochina.com>. This subscription database provides access to English translations and original Chinese versions of statutes, regulations and cases from the People's Republic of China, with basic laws of the National People's Congress and regulations of the State Council from 1949 to present and selected cases of the Supreme People's Court and Supreme People's Procurate.
- **France**: JurisClasseur (Lexis) <http://www.juris-classeur.com>. This subscription database provides extensive treatment of searchable and browsable French legislation and case law in addition to French legal periodicals dating back to the 1970s.
- **Germany**: Beck Online <http://www.beck.de>. Beck Online provides access to German case law, legislation, and commentary (by subscription).
- **Singapore**: Singapore Lawnet Legal Workbench <http://www.lawnet.com.sg>. This commercial database for the law of Singapore provides full-text access to statutes, regulations, and case law from Singapore (including cases from the *Singapore Law Reports* and the *Malayan Law Journal*), as well as treaties and secondary sources.

F. SAMPLE PROBLEMS AND SUGGESTED APPROACHES

Set out in this section are the following four hypothetical problems that a Canadian legal researcher might typically come across, along with suggested approaches to finding information on the Internet to answer these questions.

How do I serve Ontario court papers on a Swedish company?

There are several possible approaches to answering this question. Ontario litigators might think of checking Rule 17 (Service outside of Ontario) from one of the annotated versions of the *Ontario Rules of Civil Procedure* where the Rule itself mentions the *Hague Convention on the Service Abroad of Judicial and Extrajudicial Documents in Civil or Commercial Matters* (the annotated versions of the Rules in print provide added commentary).

Simply "Googling" the name of this Convention results in finding it on the first hit. The full text of the Convention is available online and by clicking on the "Full Status" there is a link for Sweden that explains who the "contact" is within Sweden for the purpose of accepting foreign court documents under the Convention.

Alternative approaches: The *International Law Digests* (in print) from Martindale-Hubbell (part of its multi-volume Directory) have a listing for Sweden that mentions that Sweden is a party to this Convention. That might be enough to trigger one to search online for the Convention.

I have a citation to E/CN.4/Sub.2/1997/1. What is it and how can I get it?

Even if one is not certain this is a United Nations document symbol, simply "Googling" the citation retrieves the document on the first hit. The document turns out to be a 1997 Provisional Agenda from the Sub Commission on the Prevention of Discrimination and Protection of Minorities of the Commission on Human Rights. The symbol/citation translates as follows:

E   = Economic and Social Council
CN.4 = Commission on Human Rights
Sub.2 = Sub Commission on the Prevention of Discrimination and Protection of Minorities
1997 = year
1   = document number

My buddy (a Canadian) is in prison in Mexico — can he be transferred back to a Canadian jail?

A Google search containing the words (not in quotes) — mexico canada prison transfer — results in mention of bilateral treaties dealing with the transfer of offenders between countries. One of the first twenty hits is a link to the actual *Transfer of Offenders Act*, R.S.C. 1985, T-15 and

Mexico is listed in the Appendix to that Act as being a country with which Canada has entered into a treaty for the transfer of prisoners.

One could then go to the Canada Treaty Information Web site at <http://www.treaty-accord.gc.ca> and search under bilateral treaties by scrolling down the "word wheel" where one of the options is "transfer of offenders." Choosing that subject and the country "Mexico" results in a link to the full text of the *Treaty Between Canada and the United Mexican States on the Execution of Penal Sentences*, C.T.S. 1979, No. 3 (1979/03/29). This Treaty describes in detail the procedures involved.

Also, in the initial Google search, one of the Web sites listed (although not obviously relevant at first) was Corrections Canada. On its Web site, under a main link called "Programs" there is a good explanation of the topic "International Transfer of Offenders," with links to various treaties. A phone and fax number are also provided.

I heard about the *Waldman* decision at the "United Nations" dealing with the lack of funding for Jewish schooling in Ontario; I think he was represented by Toronto lawyer, Raj Anand — where can I get a copy of this decision?

Once again, Googling the words (without quotations) — waldman catholic school anand — brings a number of hits, albeit none of the first ten results are official URLs from the UN. However, the first result appears to be an unofficial version of the decision from the Human Rights Library at the University of Minnesota. Looking at that document reveals a UN document symbol of CCPR/C/67/D/694/1996.

Googling that symbol brings up the official page from within the UN site for that decision. Alternatively, if one knew it was likely a decision from the Human Rights Committee, one could browse through the UN Web site for the document.

CHAPTER 8

LEGAL RESEARCH BY TOPIC

This chapter provides information on Canadian legal resources, broken down into the following forty-five topics:

A. Aboriginal law
B. Administrative law
C. Alternative dispute resolution (ADR)
D. Banking law
E. Bankruptcy and insolvency law
F. Charities and not-for-profit law
G. Civil procedure
H. Communications law
I. Competition and anti-trust law
J. Constitutional and human rights law
K. Construction law
L. Contract and agency law
M. Corporate and partnership law
N. Criminal law
O. Crown law
P. Damages law
Q. Debtor/creditor law
R. Education law
S. Employment law
T. Environmental and natural resources law
U. Evidence law

V.   Family law
W.   Health and medical law
X.   Immigration and refugee law
Y.   Insurance law
Z.   Intellectual property/e-commerce law
AA. International and foreign law
BB. Introduction to law/legal systems
CC. Labour law
DD. Landlord and tenant/commercial leasing law
EE. Legal practice
FF. Media/defamation law
GG. Motor vehicle and transportation law
HH. Municipal and planning law
II. Occupational health and safety law
JJ. Pension law
KK. Personal property security law
LL. Privacy law
MM. Property law (real and personal)
NN. Securities law
OO. Sports and entertainment law
PP. Taxation law
QQ. Tort law
RR. Trusts, wills, and estates law
SS. Workers' compensation law

Included for each topic is a list of the following information:

- Short scope note for the topic
- Library of Congress Subject Headings
- Applicable title for the *Canadian Encyclopedic Digest* (CED)
- Applicable volume for the *Canadian Abridgment*[1] (Can. Abr.)
- Relevant Quicklaw databases, if any
- Print case law reporters (full text), if any
- Journals, if any
- CD-ROMs, if any

---

1   At the time of publication of this book, Carswell had started to publish in installments a third edition of the *Canadian Abridgment* (see the discussion in Chapter 2 for more information). As such, the references to volumes of the *Canadian Abridgment* in this chapter will be to the second edition, unless the third edition is indicated. Over the course of time, readers should consult the actual volumes of the *Canadian Abridgment* on the shelf as volumes of the second edition are converted into a third edition since the volume numbers and some topics will most likely change as the third edition is rolled out.

- Relevant Web sites, if any
- Leading textbooks

Readers should use this chapter when they are starting a new legal research project. Once the applicable broad area of law has been identified for the problem (e.g., "evidence law"), consult that particular section of this chapter to gain a quick overview of relevant resources for that topic to help reduce the risk of missing any obvious possible sources of information.

Not always included in the lists below are annotated or consolidated books of legislation (of which there are often many), which provide a convenient albeit unofficial source of legislation, usually with commentary or other value-added features, such as summaries of leading cases that have considered particular sections of legislation. To check for more recent editions of the materials listed below or for more materials, consult one of the online library catalogues listed in Chapter 2 or visit the Web sites of the major Canadian legal publishers (listed in Table 9.1).

A. ABORIGINAL LAW

Scope
: Aboriginal law in Canada is governed largely by federal legislation such as the *Indian Act*, R.S.C. 1985, c. I-5, an Act administered by the Department of Indian and Northern Affairs. Case law is highly relevant and often involves issues of constitutional law and fiduciary law.

Subject headings
: Native peoples — Canada — Legal status, laws, etc.
Indians of North America — Canada — Legal status, laws, etc.
Indigenous peoples — Canada — Legal status, laws, etc.

CED
: Title 77, Vol. 16: Indians

Can. Abr.
: Vol. 1: Aboriginal Law (3d)

Quicklaw
: Aboriginal law — Global Database: ABRT (includes individual databases, including the *Canadian Native Law Reporter* — database: CNLR)

Case law reporters
: *Canadian Native Law Reporter* (University of Saskatchewan, Native Law Centre, 1979)

Journals
: *Indigenous Law Journal* (University of Toronto, Faculty of Law, 2002)

CD-ROMs
: *Treaties with Canada/Aboriginal Land Claims: British Columbia* (Carswell)
Treaties with Canada/Aboriginal Land Claims: North (Carswell)

Treaties with Canada (Carswell)

Web Sites   Indian and Northern Affairs Canada: <http://www.ainc-inac.gc.ca>
Bora Laskin Law Library First Nations Research Guide:
<http://www.law-lib.utoronto.ca/resguide/aborig.htm>

Textbooks   Borrows, John and Leonard Rotman. *Aboriginal Legal Issues: Cases, Materials and Commentary*. 2d ed. Toronto: Butterworths, 2003.

Canada. Royal Commission on Aboriginal Peoples. *Report of the Royal Commission on Aboriginal Peoples*. Ottawa, ON: The Commission, 1996. Also available on CD-ROM and online at <http://www.ainc-inac.gc.ca/ch/rcap/index_e.html>.

Elliott, David W., ed. *Law and Aboriginal Peoples of Canada*. 4th ed. North York, ON: Captus Press, 2000.

Henderson, James (Sákéj) Youngblood, Marjorie Benson and Isobel H. Findlay. *Aboriginal Tenure in the Constitution of Canada*. Toronto: Carswell, 2000 [annual].

Imai, Shin et al. *Aboriginal Law Handbook*. 2d ed. Toronto: Carswell, 1999.

Macaulay, Mary Locke. *Aboriginal & Treaty Rights Practice*. Looseleaf. Toronto: Carswell, 2000.

Magnet, Joseph E. and Dwight A. Dorey, eds. *Aboriginal Rights Litigation*. Toronto: Butterworths, 2003.

Reiter, Robert Alan. *The Law of First Nations*. Edmonton: Juris Analytica Publishing, 1996.

Woodward, Jack. *Native Law*. Looseleaf. Toronto: Carswell, 1989.

B. ADMINISTRATIVE LAW

Scope   Administrative law in Canada is a well-defined area of law due to the proliferation of government regulatory bodies in the past half-decade. Much of administrative law arises in the common law through decisions of both provincial and federal courts and administrative tribunals, although many regulatory bodies, and the procedures they must follow, are governed by legislation. In addition, most jurisdictions have legislation, such as the *Judicial Review Procedure Act*, R.S.B.C. 1996, c. 241, specifically governing procedure before, or appealing ,from regulatory bodies.

Subject headings   Administrative law — Canada
Judicial review of administrative acts — Canada

CED   Title 3, Vol. 1: Administrative Law

Title 119.1, Vol. 27: Public Inquiries
Title 120, Vol. 27: Public Utilities
Title 125, Vol. 28: References and Inquiries

Can. Abr.   Vol. 1: Administrative Law (3d)

Quicklaw   Administrative law — Global Database: ADMT (includes individual databases)

Caselaw   *Administrative Law Reports* (Carswell, 1983)
reporters   *Reid's Administrative Law* (Administrative Law Publishing, 1992)

Journals   *Canadian Journal of Administrative Law & Practice* (Carswell, 1987). Available on WestlaweCARSWELL (database: CJALP) from v. 11, 1997–98.

Textbooks   Blais, Marie-Hélène et al. *Standards of Review of Federal Administrative Tribunals*. Toronto: Butterworths, 2003.

Blake, Sara. *Administrative Law in Canada*. 3d ed. Toronto: Butterworths, 2001.

Braverman, Lisa S. *Administrative Tribunals: A Legal Handbook*. Toronto: Canada Law Book, 2002.

Brown, Donald J.M. *Judicial Review of Administrative Action in Canada*. Looseleaf. Toronto: Canvasback Publishing, 1998.

Dussault, René and Louis Borgeat. *Administrative Law: A Treatise*. 2d ed. Toronto: Carswell, 1988.

Jones, David Phillip and Anne S. de Villars. *Principles of Administrative Law*. 4th ed. Scarborough, ON: Carswell, 2004.

Kavanagh, John A. *A Guide to Judicial Review*. 2d ed. Toronto: Carswell, 1984.

Kligman, Robert. *Bias*. Toronto: Butterworths, 1998.

Macaulay, Robert W. and James L.H. Sprague. *Hearings Before Administrative Tribunals*. 2d ed. Toronto: Carswell, 2002.

Manuel, William J. and H. Christina Donszelmann. *Law of Administrative Investigations and Prosecutions*. Toronto: Canada Law Book, 1999.

Mullan, David. *Administrative Law*. Toronto: Irwin Law, 2001. Available on Quicklaw (database identifier: MULL).

Mullan, David and John M. Evans. *Administrative Law: Cases, Text and Materials*. Toronto: Emond Montgomery, 2003.

Sossin, Lorne. *Boundaries of Judicial Review: The Law of Justiciability in Canada*. Toronto: Carswell, 1999.

C. ALTERNATIVE DISPUTE RESOLUTION (ADR)

Scope   Alternative dispute resolution — or ADR — has developed into its own discipline and practice area in part because of the delays inherent in the traditional litigation system: individuals and companies need a fast, effective method to resolve disputes. ADR includes arbitration (where parties submit their dispute to one or more impartial persons for a final and binding ruling) and mediation (where a neutral person tries to mediate a settlement between the parties but does not have the power to make a binding ruling on the parties). ADR involves a combination of legislation (such as Ontario's *Arbitration Act, 1991*, S.O. 1991, c. 17, for example), the possible adoption of arbitration rules or procedures from various organizations (such as the American Arbitration Association) and contract law and advocacy skills.

Subject   Dispute resolution (Law) — Canada
headings

CED   Title 8, Vol. 1A: Arbitration

Can. Abr.   Vol. 2: Alternative Dispute Resolution (3d)

Journals   *ADR Forum* (CCH Canadian, 1994) [annual]
             Dispute Resolution Journal (American Arbitration Association, 1993).
             Journal of ADR, Mediation & Negotiation (EMIS Professional Publishing, Hertfordshire, UK). Available on Quicklaw — Database JADR.

Web Sites   ADR Institute of Canada: <http://www.adrcanada.ca>
             American Arbitration Association: <http://www.adr.org>

Textbooks   Adams, George W. *Mediating Justice: Legal Dispute Negotiations.* Toronto: CCH Canadian, 2003.
             Barin, Babak. *Carswell's Handbook of International Dispute Resolution Rules.* Toronto: Carswell, 1999.
             Boulle, Laurence and Kathleen J. Kelly. *Mediation: Principles, Process, Practice.* Canadian ed. Toronto: Butterworths, 1998.
             Chornenki, Genevieve A. *The Corporate Counsel Guide to Dispute Resolution.* Aurora, ON: Canada Law Book, 1999.
             Chornenki, Genevieve A. and Christine E. Hart. *Bypass Court: A Dispute Resolution Handbook.* 2d ed. Toronto: Butterworths, 2001.

Corry, David J. *Negotiation: The Art of Mutual Gains Bargaining.* Toronto: Canada Law Book, 2000.

Earle, Wendy J. *Drafting ADR and Arbitration Clauses for Commercial Contracts: A Solicitor's Manual.* Looseleaf. Toronto: Carswell, 2002.

Kovachich, Hélène et al. *Guide pratique de la mediation.* Toronto: Carswell, 1997.

Macfarlane, Julie et al. *Dispute Resolution: Readings and Case Studies.* 2d ed. Toronto: Emond Montgomery, 2003.

Mackenzie, Deborah and Therese Reilly. *ADR in the Corporate Environment: A Practical Guide for Designing Alternative Dispute Resolution Systems.* Toronto: CCH Canadian, 1999.

McEwan, Kenneth and Ludmila Barbara Herbst. *Commercial Arbitration in Canada.* Looseleaf. Toronto: Canada Law Book, 2004.

McLaren, Richard H. and John P. Sanderson. *Innovative Dispute Resolution: The Alternative.* Looseleaf. Toronto: Carswell, 1994.

Nelson, Robert M. *Nelson on ADR.* Scarborough, ON: Carswell, 2003.

Noble, Cinnie, L. Leslie Dizgun, and D. Paul Emond. *Effective Client Representation in Mediation Proceedings.* Toronto: Emond Montgomery, 1998.

Pirie, A.J. *Alternative Dispute Resolution.* Toronto: Irwin Law, 2000. Available on Quicklaw (database identifier: ADRP).

Silver, Michael P., with the assistance of Peter G. Barton. *Mediation and Negotiation: Representing your Clients.* Toronto: Butterworths, 2001.

Stitt, Allan J. and Richard Jackman, eds. *CCH Alternative Dispute Resolution Practice Manual.* Looseleaf. Toronto: CCH Canadian, 1996.

Stitt, Allan J. *Mediating Commercial Disputes.* Toronto: Canada Law Book, 2003.

D. BANKING LAW

Scope   Banking law in Canada is largely governed by federal legislation under the *Bank Act*, S.C. 1991, c. 46 and the *Trust and Loan Companies Act*, S.C. 1991, c. 45. Federal banks fall under the jurisdiction of the federal Department of Finance. Additional legislation can also apply, and credit unions are often governed by provincial legislation, such as the *Credit Union Act*, S.N.S. 1994, c. 4.

Subject headings	Banking law — Canada Banks and banking — Canada

CED   Title 14, Vol. 2: Banking
             Title 17, Vol. 3: Bills of Exchange
             Title 69, Vol. 14: Guarantee, Indemnity and Standby Letters of
             Credit

Can. Abr. Vol. 5: Bills of Exchange and Negotiable Instruments (3d)

Journals   *Banking & Finance Law Review* (Carswell, 1986). Available on West-
             laweCARSWELL (database: BFLR-CAN) from v. 13, 1997–1998.
             National Banking Law Review (Butterworths, 1982). Available on
             LexisNexis (database: CNBLR) from 1994.

Web Sites Department of Finance: <http://www.fin.gc.ca>

Textbooks Baxter, Ian. F.G. *Law of Banking*. 4th ed. Scarborough, ON: Car-
             swell, 1992.
             Crawford, Bradley. *Crawford and Falconbridge Banking and Bills of
             Exchange: A Treatise on the Law of Banks, Banking, Bills of
             Exchange and the Payment System in Canada*. 8th ed. Toronto:
             Canada Law Book, 1986.
             Crawford, Bradley. *Payment, Clearing and Settlement in Canada*.
             Toronto: Canada Law Book, 2002.
             David, Guy and Louise S. Pelly. *The Annotated Bank Act*. Scarbor-
             ough, ON: Carswell [annual].
             Gelfand, Brian Z. *Regulation of Financial Institutions*. Looseleaf.
             Toronto: Carswell, 1993.
             L'Heureux, Nicole. *Droit bancaire*. 3d ed. Cowansville, PQ: Edi-
             tions Y. Blais, 1999.
             Manzer, Alison R. and Jordan Bernamoff. *The Corporate Counsel
             Guide to Banking and Credit Relationships*. Aurora, ON: Cana-
             da Law Book, 1999.
             McGuinness, Kevin P. *The Law of Guarantee*. 2d ed. Toronto: Car-
             swell, 1996.
             Nicholls, Christopher C. *Corporate Finance and Canadian Law*.
             Toronto: Carswell, 2001.
             Ogilvie, Margaret H. *Canadian Banking Law*. 2d ed. Scarborough,
             ON: Carswell, 1998.
             Sarna, Lazar. *Letters of Credit: The Law and Current Practice*. 3d ed.
             Looseleaf. Toronto: Carswell, 1989.
             Teolis, John W. and C. Dawn Jetten. *Bank Act: Legislation and Com-
             mentary*. Looseleaf. Toronto: Butterworths, 1998.

Waldron, Mary Anne. *The Law of Interest in Canada*. Scarborough, ON: Carswell, 1992.

E. BANKRUPTCY AND INSOLVENCY LAW

Scope   Bankruptcy and insolvency law is generally governed by federal legislation, including the *Bankruptcy and Insolvency Act*, R.S.C. 1985, c. B-3 and the *Companies' Creditors Arrangement Act*, R.S.C. 1985, c. C-36. Provincial law also affects issues of bankruptcy and insolvency in various corporate legislation and laws governing preferences.

Subject   Bankruptcy — Canada
headings Corporate reorganizations — Canada

CED   Title 15, Vol. 2: Bankruptcy and Insolvency
               Title 124, Vol. 28: Receivers

Can. Abr. Vols. 3, 4: Bankruptcy and Insolvency

Quicklaw Insolvency law — Global Database: INVT (includes individual databases)

Case law *Canadian Bankruptcy Reports* (Carswell, 1920)
reporters

Journals *Commercial Insolvency Reporter* (Butterworths Canada, 1987). Available on LexisNexis (database: CCIR) from 1994.
              National Insolvency Review (Butterworths Canada, 1983).

CD-ROMs *Bankruptcy Partner* [CD-ROM]. Toronto: Carswell. Updated 4 times per year. Contains bankruptcy-related legislation, case law, and full text. Available in an expanded version as *InsolvencySource* on WestlaweCARSWELL (by subscription).

Web Sites Office of the Superintendent of Bankruptcy: <http://osb-bsf.ic.gc.ca>

Textbooks Bennett, Frank. *Bennett on Bankruptcy*. 8th ed. North York, ON: CCH Canadian, 2004.
               Bennett, Frank. *Bennett on Receiverships*. 2d ed. Toronto: Carswell, 1999.
               Bennett, Frank. *Bennett's A-Z Guide to Bankruptcy: A Professional's Handbook*. Toronto: CCH Canadian, 2001.
               Boucher, Bernard and Jean-Yves Fortin. *Faillite et insolvabilité: Une perspective québécoise de la jurisprudence canadienne*. Loose-leaf. Toronto: Carswell, 1997.

Honsberger, John D. *Debt Restructuring: Principles and Practice.* Looseleaf. Toronto: Canada Law Book, 1990.

Houlden, Lloyd W. and C.H. Morawetz. *Bankruptcy and Insolvency Law of Canada.* 3d ed. Looseleaf. Scarborough, ON: Carswell, 1992. Also available on CD-ROM [*Bankruptcy Partner* — also contains legislation and case law] and by Internet subscription [*InsolvencySource* — also contains legislation and case law].

Klotz, Robert A. *Bankruptcy, Insolvency and Family.* 2d ed. Toronto: Carswell, 2001.

Lamer, Francis L. *Priority of Crown Claims in Insolvency.* Looseleaf. Toronto: Carswell, 1996.

McLaren, Richard H. *Canadian Commercial Reorganization: Preventing Bankruptcy.* Looseleaf. Aurora, ON: Canada Law Book, 1994.

Sarna, Lazar. *The Law of Bankruptcy and Insolvency of Canada.* Montreal, Jewel Publications, 1997.

Sarra, Janis Pearl. *Creditor Rights and the Public Interest: Restructuring Insolvent Corporations.* Toronto: University of Toronto Press, 2003.

Sarra, Janis Pearl and Ronald B. Davis. *Director and Officer Liability in Corporate Insolvency: A Comprehensive Guide to Rights and Obligations.* Markham, ON: Butterworths, 2002.

Ziegel, Jacob, Tony Duggan, and Thomas Telfer. *Canadian Bankruptcy and Insolvency Law: Cases, Text and Materials.* Toronto: Emond Montgomery, 2003.

F. CHARITIES AND NOT-FOR-PROFIT LAW

Scope	Charities and not-for-profit law in Canada tends to centre around non-share capital corporations incorporated under the federal *Canada Corporations Act*, R.S.C. 1970, c. C-32 (at the time of publication of this book, there has been ongoing discussion of reforming this now quite dated legislation).
Subject headings	Charity laws and legislation — Canada Nonprofit organizations —Canada
CED	Title 10, Vol. 1A: Associations and Non-Profit Corporations Title 24, Vol. 4: Charities Title 26, Vol. 4: Churches and Religious Institutions Title 33.1, Vol. 5: Co-operatives

Can. Abr.   Vol. R6: Charities

Web Sites   Corporations Canada: <http://strategis.ic.gc.ca/epic/internet/incd-dgc.nsf/en/home>

Textbooks   Bourgeois, Donald J. *Charities and Not-for-Profit Fundraising Handbook*. Toronto: Butterworths, 2000.

Bourgeois, Donald J. *The Law of Charitable and Casino Gaming*. Toronto: Butterworths, 1999.

Bourgeois, Donald J. *The Law of Charitable and Not-for-Profit Organizations*. 3d ed. Toronto: Butterworths, 2002.

Burke-Robertson, R. Jane and Arthur B.C. Drache. *Non-Share Capital Corporations*. Looseleaf. Toronto: Carswell, 1992.

Drache, Arthur B.C. and Rob Blackstien. *The Charity & Not-for-Profit Sourcebook*. Looseleaf. Toronto: Carswell, 1995.

Hoffstein, Maria Elena et al. *Charities Law*. Looseleaf. Toronto: Butterworths, 2003.

Nathan, Hartley R. et al. *Wainberg's Society Meetings Including Rules of Order*. 5th ed. Toronto: CCH Canadian, 2001.

Saxe, Stewart D. and Jean A. Brough. *Charities and Not-for-Profit Employment Law Handbook*. Toronto: Butterworths, 2002.

G. CIVIL PROCEDURE

Scope   Civil procedure in Canada is generally governed by rules of court applicable to the jurisdiction in question. Thus, there are rules of court for both provincial and superior courts and for the Federal Court of Canada and Supreme Court of Canada. Included below are materials on limitation periods, something with which all lawyers should be familiar.

Subject headings   Civil procedure — [jurisdiction]
Court rules — [jurisdiction]

CED   Title 2, Vol. 1: Actions
Title 37, Vol. 6: Costs
Title 38, Vol. 6: Courts
Title 47, Vol. 9: Discovery
Title 79, Vol. 16: Injunctions
Title 82, Vol. 17: Interpleader
Title 83, Vol. 18: Judgments and Orders
Title 87, Vol. 19: Limitations of Actions
Title 105, Vol. 24: Parties

Title 111, Vol. 25: Pleadings
Title 114, Vol. 26: Practice
Title 143, Vol. 32: Trials

Can. Abr.   Vols. 8–20: Civil Practice and Procedure (3d) (includes limitation periods)

Quicklaw   Civil Procedure — Global Database: CIVT (includes individual databases)

Case law reporters   *Carswell's Practice Cases* (Carswell, 1976)

Journals   *Advocate's Quarterly* (Canada Law Book, 1978)
Canadian Class Action Review (Irwin Law, 2004)

CD-ROMs   *Civil Practice Partner* [CD-ROM]. Toronto: Carswell. Updated 4 times per year. Contains Ontario, Federal, and Supreme Court of Canada Rules of Court and *Carswell's Practice Cases*, along with other publications.
Rules Concordance and Case Locator [CD-ROM]. Toronto: Carswell, 2000. Contains full-text rules of court from all common law provinces, along with a concordance and links to full-text court decisions. The "data" from this CD-ROM are available in a modified format on *LawSource* on WestlaweCARSWELL (by subscription).

Textbooks   Selected texts on civil procedure:
Cassels, Jamie and Craig Jones. *The Law of Large-Scale Claims: Product Liability, Mass Torts, and Complex Litigation in Canada.* Toronto: Irwin Law, 2004.
Crane, Brian A. and Henry S. Brown. *Supreme Court of Canada Practice.* Scarborough, ON: Carswell [annual].
Cudmore, Gordon D. *Choate on Discovery.* 2d ed. Looseleaf. Toronto: Carswell, 1993.
Eizenga, Michael et al. *Class Actions Law and Practice.* Looseleaf. Toronto: Butterworths, 1999.
Hamer, I.W. David and Elizabeth Stewart. *Defending Class Actions in Canada.* Toronto: CCH Canadian, 2002.
Hughes, Roger T. *Annotated Federal Court Act and Rules.* Markham, ON: Butterworths [annual].
James, Morton C. and Todd L. Archibald. *Discovery: Principles in Practice.* Toronto: CCH Canadian, 2004.
Jones, Craig. *Theory of Class Actions.* Toronto: Irwin Law, 2003. Available on Quicklaw (database identifier: CLAC).

Killeen, Gordon P. and Morton C. James. *A Guide to Costs in Ontario*. Toronto: CCH Canadian, 2002.

Leon, Jeffrey S. and David C. Rosenbaum. *Ontario Civil Court Forms*. Looseleaf. Scarborough, ON: Carswell, 1993.

Lubet, Steven. Adapted for Canada by Sheila Block and Cynthia Tape. *Modern Trial Advocacy: Analysis and Practice* (Canadian edition). 2d ed. Notre Dame, IN: National Institute for Trial Advocacy, 2000. Available on Quicklaw (database identifier: MTAC).

Orkin, Mark M. *Law of Costs*. 2d ed. Looseleaf. Toronto: Canada Law Book, 1987.

Salhany, Roger E. *The Preparation and Presentation of a Civil Action*. Toronto: Butterworths, 2000.

Sgayias, David. *Federal Court Practice*. Toronto: Carswell [annual].

Sopinka, John and Mark A. Gelowitz. *The Conduct of an Appeal*. 2d ed. Toronto: Butterworths, 2000.

Stevenson, W. A. and and Jean E. Côté, with editorial assistance by Debra MacGregor et al.; researchers, J. Scott Brodie et al. *Civil Procedure Encyclopedia*. Edmonton: Juriliber, 2003.

Stockwood, David. *Civil Litigation: A Handbook*. 5th ed. Scarborough, ON: Carswell, 2004.

Van Kessel, Robert J. *Summary Judgments and Dispositions before Trial*. Toronto: Butterworths, 2002.

Ward, Branch. *Class Actions in Canada*. Looseleaf. Toronto: Canada Law Book, 1996.

Watson, Garry D. and Craig Perkins. *Holmested and Watson: Ontario Civil Procedure*. Looseleaf. Toronto: Carswell, 1984.

Watson, Garry D. and Michael McGowan. *Ontario Civil Practice*. Toronto: Carswell [annual].

Williston and Rolls' Court Forms. Looseleaf. Toronto: Butterworths, 1981.

Zuker, Marvin A. *Ontario Small Claims Court Practice*. Toronto: Carswell [annual].

Selected texts on limitation periods:

Bocska, Rosemary. *Ontario Limitation Periods: A Handbook of Limitation Periods and Other Statutory Time Limits*. 2d ed. Looseleaf. Toronto: LexisNexis Butterworths, 2003.

Dukelow, Daphne A. *Guide to Ontario and Federal Limitation Periods*. Looseleaf. Toronto: Carswell, 1998.

Joffe, Hal et al. *Federal Limitation Periods: A Handbook of Limitation Periods and Other Statutory Time Limits*. Looseleaf. Toronto: Butterworths, 1978.

Mew, Graeme. *The Law of Limitations*. 2d ed. Toronto: LexisNexis Butterworths, 2004.

Table of Federal Statutory Limitations. Looseleaf. Vancouver: University of British Columbia Law Review Society, 1999.

Williams, Jeremy S. *Limitations of Actions in Canada*. 2d ed. Toronto: Butterworths, 1980.

H. COMMUNICATIONS LAW

Scope   Communications law in Canada tends to be heavily regulated by the federal government through such government agencies as the Canadian Radio-television and Telecommunications Commission (CRTC) and by the federal *Broadcasting Act*, S.C. 1991, c. 11 and *Telecommunications Act*, S.C. 1993, c. 38. Media law and the law of defamation are discussed in a separate category below (under Media/defamation law).

Subject   Telecommunication — Law and legislation — Canada
headings

CED   Title 120, Vol. 27: Public Utilities
Title 121, Vol. 28: Radio and Television
Title 136.1, Vol. 31: Telecommunications

Can. Abr.   Vol. 23: Communications Law (3d)

Quicklaw   Telecommunications Law — Global Database: TC (includes individual databases)

Web Sites   Canadian Radio-television and Telecommunications Commission (CRTC): <http://www.crtc.gc.ca>
Centre for Innovation Law and Policy (University of Toronto): <http://www.innovationlaw.org/lawforum/pages/communications_law_and_reg.htm>

Textbooks   Biron, Dorthee and Philippe Vaillant. *Canadian Legislation on Telecommunications 1997*. Toronto: Carswell, 1997.

Handa, Sunny et al. *Communications Law in Canada*. Toronto: Butterworths, 2000.

Long, Colin, ed. *Global Telecommunications Law and Practice*. 3d ed. Looseleaf. London: Sweet & Maxwell, 2000.

Ryan, Michael H. *Canadian Telecommunications Law and Regulation*. Looseleaf. Scarborough, ON: Carswell, 1993.

I. COMPETITION AND ANTITRUST LAW

Scope   Competition and antitrust law in Canada regulates mergers and acquisitions between businesses with the policy goal of ensuring adequate competition and a healthy economy for consumers and businesses. The major competition "watchdog" in Canada is the Competition Bureau, which administers four major statutes: the *Competition Act*, R.S.C. 1985, c. C-34, the *Consumer Packaging and Labelling Act*, R.S.C. 1985, c. C-38, the *Textile Labelling Act*, R.S.C. 1985, c. T-10, and the *Precious Metals Marking Act*, R.S.C. 1985, c. P-19.

Subject   Competition, Unfair—Canada
headings   Antitrust law—Canada

CED   Title 140, Vol. 31: Trade and Commerce

Can. Abr. Vols. 21, 22: Commercial Law (3d)

Journals   *Canadian Business Law Journal* (Canada Law Book, 1975)
              Canadian Competition Record (Fraser Milner Casgrain LLP, 1993)

Web Sites Competition Bureau (Canada): <http://www.cb-bc.gc.ca>
              Competition Tribunal (Canada): <http://www.ct-tc.gc.ca>

Textbooks Addy, George N. and William L. Vanveen. *Competition Law Service*. Looseleaf. Aurora, ON: Canada Law Book, 1988.
              Affleck, Don and Wayne McCracken. *Canadian Competition Law*. Looseleaf. Toronto: Carswell, 1990.
              Campbell, Neil. *Merger Law and Practice: The Regulation of Mergers under the Competition Act*. Toronto: Carswell, 1997.
              Flavell, C.J. Michael and Christopher J. Kent. *The Canadian Competition Law Handbook*. Toronto: Carswell, 1998.
              Gourley, Albert C. *Merger Notification and Clearance in Canada*. Looseleaf. Toronto: CCH Canadian, 2003. Available in print, CD-ROM, and by Internet subscription.
              Kaiser, Gordon et al. *Competition Law of Canada*. Looseleaf. New York: M. Bender, 1988.
              Nozick, Robert S. *The Annotated Competition Act*. Toronto: Carswell [annual].

Reiter, Barry J. and Melanie Shisler. *Joint Ventures: Legal and Business Perspectives*. Toronto: Irwin Law, 1999. Available on Quicklaw (database identifier: RESH).

Stikeman Elliott LLP. *Competition Act and Commentary*. Toronto: Butterworths [annual].

Trebilcock, Michael J. et al. *The Law and Economics of Canadian Competition Policy*. Toronto: University of Toronto Press, 2002.

J. CONSTITUTIONAL AND HUMAN RIGHTS LAW

Scope   The implementation of the *Canadian Charter of Rights and Freedoms* (the *Charter*) in 1982 has increased the profile of constitutional law in Canada due to a number of high profile human rights cases being decided by the Supreme Court of Canada. Constitutional law involves a combination of the application of various federal legislation (including the *Charter* and the *Constitution Act, 1867*), provincial legislation, and case law.

Subject   Constitutional law — Canada
headings   Civil rights — Canada

CED   Title 30, Vol. 4A: Constitutional Law
           Title 74, Vol. 15: Human Rights

Can. Abr. Vol. 24: Constitutional Law (3d)
           Vol. R19 Reissue: Human Rights

Quicklaw   Constitutional Law — Global Database: CONT (includes individual databases)

Case law   *Canadian Rights Reporter* 2d series (Butterworths, 1991)
reporters *Charter of Rights Decisions* (Canada Law Book, 1982)

Journals   *Constitutional Forum* (Centre for Constitutional Studies, 1989)
           National Journal of Constitutional Law (Carswell, 1991). Available on WestlaweCARSWELL (database: NJCL) from v. 9, 1997–1998.
           Review of Constitutional Studies (Centre for Constitutional Studies, 1993)
           Supreme Court Law Review 2d series (Butterworths Canada, 1991)

Textbooks Bakan, Joel et al. *Canadian Constitutional Law*. 3d ed. Toronto: Emond Montgomery, 2003.

Barrett, Joan. *Balancing Charter Interests: Victims' Rights and Third Party Remedies*. Looseleaf. Toronto: Carswell, 2000.

Beatty, David M. *Constitutional Law in Theory and Practice*. Toronto: University of Toronto Press, 1995.

Beaudoin, Gerald A. and Errol Mendes. *The Canadian Charter of Rights and Freedoms*. 3d ed. Toronto: Carswell, 1996.

Boucher, Susanne and Kenneth Landa. *Understanding Section 8: Search, Seizure and the Canadian Constitution*. Toronto: Irwin Law, 2004.

Brun, Henri and Guy Tremblay. *Droit constitutionnel*. 4e éd. Cowansville, PQ: Éditions Y. Blais, 2002.

Canadian Charter of Rights Annotated. 6 vol. Looseleaf. Toronto: Canada Law Book, 1982.

Carswell. *The Annotated Charter of Rights and Freedoms*. Toronto: Carswell [annual].

Cooper-Stephenson, Kenneth D. *Charter Damages Claims*. Toronto: Carswell, 1990.

Funston, Bernard W. and Eugene Meehan *Canada's Constitutional Law in a Nutshell*. 3d ed. Toronto: Carswell, 2003.

Hogg, Peter W. *Constitutional Law of Canada*. 4th ed. Looseleaf. Scarborough, ON: Carswell, 1997.

Jamal, Mahmud and Matthew Taylor. *Charter of Rights in Litigation: The Direction from the Supreme Court of Canada*. Looseleaf. Toronto: Canada Law Book, 1991.

Magnet, Joseph Eliot. *Constitutional Law of Canada: Cases, Notes and Materials*. 8th ed. Edmonton: Juriliber Ltd., 2001. Available on Quicklaw (database identifier: MAG).

Magnet, Jospeh E. *Modern Constitutionalism: Equality, Identity and Democracy*. Toronto: Butterworths, 2003.

McAllister, Debra M. *Taking the Charter to Court: A Practitioner's Analysis*. Looseleaf. Toronto: Carswell, 1998.

Monahan, Patrick. *Constitutional Law*. 2d ed. Toronto: Irwin Law, 2002. Available on Quicklaw (database identifier: MONA).

Pentney, William. *Discrimination and the Law*. Looseleaf. Toronto: Carswell, 1990.

Roach, Kent. *Constitutional Remedies in Canada*. Looseleaf. Aurora, ON: Canada Law Book, 1994.

Roach, Kent. *The Supreme Court on Trial: Judicial Activism or Democractic Dialogue*. Toronto: Irwin Law, 2001.

Sharpe, Robert J. et al. *The Charter of Rights and Freedoms*. 2d ed. Toronto: Irwin Law, 2002. Available on Quicklaw (database identifier: SHAR).

Zinn, Russel W. and Patricia P. Brethour. *The Law of Human Rights in Canada: Practice and Procedure.* Looseleaf. Toronto: Canada Law Book, 1996.

K. CONSTRUCTION LAW

Scope — Construction law in Canada is governed by legislation, largely in the form of provincial builders or mechanics lien legislation, contract law, and case law.

Subject headings — Construction law — [jurisdiction]
Construction liens — [jurisdiction]
Construction contracts — [jurisdiction]
Mechanics' liens — [jurisdiction]

CED — Title 20, Vol. 3: Building Contracts
Title 30.1, Vol. 4A: Construction Liens
Title 86, Vol. 19: Liens

Can. Abr. — Vols. 25, 26: Construction Law (3d)

Quicklaw — Construction law topical — Global Database: CSTT (includes individual databases)

Case law reporters — *Construction Law Reports* (Carswell, 1983)

Journals — *Construction Law Letter* (Butterworths Canada, 1984)

Web Sites — Canadian College of Construction Lawyers: <http://www.cccl.org>
Papadopoulos, John. *Construction Law Research Guide.* Available online: <http://www.law-lib.utoronto.ca/construction/>.

Textbooks — Glaholt, Duncan W. *Conduct of a Lien Action.* Toronto: Carswell [annual].
Glaholt, Duncan W. *Construction Trusts.* Toronto: Carswell, 1999.
Glaholt, Duncan W. and M. David Keeshan. *Annotated Ontario Construction Lien Act.* Toronto: Carswell [annual].
Goldsmith, Immanuel, Q.C. and Heintzman, Thomas, Q.C. *Goldsmith on Canadian Building Contracts.* 4th ed. Toronto: Carswell, 1989 [supplemented annually].
Kirsh, Harvey J. *Kirsh's Construction Law Lien Finder.* Looseleaf. Toronto: Butterworths, 1992.
Kirsh, Harvey J. *Kirsh's Guide to Construction Liens in Ontario.* 2d ed. Toronto: Butterworth's, 1995.

Kirsh, Harvey J. and Lori A. Roth. *Kirsh and Roth: The Annotated Construction Contract (CCDC 2-1994)*. Aurora, ON: Canada Law Book, 1997.

Macklem, Douglas N. and David I. Bristow. *Construction Builders' and Mechanics' Liens in Canada*. 6th ed. Looseleaf. Toronto: Carswell, 1990.

Marston, D.L. *Law for Professional Engineers*. 3d ed. Toronto: McGraw-Hill Ryerson, 1996.

McGuinness, Kevin P. *Construction Lien Remedies in Ontario*. 2d ed. Toronto: Carswell, 1997.

McLachlin, Beverley M. et al., *The Canadian Law of Architecture and Engineering*, 2d ed. Toronto: Butterworths, 1994.

Sandori, Paul and William M. Pigott. *Bidding and Tendering: What is the Law?* 2d ed. Toronto: Butterworths, 2000.

Wise, Howard M. *The Manual of Construction Law*. Looseleaf. Toronto: Carswell, 1994.

L. CONTRACT AND AGENCY LAW

Scope — Contract law in Canada is governed largely by judge-made common law, although there is some legislation that affects contracts, including statutes of fraud legislation, consumer protection legislation, and sale of goods act legislation (usually provincial legislation). Some regard is still granted to classic English textbooks on contract law in Canada, but there is now a large body of Canadian law on point to lessen the need to consult English authorities.

Subject headings — Contracts — Canada

CED — Title 4, Vol. 1: Agency
Title 18, Vol. 3: Bills of Sale
Title 21, Vol. 3: Bulk Sales
Title 32, Vol. 5: Contracts
Title 44, Vol. 8A: Deeds and Documents
Title 129, Vol. 29: Sale of Goods

Can. Abr. — Vols. 21, 22: Commerical Law (3d) (for agency, bulk sales, sale of goods)
Vols. 27, 28: Contracts (3d)

Case law — *Business Law Reports* (Carswell, 1977)

reporters

Textbooks   Boyle, Christine and David R. Percy. *Contracts: Cases and Commentaries*. 6th ed. Toronto: Carswell, 1999.

Fitzgerald, Jean. *Fundamentals of Contract Law*. Toronto: Emond Montgomery, 2000.

Fridman, G.H.L. *The Law of Contract*. 4th ed. Scarborough, ON: Carswell, 1999.

Snyder, Ronald M. and Harvin D. Pitch. *Damages for Breach of Contract*. 2d ed. Looseleaf. Toronto: Carswell, 1989.

Swan, John, Barry Reiter, and Nicholas C. Bala. *Contracts: Cases, Notes & Materials*. 6th ed. Markham, ON: Butterworths, 2002.

Trebilcock, Michael J. *The Limits of Freedom of Contract*. Cambridge, MA: Harvard University Press, 1993.

Waddams, S.M., M.J. Trebilcock, and M.A. Waldron. *Cases and Materials on Contracts*. 2d ed. Toronto: Emond Montgomery, 2000.

Waddams, S.M. *The Law of Contracts*. 4th ed. Aurora, Ontario: Canada Law Book, 1999.

M. CORPORATE AND PARTNERSHIP LAW

Scope   Corporate law in Canada is governed by both federal legislation (such as the *Canada Business Corporations Act*, R.S.C. 1985, c. C-44) and applicable provincial legislation (such as the *Company Act*, R.S.B.C. 1996, c. 62, for British Columbia companies), depending on whether the company is incorporated or carries on business federally or provincially. Partnership law in Canada is closely mirrored on English law as reflected in various provincial partnership statutes. Corporate and partnership law often involve issues of "commercial law," which includes aspects of contract law, competition law (each discussed above as a separate topic), and personal property security law (discussed below as a separate topic). Charities and not-for-profit corporations are discussed above as a separate topic.

Subject   Corporation law — Canada
headings   Corporations — Canada
Stockholders — Legal status, laws, etc. — Canada
Directors of corporations — Legal status, laws, etc. — Canada

CED   Title 36, Vol. 6: Corporations
Title 106, Vol. 24: Partnership

Can. Abr.   Vols. 6, 7: Business Associations (3d)

Quicklaw   Corporate law — Global Database: CORT (includes individual databases)

Case law   *Business Law Reports* (Carswell, 1997)
reporters

Journals   *Corporate Brief* (CCH Canadian, 1994)
Directors Briefing (CCH Canadian, 1995)

CD-ROMs   *Corporate Law Partner (Federal and Ontario)* [CD-ROM]. Toronto: Carswell. Updated regularly. Contains relevant legislation, case law, and Carswell-published textbooks on federal and Ontario corporate law.

Textbooks   Adams, Stephen N. *Annotated Ontario Business Corporations Act.* Looseleaf. Toronto: Canada Law Book, 1990.

Adams, Stephen N. *Federal and Ontario Corporate and Business Legislation.* Toronto: Canada Law Book [annual].

Borden Ladner Gervais LLP, *British Columbia Corporation Manual.* Looseleaf. Toronto: Carswell, 1990.

Buckley, Francis H, et al. *Corporations: Principles and Policies.* 3d ed. Toronto: E. Montgomery, 1995.

Carswell. *Consolidated Canada Business Corporations Act and Regulations.* Toronto: Carswell [annual].

CCH Canadian Limited. *Alberta Corporations Law Guide.* Looseleaf. North York, Ontario: CCH Canadian, 1983. Available in print, CD-ROM, and by Internet subscription.

CCH Canadian Limited. *British Columbia Corporations Law Guide.* Looseleaf. North York, Ontario: CCH Canadian, 1974. Available in print, CD-ROM, and by Internet subscription.

CCH Canadian Limited. *Canadian Corporations Law Reporter.* Looseleaf. North York, Ontario: CCH Canadian, 1995. Available in print, CD-ROM, and by Internet subscription.

CCH Canadian Limited. *The Directors Manual.* Looseleaf. North York, Ontario: CCH Canadian, 1994. Available in print, CD-ROM, and by Internet subscription.

CCH Canadian Limited. *Ontario Corporations Law Guide.* Looseleaf. North York, Ontario: CCH Canadian, 1995. Available in print, CD-ROM, and by Internet subscription.

Dawson, Garry. *Shareholders Agreements: An Annotated Guide.* Toronto: Canada Law Book, 1997.

Ellis, Mark Vincent. *Corporate and Commercial Fiduciary Duties.* Toronto: Carswell, 1995.

Fraser, William K. *Fraser's Handbook on Company Law*. 8th ed. Scarborough, ON: Carswell, 1994.

Gray, Wayne D. *The Annotated Canada Business Corporations Act*. 2d ed. Looseleaf. Toronto: Carswell, 2002.

Gray, Wayne D. *The Annotated Ontario Business Corporations Act*. 2d ed. Looseleaf. Toronto: Carswell, 2003

Grover, Warren M. *Canada Corporation Manual*. Looseleaf. Toronto: Carswell, 1990.

Grover, Warren M. *Ontario Corporation Manual*. Looseleaf. Toronto: Carswell, 1990.

Halpern, Robert. M., ed. et al. *Advising the Family-Owned Business*. Looseleaf. Toronto: Canada Law Book, 1999.

Hansell, Carol. *Directors and Officers in Canada: Law and Practice*. Looseleaf. Toronto: Carswell, 1999.

Hansell, Carol. *What Directors Need to Know: Corporate Governance*. Toronto: Carswell, 2003.

Harris, Doug et al. *Cases and Materials on Partnerships and Canadian Business Corporations*. Toronto: Carswell, 2004.

Hepburn, Lyle and William J. Strain. *Limited Partnerships*. Looseleaf. Toronto: Carswell, 1990.

Iacovelli, Michael and Gil Lan. *Counselling Corporations and Advising Businesses*. Toronto: Butterworths, 2000.

Kerr, M. Kaye and Hubert W. King. *Procedures for Meetings and Organizations*. 3d ed. Toronto: Carswell, 1996.

Koehnen, Markus. *Oppression and Related Remedies*. Toronto: Carswell, 2004.

Kwaw, Edmund. *The Law of Corporate Finance in Canada*. Toronto: Butterworths, 1997.

Lipson, Barry D. *The Art of the Corporate Deal*. Toronto: Carswell, 2000.

Macleod Dixon LLP. *Alberta Corporation Manual*. Looseleaf. Toronto: Carswell, 1990.

Manzer, Alison R. et al. *Canadian Commercial Law Guide*. Looseleaf. North York, Ontario: CCH Canadian, 1967. Available in print, CD-ROM, and by Internet subscription.

Manzer, Alison R. et al. *A Practical Guide to Canadian Partnership Law*. Looseleaf. Toronto: Canada Law Book, 1994.

McCarthy Tétrault. *Directors' and Officers' Duties and Liabilities in Canada*. Toronto, Butterworths, 1997.

McGuiness, Kevin P. and William Johnston. *The Law and Practice of Canadian Business Corporations*. Toronto: Butterworths, 1999.

Nathan, Hartley R. et al. *Canadian Corporate Secretary's Guide.* Looseleaf. Toronto: CCH Canadian, 1978. Available in print, CD-ROM, and by Internet subscription.

Nathan, Hartley R. et al. *Wainberg and Nathan's Company Meetings Including Rules of Order.* 5th ed. Toronto: CCH Canadian, 2001.

Nathan, Hartley R. and Margot Priest. *Directors' Duties in Canada: Managing Risk.* Toronto: CCH Canadian, 2002.

Nathan, Hartley R. and Mihkel E. Voore. *Corporate Meetings: Law and Practice.* Looseleaf. Scarborough, ON: Carswell, 1995.

Peterson, Dennis H. *Shareholder Remedies in Canada.* Looseleaf. Toronto: Butterworths, 1989.

Phillips, Gordon. *Personal Remedies for Corporate Injuries.* Scarborough, ON: Carswell, 1992.

Reiter, Barry J. and Melanie Shisler. *Joint Ventures: Legal and Business Perspectives.* Toronto: Irwin Law, 1999. Available on Quicklaw (database identifier: RESH).

Sutherland, Harry and David B. Horsley. *Company Law of Canada.* 6th ed. Scarborough, ON: Carswell, 1993.

VanDuzer, J. Anthony. *The Law of Partnerships and Corporations.* 2d ed. Toronto: Irwin Law, 2003. Available on Quicklaw (database identifier: VAND).

Welling, Bruce L. *Corporate Law in Canada: The Governing Principles.* 2d ed. Toronto: Butterworths, 1991.

Welling, Bruce L. et al. *Canadian Corporate Law: Cases, Notes & Materials.* 2d ed. Toronto: Butterworths, 2001.

Zaid, Frank. *Canadian Franchise Guide.* Looseleaf. Toronto: Carswell, 1990.

N. CRIMINAL LAW

Scope　　Criminal law in Canada is generally governed by federal law, most often the *Criminal Code*, R.S.C. 1985, c. C-46, the *Youth Criminal Justice Act*, S.C. 2002, c. 1, and the *Controlled Drugs and Substances Act*, S.C. 1996, c. 19. Offences under provincial statutes also exist. Case law is highly relevant. Young offenders law is also included in this section.

Subject　　Criminal law – Canada
headings　　Criminal procedure — Canada

CED　　Title 29, Vol. 4A: Conspiracy

Title 39, Vol. 7: Criminal Procedure
Title 39.1, Vol. 7A: Criminal Law (Offences)
Title 39.2, Vol. 7: Criminal Law (Defences)
Title 62.1, Vol. 13: Firearms, Weapons and Explosives
Title 65, Vol. 13: Fraud and Misrepresentation
Title 67, Vol. 14: Gaming
Title 88, Vol. 19: Liquor Control
Title 100, Vol. 23: Narcotic Control
Title 113, Vol. 26: Police
Title 116, Vol. 27: Prisons
Title 132.1, Vol. 30: Sentencing
Title 133, Vol. 30: Sheriffs and Bailiffs
Title 142, Vol. 32: Victims of Crime — Compensation
Title 147, Vol. 33: War and Emergency
Title 152, Vol. 34: Young Offenders

Can. Abr. Vol. R9-R11E Reissue: Criminal Law (includes Young Offenders Law)
Vol. R17D Reissue: Fraud
Vol. R17D: Gaming
Vol. R23: Liquor Control
Vol. R28: Narcotic and Drug Control
Vol. R30: Police
Vol. R33: Sheriffs and Bailiffs

Quicklaw Criminal law — Global Database: CRIM (includes individual databases)

Case law *Canadian Criminal Cases* (Canada Law Book, 1898)
reporters *Criminal Reports* (Carswell, 1946)

Journals *Canadian Criminal Law Review* (Carswell, 1996). Available on West-laweCARSWELL (database: CANCRIMLR) from v. 3, 1998.
Criminal Law Quarterly (Canada Law Book).

CD-ROMs *Canadian Criminal Law Library* (Canada Law Book)
Criminal Law Partner [CD-ROM]. Toronto: Carswell. Updated regularly. Contains relevant legislation, case law, and Carswell-published textbooks on criminal law. Available in an expanded version as *CriminalSource* on WestlaweCARSWELL (by subscription).

Textbooks Atrens, Jerome T. and Donald Egleston. *Criminal Procedure: Canadian Law & Practice*. Looseleaf. Toronto: Butterworths, 1981.
Bala, Nicholas. *Youth Criminal Justice Law*. Toronto: Irwin Law, 2002. Available on Quicklaw (database identifier: BAYC).

Bentley, Christoper A.W. *Criminal Practice Manual: A Practical Guide to Handling Criminal Case*. Looseleaf. Toronto: Carswell, 2000.

Cameron, Jamie. *Charter's Impact on the Criminal Justice System*. Toronto: Carswell, 1996.

Castel, Jacqueline R. *Gaming Control Law in Ontario*. Looseleaf. Toronto: Canada Law Book, 2001.

Clewley, Gary R. and Paul G. McDermott. *Sentencing: The Practitioner's Guide*. Looseleaf. Toronto: Canada Law Book, 1995.

Delisle, Ron and Don Stuart. *Learning Canadian Criminal Procedure*. 7th ed. Toronto: Carswell, 2003.

Der, Balfour Q.H. *The Jury: A Handbook of Law and Procedure*. Looseleaf. Toronto: Butterworths, 1989.

Ewaschuk, E.G. *Criminal Pleadings & Practice in Canada*. 2d ed. Looseleaf. Aurora, ON: Canada Law Book, 1987. Also available electronically (by subscription).

Friedland, Martin and Kent Roach. *Cases and Materials on Criminal Law and Procedure*. 8th ed. Toronto: Emond Montgomery, 1997.

Gibson, John L. *Canadian Criminal Code Offences*. Looseleaf. Toronto: Carswell, 1988. Available on *CriminalSource* on WestlaweCARSWELL (by subscription).

Gibson, John L. and Henry Waldcock. *Criminal Law: Evidence, Practice and Procedure*. Looseleaf. Toronto: Carswell, 1988. Available on *CriminalSource* on WestlaweCARSWELL (by subscription).

Granger, Christoper. *The Criminal Jury Trial in Canada*. 2d ed. Toronto: Carswell, 1996.

Greenspan, Edward L. and Marc Rosenberg. *Martin's Annual Criminal Code*. Toronto: Canada Law Book [annual]. See also *Martin's Related Criminal Statutes*.

Hamilton, Keith R. *Judicial Interim Release: A Bail Manual*. 4th ed. Looseleaf. Toronto: Butterworths, 1983.

Harris, Peter J. *Youth Criminal Justice Act Manual*. Looseleaf. Toronto: Canada Law Book, 2003.

Hill, S. Casey. *McWilliam's Canadian Criminal Evidence*. 4th ed. Looseleaf. Toronto: Canada Law Book, 2003.

Hubbard, Robert W. et al. *Wiretapping and Other Electronic Surveillance: Law and Procedure*. Looseleaf. Toronto: Canada Law Book, 2000.

Hubbard, Robert W. et al. *Money Laundering and Proceeds of Crime*. Toronto: Irwin Law, 2004.

Hutchison, Scott C. *Search and Seizure Law in Canada*. Looseleaf. Toronto: Carswell, 1991.

Jackman, Barbara L. et al. *Canadian Public Security Law Guide*. Looseleaf. Toronto: CCH Canadian, 2003. Available in print, on CD-ROM, and by Internet subscription.

Katz, Joel I. *The Art of Bail: Strategy and Practice*. Toronto: Butterworths, 1999.

Levy, Earl J. *Examination of Witnesses in Criminal Cases*. 5th ed. Toronto: Carswell, 2004.

MacFarlane, Bruce A. et al. *Drug Offences in Canada*. 3d ed. Looseleaf. Toronto: Canada Law Book, 1996.

Maleszyk, Anna. *Crimes Against Children: Prosecution and Defence*. Looseleaf. Aurora, ON: Canada Law Book, 2001.

Manson, Allan. *The Law of Sentencing*. Toronto: Irwin Law, 2001. Available on Quicklaw (database identifier: MANS).

McLeod, R.M. et al. *Canadian Charter of Rights: the Prosecution and Defence of Criminal and Other Statutory Offences*. Looseleaf. Toronto: Carswell, 1988.

Mewett, Alan and Morris Manning. *Criminal Law*. 3d ed. Toronto: Butterworths, 1994.

Mewett, Alan and Shaun Nakatsuru. *An Introduction to the Criminal Process*. 4th ed. Toronto: Carswell, 2000.

Paciocco, David M. *Getting Away with Murder: The Canadian Criminal Justice System*. Toronto: Irwin Law, 2000.

Pickard, Toni and Phil Goldman. *Dimensions of Criminal Law*. 3d ed. Toronto: Emond Montgomery, 2002.

Pink, Joel E. and David Perrier. *From Crime to Punishment: An Introduction to the Criminal Law System*. 5th ed. Toronto: Carswell, 2003.

Platt, Priscilla. *Young Offenders Service*. Looseleaf. Toronto: Butterworths, 1984.

Proulx, Michel and David Layton. *Ethics and Canadian Criminal Law*. Toronto: Irwin Law, 2001. Available on Quicklaw (database identifier: ECCL).

Roach, Kent. *Criminal Law*. 3d ed. Toronto: Irwin Law, 2004. Second edition available on Quicklaw (database identifier: ROA2).

Rodrigues, Gary P. *Crankshaw's Criminal Code*. 8th ed. Looseleaf. Toronto: Carswell, 1979.

Ruby, Clayton C. *Sentencing*. 6th ed. Toronto: Butterworths, 2004.

Salhany, Roger E. *Canadian Criminal Procedure*. 6th ed. Looseleaf. Toronto: Canada Law Book, 1994.

Salhany, Roger E. *Police Manual of Arrest, Seizure and Interrogation.* 8th ed. Toronto: Carswell, 2002.

Segal, Murray D. *Disclosure and Production in Criminal Cases.* Looseleaf. Toronto: Carswell, 1996. Available on *Criminal-Source* on WestlaweCARSWELL (by subscription).

Stuart, Don. *Canadian Criminal Law: A Treatise.* 4th ed. Toronto: Carswell, 2001.

Stuart, Don. *Charter Justice in Canadian Criminal Law.* 3d ed. Toronto: Carswell, 2001.

Stuart, Don and Ron Delisle. *Learning Canadian Criminal Law.* 9th ed. Toronto: Carswell, 2004.

Tanovich, David M. et al. *Jury Selection in Criminal Trials: Skills, Science, and the Law.* Toronto: Irwin Law, 1997. Available on Quicklaw (database identifier: JURS).

Trotter, Gary T. *The Law of Bail in Canada.* 2d ed. Toronto: Carswell, 1999.

Tuck-Jackson, Andrea E.E. et al., eds. *Annotated Youth Criminal Justice Act.* Looseleaf. Toronto: Butterworths, 2003.

Watt, David. *Watt's Manual of Criminal Evidence.* Toronto: Carswell [annual]. Available on *CriminalSource* on WestlaweCAR-SWELL (by subscription).

Watt, David and Michelle K. Fuerst. *Annotated Tremeear's Criminal Code.* Toronto: Carswell [annual].

O. CROWN LAW

Scope   Crown law in Canada is still influenced by British law, although the law has developed on its own in Canada, partly as a result of federal legislation, such as the *Crown Liability and Proceedings Act,* R.S.C. 1985, c. C-50 and various provincial statutes, such as Ontario's *Public Authorities Protection Act,* R.S.O. 1990, c. P.38. The government — whether federal, provincial, or municipal — may often have the benefit of special limitation periods when being sued. Care should always be taken to check for applicable limitation periods when suing the government (limitation periods are discussed in the section above on civil procedure).

Subject   Government liability — Canada
headings   Privileges and immunities — Canada

CED   Title 40, Vol. 8: Crown
               Title 115, Vol. 27: Prerogative Remedies

Title 118, Vol. 27: Public Authorities and Public Officers
Title 147, Vol. 33: War and Emergency

Can. Abr.   Vol. R12: Crown

Case law   *Federal Court Reports*
reporters

Journals   *Ottawa Letter* (CCH Canadian, 1977)

Textbooks   Cooper, Terrance G. *Crown Privilege*. Aurora, ON: Canada Law
Book, 1990.
Hogg, Peter W. and Patrick J. Monahan. *Liability of the Crown*. 3d
ed. Toronto: Carswell, 2000.
Lordon, Paul. *Crown Law*. Toronto, Butterworths, 1991.
Noonan, Peter W. *The Crown and Constitutional Law in Canada*.
Calgary: Sripnoon Publications, 1998.
Sgayias, David et al. *The 1995 Annotated Crown Liability and Pro-
ceedings Act*. Scarborough, ON: Carswell, 1995.

P. DAMAGES LAW

Scope   Damages law is governed by a combination of case law and (largely) provincial legislation too numerous to list here. British textbooks, such as *McGregor on Damages* (17th ed., Sweet & Maxwell),
are also useful.

Subject   Damages — Canada
headings   Injunctions — Canada
Remedies (law) — Canada
Restitution — Canada
Specific performance — Canada

CED   Title 30, Vol. 5: Contempt of Court
Title 42, Vol. 8A: Damages
Title 55, Vol. 10: Equity
Title 56, Vol. 10: Estoppel
Title 79, Vol. 16: Injunctions
Title 95, Vol. 21: Mistake
Title 127, Vol. 29: Restitution
Title 135, Vol. 31: Specific Performance
Title 145.1, Vol. 33: Victims of Crime — Compensation

Can. Abr.   Vol. R12A, R12B Reissue: Damages
Vol. R20 Reissue: Injunctions

Vol. 31: Equity (ed)
Vol. R32A: Restitution
Vol. R33 Reissue: Specific Performance
Vol, 35: Estoppel (3d)

Quicklaw   Quantum of Damages — Global Database: QPIT (includes individual databases)

CD-ROMs   *Personal Injury Damages Partner* [CD-ROM]. Toronto: Carswell. Updated regularly. Contains relevant case law and commentary from Carswell textbooks on damages law.

Textbooks   Berryman, Jeffrey. *The Law of Equitable Remedies*. Toronto: Irwin Law, 2000. Available on Quicklaw (database identifier: BERR).

Brown, Cara. *Damages: Estimating Pecuniary Loss*. Looseleaf. Toronto: Canada Law Book, 2001.

Bruce, C.J. *Assessment of Personal Injury Damages*. 3d ed. Toronto: Butterworths, 1999.

Cassels, Jamie. *Remedies: The Law of Damages*. Toronto: Irwin Law, 2000. Available on Quicklaw (database identifier: CASS).

Cooper-Stephenson, Ken. *Personal Injury Damages in Canada*. 2d ed. Toronto: Carswell, 1996.

Fitzgerald, Oonagh E. *Understanding Charter Remedies: A Practitioner's Guide*. Looseleaf. Scarborough, ON: Carswell, 1994.

Fridman, G.H.L. *Restitution*. 2d ed. Toronto: Carswell, 1992.

Goldsmith, Immanuel. *Damages for Personal Injury and Death in Canada*. Toronto: Carswell, 1959 [annual supplements].

Klar, Lewis N. *Remedies in Tort*. Looseleaf. Toronto: Carswell, 1987.

Law Society of Upper Canada. *Special Lectures: Law of Remedies: Principles and Proofs*. Scarborough, ON: Carswell, 1995.

Maddaugh, Peter D. and John D. McCamus. *The Law of Restitution*. 2d ed. Toronto: Canada Law Book, 2004. Also available in a looseleaf edition.

Miller, Jeffrey. *The Law of Contempt in Canada*. Toronto: Carswell, 1997.

Perell, Paul M. and Bruce H. Engell. *Remedies and the Sale of Land*. 2d ed. Toronto: Butterworths, 1998.

Roach, Kent. *Constitutional Remedies in Canada*. Looseleaf. Aurora, ON: Canada Law Book, 1994.

Sharpe. Robert J. *Injunctions and Specific Performance*. 3d ed. Aurora, ON: Canada Law Book, 2002. Also available in a looseleaf edition.

Snyder, Ronald M. and Harvin D. Pitch. *Damages for Breach of Contract*. Looseleaf. 2d ed. Toronto: Carswell, 1989.

Spry, Ian. *Equitable Remedies*. 6th ed. Toronto: Carswell, 2004.

Waddams, S.M. *The Law of Damages*. 3d ed. Aurora, ON: Canada Law Book, 1997.

Q. DEBTOR/CREDITOR LAW

Scope   Debtor/creditor law is affected by both case law and provincial (and federal) legislation too numerous to list here. In addition, in enforcing or defending a debt, it is often useful to have a good understanding of civil procedure, discussed above. Bankruptcy and insolvency is also discussed above as a separate topic.

Subject   Debtor and creditor — Canada
headings   Fraudulent conveyances — Canada

CED   Title 43, Vol. 8A: Debtor and Creditor
Title 58, Vol. 12: Execution
Title 66, Vol. 13: Fraudulent Conveyances and Preferences
Title 133, Vol. 30: Sheriffs and Bailiffs

Can. Abr.   Vols. 29, 30: Debtors and Creditors (3d)

Journals   *National Debtor-Creditor Review* (Butterworths Canada). Available on LexisNexis (database: CNCDR) from 1994.

Textbooks Bennett, Frank. *Bennett on Collection*. 5th ed. Toronto: Carswell, 2003.

Bennett, Frank. *Bennett on Creditors' and Debtors' Rights and Remedies*. 4th ed. Scarborough, ON: Carswell, 1994.

Dunlop, Charles R.B. *Creditor-Debtor Law in Canada*. 2d ed. Scarborough, ON: Carswell, 1995.

Fraser, Marcia J. *Debt Collection: A Step-by-Step Guide*. Looseleaf. Aurora, ON: Canada Law Book, 1989.

Kershman, Stanley J. *Credit Solutions: Kershman on Advising Secured and Unsecured Creditors*. Toronto: Carswell, 2001.

McConnell, H. Rose. *A Guide to Collection Procedures in Ontario*. Toronto: CCH Canadian, 2002.

Meehan, Eugene et al. *Creditors' Remedies in Ontario*. Toronto: Butterworths, 1994.

O'Reilly, Miles D. and Steven G. Cloutier. *Advising Individual Debtors in Ontario*. Toronto: Carswell, 1994 [annual].

Stewart, George R. et al. *Fraudulent Conveyances and Preferences*. Looseleaf. Scarborough, ON: Carswell, 1994.

Tweedie, Michael G. *Debt Litigation*. Looseleaf. Toronto: Canada Law Book, 2004.

R. EDUCATION LAW

Scope   Education law is governed by both legislation (largely provincial) and case law. It encompasses other areas of law including constitutional law and employment law.

Subject   Educational law and legislation — Canada
headings

CED   Title 52, Vol. 10: Education

Can. Abr.   Vol. 31: Education Law (3d)

Quicklaw   Shibley Righton Education Case Law Digests — SRED

Journals   *Education & Law Journal* (Carswell, 1988). Available on Westlawe-CARSWELL (database: EDUCLJ) from v. 7, 1995–1996.
                  Education Law Reporter (Education Law Infosource, 1997).
                  Risk Management in Canadian Education (Butterworths, 2000).

Textbooks   Bowers, Grant and Rena Knox; Marvin A. Zuker, consulting editor. *Sexual Misconduct in Education: Prevention, Reporting and Discipline*. Toronto: Butterworths, 2003.

                  Bowlby, Brenda et al. *An Educator's Guide to Special Education Law*. Aurora, ON: Aurora Professional Press, 2001.

                  Brown, Anthony F. *Legal Handbook for Educators*. 5th Toronto: Carswell, 2004.

                  Brown, Anthony F. and Marvin A. Zuker. *Education Law*. 3d ed. Toronto: Carswell, 2002.

                  Brown, David M. *An Educator's Guide to Independent Schools*. Aurora, ON: Aurora Professional Press, 1998.

                  Hurlbert, Earl Leroy and Margot Ann Hurlbert. *School Law under the Charter of Rights and Freedoms*. 2d ed. Calgary: University of Calgary Press, 1992.

                  Keel, Robert G. *Student Rights and Responsibilities: Attendance and Discipline*. Toronto: Emond Montgomery, 1998.

                  Keel, Robert G. and Nadya Tymochenko. *An Educator's Guide to Managing Sexual Misconduct in School*. Aurora, ON: Aurora Professional Press, 2003.

Mackay, Wayne. *Education Law in Canada*. Toronto: Emond Montgomery, 1984.

Mackay, Wayne and Gregory M. Dickinson. *Beyond the "Careful Parent": Tort Liability in Education*. Toronto: Emond Montgomery, 1998.

Mackay, Wayne and Lyle I. Sutherland. *Teachers and the Law: A Practical Guide for Educators*. Toronto: Emond Montgomery, 1992.

McIntyre, Elizabeth J. and David I. Bloom. *An Educator's Guide to the Ontario College of Teachers*. Aurora, ON: Aurora Professional Press, 2002.

Roher, Eric M. *An Educator's Guide to Violence in Schools*. Aurora, ON: Aurora Professional Press, 2000.

Roher, Eric M. and Simon A. Wormwell. *An Educator's Guide to the Role of the Principal*. Aurora, ON: Aurora Professional Press, 2000.

Shilton, Elizabeth J. and Karen Schucher. *Education Labour and Employment Law in Ontario*. 2d ed. Looseleaf. Toronto: Canada Law Book, 2001.

Sussel, Terri A. *Canada's Legal Revolution: Public Education, The Charter and Human Rights*. Toronto: Emond Montgomery, 1995.

Trépanier, Jennifer E. *Student Discipline: A Guide to the Safe Schools Act*. Toronto: Butterworths, 2003.

S. EMPLOYMENT LAW

Scope   Employment law in Canada is governed by both common law principles (what constitutes just cause for dismissal of a senior employee?) and legislation (both provincial and federal, depending on whether the employment is governed by federal or provincial laws). Typical of a provincial statute is the Ontario *Employment Standards Act, 2000*, S.O. 2000, c. 41. Employment law tends to cover only non-unionized employees, whereas labour law (discussed below) covers unionized employees.

Subject   Employees — Dismissal of — Law and legislation — Canada
headings Labor laws and legislation — Canada

CED   Title 90, Vol. 20: Master and Servant
              Title 102.1, Vol. 23: Occupational Health and Safety
              Title 145, Vol. 33: Unemployment Insurance
              Title 151, Vol. 34: Workers' Compensation

Can. Abr. Vol. R14A, R14AA Reissue: Employment Law

Quicklaw Employment law — Global Database: EMPL (includes individual databases)

Case law *Canadian Cases on Employment Law* (Carswell, 1983)
reporters

CD-ROMs *Employment Law Partner* [CD-ROM]. Toronto: Carswell. Updated regularly. Contains relevant legislation, case law, and Carswell-published textbooks on employment law.
Wrongful Dismissal Notice Searcher (Ellen Mole, Butterworths)
Wrongful Dismissal Database (Fisher and Benaroche, Carswell)

Journals *Canadian Labour & Employment Law Journal* (Lancaster House)
Employment and Labour Law Reporter (Butterworths, 1991). Available on LexisNexis (database: CELLR) from 1994.
Employment Bulletin: Legal Issues in the Workplace (Canada Law Book, 1991)
The Canadian Employer (Newsletter) (Carswell, 2004)

Textbooks Aggarwal, Arjun P. and Madhu M. Gupta. *Sexual Harassment in the Workplace*. 3d ed. Toronto: Butterworths, 2000.
Ball, Stacey Reginald. *Canadian Employment Law*. Looseleaf. Toronto: Canada Law Book, 1996. Also available via an Internet subscription or on CD-ROM.
Bernardi, Lauren M. *Powerful Employment Policies*. Looseleaf. Toronto: Canada Law Book, 2001.
Bishop, Peter. *Winning in the Workplace: ADR Strategies for the Workplace*. Toronto: Carswell, 1994.
Chauvin, P.F. et al. *Canadian Employment Law Factbook*. Looseleaf. Toronto: Carswell, 1992.
Corry, David J. and James M. Petrie. *Conducting a Wrongful Dismissal Action*. Calgary, AB: Carswell [annual].
D'Andrea, James A. *Employee Obligations in Canada*. Looseleaf. Toronto: Canada Law Book, 2003.
Echlin, Randall Scott and Matthew L.O. Certosimo. *Just Cause: The Law of Summary Dismissal in Canada*. Looseleaf. Toronto: Canada Law Book, 2000.
Echlin, Randall Scott et al. *Quitting for Good Reason: The Law Of Constructive Dismissal in Canada*, Toronto: Canada Law Book, 2001.
England, Geoffrey. *Individual Employment Law*. Toronto: Irwin Law, 2000. Available on Quicklaw (database identifier: ENGE).
England, Geoffrey et al. *Employment Law in Canada*. 3d ed. Looseleaf. Markham, ON: Butterworths, 1998.

Grosman, Brian A. and John R. Martin. *Discrimination in Employment in Ontario*. Toronto: Canada Law Book, 1994.

Grosman, Norman M. *Federal Employment Law in Canada*. Toronto: Carswell, 1990.

Harris, David. *Wrongful Dismissal*. 3d ed. Looseleaf. Toronto: Carswell, 1984.

Heenan Blaikie LLP. *Qudbec Labour and Employment Law: Frequently Asked Questions*. Toronto: Carswell, 2002.

Knight, James G. et al. *Employment Litigation Manual*. Looseleaf. Toronto: Butterworths, 2004.

Levitt, Howard A. *The Law of Dismissal in Canada*. 3d ed. Looseleaf. Aurora, ON: Canada Law Book, 2003.

Litherland, Geoffrey J. *An Employer's Guide to Dismissal*. Aurora, ON: Aurora Professional Press, 2000.

Manning, Melanie. *Pregnancy, Workplace and the Law*. Toronto: Canada Law Book, 2003.

Mole, Ellen E. *The Wrongful Dismissal Handbook*. 2d ed. Toronto: Butterworths, 1997.

Mole, Ellen E. *The Wrongful Dismissal Practice Manual*. Looseleaf. Toronto: Butterworths, 1997.

Ontario Ministry of Labour, Employment Standards Branch. *Employment Standards Act 2000 — Policy and Interpretation Manual*. Looseleaf. Toronto: Carswell, 2001. Also available on CD-ROM.

O'Reilly, John C. *An Employer's Guide to Surveillance, Searches and Medical Examinations*. Toronto: Carswell, 2003.

Parry, Kimberly A. and David A. Ryan. *Employment Standards Handbook*. 3d ed. Looseleaf. Toronto: Canada Law Book, 2002.

Parry, Robert M. *A Practical Guide to Employment Standards in Ontario*. 2d ed. Aurora, ON: Aurora Professional Press, 1997.

Sproat, John R. *Employment Law Manual: Wrongful Dismissal, Human Rights and Employment Standards*. Scarborough, ON: Carswell, 1995.

Sproat, John R. *Human Rights in Employment Law*. Toronto: Carswell, 1995.

Sproat, John R. *Wrongful Dismissal Handbook*. 3d ed. Toronto: Carswell, 2004.

Steele, Gregory K. and Kenneth W. Thornicroft. *Employment Covenants and Confidential Information*. Toronto: Butterworths, 2002.

T. ENVIRONMENTAL AND NATURAL RESOURCES LAW

Scope Environmental law is governed by federal and provincial legislation. Examples include the federal *Canadian Environmental Assessment Act*, S.C. 1992, c. 37, the *Canadian Environmental Protection Act, 1999*, S.C. 1999, c. 33, and the *Environmental Protection and Enhancement Act*, R.S.A. 2000, c. E-12. Environmental law is heavily regulated in Canada and first-time researchers should ensure they have not overlooked any applicable statute or regulation. Included below are materials that cover natural resources and oil and gas law.

Subject headings Environmental law — Canada
Environmental policy — Canada

CED Title 54, Vol. 10: Environmental Law
Title 63, Vol. 13: Fires
Title 64, Vol. 13: Fish and Game
Title 94, Vol. 20: Mines and Minerals
Title 103, Vol. 23: Oil and Gas
Title 137, Vol. 31: Timber
Title 148, Vol. 33: Waters and Watercourses

Can. Abr. Vol. 17D Reissue: Fires
Vol. 17D Reissue: Fish and Wildlife
Vol. R18: Grain Laws
Vol. R24: Mines and Minerals
Vol. R29: Oil and Gas
Vol. 31: Environmental Law (3d)
Vol. R34A Reissue: Timber
Vol. R35: Waters and Watercourses

Quicklaw Environmental law — Global Database: ENV (includes individual databases)

Case law reporters *Canadian Environmental Law Reports* (Carswell, 1986)

CD-ROMs Carswell. *Treaties with Canada/Environmental* [CD-ROM]. Toronto: Carswell [updated regularly].
ECO/LOG Canadian Environmental Legislation [CD-ROM]. Don Mills, ON: Southam Information Products, 1997. Also available in print.

Web Sites   Canadian Environmental Law Association: <http://www.cela.ca>

Journals   *Canadian Journal of Environmental Law & Practice* (Carswell, 1990). Available on WestlaweCARSWELL (database: JELP-CAN) from v. 7, 1997.

Environment Policy & Law (Environment Policy & Law, 1990)

Textbooks   Benidickson, Jamie. *Environmental Law*. 2d ed. Toronto: Irwin Law, 2002. Available on Quicklaw (database identifier: BENI).

Berger, Stanley D. *Prosecution and Defence of Environmental Offences*. Looseleaf. Toronto: Canada Law Book, 2002.

Boyd, David R. *Unnatural Law: Rethinking Canadian Environmental Law and Policy*. Vancouver: UBC Press, 2003.

Cameron, Duncan et al. *Annotated Guide to the Canadian Environmental Protection Act*. Looseleaf. Toronto: Canada Law Book, 2004.

Canada Law Book. *Canadian Environmental Legislation*. Aurora, ON: Canada Law Book [annual].

Canadian Institute of Resources Law. *Canada Energy Law Service*. Looseleaf. Toronto: Carswell, 1990. There is a 2-volume federal component and a 1-volume Alberta component of this service.

Canadian Oil and Gas Law. 10 vols. 2d ed. Looseleaf. Toronto: Butterworths, 1954.

Coburn, Frederick and Garth Manning. *Toxic Real Estate Manual*. Looseleaf. Toronto: Canada Law Book, 1994.

Estrin, David. *Business Guide to Environmental Law*. Looseleaf. Toronto: Carswell, 1993.

Estrin, David and John Swaigen. *Environment on Trial: A Guide to Ontario Environmental Law and Policy*. 3d ed. Toronto: Emond Montgomery, 1993.

Faieta, Mario D. et al. *Environmental Harm: Civil Actions and Compensation*. Toronto: Butterworths, 1996.

Ferguson, Reg. *WHMIS Compliance Manual*. Looseleaf. Toronto: Carswell, 1989.

Hobby, Beverly et al. *Canadian Environmental Assessment Act: An Annotated Guide*. Looseleaf. Toronto: Canada Law Book, 1997.

Hughes, Elaine L., ed. et al. *Environmental Law and Policy*. 3d ed. Toronto: E. Montgomery, 2003.

Lucas, Alastair and Roger Cotton. *Canadian Environmental Law*, 2d ed. Looseleaf. Toronto: Butterworths, 2004.

Mancell, Garry E. and Brian D. Gilfillan. *Davis & Company's British Columbia Forestry Law: An Annotated Guide to the Forest Practices Code & Forest Act*. Looseleaf. Toronto: Canada Law Book, 1997.

Miller Thomson LLP. *Miller Thomson's Environmental Law Dictionary*. Toronto: Carswell, 1995.

Muldoon, Paul and Richard Lindgren, *The Environmental Bill of Rights: A Practical Guide*. Toronto: Emond Montgomery, 1995.

Northey, Rod. *The Annotated Canadian Environmental Assessment Act and EARP Guidelines Order*. Scarborough, ON: Carswell, 1994.

Pardy, Bruce. *Environmental Law: A Guide to Concepts*. Toronto, Butterworths, 1996.

Pickfield, Peter. *Environmental Approvals in Canada: Practice and Procedure*. Looseleaf. Toronto: Butterworths, 1989.

Saxe, Dianne. *Environmental Offences: Corporate Responsibility and Executive Liability*. Aurora, ON: Canada Law Book, 1990.

Saxe, Dianne. *Ontario Environmental Protection Act Annotated*. Looseleaf. Aurora, ON: Canada Law Book, 1990.

Swaigen, John. *Regulatory Offences in Canada: Liability & Defences*. Scarborough, ON: Carswell, 1992.

Theisen, Eric J. *Guide and Explanation to the Canadian Transportation of Dangerous Goods Act and Regulations*. Looseleaf. Toronto: Carswell, 1992.

Wilson, Paul C., ed. *Canadian Environmental Law Guide*. Looseleaf. Vancouver: STP Specialty Technical Publishers, 1996.

U. EVIDENCE LAW

Scope   Evidence law governs the rules by which courts and other adjudicate bodies are governed regarding the admission of evidence before them. There is a federal *Evidence Act* in addition to provincial evidence Acts. This area of law is also strongly influenced by case law.

Subject headings   Evidence (law) — Canada

CED   Title 57, Vol. 11: Evidence

Can. Abr.   Vol. R15, R15A, R15B, R15C Reissue: Evidence

Quicklaw   Evidence in Civil Cases — Global Database: EVIQ (includes individual databases)

Textbooks   Arboleda-Flórez, Julio and Christine Deynaka. *Forensic Psychiatric Evidence*. Toronto: Butterworths, 1999.

Boyle, Christine et al. *The Law of Evidence: Fact Finding, Fairness, and Advocacy*. Toronto: Emond Montgomery, 1999.

Carswell. *Annotated Canadian Evidence Acts*. Toronto: Carswell [annual].

Chayko, Garry, ed. *Forensic Evidence in Canada*. 2d ed. Toronto: Canada Law Book, 1999.

Corbin, Ruth M. et al. *Trial by Survey: Survey Evidence & the Law*. Toronto: Carswell, 2000.

Cudmore, Gordon. *Civil Evidence Handbook*. Looseleaf. Toronto: Carswell, 1987.

Delisle, Ronald J. *Canadian Evidence Law in a Nutshell*. 2d ed. Toronto: Carswell, 2002.

Delisle, Ronald J. *Evidence: Principles and Problems*. 6th ed. Toronto: Carswell, 2001.

Deutscher, David and Heather Leonoff. *Identification Evidence*. Toronto: Carswell, 1991.

Doherty, Michael P. *The Portable Guide to Evidence*. Toronto: Carswell, 2001.

Freiman, Mark J. and Mark L. Berenblut. *The Litigator's Guide to Expert Witnesses*. Toronto: Canada Law Book, 1997.

Gahtan, Alan M. *Electronic Evidence, 1999*. Toronto: Carswell, 1999.

Gold, Alan D. *Expert Evidence in Criminal Law*. Toronto: Irwin Law, 2003.

Goldstein, Elliott. *Visual Evidence: A Practitioner's Manual*. Looseleaf. Toronto: Carswell, 1991.

Hageman, Cecilia et al. *DNA Handbook*. Toronto: Butterworths, 2002.

Hill, S. Casey. *McWilliam's Canadian Criminal Evidence*. 4th ed. Looseleaf. Toronto: Canada Law Book, 2003.

Mewett, Alan W. and Peter Sankoff. *Witnesses*. Looseleaf. Toronto: Carswell, 1991.

Morton, James C. *Pocket Guide to Evidence*. 2d ed. Toronto: Butterworths, 2002.

Paciocco, David M. and Lee Stuesser. *The Law of Evidence*. 3d ed. Toronto: Irwin Law, 2002. Available on Quicklaw (database identifier: PASE).

Rose, David and Lisa Goos. *DNA: A Practical Guide*. Looseleaf. Toronto: Carswell, 2004.

Salhany, Roger E. *The Practical Guide to Evidence in Criminal Cases*. 6th ed. Toronto: Carswell, 2002.

Schiff, Stanley. *Evidence in the Litigation Process*. Toronto: Carswell, 1993.

Sopinka, John et al. *The Law of Evidence in Canada*. 2d ed. Toronto: Butterworths, 1998.

Stewart, Hamish. *Evidence: A Canadian Casebook*. Toronto: Emond Montgomery, 2002.

White, Robert B. *The Art of Using Expert Evidence*. Toronto: Canada Law Book, 1997.

V. FAMILY LAW

Scope   Family law is split between federal jurisdiction over divorce law under the *Divorce Act*, R.S.C. 1985, c. 3 (4th Supp.) and various provincial laws governing marriage, separation, and custody that are too numerous to list here.

Subject   Divorce — Law and legislation — Canada
headings   Domestic relations — [jurisdiction]

CED   Title 49, Vol. 9: Divorce and Nullity
Title 62, Vol. 13: Family Law
Title 78, Vol. 16: Infants and Children
Title 146, Vol. 33: Vital Statistics

Can. Abr.   Vols. 36–47: Family Law (3d)

Quicklaw   Family law — Global Database: FAM (includes individual databases)

Case law   *Reports of Family Law* (Carswell, 1971)
reporters

Journals   *Annual Review of Family Law* (Carswell, 1992)
Canadian Family Law Matters (CCH Canadian, 1978)
Canadian Family Law Quarterly: A Journal for Practitioners (Carswell, 1986)
Canadian Journal of Family Law (Carswell, 1978). Available on Quicklaw (database: CJFL) from 1990; LexisNexis (database: CANJFL) from 1996.
Money & Family Law (Carswell)
Ontario Family Law Reporter Newsletter (Butterworths Canada, 1987)

CD-ROMs   *Family Law Library* (Canada Law Book). Also available on the Internet (by subscription).

Family Law Partner [CD-ROM]. Toronto: Carswell. Updated regularly. Contains relevant legislation, case law, and Carswell-published textbooks on family law. Available in an expanded version as *FamilySource* on WestlaweCARSWELL (by subscription).

Canadian Family Law Guide (CCH Canadian). Also available on CCHOnline (by subscription).

Textbooks Benotto, Mary Lou and Williams and Partners. *Income Tax and Family Law Handbook*. Looseleaf. Toronto: Butterworths, 1988.

Bernstein, Marvin M. et al. *Child Protection Law in Canada*. Looseleaf. Toronto: Carswell, 1990. Available on *FamilySource* on WestlaweCARSWELL (by subscription).

Bernstein, Marvin M. and Lynn M. Kirwin. *Child Protection: Practice and Procedure*. Toronto: Carswell, 1996.

Botnick, David I. *Ontario: Marriage, Separation and Divorce: Understand Your Rights*. 10th ed. North Vancouver, BC: Self-Counsel Press, 2003.

Brodeur, Marie-Josée and Catherine La Rosa. *Loi sur le divorce annotée*. Toronto: Carswell, 2000.

Butterworths Canada. *Alberta Family Service*. Looseleaf. Vancouver: Butterworths, 1982. Also available for British Columbia and Ontario.

CCH Canadian Limited. *Canadian Family Law Guide*. Looseleaf. Toronto: CCH Canadian, 1976. Also available on CD-ROM and on *CCH Online* (by subscription).

Christopher, T. Catherine. *The Law of Domestic Conflict in Canada*. Looseleaf. Toronto: Carswell, 2002.

Cochrane, Michael G. *Family Law in Ontario: A Practical Guide for Lawyers and Law Clerks*. Looseleaf. Toronto: Canada Law Book, 1990.

Fodden, Simon. *Family Law*. Toronto: Irwin Law, 1999. Available on Quicklaw (database identifier: FODD).

Freedman, Andrew J. et al. *Financial Principles of Family Law*. Looseleaf. Toronto: Carswell, 2001.

Hainsworth, Terry W. *Child Support Guidelines Service*. Looseleaf. Toronto: Canada Law Book, 1998. Also available on CD-ROM or by Internet subscription.

Hainsworth, Terry W. *Divorce Act Manual*. Looseleaf. Aurora, ON: Canada Law Book, 1994.

Hainsworth, Terry W. *Ontario Family Law Act Manual*. 2d ed. Looseleaf. Toronto: Canada Law Book, 1992. Also available on CD-ROM or by Internet subscription.

Harvey, Cameron. *The Law of Dependants' Relief in Canada*. Toronto: Carswell, 1999.

Holland, Winifred and Barbro Stalbecker-Pountney. *Cohabitation: The Law in Canada*. Looseleaf. Toronto: Carswell, 1990.

Klotz, Robert A. *Bankruptcy, Insolvency and Family Law*. 2d ed. Toronto: Carswell, 2001.

Landau, Barbara et al. *Family Mediation Handbook*. 2d ed. Toronto: Butterworths, 1997.

MacDonald, James C. and Lee K. Ferrier. *Canadian Divorce Law and Practice*. 2d ed. Looseleaf. Toronto: Carswell, 1988. Available on *FamilySource* on WestlaweCARSWELL (by subscription).

MacDonald, James C. and Ann C. Wilton. *The Annotated Divorce Act*. Scarborough, ON: Carswell [annual]. Carswell also publishes annotated legislation titles for family law legislation in Ontario.

MacDonald, James C. and Ann C. Wilton. *Child Support Guidelines: Law and Practice*. Looseleaf. Toronto: Carswell, 1998.

MacDonald, James C. and Ann C. Wilton. *Family Law Act of Ontario*. Revised ed. Looseleaf. Toronto: Carswell, 1998. Available on *FamilySource* on WestlaweCARSWELL (by subscription).

McLeod, James G. *Child Custody Law and Practice*. Looseleaf. Toronto: Carswell, 1992. Available on *FamilySource* on WestlaweCARSWELL (by subscription).

McLeod, James G. and Alfred A. Mamo. *Matrimonial Property Law in Canada*. Looseleaf. Toronto: Carswell, 1988. Available on *FamilySource* on WestlaweCARSWELL (by subscription).

Mossman, Mary Jane. *Families and the Law in Canada: Cases and Commentary*. Toronto: Emond Montgomery, 2004.

Noble, Cinnie. *Family Mediation: A Guide for Lawyers*. Toronto: Canada Law Book, 1999.

Payne, Julien D. *Child Support in Canada*. 3d ed. Available on Quicklaw (database identifier: PDCS).

Payne, Julien D. *Payne on Divorce*. 4th ed. Scarborough, ON: Carswell, 1996.

Payne, Julien D. and Marylin A. Payne. *Canadian Family Law in a Nutshell*. Toronto: Irwin Law, 2001. Available on Quicklaw (database identifier: PAYN).

Payne, Julien D. and Marylin A. Payne. *Child Support Guidelines in Canada, 2004*. Toronto: Irwin Law, 2004.

Payne, Julien D. and Marylin A. Payne. *Introduction to Canadian Family Law*. Scarborough, ON: Carswell, 1994.

Sawyer, Alison. *Divorce Guide for Canada*. North Vancouver, BC: Self-Counsel Press, 2002.

Shields, Richard W. *Collaborative Family Law: Another Way to Resolve Family Law Dipsutes*. Toronto: Carswell, 2003.

Stark, Hugh G. and Kirstie J. Maclise. *Domestic Contracts*. Looseleaf. Toronto: Carswell, 1988. Available on *FamilySource* on WestlaweCARSWELL (by subscription).

Stewart, Douglas and Mary Lou Benotto. *Preparation of Domestic Contracts*. Aurora, ON: Canada Law Book, 1995.

Wallace, Patricia H. and Debra Wallace. *Effective Advocacy in Family Law*. Toronto: Butterworths, 2004.

Wilson, Jeffrey. *Wilson on Children and the Law*. 3d ed. Looseleaf. Toronto: Butterworths, 1994.

Wilton, Ann C. and Judy Miyauchi. *Enforcement of Family Law Orders and Agreements: Law and Practice*. Looseleaf. Toronto: Carswell, 1989. Available on FamilySource on WestlaweCARSWELL (by subscription).

W. HEALTH AND MEDICAL LAW

Scope   Health law in Canada is governed by a variety of federal and provincial legislation, policy, and case law.

Subject   Medical laws and legislation — Canada
headings   Medical jurisprudence — Canada
Mental health laws — Canada
Physicians — Malpractice — Canada
Tort liability of hospitals — Canada

CED   Title 72, Vol. 15: Hospitals and Health Care
Title 93, Vol. 20: Mental Incompetency
Title 117, Vol. 27: Professions and Occupations
Title 119, Vol. 27: Public Health and Welfare

Can. Abr.   Vol. R18: Health Law
Vol. R24: Mental Incompetency

Quicklaw   Health Law Topical — Global Database: HTHT (includes individual databases)

Journals   *Health Law in Canada* (Toronto: Butterworths, 1980). Available on LexisNexis (database: CHL) from 1994.

Health Law Journal (Edmonton, AB: Health Law Institute, 1991). Available on Quicklaw (database identifier: HLJA) from 1993.

Health Law Review (Edmonton, AB: Health Law Institute, 1991). Available on Quicklaw (database identifier: HLRA) from 1991.

Legal Medical Quarterly (Toronto: Jonah Publications, 1977).

Risk Management in Canadian Health Care Newsletter (Toronto: Butterworths, 1999).

Telehealth Law Newsletter. (Toronto: Butterworths, 2000).

Web Sites   Health Law Institute (Dalhousie University): <http://is.dal.ca/~wwwlaw/hli/index.html>

Textbooks   Berry, Marie. *Canadian Pharmacy Law*. Looseleaf. Toronto: Butterworths, 1995.

Bloom, Hy and Michael Bay. *A Practical Guide to Mental Health, Capacity and Consent Law of Ontario*. Toronto: Carswell, 1996.

Downie, Jocelyn et al. *Canadian Health Law and Policy*. 2d ed. Toronto: Butterworths, 2002.

Downie, Jocelyn et al. *Dental Law in Canada*. Toronto: Butterworths, 2004.

Dykeman, Mary Jane. *Canadian Health Law Practice Manual*. Looseleaf. Toronto: Butterworths, 2000.

Emson, H.E. *The Doctor and the Law: A Practical Guide for the Canadian Physician*. 3d ed. Toronto: Butterworths, 1995.

Grant, Anne E. and Aileen A. Ashman. *Nurse's Practical Guide to the Law*. Toronto: Canada Law Book, 1997.

Gray, John E. et al. *Canadian Mental Health Law and Policy*. Toronto: Butterworths, 2000.

Knoopers, Bartha Maria et al. *Legal Rights and Human Genetic Material*. Toronto: Emond Montgomery, 1996.

Marshall, T.D. *The Law of Human Experimentation*. Toronto: Butterworths, 2000.

McPhedran, Marilou and Wendy Sutton. *Preventing Sexual Abuse of Patients: A Legal Guide for Health Care Professionals*. Toronto: Butterworths, 2004.

McTeer, Maureen A. *Tough Choices: Living and Dying in the 21st Century*. Toronto: Irwin Law, 1999. Available on Quicklaw (database identifier: MCTE).

Morris, John J. *Canadian Nurses and the Law*. 2d ed. Toronto: Butterworths, 1999.

Morris, John J. *Law for Canadian Health Care Administrators.* Toronto: Butterworths, 1996.

Robertson, Gerald B. *Mental Disability and the Law in Canada.* 2d ed. Toronto: Carswell, 1994.

Robertson, Gerald B. and Ellen I. Picard. *Legal Liability of Doctors and Hospitals.* 3d ed. Toronto: Carswell, 1996.

Rozovsky, Lorne E. *Canadian Law of Consent to Treatment.* 3d ed. Toronto: Butterworths, 2003.

Rozovsky, Lorne E. and Noel Inions. *Canadian Health Information: A Practical Legal and Risk Management Guide.* 3d ed. Toronto: Butterworths, 2002.

Sneiderman, Barney et al. *Canadian Medical Law: An Introduction for Physicians, Nurses and Other Health Care Professionals.* 3d ed. Toronto: Carswell, 2003.

Steinecke, Richard. *A Complete Guide to the Regulated Health Professions Act.* Looseleaf. Toronto: Butterworths, 1995.

X. IMMIGRATION AND REFUGEE LAW

Scope Immigration and refugee law is governed primarily by federal law, including the *Immigration and Refugee Protection Act,* S.C. 2001, c. 27 and the *Citizenship Act,* R.S.C. 1985, c. C-29.

Subject headings Citizenship — Canada
Refugees — Legal status, laws, etc. — Canada
Emigration and immigration law — Canada

CED Title 61, Vol. 12: Extradition
Title 75, Vol. 15: Immigration and Refugees

Can. Abr. Vol. R1B: Aliens, Immigration and Citizenship

Quicklaw Immigration and refugee law — Global Database: IMRE (includes individual databases)

Case law reporters *Immigration Law Reporter* (Carswell, 1985).

Journals *Canada's Immigration and Citizenship Bulletin* (Canada Law Book, 1989)

Web Sites Citizenship and Immigration Canada: <http://www.cic.gc.ca>
Immigration and Refugee Board of Canada: <http://www.cisr-irb.gc.ca>

Textbooks Bagambiire, Davies B.N. *Canadian Immigration and Refugee Law.* Aurora, ON: Canada Law Book, 1996.

Bart, Jacqueline R. et al. *Canada/U.S. Relocation Manual: Immigration, Customs, Employment and Taxation.* Looseleaf. Toronto: Carswell, 1998.

Bart, Jacqueline R. and David A. Bruner. *Permanent Residence.* Toronto: Carswell, 1998.

Bart, Jacqueline R. and Benjamin J. Trister. *Work Permits and Visas.* Toronto: Carswell [annual].

Berezowski, Nan M. and Benjamin J. Trister. *Citizenship.* Toronto: Carswell, 1996.

Berman, Samuel and Caroline McChesney. *Refugee Determination Proceedings.* Toronto: Carswell [annual].

Galloway, Donald. *Immigration Law.* Concord, ON: Irwin Law, 1997. Available on Quicklaw (database identifier: GALO).

Hathaway, James C. *The Law of Refugee Status.* Toronto: Butterworths, 1991.

Jackman, Barbara L. et al. *Canadian Public Security Law Guide.* Looseleaf. Toronto: CCH Canadian, 2003. Available in print, on CD-ROM, and by Internet subscription.

Kranc, Benjamin A. *Human Resources Guide to Immigration.* Looseleaf. Toronto: Canada Law Book, 2003.

Marrocco, Frank N. *The Annotated Citizenship Act.* Toronto: Carswell [annual].

Marrocco, Frank N. and Henry M. Goslett. *The Annotated Immigration Act.* Toronto: Carswell [annual].

Waldman, Lorne. *Canadian Immigration and Refugee Law and Practice, 2004 edition.* Toronto: Butterworths, 2003.

Waldman, Lorne. *The Definition of Convention Refugee.* Toronto: Butterworths, 2001.

Waldman, Lorne. *Immigration Law and Practice.* Looseleaf. Toronto: Butterworths, 1992.

Wlodyka, Andrew Z. and John D. Gardner. *Appeals Before the Immigration Appeal Division.* Toronto: Carswell, 1996.

Zambelli, Pia. *The Refugee Convention: A Compendium of Canadian and American Cases.* Toronto: Carswell [annual].

Y. INSURANCE LAW

Scope Insurance law in Canada is governed largely by provincial legislation (such as British Columbia's *Insurance Act*, R.S.B.C. 1996, c. 226), while insurance companies are governed by federal legislation (such as the *Insurance Companies Act*, S.C. 1991, c. 47).

Subject Insurance law — Canada
headings Insurance, liability — Canada

CED Title 80, Vol. 17: Insurance Law

Can. Abr. Vol. R20A-R20C Reissue: Insurance Law

Quicklaw Insurance law — Global Database: INS (includes individual databases)

Case law *Canadian Cases on the Law of Insurance* (Carswell, 1983)
reporters *Canadian Insurance Law Reporter* (CCH Canadian, 1934)
    Ontario Accident Benefit Case Summaries (CCH Canadian, 1994)

Journals *Canadian Insurance Law Review* (Carswell, 1988–1996)
    Canadian Journal of Insurance Law (Jewel Publications, 1983)

Textbooks Boivin, Denis. *Insurance Law*. Toronto, Irwin Law, 2004
    Bossin, Alan I. *Duties of Insurance Agents and Brokers: A Guide to Managing Responsiblities*. Toronto: Canada Law Book, 1995.
    Brown, Craig. *Canadian Insurance Contracts Law in a Nutshell*. Toronto: Carswell, 1995.
    Brown, Craig. *Insurance Law in Canada*. 2d ed. Scarborough, ON: Carswell, 1999.
    Brown, Craig. *Introduction to Canadian Insurance Law*. Toronto: Butterworths, 2003.
    Hayles , Richard. *Disability Insurance: Canadian Law and Business Practice*. Toronto: Carswell, 1998.
    Hilliker, Gordon G. *Insurance Bad Faith*. Toronto: Butterworths, 2004.
    Hilliker, Gordon G. *Liability Insurance Law in Canada*. 3d ed. Toronto: Butterworths, 2001.
    Leckie, Ann and Manjit Grewal et al. *Disability Claims Management*. 2d ed. Toronto: Butterworths, 2001.
    Lichty, Mark G. and Marcus B. Snowden. *Annotated Commercial General Liability Policy*. Looseleaf. Toronto: Canada Law Book, 1997.

McNairn, Colin H.H. *Consolidated Insurance Companies Act of Canada Regulations and Guidelines*. Scarborough, ON: Carswell, [annual].

Norwood, David and John P. Weir. *Norwood on Life Insurance Law in Canada*. 3d ed. Scarborough, ON: Carswell, 2002.

Sanderson, Heather A. *Commercial General Liability Insurance*. Toronto: Butterworths, 2000.

Scott, Kenneth W. and R. Bruce Reynolds. *Scott and Reynolds on Surety Bonds*. Looseleaf. Toronto: Carswell, 1993.

Strathy, George R. and George C. Moore. *The Law and Practice of Marine Insurance in Canada*. Toronto: Butterworths, 2003.

Weir, John P. *The Annotated Insurance Act of Ontario*. Looseleaf. Toronto: Carswell, 1988.

Z. INTELLECTUAL PROPERTY/E-COMMERCE LAW

Scope Intellectual property laws in Canada generally fall under federal jurisdiction and are regulated by such Acts as the *Copyright Act*, R.S.C. 1985, c. C-42, the *Trade-Marks Act*, R.S.C. 1985, c. T-13, and the *Patent Act*, R.S.C. 1985, c. P-4.

Subject headings
Copyright — Canada
Trademarks — Canada
Patent laws and legislation — Canada
Intellectual property — Canada

CED Title 34, Vol. 5: Copyright
Title 107, Vol. 24: Patents of Invention
Title 141, Vol. 32: Trade Marks and Industrial Designs

Can. Abr. Vol. R20D, R20E Reissue: Intellectual Property

Quicklaw Intellectual property law — Global Database: IP (includes individual databases)

Case law reporters *Canadian Patent Reporter* (Canada Law Book, 1971)

CD-ROMs *Canadian Patent Reporter* (Canada Law Book)
Copyright & New Media Law Newsletter (Lesley Ellen Harris, 1997)
Intellectual Property Library (Butterworths)

Journals   *Canadian Intellectual Property Review* (Patent and Trademark Institute of Canada, 1956).

Canadian Journal of Law and Technology (CCH Canadian, 2002). Available in print and on *CCH Online* (by subscription).

Intellectual Property Journal (Carswell, 1984). Available on WestlaweCARSWELL (database: IPJ-CAN) from v. 12, 1997.

Web Sites Canadian Intellectual Property Office (CIPO): <http://cipo.gc.ca>

Centre for Innovation Law and Policy — Innovation Law Forum: <http://www.innovationlaw.org/lawforum/forumindex.htm>

Textbooks Burshtein, Sheldon. *The Corporate Counsel Guide to Intellectual Property Law.* Toronto: Canada Law Book, 2000.

Canada Law Book. *Intellectual Property Statutes: Legislative History.* Looseleaf. Toronto: Canada Law Book, 1999.

Card, Duncan. *Information Technology Transactions: Business, Management and Legal Strategies.* Toronto: Carswell, 2002.

Cornish, Diane E. *Licensing Intellectual Property Law.* Toronto: Carswell, 1995.

Deturbide, Michael and Teresa Scassa. *Electronic Commerce and Internet Law.* Toronto: CCH Canadian, 2004.

Dimock, Ronald E. *I Thought of That! A Practical Guide to Patents, Trademarks and Copyright.* Toronto: CCH Canadian, 1999.

Dimock, Ronald E. *Intellectual Property Disputes: Resolutions and Remedies.* Looseleaf. Toronto: Carswell, 2003.

Fecenko, Mark J. *Biotechnology Law: Corporate-Commercial Practice.* Toronto: Butterworths, 2002.

Gahtan, Alan M. *Internet Law: A Practical Guide for Legal and Business Professionals.* Scarborough, ON: Carswell, 1998.

Gahtan, Alan M. *Electronic Commerce: A Practitioner's Guide.* Looseleaf. Toronto: Carswell, 2003.

Gratton, Eloise. *Internet and Wireless Privacy: A Legal Guide to Global Business Practices.* Toronto: CCH Canadian, 2003.

Handa, Sunny. *Copyright Law in Canada.* Toronto: Butterworths, 2001.

Harris, Lesley-Ellen. *Canadian Copyright Law.* 3d ed. Toronto: McGraw-Hill Ryerson, 2001.

Henderson, Gordon F. et al., eds. *Copyright and Confidential Information Law of Canada.* Scarborough, ON: Carswell, 1994.

Henderson, Gordon F. et al., eds. *Patent Law of Canada.* Scarborough, ON: Carswell, 1994.

Henderson, Gordon F. et al., eds. *Trade-marks Law of Canada.* Scarborough, ON: Carswell, 1993.

Howell, Robert G. et al. *Intellectual Property Law: Cases and Materials.* Toronto: Emond Montgomery, 1999.

Hughes, Roger T. *Hughes on Copyright and Industrial Design.* Looseleaf. Toronto: Butterworths, 1984.

Hughes, Roger T. *Hughes on TradeMarks.* Looseleaf. Toronto: Butterworths, 1984.

Hughes, Roger T. and John H. Woodley. *Hughes and Woodley on Patents.* Looseleaf. Toronto: Butterworths, 1984.

Joliffe, R. Scott and A. Kelly Gill. *Fox on Canadian Law of Trademarks and Unfair Competition.* 4th ed. Looseleaf. Toronto: Carswell, 2002.

Knop, Howard P. *Security Interests in Intellectual Property.* Toronto: Carswell, 2003.

Kratz, Martin P.J. *Canada's Intellectual Property Law in a Nutshell.* Toronto: Carswell, 1998.

Kratz, Martin P.J. *Protecting Copyright and Industrial Design.* 2d ed. Toronto: Carswell, 1999.

Kratz, Martin P.J. *Obtaining Patents.* 2d ed. Toronto: Carswell, 1999.

Mann, Fraser J. *Information and Technology Law: Recent Developments for Professionals.* Scarborough, ON: Carswell, 1996 [published 5 times per year].

McKeown, John S. *Fox on Canadian Law of Copyright and Industrial Designs.* 4th ed. Looseleaf. Toronto: Carswell, 2003.

Ramsay, John T. *Ramsay on Technology Transfers and Licensing.* 2d ed. Toronto: Butterworths, 2002.

Richard, Hugues G. *Canadian Trade-Marks Act — Annotated.* Looseleaf. Toronto: Carswell, 1990.

Richard, Hugues G. and Laurent Carrière. *Canadian Copyright Act — Annotated.* Looseleaf. Toronto: Carswell, 1992.

Sookman, Barry B. *Computer, Internet and Electronic Commerce Terms: Judicial, Legislative and Technical Definitions, 2003.* Toronto: Carswell [annual].

Sookman, Barry B. *Sookman: Computer, Internet and Electronic Commerce Law.* Looseleaf. Toronto: Carswell, 1988.

Takach, George S. *Computer Law.* 2d ed. Toronto: Irwin Law, 2003. Available on Quicklaw (database identifier: TAKA).

Tamaro, Normand. *Annotated Copyright Act.* Toronto: Carswell [annual].

Tamaro, Normand. *Loi sur le droit d'auteur, texte annoté.* 6th ed. Toronto: Carswell, 2003.

Thorburn, Julie A. and Keith G. Fairburn. *Law of Confidential Business Information*. Looseleaf. Aurora, ON: Canada Law Book, 1998.

Vaver, David. *Copyright Law*. Toronto, ON: Irwin Law, 2000. Available on Quicklaw (database identifier: VACO).

Vaver, David. *Intellectual Property Law: Copyright, Patents, Trademarks*. Concord, ON: Irwin Law, 1997. Available on Quicklaw (database identifier: VAIP).

AA. INTERNATIONAL AND FOREIGN LAW

Scope   International law in Canada encompasses various international treaties and conventions that Canada has entered into governing its relationships with other countries and between Canadians and citizens of other countries. Foreign law involves the domestic laws of countries outside of Canada. International and foreign legal resources are discussed in detail in Chapter 7 (the books listed below are only a small sample).

Subject headings   International law — Canada

CED   Title 28, Vol. 4A: Conflict of Laws
Title 81, Vol. 17: International Law
Title 140, Vol. 31: Trade and Commerce and Foreign Investment in Canada

Can. Abr.   Vol. 23: Conflict of Laws (3d)
Vol. R20E: Reissue: International Law

Quicklaw   International Law Update — database identifier: ILU (1995 to date)
North American Free Trade Agreement — database indentifier: FTA
General Agreement on Tariffs and Trade (GATT) — database identifier: GATT

Journals   *Asper Review of International Business and Trade Law* (Faculty of Law, University of Manitoba) Also available on Quicklaw, database ASPR.
Bulletin (Canadian Council on International Law, 1974).
Canada-United States Law Journal (Canada-United States Law Institute, 1978).
Canadian International Lawyer (Canadian Bar Association, 1994).

Canadian Yearbook of International Law (International Law Association, Canadian Branch. University of British Columbia Press, 1963).

International Insights: A Dalhousie Journal of International Affairs (John E. Reed International Law Society, Dalhousie Law School, 1985).

Journal of International Law and International Relations (University of Toronto, Faculty of Law and Munk Centre for International Studies, 2004).

Revue québécoise de droit international (Éditions Thémis, 1984). Available on Quicklaw (database: RQDI) from 2000.

CD-ROMs *Treaties with Canada Collection* (Carswell)

Web Sites Foreign Affairs Canada: <http://www.fac-aec.gc.ca>
International Trade Canada: <http://www.itcan-cican.gc.ca>
Womens' Human Rights Resources: <http://www.law-lib.utoronto.ca/diana/mainpage.htm>

Textbooks Baer, Marvin et al. *Private International Law in Common Law Canada: Cases, Text and Materials.* 2d ed. Toronto: Emond Montgomery, 2003.

Baran, Babak. *Carswell's Handbook of International Dispute Resolution Rules.* Toronto: Carswell, 1999.

Bayefsky, Anne F. *International Human Rights Law: Use in Canadian Charter of Rights and Freedoms Litigation.* Toronto: Butterworths, 1992.

Castel. J.-G. *Introduction to Conflict of Laws.* 4th ed. Toronto: Butterworths, 2002.

Castel, J.-G. *Canadian Conflict of Laws.* 5th ed. Looseleaf. Toronto: Butterworths, 2002.

Currie, John H. *Public International Law.* Toronto: Irwin Law, 2001. Available on Quicklaw (database identifier: CURR).

Freeman, Mark and Gib van Ert. *International Human Rights Law.* Toronto: Irwin Law, 2004.

Gold, Edgar et al. *Maritime Law.* Toronto: Irwin Law, 2004.

Johnson, Jon Ragnar. *International Trade Law.* Toronto: Irwin Law, 1998. Available on Quicklaw (database identifier: JOIL).

Kindred, Hugh M. *International Law, Chiefly as Interpreted and Applied in Canada.* 6th ed. Toronto: Emond Montgomery, 2000.

Schabas, William A. *International Human Rights Law and the Canadian Charter.* 2d ed. Toronto: Carswell, 1996.

van Ert, Gibran. *Using International Law in Canadian Courts*. Kluwer Law International, 2002.

BB. INTRODUCTION TO LAW/LEGAL SYSTEMS

Scope   This section provides information for first-time law students or persons interested in studying law. Some of the texts below are American but apply, for the most part, equally well to the study of law in any jurisdiction.

Subject   Justice, Administration of — Canada
headings   Law — Canada
          Law — Studying and teaching — Canada
          Law examinations — [jurisdiction]
          Law students — Canada

CED   Title 16, Vol. 13: Barristers and Solicitors
          Title 104, Vol. 24: Parliament and Legislatures
          Title 136, Vol. 31: Statutes

Can. Abr.   Vol. R21: Judges and Courts
          Vol. R34: Statutes

Textbooks Ali, Ramsey et al. *The ABCs of Law School: A Practical Guide to Success Without Sacrifice*. Toronto: Irwin Law, 2002.

Burkhart, Ann M. and Robert A. Stein. *How to Study Law and Take Law Exams*. St. Paul, MN: West Pub. Co., 1996.

Civiletto Carey, Christian and Kristen David Adams. *The Practice of Law School: Getting In and Making the Most of Your Legal Education*. New York: ALM Pub., 2003.

Dernbach, John C., ed. *A Practical Guide to Writing Law School Essay Exams*. Littleton, CO: F.B. Rothman, 2001.

Fischl, Richard M. and Jeremy Paul. *Getting to Maybe: How to Excel on Law School Exams*. Durham, NC: Carolina Academic Press, 1999.

Fitzgerald, Patrick and Barry Wright. *Looking at Law: Canada's Legal System*. 5th ed. Toronto: Butterworths, 2000.

Gader-Shafran, Rachel. *The International Student's Survival Guide to Law School in the United States: Everything You Need to Succeed*. New York: iUniverse, 2003.

Gall, Gerald L. *The Canadian Legal System*. 4th ed. Toronto: Carswell, 1995.

Hegland, Kenney. *Introduction to the Study and Practice of Law in a Nutshell*. 4th ed. St. Paul, MN: Thomson/West, 2003.

Hutchinson, Allan C. *The Law School Book: Succeeding at Law School*. 2d ed. Toronto: Irwin Law, 2000.

Jones, Craig E. *Secrets of an Entrepreneurial Law Student and Other Strategies for Law School Success*. Toronto: Emond Montgomery, 1997.

Kissam, Philip C. *The Discipline of Law Schools: The Making of Modern Lawyers*. Durham, NC: Carolina Academic Press, 2003.

Lyon, Noel. *Inside Law School: Two Dialogues About Legal Education*. Calgary: University of Calgary Press, 1999.

Miller, Robert H. *Law School Confidential: A Complete Guide to the Law School Experience: By Students, For Students*. New York: St. Martin's Griffin, 2004.

Noyes, Shana Connell and Henry S. Noyles. *Acing Your First Year of Law School: The Ten Steps to Success You Won't Learn in Class*. Littleton, CO: Fred B. Rothman, 1999.

Romano, Diana. *The Law Students' Guide to Articling and Summer Positions in Canada*. 2d ed. Toronto: Emond Montgomery, 1997.

Shapo, Helene S. *Law School Without Fear: Strategies for Success*. 2d ed. New York: Foundation Press, 2002.

Waddams, S.M. *Introduction to the Study of Law*. 5th ed. Toronto: Carswell, 1997.

Williams, Sharon A. and Janet Walker. *A Practical Guide to Mooting*. Toronto: Emond Montgomery, 1995.

CC. LABOUR LAW

Scope   Labour law in Canada can fall under federal jurisdiction for employees working for the federal government or in the federal sector and under provincial jurisdiction for all other unionized employees. Labour law tends to cover unionized employees, whereas employment law (discussed above) tends to cover non-unionized employees. An example of typical provincial legislation would be Ontario's *Labour Relations Act*, S.O. 1995, c. 1, Sched. A.

Subject   Arbitration, industrial — Canada
headings   Collective labor agreements — Canada
Grievance arbitration — Canada
Labor laws and legislation — Canada
Trade unions — Law and legislation — Canada

CED   Title 84, Vol. 18: Labour Law
                 Title 84.1, Vol. 18: Labour Law — Federal

Can. Abr.   Vol. R21A-R22C Reissue: Labour Law

Quicklaw   Labour law — Global Database: LABT (includes individual databases)

Case law   *Canadian Labour Law Reporter* (CCH Canadian)
reporters   *Canadian Labour Relations Boards Reports* (Butterworths Canada)
                 Labour Arbitration Cases (Canada Law Book, 1948)
                 Leading Cases on Labour Arbitration (Butterworths Canada)

Journals   *Canadian Labour & Employment Law Journal* (Lancaster House)
                 CLV Reports (Canada Labour Views Reports) (Carswell)
                 College and University Employment Law Service (Lancaster House)
                 Employment and Labour Law Reporter (Butterworths, 1991)
                 Federal Labour & Employment Law Service (Lancaster House)
                 IMPACT: Labour Law & Management Practices (Canada Law Book)
                 Labour Arbitration Yearbook (Lancaster House)

CD-ROMs   *Canadian Labour Law Library* (Canada Law Book)
                 CLV Labour Arbitration Searcher (Carswell)
                 LabourSource (Carswell)

Textbooks   Adams, George W. *Canadian Labour Law*. 2d ed. Looseleaf. Toronto: Canada Law Book, 1993.

Brown, Donald J.M. and David M. Beatty. *Canadian Labour Arbitration*. 3d ed. Looseleaf. Aurora, ON: Canada Law Book, 1997. Also available on CD-ROM and by Internet subscription.

Caron, Renée. *Employment in the Federal Public Service*. Looseleaf. Toronto: Canada Law Book, 2001.

Carter, D.D. et al. *Labour Law in Canada*. 5th ed. Toronto: Butterworths, 2001.

CCH Canadian Limited. *Canadian Master Labour Guide*. 18th ed. Toronto: CCH Canadian, 2004.

Charney, Richard J. and Thomas E.F. Brady. *Judicial Review in Labour Law*. Looseleaf. Toronto: Canada Law Book, 1997.

Clarke, Graham J. *Clarke's Canadian Industrial Relations Board*. Looseleaf. Toronto: Canada Law Book, 1999.

Corry, David J. *Collective Bargaining and Agreement*. Looseleaf. Toronto: Canada Law Book, 1997.

Gorsky, M.R. et al. *Evidence and Procedure in Canadian Labour Arbitration*. Rev. ed. Looseleaf. Scarborough, ON: Carswell, 1991.

Labour Law Casebook Group. *Labour and Employment Law: Cases, Materials, and Commentary* 7th ed. Toronto, Irwin Law, 2004.

MacNeil, Michael et al. *Trade Union Law in Canada.* Looseleaf. Aurora, ON: Canada Law Book, 1994.

Poskanzer, Ethan and Jeffrey Sack. *Labour Law Terms: A Dictionary.* Toronto: Lancaster House, 1984.

Sack, Jeffrey et al. *Ontario Labour Relations Board Law and Practice.* 3d ed. Looseleaf. Toronto: Butterworths, 1997.

Sanderson, John P. *The Art of Collective Bargaining.* 2d ed. Aurora, ON: Canada Law Book, 1989.

Sanderson, John P. and Jerry W. Brown. *Labour Arbitrations and All That.* 3d ed. Toronto: Canada Law Book, 1994.

Saxe, Stewart D. and Brian C. McLean. *Collective Agreement Handbook: A Guide for Employers and Employees.* Toronto: Canada Law Book, 1999.

Shilton, Elizabeth J. and Karen Schucher. *Education Labour and Employment Law in Ontario.* 2d ed. Looseleaf. Toronto: Canada Law Book, 2001.

Sommer, Neal B. and Stewart D. Saxe. *Understanding the Labour Relations Act.* 2d ed. Toronto: Canada Law Book, 2001.

Weatherill, John F.W. *A Practical Guide to Labour Arbitration Procedure.* 2d ed. Aurora, ON: Canada Law Book, 1998.

DD. LANDLORD AND TENANT/ COMMERCIAL LEASING LAW

Scope   Landlord and tenant law is governed largely by provincial legislation, which is often then interpreted by decisions from courts or provincial tribunals. Many landlord and tenant decisions are unpublished; hence, a good source for them is Quicklaw's LTLQ database.

Subject   Landlord and tenant — [jurisdiction]
headings   Rental housing — Law and legislation — [jurisdiction]

CED   Title 48, Vol. 9: Distress
Title 85, Vol. 19: Landlord and Tenant

Can. Abr.   Vol. R22D Reissue: Landlord and Tenant

Quicklaw Landlord and Tenant Law — Global Database: LTLT (includes individual databases)

Textbooks Balfour, Richard J. *Landlord and Tenant Law*. Toronto: Emond Montgomery, 1991.

Bentley, Christoper A.W. et al. *Williams and Rhodes' Canadian Law of Landlord and Tenant*. 6th ed. Looseleaf. Toronto: Carswell, 1988.

Butkus, Mavis J. *Annotated Ontario Landlord and Tenant Statutes*. Toronto: Carswell [annual].

CCH Canadian. *Ontario Residential Tenancies*. 2d ed. Toronto: CCH Canadian, 2002.

Ferguson, Jane and Rose H. McConnell. *Evictions: A Practical Guide to Residential Evictions in Ontario*. Toronto: CCH Canadian, 2001.

Fleming, Jack. *Residential Tenancies in Ontario*. Toronto: Butterworths, 1998.

Haber, Harvey M., ed. *Assignment, Subletting and Change of Control in a Commercial Lease: A Practical Guide*. Toronto: Canada Law Book, 2002.

Haber, Harvey M. *The Commercial Lease: A Practical Guide*. 3d ed. Toronto: Canada Law Book, 1999.

Haber, Harvey M., ed. *Distress: A Commercial Landlord's Remedy*. Toronto: Canada Law Book, 2001.

Haber, Harvey M. *Landlord's Rights and Remedies in a Commercial Lease: A Practical Guide*. Toronto: Canada Law Book, 1996.

Haber, Harvey M. *Tenant's Rights and Remedies in a Commercial Lease: A Practical Guide*. Toronto: Canada Law Book, 1998.

Haber, Harvey M. *Understanding the Commercial Agreement to Lease*. Toronto: Canada Law Book, 1990.

Hall, Daniel D. *How to Win at the Ontario Rental Housing Tribunal*. Toronto: Butterworths, 2000.

Hoffer, Joseph J.M. *Practical Guide to the Tenant Protection Act*. Toronto: Canada Law Book, 1999.

Lamont, Donald H.L. *Residential Tenancies*. 6th ed. Toronto: Carswell, 2000.

Overtveld, Joy, ed. *Ontario Residential Tenancies Law*. Looseleaf. Toronto: Carswell, 1991.

EE. LEGAL PRACTICE

Scope This section sets out resources that relate to the practice of law, ranging from legal ethics, conflicts of interest, and law practice management.

Subject
headings   Attorney and client — Canada
Conflict of interests — Canada
Lawyers — Malpractice — Canada
Legal ethics — Canada
Practice of law — Canada

CED   Title 16, Vol. 3: Barristers and Solicitors
Title 117, Vol. 27: Professions and Occupations

Can. Abr.   Vol. R3B Reissue: Barristers and Solicitors
Vol. R32: Professions and Occupations

Journals   *Appeal: Review of Current Law and Law Reform* (UVIC, 1995).
Available on Quicklaw (database: UVLR).
Canadian Bar Review (Canadian Bar Association, 1923).
Canadian Lawyer (Canada Law Book, 1997).
National (Canadian Bar Association, 1974).

Web Sites   Canadian Bar Association: <http://www.cba.org>

Textbooks   Barker, Jonathan and Vivienne Denton. *The Effective Use of Technology in the Practice of Law.* Toronto: Canada Law Book, 1998.
Buckingham, Donald E. et al. *Legal Ethics in Canada: Theory and Practice.* Toronto: Harcourt Brace Canada, 1996.
CBA Code of Professional Conduct. Available online: <http://www.cba.org/CBA/activities/code/default.asp>.
Chang, Henry J. *The Canadian Lawyer's Guide to Advanced Internet Marketing.* Toronto: Carswell, 1998.
Grant, Stephen M. and Linda Rothstein. *Lawyers' Professional Liability.* Toronto: Butterworths, 1998.
Hutchinson, Allan. *Legal Ethics and Professional Responsibility.* Toronto: Irwin Law, 1999. Available on Quicklaw (database identifier: HUTC).
Jollimore, Mary. *A Lawyer's Guide to Managing the Media.* Toronto: Canada Law Book, 2000.
Lysyk, Kenneth N. and Lorne Sossin. *Barristers and Solicitors in Practice.* Looseleaf. Toronto: Butterworths, 1998.
MacKenzie, Gavin. *Lawyers & Ethics: Professional Responsibility and Discipline.* Looseleaf. Toronto: Carswell, 1993.
Manes, Ronald D. and Michael Silver. *Solicitor-Client Privilege in Canada.* Toronto: Butterworths, 1993.
Manes, Ronald D. and Michael Silver. *The Law of Confidential Communications in Canada.* Toronto: Butterworths, 1996.

Oughtred, Wendy E. *Going it Alone: A Start Up Guide for the Sole Practitioner*. Toronto: Canada Law Book, 1995.

Perrell, Paul M. *Conflicts of Interest in the Legal Profession*. Toronto: Butterworths, 1995.

Plant, Albert C. *Making Money: The Business of Law*. Toronto: Canada Law Book, 1993.

Smith, Beverley G. *Professional Conduct for Lawyers and Judges*. Fredericton, NB: Maritime Law Book, 1998.

Tjaden, Ted. *The Law of Independent Legal Advice*. Toronto: Carswell, 2000.

Zwicker, Milton W. *Developing and Managing a Successful Law Firm*. Toronto: Carswell, 1995.

FF. MEDIA/DEFAMATION LAW

Scope   This section discusses media law and the law of defamation, a topic governed by various (largely) provincial legislation and case law. See also Communications Law, discussed above.

Subject headings   Freedom of the press — Canada
Libel and slander — Canada
Mass media — Law and legislation — Canada
Press law — Canada

CED   Title 45, Vol. 8A: Defamation

Can. Abr.   Vol. R13: Defamation

Textbooks   Brown, Raymond. *Defamation Law: A Primer*. Toronto: Carswell, 2003.

Brown, Raymond. *The Law of Defamation in Canada*. 2d ed. Looseleaf. Toronto: Carswell, 1994.

Crawford, Michael G. *The Journalist's Legal Guide*, 2d ed. Toronto: Carswell, 1990.

Downard, Peter A. *Libel*. Toronto: Butterworths, 2003.

Duarte, Tony. *Canadian Film & Television Business & Legal Practice*. Looseleaf. Toronto: Canada Law Book, 2000.

Jobb, Dean. *The Fine Print: A Writer's Guide to Canadian Media Law*. Toronto: Emond Montgomery, 2004.

Jollimore, Mary. *A Lawyer's Guide to Managing the Media*. Toronto: Canada Law Book, 2000.

Martin, Robert. *Media Law*. 2d ed. Toronto: Irwin Law, 2003. First edition available on Quicklaw (database identifier: MART).

Martin, Robert. *Speaking Freely: Expression and the Law in the Commonwealth.* Toronto: Irwin Law, 1999. Available on Quicklaw (database identifier: MASF).

McConchie, Roger D. and David A. Potts. *Canadian Libel and Slander Actions.* Toronto: Irwin Law, 2004.

Porter, Julian. *Canadian Libel Practice.* Toronto: Butterworths, 1986.

Williams, Jeremy S. *The Law of Libel and Slander in Canada.* 2d ed. Toronto: Butterworths, 1987.

GG. MOTOR VEHICLE AND TRANSPORATION LAW

Scope	Motor vehicle law is governed largely by provincial legislation (with the exception of such things as federal *Criminal Code* driving offences). Case law interpreting legislation is highly relevant.
Subject headings	Insurance, No-fault automobile — Law and legislation — [jurisdiction] Motor vehicles — Law and legislation — [jurisdiction] Liability for traffic accidents — [jurisdiction] Traffic regulations — [jurisdiction]
CED	Title 12, Vol. 1A: Aviation and Air Law Title 23, Vol. 4: Carriers Title 70, Vol. 14: Highway Traffic Title 71, Vol. 14: Highways and Streets Title 122, Vol. 28: Railways Title 134, Vol. 30: Shipping
Can. Abr.	Vol. R1A Reissue: Aviation and Aeronautics Vol. R5: Carriers Vol. R19 Reissue: Highways and Traffic Vol. R 23: Maritime Law Vol. R25: Motor Vehicles Vol. R32: Railways
Quicklaw	Motor Vehicle and Transportation Law — Global Database: MVLT (includes individual databases)
Case law reporters	*Motor Vehicle Reports* (Carswell, 1979) *Ontario Accident Benefit Case Summaries* (CCH Canadian, 1994)
Journals	*Journal of Motor Vehicle Law* (Carswell, 1989)

Textbooks Flaherty, James M. *Financial Services Commission of Ontario (Motor Vehicle Insurance): Law and Practice*. Looseleaf. Toronto: Canada Law Book, 1998.

Gold, Alan D. *Defending Drinking and Driving Cases*. Toronto: Carswell [annual].

Gold, Alan D. *Drinking and Driving Law*. Toronto: Carswell, 2000.

Gold, Edgar et al. *Maritime Law*. Toronto: Irwin Law, 2004.

Gregory, Eleanor A. and George F.T. Gregory. *The Annotated British Columbia Insurance (Motor Vehicle) Act*. 2d ed. Looseleaf. Toronto: Carswell, 1990.

Hutchison, Scott C. et al. *The Law of Traffic Offences*. 2d ed. Toronto: Carswell, 1998.

Linden, Allen M. and Stephen Eric Firestone. *Butterworths Ontario Motor Vehicle Insurance Practice Manual*. Looseleaf. Toronto: Butterworths, 1995.

McLeod, R.M. et al. *Breathalyzer Law in Canada: The Prosecution and Defence of Drinking and Driving Offences*. 3d ed. Looseleaf. Toronto: Carswell, 1998.

Muir, Douglas B. and Michael Libby. *Annotated British Columbia Motor Vehicle Act*. Looseleaf. Toronto: Canada Law Book, 2000.

Oatley, Roger G. and John McLeish. *The Oatley-McLeish Guide to Personal Injury Practice in Motor Vehicle Cases*. Looseleaf. Toronto: Canada Law Book, 2002.

Segal, Murray D. *The Annotated Ontario Highway Traffic Act*. Toronto: Carswell [annual].

Segal, Murray D. *Manual of Motor Vehicle Law*. 3d ed. Looseleaf. Toronto: Carswell, 1982

HH. MUNICIPAL AND PLANNING LAW

Scope Municipal and planning law is governed almost exclusively by provincial legislation but is affected by case law and the decisions of provincial municipal and planning boards that have statutory jurisdiction to rule on matters of municipal or planning law. Be aware that municipalities and their employees are often entitled to the benefit of shorter limitation periods.

Subject headings
Eminent domain — Canada
Municipal corporations — Canada
Zoning law — Canada

CED Title 71, Vol. 14: Highways and Streets

Title 97, Vol. 21: Municipal and School Taxes
Title 98, Vol. 22: Municipal Corporations
Title 110, Vol. 25: Planning and Zoning
Title 118, Vol. 27: Public Authorities and Public Officers

Can. Abr.   Vol. R16A Reissue: Expropriation
Vol. R26, R27, R27A Reissue: Municipal Law
Vol. R32 Reissue: Public Authorities

Quicklaw   Municipal Law — Global Database: MUN (includes individual databases)

Case law   *Municipal and Planning Law Reports* (Carswell, 1976)
reporters   *Ontario Municipal Board Reports* (Canada Law Book, 1973)

Journals   *Municipal Liability Risk Management Newsletter* (Butterworths Canada)

Textbooks Boghosian, David G. and J. Murray Davison. *The Law of Municipal Liability in Canada.* Looseleaf. Toronto: Butterworths, 1999.

Buholzer, William. *British Columbia Planning Law and Practice.* 2d ed. Looseleaf. Toronto: Butterworths, 2001.

Chipman, John. *The Ontario Municipal Act: A Comprehensive Guide.* Looseleaf. Toronto: Canada Law Book, 2003.

Coates, John A. and Stephen F. Waque. *New Law of Expropriation.* Looseleaf. Toronto: Carswell, 1990.

Gill, David. *Annotated British Columbia Assessment Act.* Looseleaf. Toronto: Canada Law Book, 1997.

Gregory, Eleanor et al. *Annotated British Columbia Local Government Act and Community Charter.* Looseleaf. Toronto: Canada Law Book, 2001.

Hillel, David, ed. *Thomson Rogers on Municipal Liability.* Toronto: Canada Law Book, 1996.

Krushelnicki, Bruce W. *A Practical Guide to the Ontario Municipal Board.* Toronto: Butterworths, 2003.

MacLean, Viriginia and Thomas Richardson. *A User's Guide to Municipal By-Laws.* Toronto: Butterworths, 2001.

Makuch, Stanley M. et al. *Canadian Municipal and Planning Law,* 2d ed. Toronto: Carswell, 2004.

Mascarin, John and Paul De Francesca. *Annotated Land Development Agreements.* Looseleaf. Toronto: Carswell, 2001.

Rogers, Ian M. *Canadian Law of Planning and Zoning.* Looseleaf. Toronto: Carswell, 1988.

Rogers, Ian M. *The Law of Canadian Municipal Corporations.* 2d ed. Looseleaf. Toronto: Carswell, 1988.

Rogers, Ian M. *Municipal Councillors' Handbook.* 6th ed. Toronto: Carswell, 1993.

Rust-D'Eye, *George. The Ontario Municipal Act: A User's Manual.* Toronto: Carswell, 2004.

Todd, Eric. *The Law of Expropriation and Compensation in Canada.* 2d ed. Toronto: Carswell, 1992.

Troister, Sidney H. *The Law of Subdivision Control in Ontario: A Practical Guide to Section 50 of the Planning Act.* 2d ed. Toronto: Carswell, 1994.

Walker, Jack A. and Jerry Grad. *Ontario Property Tax Assessment Handbook.* 2d ed. Looseleaf. Toronto: Canada Law Book, 1998.

Weir Foulds LLP. *Ontario Planning Practice: Annotated Statutes and Regulations.* Looseleaf. Toronto: Canada Law Book, 1989.

II. OCCUPATIONAL HEALTH AND SAFETY LAW

Scope   Occupational health and safety is a special subset of employment law that is governed by (largely) provincial legislation — such as Ontario's *Occupational Health and Safety Act,* R.S.O. 1990, c. O.1 — aimed at ensuring safe work environments.

Subject   Industrial hygiene — Law and legislation — [jurisdiction]
headings Industrial safety — Law and legislation — [jurisdiction]

CED   Title 102.1, Vol. 23: Occupational Health and Safety

Can. Abr. Vol. 14A Reissue: Employment Law

Web Sites Canadian Centre for Occupational Health and Safety: <http://www.ccohs.ca>

Textbooks Arnott, Bruce et al. *Annotated Occupational Health and Safety Act.* Looseleaf. Toronto: Canada Law Book, 1998.

Ferguson, Reg. *WHMIS Compliance Manual.* Looseleaf. Toronto: Carswell, 1989.

Glasbeek, Sandra and Fred Campbell. *Occupational Health and Safety in Ontario Education: A Risk and Compliance Manual.* Looseleaf. Toronto: Butterworths, 2001.

Grossman, Michael. *The Law of Occupational Health and Safety in Ontario.* 2d ed. Toronto: Butterworths, 1994.

Humphrey, Charles E. and Cheryl A. Edwards. *The Employer's Health and Safety Manual — Ontario Edition.* 2d ed. Looseleaf. Toronto: Carswell, 1995.

Keith, Norman A. *Canadian Health and Safety Law: A Comprehensive Guide to the Statutes, Policies and Case Law*. Looseleaf. Toronto: Canada Law Book, 1997.

Keith, Norman A. *Practical Guide to Occupational Health and Safety Compliance in Ontario*. 2d ed. Toronto: Canada Law Book, 2000.

Robertson, Dilys. *ABCs of OH&S — Ontario*. Looseleaf. Toronto: Carswell, 1993.

Rock, Nora and Fred Campbell. *Occupational Health and Safety in Ontario Health Care: A Risk and Compliance Manual*. Looseleaf. Toronto: Butterworths, 2002.

JJ.   PENSION LAW

Scope   Pension law is a specialized subset of employment law focusing on federal and provincial pension legislation and case law interpreting that legislation. It is relevant in a number of areas of practice, particularly in family law (regarding valuation of matrimonial property), personal injury law, and employment law.

Subject   Pensions — Law and legislation — [jurisdiction]
headings   Pensions — Valuation — [jurisdiction]

CED   Title 7, Vol. 1A: Annuities
              Title 108, Vol. 25: Pensions and Retirement Benefits

Can. Abr. Vol. R30: Pensions

Case law   *Canadian Cases on Pensions and Benefits* (Carswell, 2004)
Reporters

Journals   *Compensation and Benefits Update* (Carswell, 2004)
              Estates, Trusts and Pensions Journal (Canada Law Book, 1988)

Web Sites Canada Pension Plan: <http://www.sdc.gc.ca/en/isp/cpp/cpptoc.shtml>
              Mercer Canada: <http://www.mercerhr.ca>

Textbooks CCH Canadian. *Canadian Employment Benefits and Pension Guide Reports*. Looseleaf. Toronto: CCH Canadian, 1963.
              Lloy, Douglas J. *CPP Disability Pension Guide*. Toronto: Butterworths, 2003.
              MacDonald, J. Bruce. *Carswell's Benefits Guide*. Looseleaf. Toronto: Carswell, 1999.

McSweeney, Ian J. and David S. McFarlane. *Pension Benefits Law in Ontario*. Looseleaf. Toronto: Carswell, 1996.

Mercer Human Resource Consulting. *The Mercer Pension Manual*. Looseleaf. Toronto: Carswell, 1989. Also available in a modified format as a CD-ROM called *Mercer Pension Manager*.

Patterson, Jack and Catherine D. Aitken, eds. *Pension Division and Valuation: Family Lawyers' Guide*. 2d ed. Toronto: Canada Law Book, 1995.

Seller, Susan G. *Ontario Pension Law Handbook*. Toronto: Canada Law Book, 1994.

KK. PERSONAL PROPERTY SECURITY LAW

Scope Personal property security law in Canada is a matter of provincial law that has largely been harmonized across most Canadian provinces. Case law interpreting provincial legislation is highly relevant.

Subject headings Security (Law) — [jurisdiction]
Personal property — [jurisdiction]

CED Title 112, Vol. 26: Pledges
Title 131, Vol. 29: Secured Transactions in Personal Property

Can. Abr. Vol. R6: Chattel Mortgages and Bills of Sale
Vol. R30 Reissue: Personal Property Security

Case law Reporters *Personal Property Security Act Cases* (Carswell)

Journals *Commercial Times* (CCH Canadian, 1995)
National Debtor/Creditor Review (Butterworths)

Textbooks Bennett, Frank. *Bennett on PPSA (Ontario)*. 2d ed. Toronto: CCH Canadian, 1999.

Cuming, Ronald C.C. and Roderick J. Wood. *British Columbia Personal Property Security Act Handbook*. 4th ed. Toronto: Carswell, 1999.

Cuming, Ronald C.C. and Roderick J. Wood. *Saskatchewan and Manitoba Personal Property Security Acts Handbook*. 4th ed. Toronto: Carswell, 1999.

Goldberg, Barry I. and Steven G. Golick. *Guide to Ontario Personal Property Security*. Looseleaf. Toronto: Carswell, 1990.

Kleppmann, Karl F. *Security Documents: An Annotated Guide.* Toronto: Canada Law Book, 1999.

McLaren, Richard H. *Secured Transactions in Personal Property in Canada.* 2d ed. Looseleaf. Toronto: Carswell, 1989. Also available on InsolvencySource on WestlaweCARSWELL (by subscription).

Ziegel, Jacob S. and David L. Denomme. *The Ontario Personal Property Security Act: Commentary and Analysis.* Toronto: Canada Law Book, 1994.

Ziegel, Jacob S. et al. *Secured Transactions in Personal Property and Suretyships: Cases, Texts and Materials.* 4th ed. Toronto: Emond Montgomery, 2003.

LL.   PRIVACY LAW

Scope   Privacy law is increasingly relevant in modern society. In Canada, privacy is regulated by federal statutes, such as the *Personal Information Protection and Electronic Documents Act*, S.C. 2000, c. 5 and the *Access to Information Act*, R.S.C. 1985, c. A-1 and parallel provincial statutes.

Subject   Freedom of information — Canada
headings   Privacy, Right of — Canada

CED   Title 1.1, Vol. 1: Access to Information and Protection of Privacy

Can. Abr.   Vol. R32: Public Authorities
Vol. R34A Reissue: Torts

Journals   *Canadian Privacy Law Review* (LexisNexis Canada)

Web Sites   Centre for Innovation Law and Policy:
<http://www.innovationlaw.org>
Office of the Privacy Commissioner of Canada:
<http://www.privcom.gc.ca>

Textbooks   Charnetski, William A. et al. *The Personal Information Protection and Electronic Documents Act: A Comprehensive Guide.* Toronto: Canada Law Book, 2001.

Drapeau, Michel W. and Marc-Aurèle Racicot. *Federal Access to Information Act and Privacy Legislation 2004.* Toronto: Carswell [annual].

Edwards, J.J. *Human Resources Guide to Workplace Privacy.* Toronto: Canada Law Book, 2003.

Fortier, Louis. *Canadian Legislation on Access to Information.* Toronto: Carswell [annual].

Long, Murray and Suzanne Morin. *The Canadian Privacy Law Handbook.* Looseleaf. Ottawa: ENS eLearning Solutions, 2001.

McNairn, Colin H.H. and Alexander K. Scott. *A Guide to the Personal Information Protection and Electronic Documents Act, 2004.* Toronto: Butterworths, 2004.

McNairn, Colin H.H. et al. *Privacy Law in Canada.* Toronto: Butterworths, 2001.

Perrin, Stephanie et al. *Personal Information Protection and Electronic Documents Act: An Annotated Guide.* Toronto: Irwin Law, 2001. Available on Quicklaw (database identifier: PIPE).

Platt, Priscilla et al. *Privacy Law in the Private Sector: An Annotation of the Legislation in Canada.* Looseleaf. Toronto: Canada Law Book, 2002.

Woodbury, Christopher D. and Colin H.H. McNairn. *Government Information: Access and Privacy.* Looseleaf. Toronto: Carswell, 1990.

MM. PROPERTY LAW (REAL AND PERSONAL)

Scope   Real property law is governed largely by provincial legislation too numerous to list here, although judicial interpretations of this legislation also impact real estate practice.

Subject headings   Condominiums — Law and legislation — [jurisdiction]
Mortgages — Canada
Property — Canada
Real estate business — Law and legislation — Canada
Vendors and purchasers — Canada

CED   Title 1, Vol. 1: Absentees
Title 13, Vol. 2: Bailment
Title 19, Vol. 3: Boundaries and Surveys
Title 27.1, Vol. 4A: Condominiums
Title 50, Vol. 9: Drainage
Title 51, Vol. 9: Easements
Title 60, Vol. 12: Expropriation
Title 66, Vol. 13: Fraudulent Conveyances and Preferences
Title 68, Vol. 14: Gifts
Title 96, Vol. 21: Mortgages
Title 109, Vol. 25: Perpetuities and Accumulations

Title 109.1, Vol. 25: Personal Property
Title 110, Vol. 25: Planning and Zoning
Title 123, Vol. 28: Real Property
Title 130, Vol. 29: Sale of Land

Can. Abr.   Vol. R2: Bailment and Warehousing
Vol. R5: Boundaries and Surveys
Vol. R13: Drainage
Vol. R13: Easements
Vol. R16A: Expropriation
Vol. R17D Reissue: Gifts
Vol. R24: Mortgages
Vol. R30: Perpetuities and Accumulations
Vol. R32 Reissue: Real Property
Vol. R32A Reissue: Sale of Land
Vol. R33 Reissue: Statute of Frauds

Quicklaw   Real property law — Global Database: RPLT (includes individual databases)

Case law   *Real Property Reports* (Carswell)
reporters

Textbooks   Alexandrowicz, George. *Real Estate Transactions: Cases, Text and Materials.* Toronto: Emond Montgomery, 2002.

Benson, Marjorie L. and Marie-Ann Bowden. *Understanding Property — A Guide to Canada's Property Law.* Toronto: Carswell, 1997.

Burke, Margaret R. *Ontario Real Estate Procedures.* 2d ed. Toronto: Carswell, 1994.

Butterworths Canada. *Ontario Residential Real Estate Practice Manual.* Looseleaf. Toronto: Butterworths, 1992.

CCH Canadian. *Prairie Real Estate Law Guide.* Looseleaf. Toronto: Carswell, 2004. Available in print and by Internet subscription.

Coburn, Frederick F. and Garth Manning. *Toxic Real Estate Manual.* Looseleaf. Toronto: Canada Law Book, 1994.

DiCastri, Victor. *The Law of Vendor and Purchaser.* 3d ed. Looseleaf. Toronto: Carswell, 1988.

DiCastri, Victor. *Registration of Title to Land.* Looseleaf. Toronto: Carswell, 1988.

Donahue, D.J. et al. *Real Estate Practice in Ontario.* 6th ed. Toronto: Butterworths, 2003.

Foster, William F. *Real Estate Agency Law in Canada*. 2d ed. Toronto: Carswell, 1994.

Gardiner, J. Robert. *The Condominium Act 1998: A Practical Guide*. Toronto: Canada Law Book, 2001.

Gray, Wayne S. *Marriott and Dunn: Mortgage Remedies in Ontario*. 5th ed. Looseleaf. Toronto: Carswell, 1991.

Lamont, Donald H.L. *Lamont on Real Estate Conveyancing*. Looseleaf. Toronto: Carswell, 1976.

Lipson, Barry. *The Art of the Real Estate Deal*. Scarborough, ON: Carswell, 1997.

Loeb, Audrey M. *The Condominium Act: A User's Manual*. Looseleaf. Toronto: Carswell, 2001.

Loeb, Audrey M. *Condominium Law and Administration*. 2d ed. Looseleaf. Toronto: Carswell, 1989.

MacIntosh, C.W. *Nova Scotia Real Property Practice Manual*. Looseleaf. Toronto: Butterworths, 1992.

Maguire, Robert and Rose H. McConnell. *British Columbia Real Estate Law Guide*. Looseleaf. Toronto: Carswell, 1979. Available in print, on CD-ROM, and by Internet subscription.

McCallum, Margaret and Alan M. Sinclair. *Introduction to Real Property Law*. 4th ed. Toronto: Butterworths, 1997.

McConnell, Rose. *Document Registration Guide*, 5th ed. Toronto: CCH Canadian, 2002.

McDermott, Jim et al. *Canadian Commercial Real Estate Manual*. Looseleaf. Toronto: Carswell, 1986. Available in print, on CD-ROM, and by Internet subscription.

McKenna, Bruce. *Title Insurance: A Guide to Regulation, Coverage and Claims Process in Ontario*. Toronto: CCH Canadian, 1999.

McKenna, Bruce et al. *Ontario Real Estate Law Guide*. Looseleaf. Toronto: Carswell, 1975. Available in print, on CD-ROM, and by Internet subscription.

Moore, Marguerite. *Title Searching & Conveyancing in Ontario*. 5th ed. Toronto: Butterworths, 2003.

Mossman, Mary Jane and William F. Flanagan. *Property Law: Cases and Commentary*. Toronto: Emond Montgomery, 1997.

Oosterhoff, A.H. and W.B. Rayner. *Anger and Honsberger: Law of Real Property*. 2d ed. Aurora, ON: Canada Law Book, 1985.

Perell, Paul M. and Bruce H. Engell. *Remedies and the Sale of Land*. 2d ed. Toronto: Butterworths, 1998.

Reiter, Barry J. et al. *Real Estate Law*. 4th ed. Toronto: Emond Montgomery, 1992.

Roach, Joseph E. *The Canadian Law of Mortgages of Land*. Toronto, Butterworths, 1993.

Salvatore, Bruce et al. *Agreements of Purchase and Sale*. Toronto: Butterworths, 1996.

Smythe, Scott D. and E.M. Vogt. *McCarthy Tétrault Annotated British Columbia Strata Property Act*. Looseleaf. Toronto: Canada Law Book, 2002.

Traub, Walter M. *Falconbridge on Mortgages*. 5th ed. Looseleaf. Aurora, ON: Canada Law Book, 2003.

Walma, Mark W. *Advanced Residential Real Estate Transactions*. Toronto: Emond Montgomery, 1999.

Ziff, Bruce A. *Principles of Property Law*. 3d ed. Toronto: Carswell, 2000.

Ziff, Bruce A. *A Property Law Reader: Cases, Questions and Commentary*. Toronto: Carswell, 2004.

NN. SECURITIES LAW

Scope   Securities law in Canada is highly regulated by provincial and federal securities and corporate legislation too numerous to list here.

Subject   Securities — Canada
headings   Stock exchanges — Law and legislation — Canada
Investments — Law and legislation — Canada
Mutual funds — Law and legislation — Canada

CED   Title 132, Vol. 30: Securities and Stock Exchanges

Can. Abr.   Vol. R33 Reissue: Securities and Commodities

Quicklaw   Securities regulation — Global Database: SEC (includes individual databases)

Case law   *Canadian Cases on the Law of Securities* (Carswell, 1993–1998)
reporters

Journals   *Canadian Securities Law Review* (Osler, Hoskin & Harcourt, 1995)
Corporate Securities and Finance Law Report (Jewel Publications, 1997)
Ontario Securities Commission Bulletin

CD-ROMs   *Securities Partner Plus* [CD-ROM]. Toronto: Carswell. Updated regularly. Contains securities-related legislation, case law, and full-text commentary. Available in an expanded version as *Securities-Source* on WestlaweCARSWELL (by subscription).

Web Sites   Bora Laskin Law Library Securities Law Guide: <http://www.law-lib.utoronto.ca/resguide/sec.htm>

SEDAR (Canadian stock exchange documents): <http://www.sedar.com>

SecuritiesSource: <http://www.westlawecarswell.com/securities-source> [subscription required]

Securities Protos (CCH Canadian, by subscription)

Textbooks   Borden Ladner Gervais LLP. *Securities Law and Practice*. 3d ed. Looseleaf. Toronto: Carswell, 1988. Available on *Securities-Source* on WestlaweCARSWELL (by subscription).

Canadian Securities Institute. *The Canadian Securities Course*. Toronto: Canadian Securities Institute, 2004.

Canadian Stock Exchanges Manual. North York, ON: CCH Canadian, 1994.

Gillen, Mark R. *Securities Regulation in Canada*. 2d ed. Scarborough, ON: Carswell, 1998.

Grottenthaler, Margaret E. and Philip J. Henderson. *The Law of Financial Derivatives in Canada*. Looseleaf. Toronto: Carswell, 1998.

Hendrickson, Barbara. *Canadian Institutional Investment Rules*. Toronto: CCH Canadian, 2003.

Hendrickson, Barbara. *Canadian Securities Law Reporter*. Toronto: CCH Canadian, 2003. Available in print, on CD-ROM, and by Internet subscription.

Hunter, W.T. *Canadian Financial Markets*. 3d ed. Peterborough, ON: Broadview Press, 1991.

Johnston, David L. and Kathleen Rockwell. *Canadian Securities Regulation*. 3d ed. Toronto: Butterworths, 2003.

MacIntosh, Jeff G. and Christopher Nicholls. *Securities Law*. Toronto: Irwin Law, 2002. Available on Quicklaw (database identifier: MANI).

Puri, Poonam and Jeffrey Larsen. *Corporate Governance and Securities Regulation in the 21st Century*. Toronto: Butterworths, 2004.

Puri, Poonam and Leslie McCallum. *Canadian Companies' Guide to the Sarbanes-Oxley Act*. Toronto: Butterworths, 2004.

Shiff, Arthur S. et al., eds. *Canadian Securities Law Precedents*. Looseleaf. Toronto: Carswell, 1989. Available on *Securities-Source* on WestlaweCARSWELL (by subscription).

Stikeman Elliott. *Legal for Life: Institutional Investment Rules in Canada*. 6th ed. Toronto: Carswell, 1996.

> *Toronto Stock Exchange Company Manual.* Looseleaf. North York,
> ON: CCH Canadian, 1976. Available in print, on CD-ROM,
> and by Internet subscription.

OO. SPORTS AND ENTERTAINMENT LAW

Scope   Sports and entertainment law has developed in recent years into a
              fairly specialized practice area, focusing on contracting and licens-
              ing for entertainers and athletes. Entertainment and sports lawyers
              frequently deal with contract law, intellectual property law, and
              negotiations.

Subject   Motion pictures — Law and legislation — Canada
headings   Performing arts — Law and legislation — Canada
              Recreation — Law and legislation — Canada
              Sports — Law and legislation — Canada
              Television programs — Law and legislation — Canada

CED   Title 135.1, Vol. 31: Sports

Textbooks Barnes, John. *Sports and the Law in Canada.* 3d ed. Toronto: But-
              terworths, 1996.

              Bird, Stephen and John Zauhar. *Recreation and the Law.* 2d ed.
              Toronto: Carswell, 1997.

              Duarte, Tony. *Canadian Film & Television Business & Legal Practice.*
              Looseleaf. Toronto: Canada Law Book, 2000.

              King, Jacqueline L. *Entertainment Law in Canada.* Looseleaf.
              Toronto: Butterworths, 2000.

PP.   TAXATION LAW

Scope   Taxation law in Canada is governed primarily by the federal *Income
              Tax Act,* R.S.C. 1985, c. 1 (5th Supp.) and the *Excise Tax Act,* R.S.C.
              1985, c. E-15, which are administered by Canada Revenue Agency
              (CRA). The CRA has extensive regulatory and administrative docu-
              mentation on its Web site, including forms, information circula-
              tions, and interpretation bulletins. Provincial tax legislation is also
              relevant. There is a plethora of print and online legal resources on
              Canadian taxation law that is too numerous to list here, so the list
              of books below is only a partial list. Check the Web sites of the
              Canadian legal publishers for more information.

Subject headings	Excise tax — Law and legislation — Canada Goods and services tax — Law and legislation — Canada Income tax — Law and legislation — Canada
CED	Title 41, Vol. 8: Customs and Excise Title 76, Vol. 15, 15A: Income Tax Title 128, Vol. 29: Revenue
Can. Abr.	Vol. R12: Customs Vol. R19A, R19B, R19C, R19D Reissue: Income Tax Vol. R34: Taxation
Quicklaw	Taxation law topical — Global Database: TAX (includes individual databases)
Case law reporters	*Canada Tax Cases* (Carswell, 1917) *Dominion Tax Cases* (CCH Canadian, 1920)
Journals	*Canadian Current Tax* (Toronto: Butterworths, 1960) *Canadian Tax Journal* (Toronto: Canadian Tax Foundation, 1953) *The Canadian Taxpayer* (Toronto: Carswell, 1979)
CD-ROMs	*Dominion Tax Cases* (CCH Canadian) *GST Partner* [CD-ROM]. Toronto: Carswell. Updated regularly. Contains relevant legislation, case law, and commentary from Carswell's GST Service. *TaxPartner* [CD-ROM]. Toronto: Carswell. Updated regularly. Contains relevant legislation, case law, and commentary from Carswell-authored textbooks on tax law.
Web Sites	Canada Revenue Agency: <http://www.cra-arc.gc.ca> Canada Tax Foundation: <http://www.ctf.ca> Taxnet.pro: <http://www.carswell.com/taxnetpro.asp> (by subscription)
Textbooks	Brown, Catherine A. and Cindy L. Radu. *Taxation and Estate Planning*. Looseleaf. Toronto: Carswell, 1996. Campbell, Colin. *Income Tax Administration in Canada*. Looseleaf. Scarborough, ON: Carswell, 1995. *Canada Income Tax Law and Policy*. Looseleaf. Toronto: Carswell, 1990. CCH Canadian Limited. *Canadian Master Tax Guide*. Don Mills, ON: CCH Canadian, 1946 [annual updates]. Related income tax material available from CCH Canadian in print, on CD-ROM, and by Internet subscription [see link under CCH Tax Works). Cuperfain, Joel T. and Florence Marino. *Canadian Taxation of Life Insurance*. 2d ed. Toronto: Carswell, 2004.

Drache, Arthur. *Canadian Taxation of Charities & Donations.* Looseleaf. Toronto: Carswell, 1990.

Duff, David G. *Canadian Income Tax Law: Cases, Text and Materials.* Toronto: Emond Montgomery, 2002.

Edgar, Tim et al. *Materials on Canadian Income Tax.* 12th ed. Toronto: Carswell, 2000.

Erlichman, Harry, ed. *Tax Avoidance in Canada: The General Anti-Avoidance Rule in Canada.* Toronto: Irwin Law, 2002. Available on Quicklaw (database identifier: TXAV).

Gorman, Barry. *Canadian Income Taxation: Policy and Practice.* 2d ed. Toronto: Carswell, 2001.

Hanson, Suzanne. *Canada Tax Manual.* Looseleaf. Toronto: Carswell, 1990.

Hogg, Peter H. et al. *Principles of Canadian Income Tax Law.* 4th ed. Scarborough, ON: Carswell, 2002.

Innes, William I. and Ralph Cuervo-Lorens. *Tax Evasion.* Looseleaf. Toronto: Carswell, 1995.

Krishna, Vern. *Canada's Tax Treaties.* Looseleaf. Toronto: Butterworths, 1999.

Krishna, Vern. *The Fundamentals of Canadian Income Tax.* 7th ed. Scarborough, ON: Carswell, 2002.

Krishna, Vern. *Income Tax Law.* Concord, ON: Irwin Law, 1997. Available on Quicklaw (database identifier: KRIS).

Krishna, Vern. *Canadian International Taxation.* Looseleaf. Toronto: Carswell, 1995.

McMechan, Robert and Gordon Bourgard. *Tax Court Practice.* Looseleaf. Toronto: Carswell, 1995.

PriceWaterhouseCoopers LLP. *Canadian Insurance Taxation.* 2d ed. Toronto: Butterworths, 2000.

Sherman, David M. *The Practitioner's Goods and Services Tax Annotated.* 14th ed. Toronto: Carswell, 2003.

Sherman, David M. *Canadian Tax Research: A Practical Guide.* 3d ed. Toronto: Carswell, 1997.

Sherman, David M. *The Practitioner's Income Tax Act.* Scarborough, ON: Carswell [annual].

Stikeman, H.H. *Annotated Income Tax Act.* Toronto: Carswell [annual].

Tari, A. Christina. *Federal Income Tax Litigation in Canada.* Looseleaf. Toronto: Butterworths, 1997.

Tobias, Norman C. *Taxation of Corporations, Partnerships and Trusts.* 2d ed. Toronto: Carswell, 2001.

QQ. TORT LAW

Scope   Tort law is traditionally governed by case law, although provinces in Canada are increasingly introducing "no fault" insurance schemes governing injuries arising from motor vehicle accidents. Tort law can also be affected by provincial negligence legislation, such as British Columbia's *Negligence Act*, R.S.B.C. 1996, c. 333. Also included below are books dealing with products liability.

Subject   Negligence — Canada
headings   Products liability
                Torts — Canada

CED   Title 89, Vol. 20: Malicious Prosecution and False Imprisonment
            Title 101, Vol. 23: Negligence
            Title 102, Vol. 23: Nuisance
            Title 139, Vol. 31: Torts
            Title 142, Vol. 32: Trespass

Can. Abr.   Vol. R28, R29 Reissue: Negligence
                 Vol. R34A Reissue: Torts

Quicklaw   Tort law — Global Database: TORT (includes individual databases)

Case law   *Canadian Cases on the Law of Torts* (Carswell, 1976)
reporters

Textbooks   Beaulac, Stéphane et al., eds. *The Joy of Torts*. Toronto: Butterworths, 2003.

Cassels, Jamie and Craig Jones. *The Law of Large-Scale Claims: Product Liability, Mass Torts, and Complex Litigation in Canada*. Toronto: Irwin Law, 2004.

Edgell, Dean F. *Product Liability in Canada*. Toronto: Butterworths, 2000.

Ellis, Mark Vincent. *Fiduciary Duties in Canada*. Looseleaf. Toronto: Carswell, 1990.

Feldthusen, Bruce. *Economic Negligence: The Recovery of Pure Economic Loss*. 4th ed. Toronto: Carswell, 2000.

Fridman, G.H.L. *Introduction to the Canadian Law of Torts*. Toronto: Butterworths, 2003.

Fridman, G.H.L. *The Law of Torts in Canada*. 2d ed. Toronto: Carswell, 2002.

Grace, Elizabeth K.P. and Susan M. Vella. *Civil Liability for Sexual Abuse and Violence in Canada*. Toronto: Butterworths, 2000.

Kerr, Margaret H. *Canadian Tort Law in a Nutshell*. Toronto: Carswell, 1997.

Klar, Lewis. *Tort Law*. 3d ed. Toronto: Carswell, 2003.

Klar, Lewis et al., *Remedies in Tort*. Looseleaf. Toronto: Carswell, 1987.

Linden, Allen M. *Canadian Tort Law*. 7th ed. Toronto: Butterworths, 2001.

Linden, Allen M. *Canadian Tort Law: Cases, Notes and Materials*. 12th ed. Toronto: Butterworths, 2004.

Osborne, Philip H. *The Law of Torts*. 2d ed. Toronto: Irwin Law, 2003. Available on Quicklaw (database identifier: OSBO).

Solomon, Robert M. et al. *Cases and Materials on the Law of Torts*. 6th ed. Toronto: Carswell, 2003.

Theall, Lawrence G. et al. *Product Liability: Canadian Law and Practice*. Looseleaf. Toronto: Canada Law Book, 2001.

Waddams, Stephen. *Products Liability*. 4th ed. Toronto: Carswell, 2002.

Weinrib, Ernest J. *Tort Law: Cases and Materials*. 2d ed. Toronto: E. Montgomery, 2003.

RR. TRUSTS, WILLS, AND ESTATES LAW

Scope   Trusts and estates law are generally a combination of case law and (largely provincial) legislation, originally strongly influenced by English law.

Subject   Trusts and trustees — Canada
headings   Estate planning — Canada

CED   Title 22, Vol. 3: Burial and Cremation
Title 35, Vol. 5: Coroners and Medical Examiners
Title 46, Vol. 9: Devolution of Estates
Title 59, Vol. 12: Executors and Administrators
Title 93, Vol. 20: Mental Incompetency
Title 144, Vol. 33: Trusts
Title 150, Vol. 34: Wills

Can. Abr.   Vol. R5: Burial and Cemeteries
Vol. R24: Mental Incompetency
Vol. 32: Estates and Trusts (3d)

Quicklaw   Wills, Estates & Trust law — Global Database: WETT (includes individual databases)

Case law   *Estates & Trusts Reports* (Carswell, 1977)
reporters

Journals   *Annual Review of Estate Law* (Carswell, 1996)
Estates, Trusts and Pension Journal (Canada Law Book, 1973)
Will Power (CCH Canadian, 1994)

CD-ROMs *Estates Partner (Ontario)* [CD-ROM]. Updated regularly. Contains relevant legislation, case law and Carswell-published textbooks on wills and estates.

Textbooks Allen, William P.G. and John P. Allen. *Estate Planning Handbook.* 3d ed. Scarborough, ON: Carswell, 1999.

Armstrong, Anne E.P. *Estate Administration: A Solicitor's Reference Manual.* Looseleaf. Toronto: Carswell, 1988.

Botnick, David I. *Probate Guide for Ontario.* 11th ed. North Vancouver, BC: Self-Counsel Press, 2002.

Botnick, David I. *Wills for Ontario.* 15th ed. North Vancouver, BC: Self-Counsel Press, 1997.

CCH Canadian Limited. *Canadian Estate Administration Law Guide.* Looseleaf. North York, Ontario: CCH Canadian, 1995. Available in print, on CD-ROM, and by Internet subscription.

CCH Canadian Limited. *Executor's Handbook.* 2d ed. North York, Ontario: CCH Canadian, 2003.

Crummey, Sheila M. et al. *Financial and Estate Planning for the Mature Client in Ontario.* Looseleaf. Toronto: Butterworths, 1997.

Easterbrook, Susan A. *Mediating Estate Disputes.* Toronto: Canada Law Book, 2003.

Gibbs, Karen M. et al. *The Practical Guide to Ontario Estate Administration.* 4th ed. Toronto: Carswell, 2002.

Gillen, Mark and Faye Woodman, eds. *The Law of Trusts: A Contextual Approach.* Toronto: Emond Montgomery, 2000.

Gillese, Eileen E. *The Law of Trusts.* Concord, ON: Irwin Law, 1997. Available on Quicklaw (database identifier: GILE).

Greenan, Jennifer. *The Executor's Handbook.* 2d ed. Toronto: CCH Canadian, 2003.

Harvey, Cameron. *The Law of Dependents' Relief in Canada.* Toronto: Carswell, 1999.

Howard, Judy and George Monticone. *Long-Term Care Facilities in Ontario: The Advocate's Manual.* 2d ed. Looseleaf. Toronto: Advocacy Centre for the Elderly, 2001.

Hull, Ian M. *Power of Attorney Litigation*. Looseleaf. Toronto: CCH Canadian, 2000.

Hull, Ian M. *Challenging the Validity of Wills*. Toronto: Carswell, 1996.

Hull, Rodney and Ian M. Hull. *Macdonell, Sheard and Hull on Probate Practice*. 4th ed. Toronto: Carswell, 1996.

Hunter, Fiona et al. *Financial and Estate Planning for the Mature Client in British Columbia*. Looseleaf. Toronto: Butterworths, 2000.

Jenkins, Jennifer J. *Compensation for Estate Trustees*. Toronto: Canada Law Book, 1997.

Jenkins, Jennifer J. and H. Mark Scott. *Duties of Estate Trustees, Guardians and Attorneys*. Toronto: Canada Law Book, 2000.

Kessler, James and Fiona Hunter. *Drafting Trusts and Will Trusts in Canada*. Toronto: Butterworths, 2003.

MacGregor, Mary L. *Preparation of Wills and Powers of Attorney: First Interview to Final Report*. 3d ed. Toronto: Canada Law Book, 2004.

MacKenzie, James. *Feeney's Canadian Law of Wills*. 4th ed. Looseleaf. Toronto: Butterworths, 2000.

McTeer, M.A. *Tough Choices: Living and Dying in the 21st Century*. Toronto: Irwin Law, 1999. Available on Quicklaw (database identifier: MCTE).

Oosterhoff, A.H. et al. *Oosterhoff on Trusts: Text, Commentary and Materials*. 6th ed. Toronto: Carswell, 2004.

Oosterhoff, A.H. *Oosterhoff on Wills and Succession: Text, Commentary and Materials*. 5th ed. Toronto: Carswell, 2001.

Oosterhoff, A.H. and E.E. Gillese. *Text, Commentary and Cases on Trusts*. 5th ed. Toronto: Carswell, 1998.

Rintoul, Margaret E. *Ontario Estate Administration*. 4th ed. Toronto: Butterworths, 2000.

Schnurr, Brian A. *Estate Litigation*. 2d ed. Looseleaf. Toronto: Carswell, 1994.

Scott-Harston, J.C. and P.A. Johnson. *Tax Planned Will Precedents*. 3d ed. Looseleaf. Toronto: Carswell, 1989.

Sokol, Stan J. *Mistakes in Wills in Canada*. Toronto: Carswell, 1995.

Solnik, Robyn and Mary-Alice Thompson. *Drafting Wills in Ontario: A Lawyer's Practical Guide*. Toronto: CCH Canadian, 2003.

Spenceley, Robert. *Estate Administration in Ontario: A Practical Guide*. 2d ed. Toronto: CCH Canadian, 1999.

Spenceley, Robert. *Who Will Make Decisions When You Can't? Ontario's Substitute Decisions Act*. Toronto: CCH Canadian, 1999.

Sweatman, M. Jasmine. *Guide to Powers of Attorney*. Toronto: Canada Law Book, 2002.

Thériault, Carmen, ed. *Widdifield on Executors and Trustees*. 6th ed. Looseleaf. Toronto: Carswell, 2002.

Waters, Donovan W.M. *The Law of Trusts in Canada*. 2d ed. Toronto: Carswell, 1984.

Youdan, Timothy G. *Equity, Fiduciaries and Trusts*. Toronto: Carswell, 1989.

SS. WORKERS' COMPENSATION LAW

Scope   Workers' compensation law is a specialized subset of employment and labour law that focuses on statutory regimes that determine the amount of money an injured worker is entitled to when injured on the job. It is generally governed by provincial legislation, such as *Ontario's Workplace Safety and Insurance Act, 1997*, S.O. 1997, c. 16, Sched. A, with disputes being heard before the relevant workers' compensation tribunal.

Subject headings   Workers' compensation — Law and legislation — [jurisdiction]

CED   Title 151, Vol. 34: Workers' Compensation

Can. Abr.   Vol. R14AA Reissue: Employment Law

Textbooks   Anstruther, Richard. *Employers' Guide to Ontario Workplace Safety & Insurance*. Looseleaf. Toronto: Carswell, 1999.

Dee, Garth et al. *Butterworths Workers' Compensation in Ontario Service*. Looseleaf. Toronto: Butterworths, 1993.

Gilbert, Douglas G. and L.A. Liversidge. *Workers' Compensation in Ontario: A Guide to the Workplace Safety and Insurance Act*. 3d ed. Toronto: Canada Law Book, 2001.

Moher, Michael and Jane Adam. *Ontario Workplace Insurance: Claims Management and Return to Work*. Looseleaf. Toronto: Carswell, 1998.

Robertson, Dilys. *CLV — Special Report — Accident Investigation in the Workplace*. Toronto: Carswell, 2004.

Starkman, David. *Ontario Workplace Safety and Insurance Act*. Toronto: Emond Montgomery, 1998.

CHAPTER 9

SELECTING AND ACQUIRING LEGAL RESOURCES

A. INTRODUCTION

Up to this point, this book has focused on how to use legal resources. For some legal researchers, this will suffice since the focus of their work is hands-on legal research. Other lawyers or legal researchers, however, will need to choose or recommend for acquisition particular legal resources for a law library, be it as part of a small law firm or personal collection or as part of a larger organization. Very little has been written on how to acquire legal resources.[1] While it helps to have a good working knowledge of legal resources when deciding what to acquire, there are certain things that many lawyers or legal researchers may not be aware of on this topic, matters that often fall within the expertise of a law librarian. This chapter is therefore aimed at lawyers or other legal researchers who need to make decisions about selecting and acquiring legal resources. Information is provided on the following topics:

- deciding between print and electronic resources
- criteria for selecting material for a law library

---

1 See, e.g.. Douglass T. MacEllven & Michael J. McGuire, "Law Firm Libraries" in *Legal Research Handbook*, 5th ed. (Toronto: Butterworths, 2003) 407; and the resources listed at the end of this chapter.

- managing a small law firm law library
- negotiating licences for electronic resources

Additional resources are set out at the end of this chapter for those readers needing more detailed information on selecting and acquiring legal research resources.

B. DECIDING BETWEEN PRINT AND ELECTRONIC RESOURCES

Over the last decade or so, law libraries have faced the dilemma of deciding whether to acquire material in *print* versus material in *electronic format* (or both). In many cases, law libraries acquire both print and online resources, in part to cater to patrons who prefer one format over the other and in part to experiment with the online version of a product. In some cases, material may only be available in one format and therefore no decision between formats is required.

There are several advantages to acquiring material in print that are often regarded as disadvantages in an online environment:

- **Permanency**: Print materials can be stored or archived, thereby protecting the investment made in the books and ensuring long-term accessibility. Online materials, however, tend to be more volatile, especially on the Internet, where addresses often change and sites get shut down.
- **Ownership**: Print materials are generally bought and owned by the purchaser, unlike many online materials, which are merely licensed for access, thereby making the licencee subject to the pricing whims or viability of the publisher. If the user stops paying for licensing a CD-ROM, for example, the user usually loses access to the information, unlike print resources, which would remain available on the shelf even if the print subscription is cancelled.
- **Comfort level**: People generally prefer to read from books rather than computer screens; there is a comfort level in using print materials, whether it be in the ability to flip quickly through pages or read from page to page. In addition, most lawyers prefer the comfort of citing materials to specific pages in a book, something that is often more difficult in an online environment.
- **Wide availability**: For the foreseeable future, most law-related materials will continue to be available in print, especially books and other monographs that are less likely ever to be available in electronic format.

Despite these advantages of print materials, there are also some fairly obvious disadvantages to law-related print materials that tend to be regarded as advantages in an online environment:

- **Storage and maintenance costs**: Print materials require space to be shelved. Many law-related print publications, such as case reporters, grow larger every year. Looseleaf legal publications require staff to file the looseleaf pages on an ongoing basis. Online materials, on the other hand, tend to take up much less space, can be read from a laptop and accessed 24 hours per day.
- **Poor indexing**: Legal materials in print tend to be poorly indexed, due in part to the Canadian market for legal materials being so small, thereby giving less incentive for publishers to invest heavily in the cost of indexing print materials. Online materials, on the other hand, are searchable by keyword and often by sophisticated search strategies (e.g., by case name or by judge's name) making it easy to find relevant material in an online environment.
- **Publication delays**: There is typically a delay in publishing legal materials in print. Having current information in law is generally very important. This is a huge advantage of online legal materials where some databases are current to within 24 hours.
- **Bill back**: Lawyers generally are unable to bill back the cost of their overhead in maintaining a print law library but are able sometimes to bill back to the client the cost of online searches.[2] Thus, in theory, a law firm can run its research department and legal research by using online databases on a break-even basis where the cost of online searches is billed back to clients and there being little overhead investment in stocking and maintaining a print collection.

In deciding between print and online material, the following questions should be considered:

- Is there a strong preference for print resources among the primary users of the materials?
- Are there significant cost or content differentials between the print and online material?
- Does material need to be used primarily within the office?
- Is there storage room available for print material?
- Are staff members available to maintain the shelving and looseleaf filing of print material? Conversely, is there adequate technical systems support if you emphasize material in electronic format?

---

2   See the discussion of this topic and a list of cases in which court costs have been awarded for legal research in Chapter 1, section A.

- How computer literate are the primary users of the material?
- How receptive will your clients be to being billed for online searches?
- Are there publicly available law libraries nearby that can be used?

There are no obvious answers regarding whether one should prefer print or online materials. The decision is often made on the following major criteria: the ability to store and maintain a print collection, the computer literacy of the primary users of the material, and the types and topics of material being acquired.

C. CRITERIA FOR SELECTION OF MATERIAL

Unfortunately, legal materials do not select themselves. From large academic law libraries to small law firm libraries, decisions must be made about what sort of materials to acquire, how much to spend, and who will maintain the collection once it is acquired.

Legal materials to be acquired can be broken down into the following broad categories:

- **Legislation**: Of most importance for the selection of legislation is federal legislation and legislation for the province in which the material is being acquired. Larger law libraries will also maintain legislation from other provinces. Consider using online sources for legislation (e.g., CD-ROMs, government Web sites, Quicklaw, Lexis-Nexis, Canada Law Book, or WestlaweCARSWELL) unless print is strongly desired (if print materials are not being kept, you must consider how you will access older legislation in print — is there a nearby courthouse or law school law library that maintains a complete archive of historical legislation?). If print is chosen, consider your space needs for ever-expanding material. Regarding draft legislation in the form of bills, there is a move now towards relying upon Quicklaw, *CCH Legislative Pulse*, or government Web sites for such information instead of subscribing to print versions of bills. Once again, this decision will often be made on user preferences.
- **Case law**: Choices here for Canadian case law include national reporters (*Supreme Court Reports*, *Federal Court Reports*, *Dominion Law Reports*, and *National Reporter*), regional reporters (*Western Weekly Reports* or *Atlantic Provinces Reports*), and provincial reporters or topical reporters. Once again, consider obtaining electronic sources of case law (CD-ROM or commercial legal databases, for example) unless print is strongly desired. Chapter 8 identifies some of the major topical case law reporters.

- **Textbooks**: Textbooks are discussed in Chapter 2, section A and are listed by topic in Chapter 8. Since most books are still being published in print only, the decision to be made with books is often between preferring bound versus looseleaf publications. With looseleaf services comes the advantage of information being kept current. The disadvantage, of course, is the added cost of maintaining the subscription and of filing the updated supplemental pages (and the cost of replacing missing or stolen pages). Table 9.1 sets out the Web sites of some of the major Canadian legal publishers whose sites can be searched for textbooks, usually by topic, author, title, or keyword. Alternatively, use the list of textbooks by topic in Chapter 8 to help decide which sort of materials may be required.

Table 9.1
Web Sites of Major Canadian Legal Publishers

Publisher	Web Site Address
Butterworths Canada	http://www.lexisnexis.ca
Canada Law Book	http://www.canadalawbook.ca
Carswell	http://www.carswell.com
CCH Canadian	http://www.cch.ca
Éditions Yvon Blais	http://www.editionsyvonblais.qc.ca
Emond Montgomery	http:/www.emp.on.ca
Irwin Law	http://www.irwinlaw.com
Lancaster House	http://www.lancasterhouse.com
Maritime Law Book	http://www.mlb.nb.ca
Quicklaw	http://www.lexisnexis.ca/ql/en/about/about.html
Self-Counsel Press	http://www.self-counsel.com
SOQUIJ	http://www.soquij.qc.ca
Wilson & LaFleur	http://www.wilsonlafleur.com

- **Reference materials**: There are a wide variety of reference materials that lawyers or legal researchers should consider acquiring, including encyclopedias, legal dictionaries, legal directories, applicable Rules of Court, and forms and precedents materials. Chapter 2 discusses these materials in more detail and should be consulted. Reference materials are increasingly available in electronic format.

    In general, when selecting any type of legal material, consider the following criteria:

- **Reputation of the author**: Is the author a lawyer or legal academic? Is the author known in his or her area of expertise? Has the author published before?

- **Reputation of the publisher**: The reputation of the publishers listed in Table 9.1 is strong for legal materials and these publishers can be relied upon to publish good quality material. When selecting law-related material from other publishers it is important to consider the reputation of that publisher for publishing reliable material.

- **Relevance of topic**: Only the largest law library will be able to acquire legal materials for all legal topics. Selection must often therefore be made based on users' needs and on what materials are essential for the lawyers or researchers using the collection.

- **Looseleaf versus bound**: As discussed above, decisions must often be made between looseleaf material and bound material. While looseleaf material has the advantage of being current, it costs time and money to continue the subscription and to ensure that the looseleaf filing is being properly done.

- **Standing orders**: Many publishers will encourage law libraries to subscribe to material that is published annually on a "standing order" basis. This means that material will automatically be shipped and invoiced when it is published. While this has its advantages, it can also result in less control to the law library. In addition, libraries on a budget may wish to consider a cost-saving measure by not ordering paper "supplements" to textbooks and waiting instead for a new "hard cover" edition to be issued.

- **Print versus online**: When assessing whether to acquire legal material in print or online (or both), it is important to evaluate whether one version provides the same or enhanced coverage compared to the other version and whether both versions are required in any event due to differing user needs and abilities.

There are a number of tools to help in the selection of materials. Publishers are more than happy to send out catalogues and brochures regarding their publications. The problem, if anything, is getting too much of this material. Another method is to simply check the Web sites of the Canadian legal publishers periodically or to check the publishers' advertisements that are found in a number of law-related publications. Some of the larger academic law libraries use "book-buying" agents (such as YBP Library Services) to create "approval plans" based on a profile of the individual library and the types of materials the library would like to acquire. Once set up, the agent will provide the library will customized "slips" of new titles for possible purchase by the library. For busy law firms, the easiest thing to do is hire a law librarian to make these sorts of decision for the firm.

D. MANAGING A SMALL LAW LAW LIBRARY

Legal researchers are often involved in the organization or running of a law firm's law library. For larger firms, a decision may be made to hire a part-time or full-time law librarian. As a rough rule of thumb, firms of say thirty-five to forty-five lawyers can usually justify the need for a full-time librarian to manage their in-house law library. Larger firms will often have a team of librarians and other library technicians managing their library. Smaller firms will often make do with a part-time librarian or will simply have some other person within the organization manage the library collection.

There are several things to consider about managing a small law firm law library:

- **Hiring a law librarian**: In Canada, a librarian is usually someone with a two-year Master's degree from a University library school program that is accredited by the American Library Association. The training would include a number of things, including how to catalogue and classify information, how to manage a library, how to provide reference and research services, and how to create and update Web pages. In some cases, courses are offered specifically on law librarianship.[3] To place an advertisement to hire a law librarian in Canada, there is the Jobs Web site at the Faculty of Information Studies[4] and the Jobline of the Foothills Library Association (emphasizing positions in Western Canada).[5] When advertising for a law librarian it is critical to be specific in the technical skills that are expected (e.g., online searching, cataloguing, Internet authoring).

- **Maintenance**: Regardless of who is hired to manage a law firm's library, there are many things that the person must manage and maintain, including the selection and acquisition of material, cataloguing and labelling of material, shelving of material, weeding of material, and selective dissemination of information (informing users about new material relevant to their research needs). The larg-

---

3   The author has regularly taught a course on law librarianship at the Faculty of Information Studies, University of Toronto — see the course Web site at <http://www.fis.utoronto.ca/courses/LIS/2133/>.

4   See online: Faculty of Information Studies <http://plc.fis.utoronto.ca/resources/jobsite//index.htm>.

5   See online: Foothills Library Association <http://www.fla.org/jobline.html>.

er the law library, the greater the need to devote resources to the maintenance of the collection.

- **Research and reference support**: Another important aspect of managing a law firm law library is to set up procedures for providing research and reference support. Will the firm have a "stand-alone" research lawyer to conduct legal research or will the work instead fall to articling students or other (typically junior) lawyers in the firm? Will the library be expected to work closely with articling students by providing them with training and support? Will the library staff offer research training to lawyers in the firm? The answer to these sorts of questions will depend on the size and type of firm. Law librarians, unless they are also lawyers, should not be giving legal advice (and should be seen not to be giving legal advice). Despite this, it is possible to bill the services of a law librarian for some aspects of research and reference support.
- **Space planning and technology**: What amount of space will the library need (allowing for growth of any print resources in the collection)? Will the library house research computers with CD-ROM drives and Internet access? Will the library materials be catalogued in an online catalogue? If so, will the catalogue be available on each lawyer's desktop or only available on a library terminal? What sort of technical support will the library need?
- **Web site and Intranet**: Increasingly, in-house law libraries play a key role in the firm's Web site and intranet as a means to disseminate information both externally and internally. Many organizations are now appreciating the value of institutionalizing their shared knowledge. This can be done in several ways regarding legal research: the firm — through a law librarian — can organize searchable or browsable databases of the firm's legal research memos, opinion letters, forms, and agreements. In addition, the firm can use an Intranet to share information among lawyers within the firm, including information on clients, on practice management, and on current awareness. When hiring a law librarian, it is therefore important to consider the Internet authoring skills of any applicants.

E. NEGOTIATING LICENCES FOR ELECTRONIC RESOURCES

As discussed above, a major disadvantage of electronic resources is the general lack of ownership of the materials being paid for. One is paying for *access* to the material, not ownership. Thus, once one stops paying for the CD-ROM or access to the database, there is generally no further access (for CD-ROMs, this happens where there is a built-in "time bomb" feature to disable the CD-ROM after the expiry of the licence period). Some care must therefore be taken when entering into licence agreements for CD-ROMs or online databases. The following points are usually the major issues that arise when entering into licence agreements to acquire law-related resources in electronic format:

- **Audience? Single user versus multiple users?** Most publishers quite naturally charge more when electronic resources are being accessed by multiple users. It is usually quite obvious when "single user" access is required, especially for sole practitioners or smaller law firms, and the cost of obtaining single user access is usually straightforward. What can often require negotiation and some explanation is when the electronic resource will regularly be used by more than one person via a computer network. Some vendors have policies to automatically calculate the number of licensed users based on the number of lawyers in the firm, even where not all lawyers in the firm will use the product. It therefore becomes necessary to evaluate how much the particular resource will be used and by how many people at the same time.
- **Controlling multi-user access**: For commercial online databases, passwords are often assigned to individual users, something that allows tracking of searches by individuals. In some settings, particularly academic law libraries, passwords to some law-related Internet subscription databases can be controlled by an IP (Internet Protocol) address, thereby allowing any user within the organization to access the database. Regardless, care must be taken to prudently manage passwords to online databases, including access to the firm's intranet or other internal computer file folders that are related to legal research.
- **Hardware and software requirements**: In acquiring CD-ROMs, it is important to check any specific hardware or software requirements for the product. The move to electronic resources in legal research saves space and labour costs associated with print law-related materials but does involve heavy investments in hardware technology. For larger firms, such matters will often be handled through technology departments that will assess the firm's technical needs. Fortunately, many legal publishers are moving away from CD-ROM technology to Internet platforms, lessening or eliminating the need for expensive CD-ROM towers to network the CD-ROMs. For Inter-

net subscriptions, it is important to check whether the product requires a newer version of a Web browser interface.

- **Training and support**: It is important to check what level and sort of training the vendors will provide for use of their products. Do they provide training in your office or are you required to attend at their training centre? Is their training free? Do they provide useful handouts and training guides? With online databases made available through a Web browser there is often a much smaller learning curve due to the more intuitive browser interfaces (compared to older DOS-based interfaces). Web browser interfaces often also include good online help or "how to" type information.
- **Scope of content**: Is the electronic resource being acquired full text? Does the online version contain the same or different information from the print equivalent, if any? What sort of search engine is used to find information? How easy is it to find information in the database?
- **Coverage**: What is the coverage of the electronic resources? How current is the resource? How often is it updated?
- **Costs**: How does the vendor bill for access to its electronic resources? Is it an hourly rate? If so, does it vary depending on what database you access? Is it based on the transaction and what information is downloaded? If so, is it easy to know in advance the cost of particular transactions? Does the vendor bill a monthly flat rate fee? If so, how is the flat rate fee calculated and how often is it adjusted and on what basis is it adjusted?
- **Terms of licence**: What rights is the vendor/licenser granting regarding the downloading and storing of information? Is the vendor giving any representations or warranties regarding the information it is licensing? Is the licensee required to indemnify the vendor regarding any claims being made by a third party against the vendor regarding any alleged misuse by the licensee of the product?

By addressing these sorts of issues when negotiating acquisition of electronic resources, it is hoped that the researcher or law firm will be in a better position to negotiate terms that improve access to electronic resources.

F. CONCLUSIONS

The legal research and legal publishing fields are undergoing great change in recent times due to the impact of the Internet and other computer technology. While these changes have greatly improved the work lives of lawyers and legal researchers, they have added to the complexity of decisions that must be made regarding the acquisition of print and electronic legal resources. Change (and potential chaos) will likely reign over the next few years as lawyers and legal researchers decide between print and electronic resources and how to rationalize material (if at all) during this period of change.

G. ADDITIONAL RESOURCES

Set out below are some additional resources on selecting and acquiring legal resources and managing a law library.

Ahlers, Glen-Peter. *The History of Law School Libraries in the United States: From Laboratory to Cyberspace.* Buffalo, NY: William S. Hein & Co., 2002.

Danner, Richard A. *Strategic Planning: A Law Library Management Tool for the 90's and Beyond.* 2d ed. Dobbs Ferry, NY: Glanville Publishers, 1997.

Dragich, Martha J. and Peter C. Schanck. eds., *Law Library Staff Organization and Administration.* Littleton, CO: F.B. Rothman, 1990.

Fenner, Audrey, ed. *Selecting Materials for Library Collections.* Binghamton, NY: Haworth Information Press, 2004.

Harris, Lesley Ellen. *Licensing Digital Content: A Practical Guide for Librarians.* Chicago: American Library Association, 2002.

Hazelton, Penny A. "How Much of Your Print Collection Is Really on Westlaw or Lexis-Nexis?" (1999) 18 Legal Ref. Serv. Q. 3.

Licensing Digital Information: A Resource for Librarians. <http://www.library.yale.edu/~llicense/>. This Web site is the home page of the LibLicense listserv and contains useful information on licensing electronic resources, along with a detailed bibliography of additional materials.

Licensingmodels.com. <http://www.licensingmodels.com>. This Web site contains public domain sample licence agreements for licensing electronic resources aimed at four types of licensees: single academic institutions, academic consortia, public libraries, and corporate and special libraries.

MacEllven, Douglass T. et al. *Guide to Purchasing Law Reports.* Ottawa, Ont.: Canadian Law Information Council, 1985.

Managing the Law Library: Positioning for Change. New York: Practising Law Institute, 1997.

Marke, Julius J. and Richard Sloane. *Legal Research and Law Library Management.* Rev. ed. Looseleaf. New York: Law Journal Seminars-Press, 1990.

Matheson, Scott. "Access versus Ownership: A Changing Model of Intellectual Property" (2002) 21 Legal Ref. Serv. Q. 151.

Megantz, Robert C. *How to License Technology.* New York: John Wiley & Sons, 1996.

Most, Marguerite. "Electronic Law Journals in the Academic Law Library — Law Reviews and Beyond" (2002) 21 Legal Ref. Serv. Q. 189.

Not a Box but a Window: Law Libraries and Legal Education in a Virtual World. Toronto: Faculty of Law, University of Toronto, 2001.

Pace, Andrew K. *The Ultimate Digital Library: Where the New Information Players Meet.* Chicago: American Library Association, 2003.

Panella, Deborah S. *Basics of Law Librarianship.* New York: Haworth Press, 1991.

Ramsay, John T. *Ramsay on Technology Transfers and Licensing.* 2d ed. Toronto: Butterworths, 2002.

Robinson, Douglas. "Negotiating Licensing Agreements for Electronic Resources: A Selective Bibliography" Bibliography Series #7 (ISSN: 1203-2468). Available online: <http://www.collectionscanada.ca/6/7/s7-2604-e.html>.

Russell, Gordon. "Re-Engineering the Law Library Resources Today for Tomorrow's Users: A Response to 'How Much of Your Collection is Really on Westlaw or Lexis-Nexis?'" (2002) 21 Legal Ref. Serv. Q. 29.

Tjaden, Ted. "The Role of the Law Librarian in the Design, Maintenance and Promotion of Internet Sites" (1999) 18 Toronto Association of Law Libraries Newsletter 2.

CHAPTER 10

LEGAL RESEARCH AND WRITING MALPRACTICE

A. INTRODUCTION

The concept of legal research malpractice and the extent to which a lawyer has adequately carried out legal research on behalf of a client is not widely discussed in Canada, although there have been several cases where the topic has been raised. The issue, however, has been more widely litigated in the United States and there is every reason to believe that Canadian courts will readily apply principles of legal research malpractice in appropriate cases where a lawyer has failed to conduct legal research or has done so incompetently. What is less certain is the extent to which Canadian courts will impose a duty on lawyers to conduct online legal research in appropriate cases. Given the increase of material online, and given the depth, accuracy, and speed of commercial online law-related databases, it is likely that courts will regard online legal research skills as a standard by which all lawyers and legal researchers should be judged.

In Chapter 1, section A, brief mention was made of the importance of legal research as a skill that every competent lawyer should possess. The very essence of lawyering assumes that the lawyer, as a legal specialist, either knows the law or can identify and find the relevant law in order to provide a competent legal opinion to the client. In recent years, continuing legal education or life-long learning for lawyers has been an important issue for Canadian provincial law societies and the liability insurers for Canadian lawyers. While there are relatively few cases dealing specifically with legal research malpractice, it is reasonable to assume that the improvement by all lawyers of legal research skills and the other competencies identified by the Law Society of Upper Canada can only reduce the incidences of malpractice claims against lawyers. This chapter looks at Canadian and American cases dealing with legal research malpractice and the consequences of sloppy drafting of court documents, and then attempts to provide some basic tips that lawyers can apply to reduce the risk of being liable for legal research and writing malpractice.

B. CANADIAN CASES ON LEGAL RESEARCH MALPRACTICE

As a general rule, lawyers are required to bring reasonable care, skill, and knowledge to the performance of the professional services they have undertaken to perform.[1] Chapter II(b) (Competence and Quality of Service) of the Canadian Bar Association *Code of Professional Conduct*, for example, admonishes the lawyer to "serve the client in a conscientious, diligent and efficient manner so as to provide a quality of service at least equal to that which lawyers would expect of a competent lawyer in a like situation."[2]

From this general standard of care, Canadian courts have specifically discussed the standard of care required for conducting legal research. In *Central & Eastern Trust Co. v. Rafuse*, for example, at issue was whether the lawyers were negligent in failing to ensure that their clients' mortgage security constituted a valid charge in a situation where the mortgage was later held to be void under Nova Scotia corporate legislation. In holding that the liability of lawyers could arise in both tort and contract for negligently performing services for which they were retained, the Court went further to hold that the lawyers in that particular case were negligent for failing to have ascertained the existence of the relevant corporate legislation that would have affected the enforceability of the mortgage. In so holding, the Supreme Court of Canada applied both American and British law in suggesting that a lawyer, to avoid being negligent, may have a duty to adequately research the law in order to properly advise a client:

---

1   See *Central & Eastern Trust Co. v. Rafuse*, [1986] 2 S.C.R. 147 at 208 [*Rafuse*].
2   (Ottawa: Canadian Bar Association, 1988) at 5.

The requirement of professional competence that was particularly involved in this case was reasonable knowledge of the applicable or relevant law. A solicitor is not required to know all the law applicable to the performance of a particular legal service, in the sense that he must carry it around with him as part of his "working knowledge," without the need of further research, but he must have a sufficient knowledge of the fundamental issues or principles of law applicable to the particular work he has undertaken to enable him to perceive the need to ascertain the law on relevant points. The duty in respect of knowledge is stated in 7 Am. Jur. 2d, "Attorneys at Law" ¶200, in a passage that was quoted by Jones J.A. in the Appeal Division, as follows [[at pp. 269–70]: pp. 269, 147 D.L.R.]: "An attorney is expected to possess knowledge of those plain and elementary principles of law which are commonly known by well-informed attorneys, and to discover those additional rules of law which, although not commonly known, may readily be found by standard research techniques." See *Charlesworth and Percy on Negligence* (7th ed., 1983), pp. 577–78 to similar effect, where it is said: "Although a solicitor is not bound to know the contents of every statute of the realm, there are some statutes, about which it is his duty to know. The test for deciding what he ought to know is to apply the standard of knowledge of a reasonably competent solicitor." The duty or requirement of professional competence in respect of knowledge is put by Jackson and Powell, *Professional Negligence* (1982), at pp. 145–46 as follows: "Although a solicitor is not 'bound to know all the law,' he ought generally to know where and how to find out the law in so far as it affects matters within his field of practice. However, before the solicitor is held liable for failing to look a point up, circumstances must be shown which would have alerted the reasonably prudent solicitor to the point which ought to be researched."[3]

Similar judicial sentiment was expressed in *World Wide Treasure Adventures Inc. v. Trivia Games Inc.*, in which the court applied the *Rafuse* decision in holding the negligent lawyer liable for his client's costs in a botched application for an interim injunction. The court ruled in essence that if the lawyer had properly conducted legal research, he would have uncovered the burden of proof facing his client and would not have proceeded (or presumably have more carefully advised the client of the risks of failing if the injunction application proceeded):

---

3   Above note 1 at 208–9.

In my opinion the conduct of the Plaintiff's solicitors in this case fell far short of the reasonable care, skill and knowledge which the Plaintiff was entitled to expect. The *American Cyanamid* principles ought by now to be part of the working knowledge of a competent counsel in this jurisdiction. *If they are not, then any counsel contemplating an injunction application ought to be able to perceive the need to research the law before preparing the material to be filed. It may be that the Aetna Financial case is not as well known, however a moderate amount of research would quickly have brought it to light, and that research should have been undertaken as part of the preparation for a bid for what are known to competent counsel to be extraordinary remedies not lightly granted by the Court.* It is for these reasons, and in accordance with the principles I have read from the *Rafuse* case that I conclude that the Plaintiff's solicitors were negligent in the performance of their duty to him.[4]

Likewise, in *285614 Alberta Ltd. v. Burnet Duckworth & Palmer*, the law firm was held liable to the client for the firm's professional negligence in structuring a shareholder's loan to allow the clients to purchase a home by securing the loan with a demand promissory note, something that later resulted in the client being subject to adverse income tax consequences. In holding the law firm liable, the court concluded that the lawyer responsible had failed to adequately research the issue regarding the income tax effect of the demand promissory note:

In my view, Spackman did breach the standard of care of a reasonably competent lawyer both in failing to adequately consider or research the requirements of the legislation, and in failing to advise Mrs. Maplesden of the potential for tax consequences.[5]

In *Renner v. O'Connell*,[6] the client was "taxing" his lawyer's account as being excessive. The account was reduced, in part, because the lawyer did not provide exhaustive research for the legal opinion required by the retainer as the lawyer failed to make use of online legal databases.

---

4   (1987), 16 B.C.L.R. (2d) 135 at 141–42 (S.C.) [emphasis added].

5   [1993] 4 W.W.R. 374 at 384 (Alta. Q.B.). For a case to the contrary in which the lawyer was not held to be negligent because he had adequately researched the quantum of the client's potential damages (despite a jury subsequently awarding a higher amount) see *Maillet v. Haliburton & Comeau* (1983), 55 N.S.R. (2d) 311 (S.C.T.D.).

6   (1989), 97 N.B.R. (2d) 200, 245 A.P.R. 200 (Q.B.).

Although no negligence per se was involved in *Gibb v. Jiwan*,[7] the court spent a fair bit of time chastising counsel and suggesting that there would be negative costs implications for their failure to properly conduct research and uncover relatively straightforward commentary and case law on a point of law involving priority interests in land involving a prior unregistered interest:

> Counsel cannot fulfil their duties to the client or the court unless they conduct reasonable research on points of law which are known in advance to be contentious. The court must rely on counsel to conduct reasonably complete research on points of law they raise. That is part of counsel's professional duty. It is desirable that counsel look up difficult or important points on Quicklaw but I can appreciate that this may not be economical in many cases. However, in my view it is not acceptable for any counsel or articling student to come to court intending to argue a contentious point of law without first researching the point at least to the extent of looking up the issue in basic reference books.
>
> In a case like this where counsel know there is a contest as to which cases may be authoritative, I think they also have a duty to cite up cases they rely on to determine whether they are still good law. (I recall that citing up a case was one of the first things I learned in law school and its importance in litigation was emphasized repeatedly during articles.)
>
> The judicial system cannot function effectively unless counsel fulfil this duty because judges cannot possibly know the law on all issues which come before them. Counsel must bear in mind that most justices in the General Division are generalists and hear cases of all kinds.[8]

The judge in *Gibb v. Jiwan* pointed out how easy it was for him to find the relevant case law by looking in the index to Carswell's *Canadian Abridgment* and *Canadian Encyclopedic Digest* and by checking out textbooks on debtor/creditor law and real property law.

---

7   [1996] O.J. No. 1370 (Gen. Div.).
8   *Ibid.* ¶ 34–36.

C. AMERICAN CASES ON LEGAL RESEARCH MALPRACTICE

American cases dealing with legal research malpractice raise similar issues as the foregoing Canadian cases despite the fact that none of these American cases appear to have been considered or applied by any Canadian court. American courts have regularly held that a lawyer is under a duty to his or her client to conduct adequate legal research in order to fully advise the client of his or her rights and/or may risk being held liable in damages for research malpractice.[9]

---

9   *Janik v. Rudy, Exelrod & Zieff*, 2004 WL 1386171 (Cal. App. 2004) [labour law class action law suit, failure to uncover alternative theory of recovery]; *Village Nurseries v. Greenbaum*, 101 Cal. App. 4th 26 (2002) [bankruptcy liens, lawyer liable, failed to establish that his advice was based on informed judgment at the time he advised his client]; *Frank v. Pepe*, 717 N.Y.S. 2d 873 (2000) [divorce action]; *Lieber v. ITT Hartford Ins. Center, Inc.*, 15 P. 3d 1030 (Utah 2000) [insurance company brief inaccurate]; *Shopsin v. Siben & Siben*, 702 N.Y.S. 2d 610 (App. Div. 2000) [real estate transaction]; *Sun Valley Potatoes, Inc. v. Rosholt, Robertson & Tucker*, 981 P. 2d 236 (Idaho 1999) [conduct of counsel at trial]; *McCoy v. Tepper*, 690 N.Y.S. 2d 678 (App. Div. 1999) [limitation period]; *Schutts v. Bentley Nevada Corp.*, 966 F. Supp. 1549 (D. Nev. 1997) [lawyer's liability for costs for filing weak employment law/discrimination claim]; *Fiorentino v. Rapoport*, 693 A. 2d 208 (Pa. Super. Ct. 1997) [corporate matter]; *Massey v. Prince George's County*, 918 F .Supp. 905 (D. Md. 1996) [dog bite case law, under ethical rule requiring attorney to provide competent representation, attorney must have ability to research law, court specifically comments on the ease of "natural language" searches on Westlaw]; *Hart v. Carro, Spanbock, Kaster & Cuiffo*, 620 N.Y.S. 2d 847 (App. Div. 1995) [negligence relating to stock purchase transaction]; *Finkelstein v. Collier*, 636 So. 2d 1053 (La. App. 5th Cir. 1994) [negligence in missing limitation in tort claim]; *Harline v. Barker*, 854 P. 2d 595 (Utah Ct. App. 1993) [negligence relating to lack of knowledge of bankruptcy court procedure]; *Niziolek v. Chicago Transit Authority*, 620 N.E.2d 1097 (Ill. App. Ct. 1993) [limitation period]; *Collas v. Garnick*, 624 A. 2d 117 (Pa. Super. Ct. 1993) [settlement of lawsuit]; *Youngworth v. Stark*, 283 Cal. Rptr. 668 (Ct. App. 1991) [civil procedure, "local rules"]; *Copeland Lumber Yards, Inc. v. Kincaid*, 684 P. 2d 13 (Or. Ct. App. 1984) [limitation period]; *Horne v. Peckham*, 158 Cal. Rptr. 714 (Ct. App. 1979) [negligence in drafting trust agreement without due regard to tax implications]; *Smith v. Lewis*, 530 P. 2d 589 (Cal. 1975) [family law, division of property]. See also *American Jurisprudence* at § 215: "An attorney is expected to possess knowledge of those plain and elementary principles of law which are commonly known by well-informed attorneys, and to discover those additional rules of law which, although not commonly known, may readily be found by standard research techniques. Thus, if the law on a subject is well and clearly defined and has existed and been published long enough to justify the belief that it was known to the profession, a lawyer who disregards the rule or is ignorant of it is liable for losses caused by such negligence or want of skill." [footnotes omitted].

In the oft-cited *Smith v. Lewis*, for example, the defendant lawyer was held liable in negligence for failing to research and properly advise his client regarding the likelihood of the client's pension being "community property":

> In any event, as indicated above, had defendant conducted minimal research into either hornbook or case law, he would have discovered with modest effort that General Smith's state retirement benefits were likely to be treated as community property and that his federal benefits at least arguably belonged to the community as well . . . . Even as to doubtful matters, an attorney is expected to perform sufficient research to enable him to make an informed and intelligent judgment on behalf of his client.[10]

Likewise, in *Horne v. Peckham*,[11] the lawyer was found liable for his negligence in drafting a trust agreement that had negative tax consequences for the client, consequences that would have been obvious if the lawyer had conducted basic legal research. In holding the lawyer liable, the court pointed out the lawyer's duty to either research the law or at least make the client aware of the uncertainty with the law by stating that "an attorney has a duty to avoid involving his client in murky areas of the law if research reveals alternative courses of conduct."[12]

In the United States, however, courts have dismissed legal research malpractice claims against lawyers where the law in question was unsettled, the lawyer at least made good faith efforts to determine the law, and made a mistake of law or error in judgment on a point on which reasonable lawyers might differ, or the lawyer, although subsequently wrong in his or her opinion, at least made the client aware at the time of the risk of the law being reversed or changed in the future.[13]

---

10   530 P. 2d 589 at 596 (Cal. 1975).

11   158 Cal. Rptr. 714 (Ct. App. 1979).

12   *Ibid.* at 720.

13   *Bergstrom v. Noah*, 974 P. 2d 531 (Kan. 1999) [alleged error regarding trial strategy]; *Villavicencio v. State*, 719 So. 2d 322 (Fla. Dist. Ct. App. 1998) [defence counsel's alleged lack of knowledge of criminal procedure]; *Wood v. McGrath, North, Mullin & Kratz, P.C.*, 589 N.W. 2d 103 (Neb. 1999) [family law settlement agreement, lawyer allegedly failed to advise client of uncertainties]; *Collins v. Miller & Miller, Ltd.*, 943 P. 2d 747 (Ariz. Ct. App. 1996) [limitations period]; *U.S. v. Vastola*, 25 F. 3d 164 (3d Cir. 1994) [prosecutor conducted adequate legal research regarding sealing of wiretap evidence]; *Bush v. O'Connor*, 791 P. 2d 915 (Wash. Ct. App. 1990) [civil procedure, limitation period]; *Meir v. Kirk, Pinkerton, McClelland, Savary & Carr, P.A.*, 561 So. 2d 399 (Fla. Dist. Ct. App. 1990) [limitation period]; *Molever v. Roush*, 152 Ariz. 367, 732 P. 2d 1105 (Ct. App.

D. CONSEQUENCES OF CARELESS DRAFTING

The consequences of inadequate research can be devastating to both the client and ultimately the lawyer in the form of embarrassment and potential professional liability. Equally embarrassing are those situations where courts have sanctioned lawyers for their careless drafting of court documents, such as motions, pleadings, and factums (or briefs). There are a number of Canadian and American decisions in which courts have denied costs to lawyers (and their clients) as a form of punishment for sloppy legal writing that has caused confusion or extra work for the court or the other party; some American decisions go further and sanction or penalize the individual lawyer.

In *Toll v. Marjanovic*, for example, even though the defendant's lawyer was ultimately successful on a summary judgment motion to dismiss the plaintiff's application for specific performance, the court denied the defendant costs on this motion due to the sloppy nature of the motion materials prepared by the defendant's lawyer:

> The fact that there was confusion generated by the drafting of the notice of motion, which came close to requiring an adjournment of the motion after the better part of the argument had taken place, inevitably means that there was a waste of some time and effort resulting in avoidable costs being incurred. The defendant must bear the consequences of that result.[14]

In *AMJ Campbell Inc. v. Kord Products Inc.*,[15] even though there was no suggestion of sloppy drafting, the court had to resolve a dispute over the drafting of a letter of intent. In what is known as the "million dollar comma case," at issue was the insertion of a comma in the definition of "Average Selling Price," which resulted in a difference to the

---

1986) [defamation action]; *Sharpe v. Superior Court, Sacramento County*, 192 Cal. Rptr. 16 (Ct. App. 1983) [family law, pension rights]; *Wright v. Williams*, 121 Cal. Rptr. 194 (Ct. App. 1975) [maritime law, documents of title]; *Young v. Bridwell*, 437 P. 2d 686 (Utah 1968) [failing to file an appeal]; *Martin v. Burns*, 429 P. 2d 660 (Ariz. 1967) [civil procedure]. See also David D. Dodge, "Lawyer Not Liable for Negligence Regarding Unsettled Issues of Law" (2000) 36 Ariz. Att'y 20 and cases cited therein.

14   [2001] O.J. No. 1529 ¶ 5 (S.C.J.). For similar results, see: *National Bank of Canada v. Pelletier* (1980), 34 N.B.R. (2d) 614 (Q.B.); *Humby Enterprises Ltd. v. A.L. Stuckless & Sons Ltd.* (2003), 225 Nfld. & P.E.I.R. 268, 2003 NLCA 20 (C.A.); *Bouteiller v. Bouteiller* (1997), 116 Man. R. (2d) 153 (Q.B.); *Royal Bank v. Robb* (1977), 19 N.S.R. (2d) 368 (C.A.).

15   (2003), 63 O.R. (3d) 375 (S.C.J.).

parties of one million dollars, depending on whether or not the comma was placed after the word "freight" in the definition. In denying rectification of the agreement, the court was satisfied that the vendor — the party now complaining about the insertion of the comma — was aware of the insertion, which was in fact inserted by its counsel in an earlier draft of the document.

In the United States, there have been a number of recent decisions in which the court has drawn attention to sloppy drafting. In *B.A.M. Development, L.L.C. v. Salt Lake County*, for example, the dissenting judge drew attention, in a footnote to the decision, to the inappropriate drafting style of the brief filed by the appellant's lawyer, a brief that used unnecessary bolding, underlining, and use of "all caps" and exclamation points:

> To the extent BAM has successfully persuaded me of the fundamental soundness of its position, that success should not be attributed, in any degree, to its counsel's unrestrained and unnecessary use of the bold, underline, and "all caps" functions of word processing or his repeated use of exclamation marks to emphasize points in his briefs. Nor are the briefs he filed in this case unique. Rather, BAM's counsel has regularly employed these devices in prior appeals to this court. While I appreciate a zealous advocate as much as anyone, such techniques, which really amount to a written form of shouting, are simply inappropriate in an appellate brief. It is counterproductive for counsel to litter his brief with burdensome material such as "WRONG! WRONG ANALYSIS! WRONG RESULT! WRONG! WRONG! WRONG!"[16]

Likewise, in *Devore v. City of Philadelphia*, the court took exception to the poorly drafted pleadings of the plaintiff's counsel, even though the plaintiff was ultimately successful in his jury trial alleging employment discrimination against the City. In addition to a substantial jury verdict, the plaintiff was awarded his costs, but the City objected to the fees submitted by the plaintiff's lawyer, a Mr. Puricelli, as being excessive, especially in light of his poor paperwork. The court agreed and significantly reduced the amount of fees Mr. Puricelli was entitled to:

> Mr. Puricelli's written work is careless, to the point of disrespectful. The Defendants have described it as "vague, ambiguous, unintelligible, verbose and repetitive." See Response, at 2. We agree. Although the Defendants have taken issue with some of the typographical

---

16   87 P. 3d 710 at 734 (Utah App. 2004).

errors present in Mr. Puricelli's filings, the problems with his pleadings have gone beyond typos.

. . .

As previously mentioned, Mr. Puricelli's filings are replete with typographical errors and we would be remiss if we did not point out some of our favorites. Throughout the litigation, Mr. Puricelli identified the court as "THE UNITED STATES DISTRICT COURT FOR THE EASTER [sic] DISTRICT OF PENNSYLVANIA." Considering the religious persuasion of the presiding officer, the "Passover" District would have been more appropriate. However, we took no personal offense at the reference. In response to the attorneys' fees petition, the Defendants note that the typographical errors in Mr. Puricelli's written work are epidemic. In response to this attack, Mr. Puricelli writes the following:

> As for there being typos, yes there have been typos, but these errors have not detracted from the arguments or results, and the rule in this case was a victory for Mr. Devore. Further, had the Defendants not tired [sic] to paper Plaintiff's counsel to death, some type [sic] would not have occurred. Furthermore, there have been omissions by the Defendants, thus they should not case [sic] stones.

If these mistakes were purposeful, they would be brilliant. However, based on the history of the case and Mr. Puricelli's filings, we know otherwise. Finally, in the most recent letter to the court, asking that we vacate the settlement agreement, Mr. Puricelli identifies the undersigned as "Honorable Jacon [sic] Hart." I appreciate the elevation to what sounds like a character in the Lord of the Rings, but alas, I am but a judge.[17]

The decision of *Re Wilkins* involved the disrespectful and sarcastic language in an appeal brief the lawyer had filed seeking an appeal:

The Court of Appeals' published Opinion in this case is quite disturbing. It is replete with misstatements of material facts, it misapplies controlling case law, and it does not even bother to discuss relevant cases that are directly on point. Clearly, such a decision should be reviewed by this Court. Not only does it work an injustice on appellant Michigan Mutual Insurance Company, it establishes dangerous

---

17   2004 WL 414085 (E.D.Pa. Feb. 20, 2004) (No CIV.A. 00-3598).

precedent in several areas of the law. This will undoubtedly create additional problems in future cases.[2]

> FN2 Indeed, the Opinion is so factually and legally inaccurate that one is left to wonder whether the Court of Appeals was determined to find for Appellee Sports, Inc., and then said whatever was necessary to reach that conclusion (regardless of whether the facts or the law supported its decision).[18]

In a 3–2 split decision, the Supreme Court of Indiana ordered a thirty-day suspension for the lawyer's use of such disrespectful language, although the dissenting judges held that the language in the footnote was speech protected by the First Amendment, even if it was "heavy-handed."[19]

Precision Specialty Metals, Inc. v. U.S., is more a situation of misleading the court rather than careless drafting, but it raises a cautionary note for all litigators. In that case, the United States Court of Appeal upheld sanctions on a Department of Justice lawyer for "misquoting and failing to quote fully from two judicial opinions in a motion for reconsideration she signed and filed."[20] In that case, the lower court — the Court of International Trade — had denied the lawyer's motion for reconsideration when she failed to file materials "forthwith" as demanded by the court (she filed them some twelve days later). In a motion for reconsideration, the lawyer signed and filed a brief setting out arguments on the definition of "forthwith." In support of her arguments, she allegedly intentionally omitted parts of the *Black's Law Dictionary* definition of "forthwith" and "cropped" parts of quotes from judicial decisions that were unfavourable to her argument and changed the meanings of the quotes. She also failed to cite a leading U.S. Supreme Court decision that defined the term as usually meaning within twenty-four hours:

> The effect of Walser's editing of this material and ignoring the Supreme Court decision that dealt with the issue — a decision that

---

18   777 N.E. 2d 714 at 715–16 (Ind. 2002).

19   *Ibid.* at 719 ff.

20   315 F. 3d 1346 at 1347 (Fed. Cir. 2003). For additional cases where counsel have been sanctioned for mis-citations, see: *Abbs v. Principi*, 237 F. 3d 1342 (Fed. Cir. 2001); and *Porter v. Farmers Supply Service*, 790 F. 2d 882 (Fed. Cir. 1986). For additional cases where counsel were sanctioned for mis-stating the law, see: *Teamsters Local No. 579 v. B & M Transit., Inc.*, 882 F. 2d 274, 280 (7th Cir. 1989); *Borowski v. DePuy, Inc.*, 850 F. 2d 297, 304–5 (7th Cir. 1988); *Jewelpak Corp. v. United States*, 297 F. 3d 1326 (Fed. Cir. 2002).

seriously weakened her argument — was to give the Court of International Trade a misleading impression of the state of the law on the point. She eliminated material that indicated that her delay in filing the motion for reconsideration had not met the court's requirement that she file "forthwith," and presented the remaining material in a way that overstated the basis for her claim that a "forthwith" filing requirement meant she could take whatever time would be reasonable in the circumstances. This distortion of the law was inconsistent with and violated the standards of Rule 11.

By signing the motion for reconsideration, Walser certified that the "claims, defenses, and other legal contentions therein are warranted by existing law." Inherent in that representation was that she stated therein the "existing law" accurately and correctly. She did not do so, however, because her omissions from and excisions of judicial authority mischaracterized what those courts had stated. The effect of her doctored quotations was to make it appear that the weight of judicial authority was that "forthwith" means "a time reasonable under the circumstances." This was quite different from the Supreme Court's statement in *Dickerman* that "[i]n matters of pleading and practice," forthwith "is usually construed, and sometimes defined by rule of court, as within twenty-four hours." By suppressing any reference to *Dickerman*, which both the Second Circuit in *McAllister* and Justice Thomas in his dissent in *Henderson* cited and which the Second Circuit quoted, Walser gave a false and misleading impression of "existing law" on the meaning of "forthwith."[21]

There are, however, a number of cases in which lawyers were *not* sanctioned for failing to uncover relevant precedents (i.e., for inadequate research).[22] In these cases, the lawyer's "offence" was not sanctionable as being an attempt to mislead the court, but in the right circumstances, might amount to a malpractice claim by the client if the lawyer's failure to adequately research resulted in a loss to the client.

The lesson from these examples is obvious: litigators must be careful to state the law accurately, avoid unnecessary sarcasm or hyperbole, and not be misleading.

---

21   *Ibid.* at 1355–56.

22   See *United States v. Stringfellow*, 911 F. 2d 225, 227 (9th Cir. 1990); *Thompson v. Duke*, 940 F. 2d 192, 197–98 (7th Cir. 1991); *Golden Eagle Distrib. Corp. v. Burroughs Corp.*, 801 F. 2d 1531, 1541–42 (9th Cir. 1986).

E. TIPS TO AVOID LEGAL RESEARCH AND WRITING MALPRACTICE

Based on the foregoing Canadian and American case law, and based on the general standards that courts apply in determining whether a lawyer was negligent in a particular transaction, there are a number of things that lawyers can do to reduce the risk of legal research malpractice. Before discussing these tips, it is useful to consider the factors that courts would take into account in determining whether a lawyer will be found liable for legal research malpractice. These factors include

- the complexity of the legal issues and whether the law is unsettled in that particular area;
- the urgency of the matter;
- the steps taken by the lawyer using either print or online resources to ascertain the law for the particular issue; and
- the relationship with the client and whether the lawyer discussed with the client the advisability of further research being done and the risk and consequences the client would face where the law is unsettled for a particular issue.

To minimize careless drafting errors, lawyers should regularly consult "forms and precedents" materials for sample pleadings and agreements and actively edit these sample documents to conform to a client's specific needs. Legal writing is discussed in detail in Chapter 11.

What is less clear in the American (and Canadian) case law is the extent to which a lawyer is obliged to conduct *online* legal research or risk being held negligent in failing to uncover relevant law.[23] Given the increasing use of computers and the availability of flat-rate fees for many of the online commercial databases, the time has likely come when a Canadian court, in the right circumstances, could easily conclude that failure to research a point of law online will result in professional negligence.

Ultimately, the focus should be on conducting good quality legal research that uses the most appropriate sources of information, whether print or online, depending on the circumstances, the issues being

---

23   See Ola Najar, "Computerized Research in the Legal Arena: Developing a Standard of Research Sufficiency in Legal Malpractice and Rule 11 Actions" (1993) 39 Wayne L. Rev. 1683; Simon Chester, "Electronic Malpractice: Does Competence Require Computer Research?" (1991) 17:8 L. Prac. Mgmt. 23; Teresa N. Pritchard, "Attorneys in the Electronic Information Age: Is there a Duty to Make the Transition?" (1988) 62 Fla. B.J. 17.

researched, the instructions from the client, and the importance of the matter. In certain situations, it may be that resort to print-based textbooks would be a prudent source of information, whereas in other situations there may be no choice but to conduct full-text keyword searches in online databases to locate otherwise hard to find information:

> Whether a lawyer should resort to Westlaw or Lexis to find the latest case or utilize other electronic media resources or go to a law library depends on the circumstances. The fact that technology provides greater efficiencies and may afford lawyers a competitive advantage does not mean that it is unethical not to use technology. In the end it is the quality of the legal work and not the speed at which it is done that matters. Given today's technologies and the inventions that will serve lawyers in the future, the practice of law still requires the exercise of judgment by the legally trained mind. Although access to law may become automated, the practice of law will not.[24]

Considering the factors discussed above that courts would likely apply to determine whether a particular lawyer was liable for legal research malpractice, it is prudent for lawyers and legal researchers to develop standard practices or checklists that will help remind them of the multiple steps involved in legal research. The legal research checklist set below provides a reminder of some of the fundamental research techniques that should be used. Equally important, of course, is ensuring that one has a correct and complete understanding of the facts that drive the legal research question and that the researcher (or lawyer to whom the researcher reports) has fully informed the client whether the law being research is settled or unsettled.

Legal Research Checklist

1. **Facts**: Do you have all of the relevant facts?
   Assumptions: What assumptions are being made?

   The facts and assumptions on which the legal research opinion is based should be set out in the legal research memorandum or in the report for the client. Where the client has documents, these should obviously be reviewed to confirm what the client has been saying and to check for things such as "choice of law" provisions (assuming it is a contractual dispute).

---

24   Mark Tuft, "Not Using New Technology: Ethical and Liability Risks? A Lawyer's Judgment Will Never Be Automated" (2003) 20 GP Solo 21 at 28.

2. **Preliminary questions and issues**:
   - Is there federal, provincial, or municipal legislation that governs this problem?
   - Is there a limitation period problem? If so, consult the applicable federal or provincial limitation legislation. If the calculation of time is involved, consult the applicable federal or provincial *Interpretation Act*.
   - How urgently is the answer needed?
   - How much time and money can be spent on research for this problem?
   - Has anyone else within the organization looked at this problem?
   - Is there someone you can speak to about this sort of research problem for guidance or ideas?

3. **Secondary research (start broad)**:
   - *Textbooks*: Check books for explanations and overviews
   - *Journals*: Check journal literature for explanations and overviews
   - *Encyclopedias of law*: Consult Canadian, British, or U.S. legal encyclopedias
   - *Reference material*: Consult dictionaries, directories, and other reference materials
   - *Case law digests*: Consult standard case law digests (*Canadian Abridgment* in print or on WestlaweCARSWELL or Quicklaw's CCS database) to ensure obvious case law is not being over-looked
   - *Internet searches*: Are there Web sites relevant to your area of research? Have you conducted a Web search on Google or other search engines?
   - *Other jurisdictions*: Have you searched for journals, textbooks, law reform commission reports, cases, or legislation from other jurisdictions, including the United Kingdom, the United States, Australia, or New Zealand?

4. **Primary research (focus and update)**:
   - Read and note up relevant case law
   - Read and note up relevant statutes and regulations
   - Keep a good dated log of the sources searched, including the syntax of online searches and the databases searched.

5. **Repeat Steps 1 to 4, as needed.**
   It is time to stop the research when you start to see references repeatedly to the same cases or same materials.

F. CONCLUSIONS

By following the basic legal research skills described in this book, it is hoped that lawyers and legal researchers can avoid, or at least minimize, the risk of being found liable for legal research malpractice. A common factor of many cases of any sort of professional negligence is likely a combination of inattention to detail, working too quickly, or making incorrect assumptions. By conducting legal research methodically and in a consistent manner that forces you to follow steps like those set out in the checklist, you should be able to avoid any possible claims at the same time as improving the effectiveness and results of your legal research.

G. RESOURCES ON LEGAL RESEARCH MALPRACTICE

Bigelow, Robert. "Be Careful How You Use Computerized Search Services" (2003) 5 The Journal of Law Office Economics and Management 17.

Butler, Marguerite L. "Rule 11 Sanctions and a Lawyer's Failure to Conduct Competent Legal Research" (2000) The Professional Lawyer 2.

Chester, Simon. "Electronic Malpractice: Does Competence Require Computer Research?" (1991) 17:8 L. Prac. Mgmt. 23.

Daiker, Duane A. "Computer-Related Legal Malpractice: An Overview of the Practitioner's Potential Liability" (1995) 69 Fla. B.J. 12.

Davis, Susan E. "Duty to Surf: Do Lawyers Have a Responsibility to Surf the Web for Every Case?" (1998) 18 California Lawyer 63.

Dodge, David D. "Lawyer Not Liable for Negligence Regarding Unsettled Issues of Law" (2000) 36 Arizona Attorney 20.

Gertner, Eric. "Case Comment: *World Wide Treasure Adventures Inc. v. Trivia Games Inc.*" (1987) 2 Legal Research Update 10.

Hamner, Claire. "Computer Assisted Legal Research and Legal Malpractice: Is the Future Here?" (1997) 16 Trial Advocate Quarterly 4.

Karpman, Diane. "Not Using New Technology: Ethical and Liability Risks? Keep up or Face Peril" (2003) 20 GP Solo 20.

MacLachlan, Lawrence Duncan. "Gandy Dancers on the Web: How the Internet Has Raised the Bar on Lawyers' Professional Responsibility to Research and Know the Law" (2000) Geo. J. Legal Ethics 607.

Macmillan, John. "The Information Age, Lawyers and Negligence" (1992) 66 Law Institute Journal 138.

Najar, Ola. "Computerized Research in the Legal Arena: Developing a Standard of Research Sufficiency in Legal Malpractice and Rule 11 Actions" (1993) 39 Wayne L. Rev. 1683.

Newman, Mark J. "Attorney Research Malpractice" (1991) 590 PLI/Comm. 11.

North, Ronwyn. "Can You Learn to Think More Carefully?" (1995) 33 Law Society Journal 31.

O'Connell, Laura A. "Legal Malpractice: Does the Lawyer have a Duty to Use Computerized Research?" (1984) 35 Federation of Insurance Counsel Quarterly 77.

Pritchard, Teresa N. "Attorneys in the Electronic Information Age: Is there a Duty to Make the Transition"? (1988) 62 Fla. B.J. 17.

Richards, J. Kent. "Lawyer Malpractice: The Duty to Perform Legal Research" (1982) 32 Federation of Insurance Counsel Quarterly 199.

Sloane, Richard. "When Ineptness Becomes Frivolous Conduct" (1996) 215 N.Y.L.J. 5.

Tuft, Mark. "Not Using New Technology: Ethical and Liability Risks? A Lawyer's Judgment Will Never Be Automated" (2003) 20 GP Solo 21.

Whiteman, Michael. "The Impact of the Internet and Other Electronic Sources on an Attorney's Duty of Competence under the Rules of Professional Conduct" (2000) Alb. L.J. Sci. & Tech. 89.

Whiteway, Ken. "Research Malpractice" (1990) 15 Can L. Libraries 51.

LEGAL WRITING

A. INTRODUCTION

There are a large number of books already published on legal writing, as seen in the lengthy list in section I at the end of this chapter. Rather than trying to duplicate the effort of other authors on this topic, an attempt is made in this chapter to highlight a few key aspects of legal writing. To start with is a discussion of effective legal writing principles. This is followed by a discussion of specific types of legal writing, including case comments, research memos, factums, drafting agreements, and court documents. Readers wanting more details on legal writing can consult the many resources listed in section I.

B. WHY LAWYERS WRITE LIKE LAWYERS

It is, of course, an indispensable part of a scrivener's business to verify the accuracy of his copy, word by word. Where there are two or more scriveners in an office, they assist each other in this examination, one reading from the copy, the other holding the original. It is a very dull, wearisome, and lethargic affair. I can readily imagine that, to some sanguine temperaments, it would be altogether intolerable.

– Herman Melville, *Bartleby, the Scrivener*

What does it mean to say that lawyers write "like lawyers?" The answer to this question is likely related in part to the reason why there are so many lawyer jokes:[1] lawyers (unfortunately) tend to use too much gobbledygook (or "legalese") when they write and speak. There are several reasons why this has been so. Perhaps the main reason is that lawyers have traditionally been quite conservative, relying upon "tried and true" past precedents.[2] This can sometimes be a good thing since it ensures consistency and safe practice. The problem with this, however, is that many older precedents used archaic language, ("This Agreement Witnesseth"), Latin phrases (*"mutatis mutandis"*), notoriously bad legalese ("the Defendant struck the *said* car"), and redundant expressions or "freight trains" ("null and void" — using void alone is sufficient).[3] Since scriveners were often paid by the numbers of words they transcribed, there was little incentive for brevity and every motivation to be as wordy as possible, as with the case with Melville's Bartleby.

Combined with these factors is the very essence of lawyering in trying to anticipate every possible scenario or risk by crossing every "t" and dotting every "i" when drafting legal documents. This is not always a bad thing but can sometimes be unnecessary, especially when it is being done unconsciously when lawyers are blindly copying past precedents.

Another reason why lawyers write like lawyers is due to the monopolistic nature of the legal profession and of its perceived elite nature. Lawyers were seen to belong to an exclusive, upper-class "club" that did not include among its members the "unlearned." The very use of legal language — especially when it is capitalized and uses Latin phrases — sounds impressive and was likely (and still is) used by some lawyers to intimidate people.

In defence of "writing like a lawyer" is the argument that lawyers often deal with complex matters that can sometimes only be described in complex terms. In addition, some Latin phrases, such as *res ipsa loquitur* (the "thing" or negligence speaks for itself) have meaning for lawyers and judges and are understood without the need for any additional explanation.

Fortunately, there has been a movement in North America and elsewhere towards the use of plain language in legal writing, a topic briefly discussed in the next section.

---

1   See, e.g., the lawyer jokes at Nolo Press' Web site at <http://www.nolo.com/humor/jokes/>.

2   Timothy Perrin, *Better Writing for Lawyers* (Toronto: Law Society of Upper Canada, 1990) at 3–4.

3   "Freight trains" is a phrase used by Perrin, *ibid.* at 136.

C. THE PLAIN LANGUAGE MOVEMENT

In the last twenty years or so there has been a gradual development of the use of plain language in legal writing. Part of this development is likely due to a rise in consumer rights and awareness, combined with an increase in the number of lawyers graduating from law schools who are no longer coming from an "elite" part of society. These factors from both within and outside of the legal profession have resulted in a growing awareness by lawyers of the advantages of using plain language in legal drafting.

The plain language movement in law, however, is not a defined group or organization but instead represents the notion that legal documents should be written using plain words that can be understood by average people. Plain language does not mean childish or simplistic language; instead, it suggests that lawyers should more carefully choose the words they use to be precise and unambiguous (assuming this is desired) yet simple and easily understood (once again, assuming this is desired).

The legal writing literature is full of horrific examples of "legalese" that tend to fall into the following categories:[4]

Table 11.1
Examples of Legalese

Archaic/Bad English	Comments
aforesaid, henceforth, hereafter, hereby, herein, hereinafter, heretofore, herewith, theretofore	These "chestnuts" are usually redundant or a signal that the sentence should be reworked.
Freight Trains	**Comments**
have and hold, save and except, keep and maintain, each and every, fit and proper, "situate, lying and being in"	These "paired" expressions are unnecessary and can usually be reduced to a single term.
Legalese	**Comments**
the undersigned, witnesseth, wherefore the Plaintiff prays that . . . , Know All Men By These Presents	Terms like these are holdovers from days past and should be dropped in favour of plain language equivalents.

Clients are often openly grateful when you use language they can easily understand. It is well worth the effort, therefore, to think consciously about your audience and the language you use as you prepare law-related documents.

---

4   These examples are culled from the various legal writing resources listed in section I, resources that should be consulted for more detail on effective legal writing.

D. CASE COMMENTS

One of the first legal writing tasks assigned to first-year law students is to write a case comment, often with little or no explanation of what a case comment is or how one goes about writing one. This section will seek to explain such matters.[5]

What is a case comment? Simply put, a case comment is a short essay that usually analyzes a single, recent decision of general interest to practising lawyers or the academic legal community. Case comments abound in a wide variety of formats and styles and are not necessarily called "case comments." It is quite easy to find case comments by using legal periodical indices such as the online version of the *Index to Canadian Legal Literature* (discussed in detail in Chapter 2, section B). One need merely type in the case name (i.e., the style of cause or the names of the parties) and this will generally identify or list any articles giving significant treatment to that case. Figure 11.1 sets out an example from the Quicklaw database "ICLL" (for the *Index to Canadian Legal Literature*) where a search was conducted on "semelhago /5 paramadevan," which resulted in eight articles regarding that decision.

Figure 11.1
Search Results from Quicklaw's ICLL Database

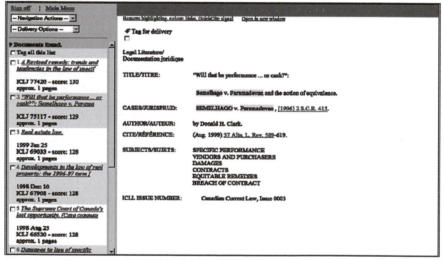

Reprinted by permission of Quicklaw Inc.

---

5   This material on case comments is based on materials prepared by Shikha Sharma, former Reference Librarian, Bora Laskin Law Library, Faculty of Law, University of Toronto and training sessions developed by her and the author.

There are usually no strict requirements or rules for writing a case comment unless one is submitting it for publication in a journal that has its own specific requirements (e.g., regarding formatting or foot-noting). That being said, a typical case comment ordinarily has the following characteristics:

- **Facts**: There is usually a very brief recitation of the relevant facts to remind the reader about what lead to the dispute. If the facts are not highly relevant to the analysis to be made, this section of the case comment should be kept very brief.
- **Ruling/history**: A case comment usually provides a brief overview of the history of the case, along with the ruling of the court. This can also usually be kept very brief.
- **Point of law**: It is fairly standard for a case comment to summarize the relevant point of law for which the case stands and to place this point of law in a larger context, where appropriate.
- **Analysis/argument**: The most important part of a case comment, and the part least susceptible to standardization, is the analysis or argument that the writer brings to the case comment. Possible approaches include but are not limited to the following ideas:

  - Faulty reasoning or conclusions — you may take the approach, supported by arguments and examples, that the court has applied faulty reasoning or reached the wrong conclusion.
  - Ground-breaking — alternatively, you may be supportive of the decision in showing how it is a ground-breaking ruling.
  - Policy issues — another approach is to analyze the decision from a policy point of view. What will the effect of the decision be on Canadian society? Does the decision have implications beyond the needs or rights of the parties to the lawsuit?
  - Grounds for appeal — if the decision is a trial or provincial Court of Appeal decision, another approach is to write the case comment from the arguments that the losing party would make if the decision were being further appealed.

There are a number of steps that can be taken to prepare for writing a case comment, :

1. **Carefully reading the decision**: It is trite advice of course for the case commentator to carefully read the decision being commented upon, but this is a critical first step and must often be repeated in order to analyze the decision carefully, and to follow up and read cases or any academic commentary cited by the court in its decision.

2. **Noting up the decision**: It is usually prudent to note up the decision being commented upon to see if other courts have yet cited the decision. If there is any judicial treatment, these subsequent decisions should ordinarily be reviewed to see if any of them have given unique or significant analysis of the case being commented upon.

3. **Journal searches**: Unless the case being commented upon is a newly released decision, it can be useful to check legal periodical indices to see if any other writers have commented on the case in question. Even if the case is new, or if there are no other case comments on the case in question, it may be fruitful to search for articles that deal with the same subject matter to see how other authors have dealt with the topic.

4. **Look to other jurisdictions**: Another possible approach is to look at how courts or academics from other jurisdictions have treated the subject matter of the case being commented upon. To find such viewpoints, use journal indices, textbooks, or encyclopedias from these foreign jurisdictions, resources that are discussed in more detail in Chapter 2.

E. RESEARCH MEMOS

Another common form of legal writing used by lawyers is the ubiquitous legal research memo (law students, as part of an assignment, are often asked to prepare a memo setting out their opinion or conclusions of law given a particular set of hypothetical facts). More so than case comments, legal research memos have no set format other than the standard opening, identifying to whom the memo is being sent, by whom, the date of the memo and the subject matter of the memo (see Chapter 12, section D for a sample legal research memo).

What separates good legal research memos from bad ones are a few basic features:

• **Purpose**: It should be obvious to the reader of the memo why the memo has been prepared. This can be most simply achieved by setting out the purpose of the memo near the beginning (e.g., "You have asked me to research whether an RSP is exigible by a creditor of the holder of the RSP.").

• **Structure**: Good memos have a natural flow or structure. If helpful, bolded headings and sub-headings should be used to divide the memo into its constituent parts (e.g., facts, law, academic commentary, analysis, and conclusions).

- **Clarity in writing**: The purpose of a research memo is to provide information clearly and directly. The goal is to help the person reading the memo to make a decision about a particular legal problem, such as whether or not to start an action on behalf of a client. Anything in the memo that distracts from this purpose should be eliminated.
- **Footnoting**: There is no strict rule or requirement regarding the footnoting of case and legislative citations in legal research memos. Many people tend to simply cite their material in the text of the memo, without resorting to footnotes. Others, however, find that the use of footnotes is cleaner and can act more like a checklist of cases cited, making it easier to retrieve those cases later, if needed, for a book of authorities if the matter proceeds to a court hearing.
- **Statement of research limitations**: As a general rule, to the extent the legal research memo is a document internal only to the law firm, it is ordinarily important for the writer to explore both sides of any issue being researched and to point out both strengths and weaknesses, along with any limitations on the research being done (i.e., a lack of time) or areas for further research if the matter proceeds further.

Many law firms will archive legal research memos by storing copies of them in separate folders or online databases. This allows the firm to retrieve the memo later if a similar issue arises on a different file.

F. FACTUMS

Factums — or *facta* for the Latin perfectionists — are written arguments or briefs filed in court to advocate a client's legal position before the court. There are technical requirements prescribed by the rules of court for most jurisdictions regarding the length, content, and format of factums. In law school, law students are usually required to participate in a moot court hearing — a mock appeal-level hearing — and as part of this process are required to prepare and file factums. Moot court factum requirements are often prescribed individually by the law school but often mirror "real life" factums.

Much has already been written in the legal literature regarding factum preparation (see the resources listed at the end of this chapter), so what follows in this section is nothing more than a simple overview of tips for drafting effective court factums. Readers needing more details should consult the resources at the end of this chapter and any specific court rule requirements of the applicable jurisdiction.

The following pointers apply to most factums, regardless of jurisdiction or level of court. Ultimately, one must always check specific requirements before preparing and filing a factum:

- **What is a factum?** A factum is a concise statement, without argument, of the facts and law a party relies upon in an argument before the court.[6] The style of factums in Canada is regarded as a hybrid of the British and American legal practice. The British practice tends to emphasize oral advocacy over written advocacy, such that barristers in England ordinarily use only written "skeletal arguments" on appeal matters, which tend to be only general outlines of their position, requiring instead that they rely upon their oral advocacy. The American practice, however, is to emphasize written argument, since on many applications, counsel may not even be called upon to make submissions or may be under strict time limitations for oral argument. The court will instead rely upon written material filed in advance of the hearing to make their ruling. In Canada, factums are not usually as detailed as the American approach and are often meant as an outline of counsel's position on the facts and the law. Remaining concise is still very important in Canada, no matter how complicated the issues may be. And despite the admonition in some court rules that a factum is "without argument," realize that most lawyers violate this part of the rules by including argument in the "Law" section of their factum.

- **Structure**: Typical factum requirements suggest an outline or structure that divides the written argument into the following parts:
  - **Introduction**: This part of the factum briefly introduces the party to the lawsuit and the type of relief that is being sought.
  - **Facts**: This part of the factum sets out a concise statement of the relevant facts. Here, do not include extraneous information. Consider using charts or tables if you are compiling a chronology of events. All facts must be supported by affidavit evidence or material forming part of the court record.
  - **Issues and the Law**: This part of the factum sets out the issues and legal argument. Stating the issues as statements rather than questions is often more forceful. (e.g., "The trial judge erred in her charge to the jury on the issue of reasonable doubt.") The legal argument is often more effective if divided into sections with separate headings. Be forceful in your arguments and support all

---

6   See, e.g., Rule 20.03 of the Ontario *Rules of Civil Procedure*, R.R.O. 1990, Reg. 194.

legal propositions with pinpoint citations to relevant case law, preferably from the same or higher jurisdictions.
– **Order sought**: This part of the factum sets out the terms of the order the court is being asked to grant.

• **Practice tips**: Effective counsel keep their own library of factums to re-deploy and adapt for future hearings, especially for commonly encountered applications such as leave to appeal hearings or applications for security for costs. In addition, factums are often only required for contentious hearings. If the court allows, it is sometimes effective to prepare a factum or an outline of your argument even if it is not required. This helps to focus your arguments, and if the judge has read the court file before the hearing, this will help focus the judge's mind on your arguments. In the future, expect to see requirements in most jurisdictions for counsel to also file an electronic version of the factum, along with electronic versions of cases being relied upon.

G. DRAFTING AGREEMENTS AND COURT DOCUMENTS

Agreements and pleadings are the final major category of legal writing to be discussed in this book. Agreements fall within the realm of traditional solicitor's work — drafting contracts, wills, and corporate documents. Pleadings fall within the realm of traditional barrister's work — drafting court documents, such as pleadings and affidavits, on behalf of a client. Resources on drafting agreements and pleadings are listed in section A.

Agreements. Lawyers rarely draft agreements from scratch. They are heavily dependent upon forms and precedents available from various commercial publications and are often more formally compiled by individual lawyers and law firms and kept internally by the firm. Precedents can be particularly useful for "boilerplate" provisions, which are those standard provisions found at the end of agreements. Boilerplate provisions often include such topics as governing law, resolution of disputes by arbitration, provisions for modifying the agreement, "entire agreement" provisions, warranty provisions, provisions for Acts of God ("force majeure" clauses), time being of the essence, and restrictions on assignment of the agreement. Although boilerplate provisions are not ordinarily required by law, prudence warrants their inclusion in most agreements since these provisions usually anticipate what might otherwise be unforeseen events. As with reliance on any precedent, care must be taken not to slavishly copy the language from the precedent without first adapting it, where necessary, to suit the needs of the client entering into the agreement. There are two major "forms and precedents" sets in Canada — one offered by Butterworths Canada (*Canadian Forms and Precedents*) and the other offered by Canada Law Book (*O'Brien's Encyclopedia of Forms*).

There are currently seven titles or topics in the Butterworths Canada *Canadian Forms & Precedents* series (blue and red binders):

- *Canadian Forms & Precedents: Commercial Transactions.* 3 vols. Looseleaf. Toronto: Butterworths Canada. Also available on CD-ROM.
- Dolan, Terence M. et al. *Canadian Forms & Precedents: Debtor/Creditor.* Looseleaf. Toronto: Butterworths Canada. Also available on CD-ROM.
- Fraser, James D.M. and Lawrence H. Iron. *Canadian Forms & Precedents: Commercial Tenancies.* Toronto: Butterworths Canada, 2004.
- MacLean, Virginia and Jennifer Smout. *Canadian Forms & Precedents: Land Development.* Looseleaf. Toronto: Butterworths Canada. Also available on CD-ROM.
- Rintoul, Margaret E. *Canadian Forms & Precedents: Estates Administration and Litigation.* 2 vols. Looseleaf. Toronto: Butterworths Canada. Also available on CD-ROM.
- Rintoul, Margaret E. *Canadian Forms & Precedents: Wills.* Looseleaf. Toronto: Butterworths Canada. Also available on CD-ROM.
- Smith, R. Bruce and Tina M. Woodside. *Canadian Forms & Precedents: Banking & Finance.* 5 vols. Looseleaf. Toronto: Butterworths Canada. Also available on CD-ROM.

Canada Law Book has a large, multi-volume series called *O'Brien's Encyclopedia of Forms* (burgundy binders). The set is currently divided into ten "divisions" or topics, with the forms and precedents being written and commented on by leading practitioners within each field (disks are included):

- Division I: Commercial and General
- Division II: Corporations
- Division III: Conveyancing and Mortgages
- Division IV: Leases
- Division V: Wills and Trusts
- Division VI: Ontario — Family Law
- Division VII: Labour and Employment Law
- Division VIII: Ontario Court Forms

- Division IX: Municipal Corporations
- Division X: Computers and Information Technology

There is a separate "Master Subject Index" volume that provides more detailed access points to help you decide which Division or volume to access. Canada Law Book has recently launched an Internet subscription version of this product called *O'Briens Internet*[7] in which it will be rolling out its forms and precedents, by subscription, in an interactive format that allows subscribers to fill out forms and precedents via a Web browser and then save them into their desired word processing format.

In addition, the following individual titles provide excellent guidance on drafting commercial documents for the various topics represented by their titles:

- Abe, Lisa K. *Internet and E-commerce Agreements: Drafting and Negotiating Tips*. Toronto: Butterworths, 2001 (includes disk).
- Dawson, Garry. *Shareholders Agreements: An Annotated Guide*. Toronto: Canada Law Book, 1997 (includes disk).
- Earle, Wendy J. *Drafting Arbitration and ADR Clauses for Commercial Contracts: A Solicitor's Manual*. Looseleaf. Toronto: Carswell, 2001.
- Elderkin, Cynthia L. and Julia S. Shin Doi. *Behind and Beyond Boilerplate: Drafting Commercial Agreements*. Toronto: Carswell, 1998.
- Ewasiuk, Ricky W. *Drafting Shareholders' Agreements: A Guide*. Toronto: Carswell, 1998.
- Kessler, James and Fiona Hunter. *Drafting Trusts and Will Trusts in Canada*. Toronto: Butterworths, 2003 (includes CD-ROM).
- Klotz, James M. *International Sales Agreements: An Annotated Drafting and Negotiation Guide*. Toronto: Canada Law Book 1997 (includes disk).

Pleadings. Pleadings, which are court documents filed on behalf of a client, present a wonderful opportunity for litigation lawyers to be effective legal drafters. Unfortunately, this opportunity is sometimes missed (often due to time constraints) when lawyers fail to appreciate the two main (related) purposes of pleadings: (i) to tell the judge a compelling and easy-to-understand story; and (ii) to resolutely advocate the client's position and win the argument. This opportunity is most often missed when lawyers blindly copy precedents without adapting them to the client's individual situation or when lawyers fail to write vigorously and concisely (i.e., they ramble on incessantly without purpose).

---

7   Online: O'Brien's Forms <http://www.obriensforms.com>.

The move to plain language in court documents is welcomed by judges where documents are organized with headings, are written with short sentences, and do not ramble on. Smart lawyers favour the active voice over the passive voice to make their pleadings easier to read and more forceful. Fortunately, there are a number of useful resources to help litigators with drafting:

- Ewaschuk, E.G. *Criminal Pleadings & Practice in Canada*. 2d ed. Looseleaf. Toronto: Canada Law Book, 1987.
- *How Do You Plead? Breaking the Bonds of Boilerplate*. Toronto: Department of Continuing Legal Education, Law Society of Upper Canada, 1994.
- Leon, Jeffrey S. and David C. Rosenbaum. *Ontario Civil Court Forms*. Looseleaf. Toronto: Carswell, 1993.
- Lord Brennan et al., eds. *Bullen & Leake & Jacob's Precedents of Pleadings*. 15th ed. London: Sweet & Maxwell, 2003.
- *Williston and Rolls Court Forms*. 2d ed. 4 vols. Looseleaf. Toronto: Butterworths.
- Wilson, Carol Ann. *Plain Language Pleadings*. Upper Saddle River, NJ: Prentice Hall, 1996.

H. CONCLUSIONS

Most legal researchers will undoubtedly apply their research in some form of legal writing, such as a research memo, an opinion letter to a client, or in a court pleading. Most legal writing is not mandated to follow particular forms, perhaps with the exceptions of court factums, court forms and other forms of documents, or contracts, the contents of which are regulated by legislation. It is hoped that this chapter has provided a good overview of legal writing issues and that the bibliography that follows can provide readers with additional resources that can answer more detailed questions about legal writing.

I. BIBLIOGRAPHY OF LEGAL WRITING MATERIAL

The section lists some of the more recent publications that discuss legal writing, essays and research papers, factums and court briefs, and agreements. Many of these materials are held by academic law libraries or are available directly from the respective publishers.

1) Legal Writing

Asprey, Michele M. *Plain Language for Lawyers*. 2d ed. Annandale, NSW: Federation Press, 1996.

Beaudoin, Louis. *Expressions juridiques en un clin d'oeil*. Cowansville, PQ: Éditions Y. Blais, 2000.

Berry, Carole C. *Effective Appellate Advocacy: Brief Writing and Oral Argument*. St. Paul, MN: Thomson/West, 2003.

Block, Gertrude. *Effective Legal Writing: For Law Students and Lawyers*. 4th ed. Westbury, NY: Foundation Press, 1992.

Bouchoux, Deborah E. *Legal Research and Writing for Paralegals*. New York: Aspen Law & Business, 2002.

Brostoff, Teresa. *Legal English: An Introduction to the Legal Language and Culture of the United States*. Dobbs Ferry, NY: Oceana Publications, 2000.

Butt, Peter. *Modern Legal Drafting: A Guide to Using Clearer Language*. New York: Cambridge University Press, 2002.

Calleros, Charles R. *Legal Method and Writing*. New York: Aspen Law & Business, 2002.

Charrow, Veda et al. *Clear and Effective Legal Writing*. New York: Aspen Law & Business, 2002.

Clary, Bradley G. and Pamela Lysaght. *Successful Legal Analysis and Writing: The Fundamentals*. St. Paul, MN: Thomson/West, 2003.

Dave, Sandeep. *Plain Language in Law*. Available Online: <http://www.llrx.com/features/plainlanguage.htm>.

Dernbach, John C., ed. *A Practical Guide to Legal Writing and Legal Method*. 2d ed. Littleton, CO: F.B. Rothman, 1994.

Dick, Robert C. *Legal Drafting in Plain Language*. 3d ed. Scarborough, ON: Carswell, 1995.

Dworsky, Alan L. *The Little Book on Legal Writing*. 2d ed. Littleton, CO: F.B. Rothman, 1992.

Edwards, Linda Holdeman. *Legal Writing: Process, Analysis & Organization*. New York: Aspen Law & Business, 2002.

Ellinport, Jeffrey M. *Tools of the Trade: Practical Legal Writing for the 21st Century*. Bethesda, MD: Austin & Winfield, 1997.

Fitzgerald, Maureen F. *Legal Problem Solving: Reasoning, Research and Writing*. Toronto: Butterworths, 2001.

Garner, Bryan A. *Elements of Legal Style*. New York: Oxford University Press, 2002.

Garner, Bryan A. with Jeff Newman and Tiger Jackson. *The Redbook: A Manual on Legal Style*. St. Paul, MN: West Group, 2002.

Gender-free Legal Writing: Managing the Personal Pronouns. Vancouver: British Columbia Law Institute, 1998.

Goldstein, Tom and Jethro K. Lieberman. *The Lawyer's Guide to Writing Well*. 2d ed. Berkeley: University of California Press, 2002.

Gordon, Suzanne. *The Law Workbook: Developing Skills for Legal Research and Writing*. Toronto: Emond Montgomery Publications, 2001.

Haggard, Thomas R. *The Lawyer's Book of Rules for Effective Legal Writing*. Littleton, CO: F.B. Rothman, 1997.

Haggard, Thomas R. *Legal Drafting in a Nutshell*. St. Paul, CO: West Pub. Co., 1996.

Haggard, Thomas R. *The Scrivener: A Primer on Legal Writing*. Columbia, SC: University of South Carolina, School of Law, 2000.

Johns, Margaret Z. *Professional Writing for Lawyers: Skills and Responsibilities*. Durham, NC: Carolina Academic Press, 1998.

LeClercq, Terri. *Guide to Legal Writing Style*. New York: Aspen Law & Business, 2000.

Mowat, Christine. *A Plain Language Handbook for Legal Writers*. Scarborough, ON: Carswell, 1999.

Neumann, Richard K. *Legal Reasoning and Legal Writing: Structure, Strategy and Style*. Gaithersburg: Aspen Law & Business, 2001.

Oates, Laurel Currie et al. *The Legal Writing Handbook: Analysis, Research and Writing*. New York: Aspen Law & Business, 2002.

Perrin, Timothy. *Better Writing for Lawyers*. Toronto: Law Society of Upper Canada, 1990.

Ray, Mary Bernard. *Legal Writing: Getting it Right and Getting it Written*. St. Paul, MN: West Group, 2000.

Ray, Mary Barnard and Barbara J. Cox. *Beyond the Basics: A Text for Advanced Legal Writing*. St. Paul, MN: Thomson/West, 2003.

Richmond, Jane. *Legal Writing: Form & Function*. Notre Dame, IN: National Institute for Trial Advocacy, 2001.

Rossini, Christine. *English as a Legal Language*. New York: Kluwer Law International, 1998.

Roznovschi, Mirela. *Toward a Cyberlegal Culture*. Ardsley, NY: Transnational Pub, 2001.

Schiess, Wayne. *Writing for the Legal Audience*. Durham, NC: Carolina Academic Press, 2003.

Shapo, Helene S. et al. *Writing and Analysis in the Law*. Westbury, NY: Foundation Press, 1989.

Smith, Michael R. *Advanced Legal Writing: Theories and Strategies in Persuasive Writing*. New York: Aspen Law & Business, 2002.

Stephens, Cheryl M. *Plain Language Legal Writing*. Vancouver: ASAP Legal Pub., 1999.

Swales, John and Christine B. Feak. *English in Today's Research World: A Writing Guide*. Ann Arbour, MI: University of Michigan Press, 2000.

Tiersma, Peter Meijes. *Legal Language*. Chicago: University of Chicago Press, 1999.

Volokh, Eugene. *Academic Legal Writing: Law Review Articles, Student Notes, and Seminar Papers*. New York: Foundation Press, 2003.

Wojcik, Mark E. *Introduction to Legal English: An Introduction to Legal Terminology, Reasoning, and Writing in Plain English*. Washington, DC: International Law Institute, 1998.

Wydick, Richard C. *Plain English for Lawyers*. 4th ed. Durham, NC: Carolina Academic Press, 1998.

2) Essays/Research Papers

Booth, Wayne C. et al. *The Craft of Research*. 2d ed. Chicago: University of Chicago Press, 2003.

Chicago Manual of Style. 15th ed. Chicago: University of Chicago Press, 2003.

Fajans, Elizabeth. *Scholarly Writing for Law Students: Seminar Papers, Law Review Notes, and Law Review Competition*. St. Paul, MN: West Group, 1995.

Lester, James D. *Writing Research Papers: A Complete Guide*. 9th ed. New York: Longman, 1999.

Soles, Derek. *Writing an Academic Essay: How to Plan, Draft, Revise and Edit your Essay*. Taunton: Studymates, 2003.

Turabian, Kate. *A Manual for Writers of Term Papers, Theses and Dissertations*. 6th ed. Chicago: University of Chicago Press, 1996.

Volokh, Eugene. *Academic Legal Writing: Law Review Articles, Student Notes, and Seminar Papers*. New York: Foundation Press, 2003.

3) Factums/Moot Court Briefs

Beazley, Mary Beth. *A Practical Guide to Appellate Advocacy*. New York: Aspen Law and Business, 2002.

Brand, Norman and John O. White. *Legal Writing: The Strategy of Persuasion*. 3d ed. New York: St. Martin's Press, 1994.

Bucholtz, Barbara K. *The Little Black Book: A Do-It-Yourself Guide for Law School Competitions*. Durham, NC: Carolina Academic Press, 2002.

Bullen & Leake & Jacob's Precedents of Pleadings. 14th ed. London: Sweet & Maxwell, 2001.

Ciampi, Maria L. and William H. Manz. *The Question Presented: Model Appellate Briefs*. Cincinnati, OH: Anderson Publishing Co, 2000.

Cromwell, T.A, ed. *Preparation of Factums*. Aurora, ON: Canada Law Book, 1996.

Facts on Factums. Toronto: Dept. of Continuing Education, Law Society of Upper Canada, 1995.

Fontham, Michael et al. *Persuasive Written and Oral Advocacy in Trial and Appellate Courts*. New York: Aspen Law and Business, 2002.

Foy, Patrick G. et al. *Factums in Civil Appeals, 1985*. Vancouver: Continuing Legal Education Society of British Columbia, 1985.

Garner, Bryan A. *The Winning Brief: 100 Tips for Persuasive Briefing in Trial and Appellate Courts*. New York: Oxford University Press, 1999.

Giles, Jack. "The Do's and Don'ts of the Respondent's Factum" in *Appellate Court Practice*. Vancouver: Continuing Legal Education Society of British Columbia, 1994.

Glaser, Cathy et al. *Lawyer's Craft: An Introduction to Legal Analysis, Writing, Research and Advocacy*. Cincinnati, OH: Anderson Publishing Co., 2004.

Gold, Alan D. "Factums" in *Indictable Appeals in Ontario*. Scarborough, ON: Carswell, 1994.

How Do You Plead? Breaking the Bonds of Boilerplate? Toronto: Department of Continuing Legal Education, Law Society of Upper Canada, 1994.

Jeffrey, Leon S. and D.C. Rosenbaum. *Ontario Civil Court Forms*. Looseleaf. Toronto: Carswell, 1993.

Knibb, David G. *Federal Court of Appeals Manual*. St. Paul, MN: West Publishing Co., 1981.

Morton, James C. and Michael E. Freeman. *Written Advocacy*. Toronto: Butterworths, 2000.

Moskovitz, Myron. *Winning an Appeal*. Rev. ed. Charlottesville, VA: Butterworths, 1985.

Perell, Paul M. *Written Advocacy*. Toronto: Law Society of Upper Canada, 1994.

Schultz, Nancy L. and Louis J. Sirico, Jr. *Legal Writing and Other Lawyering Skills*. 4th ed. Newark, NJ: LexisNexis, 2004.

Smith, Michael R. *Advanced Legal Writing: Theories and Strategies in Persuasive Writing*. New York: Aspen Law and Business, 2002.

Sopinka, John and Mark A. Gelowitz. *The Conduct of an Appeal*. 2d ed. Toronto: Butterworths, 2000.

Stern, Robert L. *Appellate Practice in the United States*. 2d ed. Washington, DC: Bureau of National Affairs, 1989.

Wilson, Carol Ann. *Plain Language Pleadings*. Upper Saddle River, NJ: Prentice Hall, 1996.

4) Legal Agreements

Abe, Lisa K. *Internet and E-commerce Agreements: Drafting and Negotiating Tips*. Toronto: Butterworths, 2001 (includes disk).

Canadian Forms & Precedents 4th ed. Looseleaf. Toronto: Butterworths, 2001 — various topics. Also available on CD-ROM.

Child, Barbara. *Drafting Legal Documents: Principles and Practices*. 2d ed. St. Paul, MN: West Publishing, 1992.

Commercial Agreements Drafting. Vancouver: Continuing Legal Education Society of British Columbia, 1991.

Dawson, Garry. *Shareholders Agreements: An Annotated Guide*. Toronto: Canada Law Book, 1997 (includes disk).

Earle, Wendy J. *Drafting Arbitration and ADR Clauses for Commercial Contracts: A Solicitor's Manual*. Looseleaf. Toronto: Carswell, 2001.

Elderkin, Cynthia L & Julia S. Shin. *Behind and Beyond Boilerplate: Drafting Commercial Agreements*. Scarborough, ON: Carswell, 1998.

Encyclopaedia of Forms and Precedents other than Court Forms. 4th ed. Toronto: Butterworths, 1964.

Ewasiuk, Ricky W. *Drafting Shareholders' Agreements: A Guide*. Toronto: Carswell, 1998.

Fox, William F. *International Commercial Agreements: A Primer on Drafting, Negotiating, and Resolving Disputes*. 3d ed. The Hague: Kluwer Law International, 1998.

Kessler, James and Fiona Hunter. *Drafting Trusts and Will Trusts in Canada*. Toronto: Butterworths, 2003 (includes CD-ROM).

Klotz, James M. *International Sales Agreements: An Annotated Drafting and Negotiation Guide*. Toronto: Canada Law Book 1997 (includes disk).

O'Brien, A.H. *O'Brien's Encyclopedia of Forms*. 11th ed. Looseleaf. Aurora, ON: Canada Law Book, 1987.

CHAPTER 12

PUTTING IT ALL TOGETHER — A SAMPLE RESEARCH PROBLEM AND MEMORANDUM OF LAW

A. INTRODUCTION

This chapter sets out a hypothetical legal problem and then seeks to answer it using the Legal Research Checklist in Chapter 10, section E and the other resources and techniques described in this book. This research culminates in a sample law office memo set out below in section D.

B. HYPOTHETICAL PROBLEM[1]

You work as a student at the law firm of Smith and Jones. A client of the firm wishes to operate a bungee-jumping company in Flavelle, Ontario in which customers would pay $80.00 per person to jump off the Flavelle Ravine Bridge with a bungee cord wrapped around their legs. The company is worried about its liability if any of its customers were injured while bungee jumping and whether it can protect itself by having its customers sign "liability waivers" (also known as "limita-

---

1   The law firm, company, and city are fictitious. I have used this hypothetical problem for a number of years in my legal research courses for law students and library science students. I am therefore indebted to the numerous students who, through their efforts, have provided me with insight into this problem. The research and resulting law office memo in this chapter are, however, based on my own work.

tions of liability" or "disclaimers"). A lawyer at the firm has asked you to (1) research the law in Canada regarding the enforceability of liability waivers at sporting and recreational events; (2) report on the results of your research; and (3) set out steps the company might want to take to help ensure the enforceability of any liability waivers it might use in its business.

C. ANALYSIS AND APPROACH

Since legal research remains an art rather than a science, there is never only one correct way to answer a problem. Instead, so long as one takes a methodical and thorough approach using the major secondary and primary legal resources, there is usually some assurance of finding relevant legal information.

1) Step 1: Facts

Do you have all of the relevant facts? What assumptions are being made? This is the first step of the Legal Research Checklist and also corresponds to the first step of the "FILAC" legal research process discussed in more detail in Chapter 1, section B.

Arguably, the legal researcher can take the position that he or she need only research the problem as presented, without having to worry about other possibly relevant facts. This can be dangerous, however, since a change in facts can change the issues that need to be researched. In many cases, the person who is the lawyer for the client is also the same person who conducts the legal research, so there is less chance for miscommunication or a misunderstanding of relevant facts. Where the researcher is different than the client's lawyer, however, it is important for the researcher to anticipate questions that may be relevant to the legal issues and to communicate any concerns to the lawyer responsible for the client's file. In the hypothetical scenario above, the legal researcher might consider some of the following questions before beginning the research; alternatively, some of these questions might only arise after the research has begun. It would ordinarily be prudent for the legal researcher to raise these questions or issues with the lawyer (or the client, if appropriate) as the research progresses:

- Is the client in fact a company? If so, is it a private or public company? In what jurisdiction is it incorporated? How heavily capitalized is it? Does it follow corporate formalities?

- What is the physical layout of the Flavelle Ravine Bridge? What arrangements, if any, does the client have to occupy the bridge to operate its business? Does the client own the bridge or lease it? If the client does not own the bridge or the land surrounding it, who does?
- Is bungee jumping a regulated industry? Are there standards governing the quality of the bungee-jumping cords? Does the government mandate any training for those operating a bungee-jumping business?

The issue of the capitalization of the company, for example, relates to the risk of a court piercing the corporate veil and finding the individual directors and operators of the company personally liable if there ever were an accident (i.e., the client might need to be told to ensure that it is properly capitalized and that it follow all corporate formalities if it wishes to minimize the risk of directors and officers being held personally liable).

2) Step 2: Preliminary Questions and Issues

Once you have considered the facts, it is then important to ask yourself some preliminary questions to help identify the relevant issues. This corresponds to the second step of the "FILAC" legal research process discussed in more detail in Chapter 1, section B.

The first two preliminary questions in this step of the Legal Research Checklist are basic questions that should be asked at the start of any legal research problem, even if the research has not formally begun:

a) Is there federal, provincial, or municipal legislation that governs this problem?

At this stage, many researchers may not know the answer to this question from first-hand knowledge. If so, it is worth keeping this question in mind as the research progresses. If you were not already aware from personal knowledge of the concept of "occupiers' liability," you would have no choice but to stumble across this concept after consulting secondary resources such as books or journal articles. This would therefore lead to the discovery of Ontario's *Occupiers' Liability Act*,[2] any relevant commentary on it, and cases interpreting its provisions (see the research below under Step 4 of the Legal Research Checklist for

---

2   R.S.O. 1990, c. O-2.

more detail on this Act, which sets out a standard of care that all occupiers must meet).

The point to make for now is that many, if not most, legal problems are affected by legislation and it is therefore important to always consider what legislation might apply to the problem. In reality, there is a good chance the instructing lawyer or client may already be familiar with any relevant statutes or regulations governing the company's operations. It would therefore be worth asking the instructing lawyer or the client about this, if only to save time and avoid unnecessary work or research.

b) Is there a limitation period problem?

Once again, the answer to this question may not be immediately obvious but you should consider potential limitation period issues for every legal research problem. If the client is facing a deadline by which to sue and you or your firm miss the filing deadline pending your research and investigation into the client's more substantive rights, your work on the substantive issues would be wasted and you or your firm would risk being liable for professional negligence in failing to identify the client's limitation period problem.

Since this hypothetical problem anticipates avoiding disputes and is not based on an actual claim, no limitation problem exists per se. Despite this, the client may not be aware of new limitations legislation in Ontario. Section 4 of Ontario's *Limitations Act, 2002*,[3] for example, sets out a basic limitation period of two years that would likely apply if any person were to sue the client for a bungee-jumping accident:

> 4. Unless this Act provides otherwise, a proceeding shall not be commenced in respect of a claim after the second anniversary of the day on which the claim was discovered.

Section 5 of this new Act also codifies the discoverability principle (i.e., that the claim is discovered only when the person knew about it or ought to have known about it). In most accidents involving bungee jumping, it would be fairly obvious when the possible claim was discovered. Even though this hypothetical problem does not raise limitation issues, the instructing lawyer might want to simply include this information when reporting to the client.

Fortunately, identifying limitation period problems gets easier with experience. For Ontario, with its new limitations legislation, consulting up-to-date limitations textbooks (listed in Chapter 8, section G) can be useful for any research problem. Unless the limitation period is

---

3   S.O. 2002, c. 24, Sched. B.

an issue, it is not always mentioned in a legal research memo on the more substantive issues, but it is worth identifying possible limitation periods for the lawyer responsible for the client's file and ensuring that this information is entered into the law firm's limitation period "bring forward" diary/computer system.

The other points mentioned in this section of the Legal Research Checklist have you consider how urgently the research is needed, how much time and money can be spent, and whether this research has already been done on another file in the law firm or whether there is someone with expertise on the subject that you can speak to, all important things to consider before beginning the substantive research.

At this stage, it is normal to try to identify the issues that need to be researched. For this problem, with what is known at present, it might be reasonable to frame the issues as follows, keeping in mind the possible need to re-define them as the research progresses:

- To what extent do courts in Canada/Ontario uphold waivers or disclaimers in sporting or recreational accidents?
- What steps can the client take to minimize the risk of being held liable for the injury or death of a customer?

3) Step 3: Secondary Research (Start Broad)

By systematically reviewing standard secondary legal resources, you increase the chance of finding commentary that can lead to relevant cases and legislation. This stage of the research roughly corresponds to the third "legal research" step in the FILAC approach. What follows next is a partial listing of some of the background resources used for this hypothetical research problem, using the categories in the Legal Research Checklist.

a) Textbooks
Generally speaking, law-related books are an excellent starting point for any research. You should assume that for any legal issue, someone, somewhere, has written a book on the topic.

A "title keyword" search was conducted on the University of Toronto Library Online Catalogue <://webcat.library.utoronto.ca> using the following keywords, truncated with the "$" sign:[4]

---

4   Truncation tools vary across databases. On Quicklaw and WestlaweCARSWELL, for example, the truncation tool is an exclamation mark ("!"). In the example above, the search would look for variations on the truncated words: liab$ = lia-

liab$ and (sport$ or recreation$)[5]

This search resulted in sixteen hits or titles, some of which seem extremely relevant and include the following:

- Law Reform Commission of British Columbia. *Report on Recreational Injuries: Liability and Waivers in Commercial Leisure Activities.* Vancouver: The Commission, 1994.
- *Liability and Negligence: A Specialized Bibliography from the SPORT Database.* Gloucester, ON: Sport Information Resource Centre, 1991.

Even if neither book is perfectly on point, the detailed records for each item indicate that official Library of Congress Subject Headings for these books are "Liability for sports accidents — [jurisdiction]" and "Sports-accidents."

When you uncover a relevant Library of Congress Subject Heading, re-running a search to browse on that subject heading can be useful. In this example, browsing on "Liability for sports accidents — Canada" results in the following two potentially relevant books:

- Hanna, Glenda. *Outdoor Pursuits Programming: Legal Liability and Risk Management.* Edmonton: University of Alberta Press, 1991.
- Opie, Hayden. *Compensation for Physical Injury Sustained by Participants in Sport.* LL.M. Thesis, University of Toronto, 1985.

If one knew at this stage that occupiers' liability was relevant, one could search for books specifically on that subject — which was done — however, the results were slightly disappointing with their being mainly older law reform commission reports from various jurisdictions and older Canadian/Ontario textbooks that were likely too out-of-date to be useful. There is an excellent chapter on occupiers' liability in *Remedies in Tort*,[6] but one needs to know that from personal knowledge

---

bility, liable; sport$ = sport, sports, sporting; and recreation$ = recreation and recreational, for example.

5   A keyword search in the University catalogue on the word "bungee" resulted in zero hits (it never hurts to try a specific search to see what you might get). A keyword search in the National Library of Canada catalogue resulted in several hits, which revealed that "Bungee jumping" is itself an official Library of Congress Subject Heading. When browsing on that subject heading in the National Library of Canada catalogue, there was the following single entry under "Bungee jumping — Ontario — Safety measures": Mary Spencer, *Report of the Task Force on Bungee Jumping* (Toronto: Ministry of Consumer and Commercial Relations, 1993). The National Library of Canada catalogue indicated that this title was available for interlibrary loan from Ryerson University.

6   Lewis N. Klar et al., eds., *Remedies in Tort*, looseleaf (Toronto: Carswell, 1987).

of the law that this issue would be covered in a torts book, since uncovering that chapter is not easily done from a catalogue search alone. One excellent feature in *Remedies in Tort* — which is a looseleaf and hence current — is the bibliographies at the end of each chapter, which can lead you to other relevant books or journal articles. Another useful feature — although not relevant for this research — is the sample pleadings at the end of each chapter.

There were also several references in other secondary sources (discussed below) that mentioned Professor Barnes' book, *Sports and the Law in Canada*.[7] Its Library of Congress Subject Heading is "Sports — Law and legislation — Canada." Under that heading was found another relevant book called *Recreation and the Law*,[8] both of which had relevant passages on disclaimer clauses.

By this stage, the researcher should have enough clues that tort law and contract law are also broad areas of law that apply to this problem. This should trigger the idea of checking basic Canadian textbooks on contract law (listed in Chapter 8, section L) and tort law (listed in Chapter 8, section QQ). For example, a review of Professor Fridman's *The Law of Contract in Canada* quickly discloses that his Chapter 15 on the topic of "Breach" has an entire section dealing with exclusion clauses.[9]

For tort law books, there are numerous examples of relevant commentary. In the index to Professor Osborne's *The Law of Torts*, there are entries under the term "Negligence" for voluntary assumption of risk and waivers.[10] The index to Mr. Justice Linden's *Canadian Tort Law* also has entries under "voluntary assumption of risk" relating to various types of sports.[11] And as already mentioned above, *Remedies in Tort* has an excellent chapter on occupiers' liability.

The relevant passages from the foregoing textbooks were relatively easy to find (using the index or Tables of Contents in each book). If these access points were not obvious enough, another good access point was the Table of Cases to look up known, relevant cases to see if they were discussed in the book. Even if you did not have a known case at hand when starting this stage of the research, you would soon come

---

7   John Barnes, *Sports and the Law*, 3d ed. (Toronto: Butterworths, 1996).

8   Stephen Bird & John Zauhar, *Recreation and the Law* (Toronto: Carswell, 1992).

9   G.H.L. Fridman, *The Law of Contract in Canada*, 4th ed. (Toronto: Carswell, 1999) at 608–37.

10   Philip H. Osborne, *The Law of Torts*, 2d ed. (Toronto: Irwin Law, 2003) at 102–5.

11   Allen M. Linden, *Canadian Tort Law*, 7th ed. (Toronto: Butterworths, 2001) at 474–78.

across references to cases such as *Crocker v. Sundance Northwest Resorts Ltd.*[12] as being a relevant Supreme Court of Canada decision. Looking up this decision in the Table of Cases of the torts books, for example, leads to the same or similar page references as the index entries under "voluntary assumption of risk."

All of these textbooks provide an excellent overview of the law and identify relevant legislation and case law. Reference will be made to some of this material in the sample memo in section D.

b) Journals

Law journals are another excellent source of commentary and will typically discuss relevant case law and legislation, often from a critical or analytical point of view.

A search for article citations in the *Index to Canadian Legal Literature*[13] on WestlaweCARSWELL (database identifier: ICLL) revealed a number of relevant hits.[14] The following Boolean operator search commands were used:

> (sport! or recreation!) and (liab! or negl!)

This resulted in thirty-three hits, perhaps a large result, but the following items were identified as being potentially relevant from this list of thirty-three results:

- *Occupiers' Liability: Recreational Use of Land.* Edmonton: Alberta Law Reform Institute, 2000 (February 2000. Final Report No. 81).
- Thiele, Stephen A. "Sports and Torts: Injuring a Fellow Participant Can be Costly" (2000) 23 Advocates' Q. 348.
- Bowal, Peter. "For the Thrill of One's Life: Legal Liability for Shattered Adventures" (1999) 23:5 L. Now No. 27.
- Kligman, Robert D. "Tort Liability for Sports Injuries" (1989) 1 C.I.L.R. 153.

---

12   [1988] 1 S.C.R. 1186.
13   The *Index to Canadian Legal Literature* is also available on Quicklaw (database: ICLL).
14   Since the online *Index to Canadian Legal Literature* only indexes articles from 1985 to current, it is ordinarily prudent to consider also searching the print version of the *Index* and the print version of the *Index to Canadian Legal Periodical Literature* for older articles (this was done for this hypothetical problem looking under the subject headings of "NEGLIGENCE" and "CONTRACTS" but it was felt that none of the material indexed in the older print indexes added anything to the analysis). Some major journals, such as the *Canadian Bar Review*, also have their own journal indexes in print that index every article for that journal.

Also included in this list of thirty-three results were references to some of the books uncovered above during the "book search" in the library catalogue (since the *Index to Canadian Legal Literature* indexes more than just law journal articles).

In the "encyclopedia" research (discussed below), references to further journal articles were also discovered,[15] including the following:

- Neumann, Jeffrey J. "Disclaimer Clauses and Personal Injury" (1991) 55 Sask. L. Rev. 312.
- Tomlinson, J.D. and G. Grant Machum. "The Contractual Waiver of Liability in Ski Resort Negligence Claims" (1997) 15 Can. J. Ins. L. 49.

In addition to searching on the Boolean operators listed above in the journal index, it would be possible to search on keywords relating to disclaimers, exclusions of liability, and waivers of liability; doing so, results in some of the same articles and additional ones.

Although journal indexes are usually the better starting place to look for journal articles, it is often a good idea to complement your journal index searching with searches of full-text journal databases, such as the JOUR database on Quicklaw or the CANADA-JLR database on WestlaweCARSWELL, which can pick up individual references to keywords or concepts that might be at too specific level of detail to be indexed in the journal index. For example, a search on the word "bungee" in Quicklaw's JOUR database resulted in five hits (four of them were false hits and the fifth was a medical story documenting the temporary blindness suffered by a bungee jumper in England due to haemorrhaging in the foveal region of both eyes). Searches in these full-text journal databases on the "disclaimer" concept in sports (and variations on those terms) resulted in a number of hits, including many that were already found using the journal indexes with none of the "extra" results being that relevant or applicable to this research.

A search on the *Canadian Law Symposia Index* on Quicklaw (database identifier: CLSI) using the same Boolean search as for the *Index to Canadian Legal Literature* resulted in ten hits for continuing legal education seminars. The following two hits seemed to be the most relevant or interesting:

- Olah, John A. "Sports Liability: The Operator's Nightmare" in *Sports in the Courts*. Toronto: Canadian Bar Association — Ontario, Continuing Legal Education, 1987.

---

15   See, e.g., §96 (Supp.) in "Sports" in *Canadian Encyclopedic Digest* (Toronto: Carswell, 2000).

- *Recreational Facilities Liability: Maximizing Protection, Minimizing Exposure*. Toronto: Canadian Institute, 1993.

Although searching for journal articles from other jurisdictions may not always be necessary or available for every "Canadian" legal research point being investigated, in this example, searches were done using the University of Toronto's online version of *LegalTrac* (largely American articles but this database indexes law-related articles from all jurisdictions) and the law school's version of AGIS (the Attorney-General's Information Services), which emphasize the indexing of Australian and New Zealand law journal articles from 1975 to the present.

Because the results from the search on the *Index to Canadian Legal Literature* seemed sufficient for now, the search on *LegalTrac* was only on the term "bungee" (and it was decided not to bother searching on the "waiver of liability" concept since there appeared to be enough Canadian material on point). There were six results on the "bungee" search, some of which would likely be worth reviewing even if not entirely applicable to the client's operations in Ontario:

- Postel, Theodore. "Bungee Operator Owes No Duty to Passing Motorist" (1999) 145 Chicago Daily Law Bulletin 137.
- Ehrhardt, Thomas H. "What Price Human Flight? Bungee Jumping Accidents Indicate Need for More Expeditious Regulation of Potentially Hazardous Activities" (1994) 25 Rutgers L.J. 853.
- Oakes, Cindy. "Florida's Bungee Jumping Regulations: Why Other States Should Take the Plunge" (1993) 16 Hastings Comm. & Ent. L.J. 189.

A search on the word "bungee" in AGIS resulted in zero hits, perhaps somewhat surprising since modern bungee jumping has a strong tradition in that region (a search in AGIS on various keywords relating to disclaimers in sporting events resulted in a number of hits but did not seem worth pursuing for this problem).

c)   Encyclopedias

Law-related encyclopedias are also an excellent way to get an overview of an area of law and to identify leading cases and relevant legislation. In Canada, there is the *Canadian Encyclopedic Digest* (Carswell), available in print, on CD-ROM, and on WestlaweCARSWELL.

The print *Index* was consulted under various entry points. There was no entry under "EXCLUSION OF LIABILITY" but under "EXCLUSION CLAUSE" was a "see" reference to "CONTRACTS." Under that heading was an entry for "exculpatory clauses" with various sub-entries for "negligence" (5-32 §§ 395, 566.1 (Supp.), 567, 569, 853–57) and "waiver" (5-32 §§ 58.5 (Supp.), 821). The "page" references above for these entries refer first to the volume (5), the title or topic (32, being "Contracts"), and the various paragraph numbers in that title or topic (preceded by the "§" symbol).

In the print *Index*, under the term "NEGLIGENCE," there were numerous, relevant entry points. Under "exclusion clauses" were "see" references to contracts, breach of; occupier's liability; sports related injuries; *volenti non fit injuria*.

If one thought of it, in the print *Index* under the term "SPORTS" there were also numerous entries, including "civil liability — exclusion of liability," "occupier's liability," "parents' liability," and individual entries for individual (high-risk) sports.

All of the various entries above provide a good overview of both the legislative and common law framework for this topic, particularly §96 of the "Sports" title of the CED. References are made in the CED in the footnotes to applicable legislation and leading cases and will be commented on in more detail in the sample memo in section D, below.

The print version of the CED is very easy to use. The same information above could have also been found using the CED on CD-ROM or on WestlaweCARSWELL searching by keywords or browsing through the Table of Contents under the applicable titles. Additionally, if one had already uncovered the names of relevant cases (such as *Crocker v. Sundance Northwest Resorts Ltd.*, mentioned above), it is possible to check the print version of the CED to see where the case is mentioned; alternatively, one could simply search on the case name in the CD-ROM or online version. This is an effective way to pinpoint the relevant sections within the encyclopedia on the theory that where a known case is mentioned or discovered, it is likely that the commentary on that case will also refer to other relevant cases.

d) Reference Tools

For this hypothetical problem, it is not likely that helpful to consult reference tools such as legal dictionaries, words and phrases services, or legal directories, given that there seems to be sufficient background material from other resources already identified. If during the course of research you came across the phrase "*volenti non fit injuria*" (as you likely would), you could look up this phrase in Carswell's *Words and Phrases* to get extended references to various Canadian cases that have interpreted this phrase, including a number of cases discussed in other secondary resources.

In addition, the resourceful researcher can always make use of legal directories in the following manner: say, for example, that you are in a small community and do not have access to a library that contains some of the material identified above. Why not try e-mailing one of the authors of the material by using a legal directory to find their e-mail address to see if they can provide you with the materials? You would be surprised at how willing most authors are to help.

e) Case Law Digests

The *General Index* of the *Canadian Abridgment* (2d) was checked for a variety of possible access points. After several unsuccessful attempts at finding more specific terms (such as "disclaimers" or "liability waivers"), several entries were found under the broader heading of "Negligence," referring the reader to Volume R29 and its Supplement, including the following:

Negligence:
- Exculpatory clauses: **R29 Reis.** 5577–5595, **R29 Supp.** 172–178
- Occupiers' liability: various entries in **R29 Reis.** And **R29 Supp.**
- Particular situations, amusement or other public park: **R29 Reis.** 6709–6726, **R29 Supp.** 304–307

These index entries translate into the following topics:

Negligence — Defences (V) — Exculpatory clauses (2) (Negligence, V.2)

Negligence — Defences (V) — Volenti non fit injuria (6) — Sporting events (g) (Negligence, V.6.g)

Negligence — Occupier's Liability (VI) — Particular situations (3) — Amusement or other public parks (a) (Negligence, VI.3.a)

Under the broad heading of "Contracts," the following entry referred the reader to the new third edition of Volume 27 for Contracts:

Contracts
- Construction and interpretation, disclaimer clauses: **CON** 27.2979–3009

This index entry translates into the following topic:

Contracts — Construction and Interpretation (VII) — Disclaimer clauses (9) (Contracts, VII.9)

In the "Table of Classification" under the entry for Contracts, VII.9, there is a reference to *duty to bring attention to stringent print terms, see III.4* (which is the topic "Contracts — Formation of Contract (III) — Communication and acceptance of specific terms (4) (Contracts, III.4).

Alternatively, rather than using the print *General Index to the Canadian Abridgment*, if you had access to the CD-ROM or Internet versions of the *Canadian Abridgment*, you could browse the headings online or search them for keywords within the Abridgment Scheme. Or, like the situation with the CED, if you had a known case at hand, you could look up the case (in print or online) to see where it fell within the Abridgment Scheme. Doing this with *Crocker v. Sundance Northwest Resorts Ltd.*, for example, shows that this decision has been indexed under three different topics within the *Canadian Abridgment* scheme:

- Contracts — Formation of contract (III) — Communication and acceptance of specific terms (4) (or Contracts, III.4)
- Negligence — Defences (V) — Volenti non fit injuria (6) — Waiving right of action (c) (or Negligence, V.6.c)
- Negligence — Occupiers' Liability (VI) — Duties and obligations (2) — Invitee (c) — General (i) (or Negligence, VI.2.c.i)

You could then browse these Abridgment categories for additional relevant cases.

On the WestlaweCARSWELL version, the following search was done in the Boolean mode:

> liab! and (waiv! or exclu! or disclaim!)

This resulted in a total of 122 digests (including possible duplicate entries within different categories), including four digests within Contracts, III.4 and twenty-one digests within Contracts, VII.9.

The cases found using the *Canadian Abridgment* and those mentioned in the various other secondary resources will be reviewed and noted up in Step 4 (below) and the relevant cases will be discussed in detail in the research memo.

f)   Internet Search

It is always amazing what can be uncovered from a simple search on the Internet using a search engine such as Google <www.google.ca>. Given the large volume of material already uncovered, it is likely not necessary to consider doing an Internet search for this hypothetical problem. Despite this, searches were done as shown below:

- bungee jumping canada = 41,600 hits, mainly tourism sites
- bungee jumping canada waiver = 871 hits
- bungee jumping Ontario = 9,230 hits

With the last search, one of the Web sites in the first ten results was <www.bungee.ca>, the Web site of a commercial bungee jumping operation. On its Web site is mention of the fact that it helped form the Canadian Bungee Association and helped to author safety guidelines for the organization, something which can alert you to the fact that safety standards do in fact exist.

The regulatory research that was done below on Quicklaw in Step 4 of the Legal Research Checklist identified the existence of a *Canadian Bungee — Code of Safe Practice.* A Google search was therefore done on the phrase "Canadian Bungee Code of Safe Practice" and the second hit was in fact a direct link to a PDF version of the document[16] on the Web site of the Ontario Technical Standards & Safety Organization <www.tssa.org>. Reading through the Web site of the Technical Standards & Safety Organization, you quickly discover that this government organization is responsible for regulating the safety of amusement devices in Ontario (which includes bungee-jumping operations). Links are provided to (unofficial) versions of legislation. Searching on the Web site's own search engine on the word "bungee" also retrieves interesting information. Contact information for the organization is also provided.

Because it is now so easy to do, never rule out doing at least a quick Internet search on your topic. You might be surprised by what you find.

g)   Resources from Other Jurisdictions

The final part of this section of the Legal Research Checklist exhorts the researcher to consider the need to research the law in other jurisdictions. This is important especially where you are not finding a lot of relevant Canadian federal or provincial material. The quickest way to get an overview of the law in a different jurisdiction is to check for textbooks, journal articles, or legal encyclopedia entries for the jurisdiction in question. In this particular hypothetical situation, since there appears to be no lack of material on point, it might be unnecessary to worry too much about how waivers in sporting events are enforced in other jurisdictions. Having said that, however, you should try to develop instincts when to look at the law in other jurisdictions. English law, for example, is often worth checking on issues of common law where one wishes to get a "classic" view of the law. American law is good for areas of law not yet well-developed in Canada (such as Internet law). Whenever researching the law outside of Canada, however, it is always necessary to be wary of possible differences between the law and policies in the foreign jurisdiction and Canada.

---

16   See online: Technical Standards & Safety Authority <http://www.tssa.org/amusement/pdf/bungeecodesafepractice.pdf>.

For this hypothetical problem, out of curiosity — since there tends to be a much deeper body of legal literature and case law due to the larger population and high volume of litigation in the United States — the *Index* to the *American Law Reports* was consulted (this resource is mentioned in Chapter 2, section C). There are a number of access points within the print *Index of the American Law Reports*, with the two most promising index entries being "Amusement operations" and "Limitation of liability." In addition, the *American Law Reports* are available on WestlaweCARSWELL and LexisNexis. Using either the print Index or searching in the online version on the word "bungee" (since it is such a unique word) resulted in the following annotations being the most relevant or interesting:

- Sutton, Randy J. "Validity, Construction, and Effect of Agreement Exempting Operator of Amusement Facility from Liability for Personal Injury or Death of Patron" (1997), 54 A.L.R. (5th) 513.
- Russ, Lee R. "Products Liability: General Recreational Equipment" (1990), 77 A.L.R. (4th) 1121.
- Russ, Lee R.,"Products Liability: Mechanical Amusement Rides and Devices" (1997), 77 A.L.R. (4th) 1152.
- McCarthy, Michelle Meyer. "Tort Liability Arising from Skydiving, Parachuting, or Parasailing Accident" (2001), 92 A.L.R. (5th) 473.

4) Step 4: Primary Research (Focus and Update)

Once the foregoing secondary or background resources have been reviewed, the researcher is then obliged to consult any relevant legislation or case law identified within the secondary literature and also to search for any additional legislation or case law that may have been overlooked or not yet identified in the secondary literature. It is also necessary to note up any relevant legislation or case law, a step that can sometimes identify other relevant, more recent information.

a) Legislation
Legislative research for this hypothetical problem was already briefly mentioned above when asking one of the preliminary questions — is there federal, provincial, or municipal legislation governing this problem?

To determine the extent of any provincial or federal legislation that regulates bungee jumping, various keyword searches were done on the Canadian federal and Ontario statutes and regulations databases. For example, searches on Quicklaw's RSOT database (Revised Statutes of Ontario — Entire Act Version) in the "title" field on that database on the word "recreation!" resulted in two Acts with the word recreation in the title, with neither of them being particularly relevant to the problem.[17] One of the results on a search on the word "bridge" in the "title" field in the database was the *Bridges Act*. Section 2 of that Act restricts the alteration of a bridge unless approved by the Minister of Transportation, something that might be relevant to this problem:

> 2. (1) No person, except a municipal corporation or other authority having jurisdiction over highways, shall build, place, construct, rebuild, replace or alter a bridge or other structure over or across any river or stream or part thereof, except with the approval of the Minister of Transportation.

A search on the word "bungee" in that database (all fields, not limited to title) resulted in zero hits in the statutes database[18] but a search on "bungee" in the Ontario Consolidated Regulations database, Entire Act Version (database: ONRG), resulted in three hits that referred to regulations under the *Technical Standards and Safety Act, 2000*[19] including a reference to the "Canadian Bungee Code of Safe Practice" (although that reference suggested that the regulation — being O. Reg. 428/00 — had been revoked, something which would require further investigation). The possible impact of Ontario regulations and standards on bungee jumping is discussed in more detail below in the section on Internet searching and in the memo in section D, below.

b) Case Law

At this stage of the research, it is critical for the researcher to carefully read the cases uncovered so far and to consider searching for additional or more recent cases not yet identified in the secondary resources.

In addition to the searches mentioned in Step 3 using the *Canadian Abridgment*, a number of Boolean searches were also conducted in the full-text Canadian Judgments Plus (CJP) database on Quicklaw using a variety of terms to identify cases involving the enforceability of waivers in sporting and recreational events. Full-text searching can also be done on the "global" databases for Canadian case law on each of

---

17 The two Acts are (1) the *Ministry of Tourism and Recreation Act*, R.S.O. 1990, c. M.35; and (2) the *Community Recreation Centres Act*, R.S.O. 1990, c. C.22.

18 The same search in the Consolidated Statutes of Canada, Entire-Act-Version database on Quicklaw (RSCT) and the Canada Consolidated Regulations, Entire-Reg-Version database (SORT) on the word "bungee" also resulted in zero hits.

19 S.O. 2000, c. 16.

LexisNexis and on WestlaweCARSWELL since there are differences in scope and coverage in the case law databases on each of these three products. The full-text searches that were done resulted in similar cases as those that were found above using the Abridgment Scheme in the *Canadian Abridgment.*[20]

Using Quicklaw's Quick-Cite database (identifier: QC), it was relatively quick to note up all of the Canadian cases uncovered so far to check both the judicial history of these cases (to make sure the cases had not been reversed on appeal) and to check the judicial treatment of these cases (to see how later courts may have interpreted the decisions). Noting up cases can also help you identify other cases since later cases that have considered the case being noted up are usually relevant either on the facts or the law or both.

Where time and money permit, the careful legal researcher will also note up all cases using the online citators from all three commercial databases — Quicklaw, WestlaweCARSWELL, and LexisNexis — since differences in scope, coverage, and treatment do arise among all three vendors.[21]

5) Step 5: Repeat Steps 1 to 4 (as Needed)

It is time to stop the research when you start to see references to the same cases or materials repeatedly.

Repeating Steps 1 to 4 of the Legal Research Checklist is not always done in real life, either due to a shortage of time, money, or because the issues and law were not that difficult and sufficient resources were found. In a real-life situation, unless the client had a lot of money to spend, it is unlikely that you would have been able to necessarily track down all of the resources and follow all of the steps listed above due to the costs involved. At a minimum, starting with textbooks and perhaps

---

20 Out of curiosity, a search on Quicklaw's Canadian Judgments Plus (CJP) database was done on the word "bungee," which resulted in nineteen hits, all but one of which were false hits. The first case listed, however, was a criminal prosecution in Ontario under the *Amusement Devices Act*, R.S.O 1990, c. A.20 (since repealed and replaced by the *Technical Standards and Safety Act, 2000*, S.O. 2000, c. 16) in which the accused was found guilty of violating the Act related to its bungee-jumping operations that resulted in the death of a patron — see: *R. v. Anderson Ventures LLC*, [2000] O.J. No. 5819 (C.J.).

21 See, e.g., Greg Wurzer, Aleksandra Zivanovic, & Rhonda O'Neill, "Canadian Electronic Citators: An Evaluation of their Accuracy and Efficiency" (2004) 29 Can. L. Libraries Rev. 68.

the *Canadian Encyclopedic Digest* alone may have been a sufficient starting point for researchers on a budget, followed up with checking a few of the leading cases. Regardless, it is somewhat comforting that many of the secondary resources refer to the same or similar cases, legislation and issues, something that helps confirm the analysis to be given in the legal research memo, a sample of which follows in the next section.

D. SAMPLE RESEARCH MEMO

Based on the foregoing research, the following legal research memo was drafted. Following this memo are comments on specific sections of the memo.[22] The persons named in the sample memo are fictitious and any resemblance to real life persons or situations is purely coincidental. In addition, although the memo is believed to be accurate as of the date indicated in it, readers of this book should not rely on the memo as legal advice but should instead consult their own lawyers if they have questions regarding the enforceability of waivers in specific sporting or recreational situations.

---

22 Footnotes in the memo that follow assume that the memo is separate from this chapter and the footnotes in it up to this point.

Memorandum

To: Pat Partner
From: Robin Researcher
Date: 6 August 2004

Subject: File 54-9234 — Enforcement of Waivers in Sporting Events

ABC Bungee Ontario Inc. and its Bungee-Jumping Business

Our client is ABC Bungee Ontario Inc. The company is concerned about its potential liability if customers are injured while bungee jumping. You have asked me to research the law in Canada on the enforceability of liability waivers used in sporting and recreational events and set out steps the company might take to help ensure the enforceability of any liability waivers it might use in its business.

Summary of Research Findings

Based on my research, I am of the following opinion:

1) Courts generally enforce signed waivers used by operators of sporting and recreational events to shield them from liability against negligence claims by adult participants. To be enforceable, though, the waiver and its execution should meet certain requirements:

   a) The waiver must be drawn to the attention of the customer.

   b) The waiver must be clearly written. Since courts generally construe waivers narrowly according to their terms, the waiver should be broad enough to cover all contingencies, including the persons covered (the client and its employees and agents), the types of conduct covered (negligence of employees, among other things), and the risks and injuries being waived (e.g., personal injury and death).

   c) Customers should be asked to sign the waiver at the time they pay their admission fee (to ensure adequate contractual consideration for the release). Customers must also be given sufficient time prior to jumping to read and understand the waiver and be given the option to withdraw if they choose not to accept the terms of the waiver.

   d) To avoid arguments that the customer did not understand the waiver because he or she was drunk or under the influence of drugs, the operator should not allow visibly drunk or incapacitated customers to sign (or jump).

2) Although certain recreational operators, such as ski resorts, have successfully avoided liability solely based on the waiver on the back of the ski ticket and posted notices (i.e., without there being a signed waiver), relying merely on a "ticket" waiver is risky since there are also a number of cases where ticket waivers were held to be invalid due to the lack of notice given to the participant of the terms of the waiver. Likewise, although it could be argued that participants of bungee jumping would be taken to know and willingly assume the risks of this thrill sport, relying solely on the defence of *volenti fit non injuria* (discussed below) — in the absence of a signed waiver — is also risky.

3) Courts are unlikely to enforce a waiver signed by a minor since the waiver would be held not to benefit the child. Even where a parent or guardian waives the child's rights, there is a risk that a court would not enforce the waiver in favour of the operator.

These points will be discussed in detail below in the Analysis section of this memo. At the end of this memo, I discuss drafting a suitable waiver for the client to use in its operations.

Facts and Assumptions

My research assumes the following facts:

1) The client, an Ontario company, operates a bungee-jumping business in which customers pay $80.00 per jump to jump off the Flavelle Ravine Bridge in Flavelle, Ontario, with a bungee cord wrapped around their legs.

2) The client is concerned about its potential liability if a customer is injured while bungee jumping.

I also assume that you have reviewed or will review with the client the following points that may affect its potential liability if a customer were every injured:

3) The client is adequately capitalized and follows all necessary corporate formalities to minimize the risk of directors and officers being held personally liable for any accidents. In addition, the client has obtained all permits to operate its bungee-jumping business.

4) The client has procedures in place to ensure that its bungee-jumping operations comply with the *Canadian Bungee — Code of Safe Prac-*

tice.[1] In particular, the client should ensure that it regularly inspects its equipment for defects, that its employees are properly trained and certified in all aspects of the operation, and that it uses reasonable efforts to screen customers who appear under the influence of alcohol or drugs so that they are not able to bungee jump (since alcohol or drugs may impair the customer's understanding of the waiver).

Academic Commentary

The enforceability of waivers in sporting and recreational events is well documented in textbook and law reform commission literature. Appendix A sets out a list of some of the more relevant books, which are also cited or referred to throughout this memo.

Likewise, there are a number of good journal articles and continuing legal education seminar papers that discuss this issue. These are also listed in Appendix A and are cited or referred to below, where relevant.

Legislation

The client will likely be considered an "occupier" of the bungee-jumping premises. As such, under section 3 of the *Occupiers' Liability Act,*[2] the client will owe a duty of care to see that its customers are reasonably safe while on the premises:

> 3. (1) An occupier of premises owes a duty to take such care as in all the circumstances of the case is reasonable to see that persons entering on the premises, and the property brought on the premises by those persons are reasonably safe while on the premises.
>
> (2) The duty of care provided for in subsection (1) applies whether the danger is caused by the condition of the premises or by an activity carried on on the premises.

Section 1(3) of the Act, however, would allow our client to restrict its duty as an occupier:

---

1   The safety regulations governing bungee jumping in Ontario are initially confusing to find and cite. The *Canadian Bungee — Code of Safe Practice* is part of the "Amusement Devices Code Adoption Document" from the *Codes and Standards Adopted by Reference Regulation,* O. Reg. 223/01. The *Amusement Devices Regulation,* O. Reg. 221/01, defines "bungee ride or bungee-type device." All of these regulations and standards are authorized by s. 34(1) of the *Technical Standards and Safety Act, 2000,* S.O. 2000, c. 16.

2   R.S.O. 1990, c. O-2.

> The duty of care provided for in subsection (1) applies except in so far as the occupier of premises is free to and does restrict, modify or exclude the occupier's duty.

Section 4(1) of the Act restricts the application of the duty of care where the risk is willingly assumed by the participant:

> The duty of care provided for in subsection 3 (1) does not apply in respect of risks willingly assumed by the person who enters on the premises, but in that case the occupier owes a duty to the person to not create a danger with the deliberate intent of doing harm or damage to the person or his or her property and to not act with reckless disregard of the presence of the person or his or her property.

Section 5(3) of the Act requires the occupier to take reasonable steps to bring any restriction on its duty of care to the attention of the person to whom the duty of care is owed:

> Where an occupier is free to restrict, modify or exclude the occupier's duty of care or the occupier's liability for breach thereof, the occupier shall take reasonable steps to bring such restriction, modification or exclusion to the attention of the person to whom the duty is owed.

The impact of the *Occupier's Liability Act* is discussed below in the Analysis section of this memo.

Current regulations governing bungee jumping in Ontario stem from a 1992 Task Force on Bungee Jumping formed by the Minister of Consumer and Commercial Relations. The purpose of this task force was to address safety concerns as a result of a bungee-jumping death in Peterborough, Ontario on 1 August 1992.[3] The Task Force report indicates, among other things:

- Three bungee-jumping deaths in North America (up to 1992) and a number of documented serious injuries (primarily in the United States).[4]
- Various risk sources in bungee jumping, including jump platforms and manbaskets, anchors and carabineers, bungee cords, harnesses, fall protection, and human factors.[5]

As a result of the Task Force report, it appears that the Ontario government introduced regulations under the *Amusement Devices Act* (now

---

3   Mary Spencer, *Report of the Task Force on Bungee Jumping* (Toronto: Ministry of Consumer and Commercial Relations, 1993) at 2.
4   *Ibid.* at 10–11.
5   *Ibid.* at 12–15.

called the *Technical Standards and Safety Act, 2000,* S.O. 2000, c. 16, mentioned above) to regulate safety standards in the bungee-jumping industry in Ontario. Part VI of the "Amusement Devices Code Adoption Document" is entitled "Amusement Devices Incorporating Elastic Suspension Systems, Section 25" and makes the *Canadian Bungee — Code of Safe Practice* binding on all bungee-jumping operators:

> Every bungee ride or bungee type device shall comply with the Canadian Bungee — Code of Safe Practice. (Revision 04/07/00).

The *Canadian Bungee — Code of Safe Practice* is available online.[6] This Code regulates bungee-jumping operations and is divided into sections that include the regulation of equipment, site conditions and requirements, management procedures, and jump-site personnel. In addition to the Code, there are also regulations governing the certification and training of amusement device mechanics.[7]

This Code does not appear to create an explicit statutory tort duty of care, but if there ever were a claim in negligence in Ontario against a bungee-jumping operator, a court would likely look to the Code as evidence of the standard by which bungee-jumping operators would be held.[8] It would therefore be important for our client to comply with the safety standards in the Code.

Canadian Case Law

There is a well-defined body of case law in Canada relating to the enforceability of waivers in sporting and recreational events. Many of these cases stem from skiing and white-water rafting cases in British Columbia, but there are cases from all jurisdictions, including Ontario.

I reviewed the case law mentioned in the books, journals, and encyclopedia entries listed in Appendix A in addition to reviewing case law in the *Canadian Abridgment* and by searching on each of Quicklaw, LexisNexis, and WestlaweCARSWELL.

---

6   See online: Technical Standards and Safety Association
     <http://www.tssa.org/amusement/pdf/bungeeCodeSafePractice.pdf>.
7   *Certification and Training of Amusement Device Mechanics,* O. Reg. 187/03.
8   In my print and online search for case law, I found no Canadian cases dealing with the potential liability in negligence of a bungee-jumping operator for injuries caused to a customer while bungee jumping. I did find one criminal prosecution under s. 18 of the *Amusement Devices Act* against Anderson Ventures LLC relating to the death of a bungee-jumping customer in August 1998 in Ottawa when a strap loosened from the harness and the customer plunged eighty feet to his death — see: *R. v. Anderson Ventures LLC,* [2000] O.J. No. 5819 (C.J.). The bungee-jumping operator was convicted on several of the counts.

Set out below is an overview of the most relevant cases, divided into (1) cases where the waiver was enforced; and (2) cases where the waiver was not enforced. Under each category, the most important cases are listed first.

1) Canadian Cases Where the Waiver Was Enforced

There are a number of Canadian cases where the court enforced a waiver to deny a claim for damages for someone injured in a sporting event:[9]

- *Dyck v. Man. Snowmobile Assn. Inc.*, [1985] 1 S.C.R. 589: The plaintiff was injured during a snowmobile race when a race official moved onto the race track to signal the end of the race. The court relieved the defendant of any liability for negligence because of the waiver signed by the plaintiff as part of the entry form:

  > The central fact is that a waiver clause of the kind in issue in the present case does not appear to be unreasonable. The appellant knew, or should have known, that snowmobile racing is a dangerous sport and he voluntarily participated in it . . . .

  > The appellant freely joined and participated in activities organized by an association. The association neither exercised pressure on the appellant nor unfairly took advantage of social or economic pressures on him to get him to participate in its activities. As already mentioned, the races carried with them inherent dangers of which the appellant should have been aware and it was in no way unreasonable for an organization like the association to seek to protect itself against liability from suit for damages arising out of such dangers. It follows from this that there are no grounds of public policy on which the waiver clause should be struck down, an issue also raised on behalf of the appellant [¶ 9–10].

- *Dixon v. Kamloops Exhibition Assn.*, 2003 BCCA 174: The plaintiff was injured during a practice snowmobile run at a race sponsored by

---

9　Because there appeared to be sufficient Canadian case law on point, I did not research British or American case law. For a good overview of American case law (which appears to be relatively consistent with Canadian case law) see Randy J. Sutton, "Validity, Construction, and Effect of Agreement Exempting Operator of Amusement Facility from Liability for Personal Injury or Death of Patron" (1997), 54 A.L.R. (5th) 513 and Lee R. Russ, "Products Liability: General Recreational Equipment" (1990), 77 A.L.R. (4th) 1121.

the defendant. At trial, the court ruled that the waiver the plaintiff was required to sign before racing was not clear enough to cover "practice runs." On appeal, however, the court held that the phrase "arising out of or related to the events" was intended to apply to a practice for the race in addition to the race itself.

- *Delaney v. Cascade River Holidays Ltd.* (1983), 44 B.C.L.R. 24 (C.A.): The plaintiff was killed while white-water rafting. His wife sued the defendant alleging it was negligent in failing to provide proper life-jackets for the rafters. Although the appeal court accepted the finding that the defendant was negligent, the majority dismissed the claim on the basis of the waiver of liability the plaintiff signed prior to boarding the river raft. The dissenting judge, however, ruled the release ineffective for two reasons: (1) There was no consideration for the release since the plaintiff signed it shortly before boarding the raft and after he had entered into the contract earlier that day; and (2) There was insufficient notice to the plaintiff of the terms and effect of the release, which was misleading since it only spoke of loss or damage and not the risk of personal injury or death.

- *Rauhanen v. Lee*, 2003 ABQB 84: The plaintiff was injured as a participant in a wheelchair race sponsored by the defendants. The race organizers required racers to sign a waiver that released the defendants from claims for "all injuries in any manner arising or resulting from" the race. The court upheld the waiver and dismissed the plaintiff's claim for injuries.

- *Mayer v. Big White Ski Resort Ltd.* (1998), 112 B.C.A.C. 288: The plaintiff, while skiing, collided with a snowmobile operated by an employee of the defendant ski resort and suffered a severely broken ankle. The plaintiff was a season's pass holder and had signed a waiver form at the start of the ski season when he obtained his season's pass. Even though the plaintiff did not read the release when he signed it, he had signed them in the past and the release contained a warning in bolded text. And although the defendant was relatively casual in its handling of the signed form (it did not witness the plaintiff's signature and placed it in an overflowing pile of documents), the court enforced the release, being satisfied that the defendant met its statutory obligation under B.C.'s *Occupier's Liability Act* to bring the waiver to the attention of the party signing it. For cases with similar facts and results (season's pass holders denied recovery for injuries due to their signed waivers) see *Ocsko v. Cypress Bowl Recreations Ltd.* (1992), 95 D.L.R. (4th) 701 (B.C.C.A.) and *Blomberg v. Blackcomb Skiing Enterprises Ltd.* (1992), 64 B.C.L.R. (2d) 51 (S.C.).

- *Schuster v. Blackcomb Skiing Enterprises Ltd. Partnership*, [1995] 3 W.W.R. 443 (B.C.S.C.): The plaintiff, an experienced skier who had skied at the defendant's resort in the past, suffered a fractured vertebrae during a three-day lesson and sued for her injuries. Prior to enrolling in the program, though, the defendant required her to sign a broadly worded, easy-to-read waiver that was clearly intended to release the defendant from any claims the plaintiff might have. The court dismissed the plaintiff's action on the basis that the waiver was clear and that the defendant brought the terms of the waiver to the plaintiff's attention. The court ruled that, under the circumstances present where there was a clearly worded written notice given to the plaintiff, the defendant was not obliged to give additional verbal notice.
- *McQuary v. Big White Ski Resort Ltd.*, [1993] B.C.J. No. 1956 (S.C.): The plaintiff fractured his pelvis when he landed in a culvert at the defendant's ski hill. At issue was whether the defendant had a complete defence to the plaintiff's claim based on the waiver on the back of the plaintiff's ski ticket purchased for the day and the notices the defendant had posted at the ticket window. The plaintiff acknowledged that he did not read the waiver even though he knew there was language on the back of the ticket that limited the liability of the defendant. The court, in upholding the validity of the release, was satisfied that the bright red border surrounding the waiver and the red and yellow background on the defendant's notice board were sufficient to bring the terms of the waiver to the attention of the plaintiff.
- *Karroll v. Silver Star Mountain Resorts Ltd.* (1988), 33 B.C.L.R. (2d) 160 (S.C.): The plaintiff was injured during a downhill ski race. Prior to entering the race, she signed a "release and indemnity" releasing the resort operator and its agents from liability for any injuries sustained during the race. The court dismissed the plaintiff's claim and upheld the release. The court identified a number of factors that may affect whether a resort operator has a positive duty to take reasonable steps to advise of an exclusion clause or waiver: (1) Whether the exclusion clause runs contrary to the party's normal expectations. Here, the waiver was consistent with the purpose of the contract — to permit the plaintiff to engage in a hazardous activity upon which she, of her own volition, desired to embark, while limiting the liability of the organizations that made the activity possible (¶ 27); and (2) The length and format of the contract and the time available for reading and understanding it also bear on whether a reasonable person should know that the other party did not in fact

intend to sign what he was signing (¶ 25). Here, the waiver was short, easy to understand, and the plaintiff was not hurried into signing it. The court also noted that waivers were commonly used in ski races and that the plaintiff had previously signed them for other races.

- *Clarke v. Action Driving School Ltd.*, 1996 CarswellBC 1004 (S.C.): The plaintiff was a 53-year-old doctor injured while taking motorcycle lessons from the defendant. When he registered for lessons, he was required to sign a waiver, which was witnessed by an employee of the defendant. In the waiver, the plaintiff released the defendant from "claims of every nature and kind howsoever arising." The court held that this wording was broad enough to cover the defendant's negligence. Given the plaintiff's education and intelligence, the court also ruled that the waiver was not unconscionable nor was the plaintiff in a vulnerable position when he signed it since he could have simply refused the lessons if he was uncomfortable with the waiver.

- *Simpson v. Nahanni River Adventures Ltd.*, 1997 CarswellYukon 64 (S.C.): The plaintiff sued the defendant adventure company for the death of her husband, who was killed during a flash flood while on a canoe trip organized by the defendant. Prior to the excursion, the husband had signed a waiver releasing the defendant from "any claims whatsoever." In dismissing the plaintiff's claim and upholding the validity of the waiver, the court noted the waiver's plain English and the fact that the husband, who was educated and actually read the waiver, was given ample time to read the document, a document that also invited participants to ask questions of the company, if any.

2)   Canadian Cases Where the Waiver Was Not Enforced

In lawsuits where the waiver was not enforced and the operator found liable, it was usually due to one of two reasons: either the defendant failed to bring the terms of the waiver to the attention of the plaintiff, or the waiver was deficient in its language and did not apply to the accident.

Lack of notice/communication cases:

- *Crocker v. Sundance Northwest Resorts Ltd.*, [1988] 1 S.C.R. 1186: The plaintiff, while visibly drunk, broke his neck during a tubing race on the defendant's ski hill. Because of his self-induced intoxication, the plaintiff was held 25% contributorily negligent for his injuries. The defendant, however, was found liable in negligence for failing to stop a drunk person from participating in what was a potentially dangerous event. The court ruled that Crocker did not voluntarily assume the legal or physical risk of the injury in part because of his drunken condition. The defendant was not entitled to rely upon the waiver contained in the entry form signed by Crocker before the event since the waiver was not drawn to the plaintiff's attention, he had not read it, and did not know of its existence (¶ 36).

- *Wilson v. Blue Mountain Resorts Ltd.* (1974), 4 O.R. (2d) 713 (S.C.): The plaintiff was an experienced skier injured while skiing through a gulley that had been previously marked with flags as being a hazard (the flags were not posted at the time of the accident). The defendant ski hill operator was found liable for negligence for failing to properly inspect the gulley and post warning flags. The defendant was not entitled to rely on the disclaimer on the back of the plaintiff's ticket since the defendant took no steps to bring the disclaimer to the attention of the plaintiff. In addition, the court held that the plaintiff did not knowingly accept the risk of injury since the danger in this case was not obvious.

- *Greeven v. Blackcomb Skiing Enterprises Ltd.* (1994), 22 C.C.L.T. (2d) 265 (B.C.S.C.): The plaintiff was an inexperienced skier injured due to a dangerous drop off. The defendant ski hill operator applied for a summary judgment to dismiss the plaintiff's claim on the basis that the defendant's liability was excluded by a disclaimer on the back of the plaintiff's ski ticket and various signs on the ski hill near the ticket wickets and lifts that set out the terms of the waiver. The court denied the defendant's application to dismiss the lawsuit since the defendant did not take sufficient steps to draw the limitation of liability to the attention of this particular plaintiff.

Waiver language insufficient to cover injury cases:

- *Huber v. Conquest Tours (Toronto) Ltd.* (1990), 74 O.R. (2d) 781 (Div. Ct.): The plaintiffs in this case sued the defendant tour company for a "nightmarish" holiday they had booked at a resort in the Dominican Republic that was still under construction at the time of the trip. At trial, the court found the defendant tour company liable in negligence for failing to make adequate inquiries into the readiness of the hotel resort. The Divisional Court upheld this ruling on appeal in addition to ruling that the tour company was not protected by a waiver in its brochure due to its ambiguous and awkward wording:

  This provision is found on p. 62 at the back of Conquest's brochure. It is in small print and difficult to read. It is plagued with grammatical and typographical errors, repetition, and convoluted syntax. Compared to the flyer and the descriptions of tours in the rest of the brochure, it is difficult to comprehend, if it can be comprehended at all [¶ 24].

- *Quick v. Jericho Tennis Club* (1998), 40 B.L.R. (2d) 315 (S.C.): The plaintiff was injured while participating in a tennis tournament held at the defendant's tennis club. All tournament participants had to sign a waiver. In this lawsuit, however, the court dismissed the defendant's application for summary judgment because the defendant tennis club was not specifically named or referred to in the waiver (the waiver instead stated "all claims of any kind, nature and description are waived, including past, present or future claims for injuries, if any, sustained in travelling to or from or participating in any Grand Prix tournament or against Tennis Canada, TBC, USTA & PNWTA or any other section, the SunLife Prince Grand Prix Circuit Committee, Tournament Committees and all Tournament and Circuit Sponsors").

- *Lyster v. Fortess Mountain Resorts Ltd.* (1978), 6 Alta. L.R. (2d) 338 (S.C.T.D.): The plaintiff skier was injured by a flying T-Bar cable. The cable derailed due to extremely high winds (the defendant had in fact already closed some of its runs due to the high winds). The court found the defendant liable in negligence for failing to close the T-bar due to high gusty winds. The lift ticket stated: "The Person using this ticket assumes all risks of Personal injury, loss or damage to property." The court ruled, however, that the defendant was not entitled to rely on this language to avoid liability since it did not specifically cover the negligence of its employees and resolved any doubt about the matter against the ski resort.

- *Smith v. Horizon Aero Sports Ltd.* (1981), 130 D.L.R. (3d) 91 (B.C.S.C.): The plaintiff broke her back and became paralyzed while trying to land her first parachute jump. She was trained at the defendant's parachute jumping school but the court held the defendant 70% at fault for failing to properly train the plaintiff in jump and landing procedures and failing to ensure that the plaintiff understood these procedures. The court construed the waiver signed by the plaintiff narrowly and held that the defendant was not protected by it because its language did not clearly exclude negligent training by the defendant.

- *Kettunen v. Sicamous Firemen's Club*, 1999 CarswellBC 1866 (S.C.), leave to appeal to C.A. refused 1999 BCCA 719: In this case, the plaintiff had accompanied her husband to an annual mud bog race held on the grounds of the defendant's property. Although the plaintiff was described on her husband's race application form as being part of his pit crew, she really wasn't, although she was present in the pit crew area from time-to-time. She signed a waiver as part of this process but claimed not to have understood it. She was injured when a mud bog car lost control and struck her. At issue was whether her signed waiver barred her claim for damages for her injuries. In ruling against the defendant, the court held that the defendant had not taken sufficient steps to bring the terms of the waiver to the plaintiff's attention. The court also ruled that the terms of the waiver were unclear and were not broad enough to cover the area where the accident actually occurred.

Analysis

1) Factors Affecting the Enforceability of Waivers in Sporting Accidents

In many of the foregoing cases, plaintiffs injured at recreational events sued under the applicable provincial occupiers' liability legislation, in addition to suing under general tort or negligence principles. As stated above, it is likely that our client would be considered an occupier under Ontario's *Occupiers' Liability Act* and would be held under section 3(1) of that Act to owe a duty to take such care as is reasonable to see that persons entering its premises are reasonably safe. If the client chooses to restrict this statutory duty under section 5(3), it must take reasonable steps to bring the restriction to the attention of its customers.

From the foregoing cases and commentary, it can be seen that courts will generally enforce signed waivers used by operators of sporting and recreational events to shield them from liability against negligence claims by adult participants when the participant is found to be aware of the waiver, is given time to read the waiver, and where the waiver is drafted in a manner that is understandable to the participant. When the courts do not enforce waivers, it is usually due to a deficiency in one or more of these factors, such as the participant not having sufficient notice of the waiver, being given insufficient time to read and understand the waiver, or because the language in the waiver was insufficient to name the actual tortfeasor or cover the actual risk encountered.

To be enforceable, any waiver used by our client should meet certain requirements:

a) **Notice requirements:** The waiver must be drawn to the attention of the customer.[10]

The issue of notice arises most often in "ticket" cases where, for example, the waiver is on the back of a ski ticket. The issue arises less often in situations where participanst are required to sign the waiver. Where the waiver is signed, it is more difficult for participants to claim they did not know what they were signing.[11]

b) **Content/language requirements:** The waiver must be clearly written. Since courts generally construe waivers narrowly according to their terms against those who draft them[12] the waiver should be broad enough to cover all contingencies, including clearly naming the client and its employees and agents, the types of conduct covered (negligence of employees, among other things), and the risks and injuries being waived (personal injury and death, for example).

c) **Consideration:** Customers should be asked to sign the waiver at the time they pay their admission fee (to ensure adequate contractual consideration for the release). Customers must also be given sufficient time prior to jumping to read and understand the waiver and be given the option to withdraw if they choose not to accept the terms of the waiver. Both "past consideration" and insufficient signing time were issues in the *Delaney* river-rafting case (above); the dissenting Court of Appeal judge in that case would not have enforced the waiver and held the river-rafting company liable because the participant signed the release sometime after paying his fees and only shortly before having to get on the boat, at which time he did not have much choice but to sign the waiver.

---

10 G.H.L. Fridman, *The Law of Contract in Canada*, 4th ed. (Toronto: Carswell, 1999) at 610ff; Jeffrey J. Neumann, "Disclaimer Clauses and Personal Injury" (1991) 55 Sask. L. Rev. 312 at 313ff; Robert D. Kligman, "Tort Liability for Sports Injuries" (1989) 1 C.I.L.R. 153 at 176; John Barnes, *Sports and the Law in Canada*, 3d ed. (Toronto: Butterworths, 1996) at 278; Glenda Hanna, *Outdoor Pursuits Programming: Legal Liability and Risk Management* (Edmonton: University of Alberta Press, 1991) at 131–32; Law Reform Commission of British Columbia, *Report on Recreational Injuries: Liability and Waivers in Commercial Leisure Activities* (Vancouver: The Commission, 1994) at 10; *Crocker v. Sundance Northwest Resorts Ltd.*, above at ¶ 36; *Wilson v. Blue Mountain Resorts Ltd.*, above at ¶ 15.

11 Law Reform Commission of British Columbia, *ibid.*; *Mayer v. Big White Ski Resort Ltd.*, above; *McQuary v. Big White Ski Resort Ltd.*, above at ¶ 16.

12 Law Reform Commission of British Columbia, *ibid.*: "Courts will confine the effect of waivers and exclusionary wordings on tickets to their precise terms and will not give them any broader interpretation than is necessary." See also Barnes, above note 10 at 277 and *Huber v. Conquest Tours (Toronto) Ltd.*, above at ¶ 28–29.

d) **Contractual capacity**: To avoid arguments that the customer did not understand the waiver because he or she was drunk or under the influence of drugs, the operator should not allow visibly drunk or incapacitated customers to jump. This was an issue in the *Crocker* tubing case where the court did not enforce the waiver signed by Crocker, who was visibly drunk and who likely did not understand or appreciate the terms of the waiver due to his condition.

2) Ticket Waivers and *volenti fit non injuria*

Although certain recreational operators, such as ski resorts, have successfully avoided liability solely based on the waiver on the back of the ski ticket and posted notices (i.e., without there being a signed waiver), relying merely on this type of "ticket" waiver is risky, as can be seen by the varied results in the skiing ticket cases described above, with some of those waivers being enforced and others not.

Likewise, although it could be argued that any bungee-jumping participant would be taken to know and willingly assume the risks of this thrill sport, relying solely on the defence of *volenti fit non injuria* ("there can be no wrong where a person consents") — in the absence of a signed waiver — is also risky. Courts have generally narrowed the defence of *volenti fit non injuria* to require that the plaintiff must knowingly accept both the physical and legal risks of the injury.[13]

In bungee jumping, if a customer were injured or killed due to a defective cord, it is unlikely that the defence of *volenti fit non injuria* would apply since the customer would be deemed not to have assumed the risk of defective equipment. Instead, the *volenti* defence would likely be limited to risks inherent in the sport (heart attacks due to fear, perhaps?) and not something that goes beyond the inherent risk (such as an illegal check into the boards in ice hockey).[14]

3) Waivers and Minors

Although many schools and other organizations continue to ask parents to sign waivers absolving them of liability for negligence for injuries caused to their students or minor participants, it is questionable whether parents can effectively waive their child's rights to sue for

---

13 Philip H. Osborne, *The Law of Torts*, 2d ed. (Toronto: Irwin Law, 2003) at 102–5; Neumann, above note 10 at 316–17; J.D. Tomlinson & G. Grant Machum, "The Contractual Waiver of Liability in Ski Resort Negligence Claims" (1997) 15 Can. J. Ins. L. 49 at 49–50.

14 See *Robinson v. Madison*, [1987] B.C.J. 2100 (S.C.) and Law Reform Commission of British Columbia, above note 10 at 8.

damages.[15] Clearly, if a child alone were to sign the waiver directly, it would be unenforceable since minors lack the legal capacity to contract and would likely void the contract since a waiver of legal rights would likely be considered not to benefit the child.[16]

Because there is much less certainty whether our client would be protected by a waiver signed by a parent on behalf of a child who was bungee jumping, the client may wish to restrict its clientele to adults only (if this is not already a restriction imposed by its liability insurers). If the client insists on allowing children to jump, we may wish to conduct further research on this issue.[17]

Drafting an Appropriate Waiver

There are a number of sources of sample waivers that could be used to adapt a waiver for our client's operations.[18]

To help ensure its enforceability, the waiver should be written in plain language, have a heading in bold font stating something such as "Waiver and Release of All Claims — Read Carefully," and — if possible — have a red border or other colour features to draw attention to it.[19] The waiver should release equipment failure, negligence by the

---

15   See Hanna, above note 10 at 32, citing *Butterfield v. Sibbit and Nipissing Electric Co.*, [1950] 4 D.L.R. 302 (Ont. H.C.). See also Barnes, above note 10 at 278 citing *Swanson v. Hanneson*, [1972] 3 W.W.R. 241 (Man. Q.B.), *Crawford v. Ferris*, [1953] O.W.N. 713 (H.C.J.) and *M. v. Sinclair* (1980), 15 C.C.L.T. 57 (Ont. H.C.J.). See also *Stevens v. Howitt*, [1969] 1 O.R. 761 (H.C.J.) [contrary to public policy for parent to provide waiver and indemnification on behalf of his child injured in a car accident] and Law Reform Commission of British Columbia, above note 10 at 31–32 (although the situation in British Columbia appears to be more clearly covered by legislation).

16   Barnes, above note 10 at 278. See also the *Canadian Encyclopedic Digest*, 3d, Vol. 5 (Toronto: Carswell, 2004) "Contracts," §27.

17   For example, Hanna, above note 10 at 130, raises the risk of such waivers being unenforceable but goes on to discuss the possibility of including language in the waiver to be signed by the parent or guardian that the contract (i.e., bungee jumping) is for the benefit of the child and that the parent or guardian, on behalf of the child, accepts the physical and legal risks of bungee jumping. I am concerned whether such language would be sufficient to ensure enforceability of the waiver.

18   See, e.g., Chapter 10 "Athletics," ¶ 10:15 — Sporting Event Release" and Chapter 49 "Releases" in *O'Brien's Encyclopedia of Forms* (Canada Law Book); Hanna, *ibid.* at 207–10 has a sample "Assumption of Risk Agreement" and Chapter 11 "Release Forms" in Christine Mowat, *A Plain Language Handbook for Legal Writers* (Toronto: Carswell, 1998) has an annotated plain language release.

19   A number of the tips I describe in this paragraph are suggested by Tomlinson & Machum, above note 13 at 54.

client and its employees, and should refer to the risk of personal injury and death. In a number of cases where the waiver was enforced, the court specifically referred to language in the waiver similar to "by signing this document, you are giving up the right to sue" as being clearly-worded and easily understood by those who are asked to sign it. The waiver should also contain language that customers are willingly assuming the risk of injury and an acknowledgement by the customer that this waiver excludes any duty the client might have to customers under the *Occupiers' Liability Act*.

The client may also wish to have the waiver reprinted on a prominent sign at the entrance to the bungee jump and also included in its promotional brochures. If the client caters to a large enough foreign language clientele (French or Chinese, for example) it should provide accurately translated versions of its waiver. Staff should be trained to ensure that all customers are given an opportunity to read and sign the waiver.

If you would like me to draft a sample waiver, please let me know.

Robin Researcher.

Appendix A — Resources Consulted

Books
- Barnes, John. *Sports and the Law in Canada*. 3d ed. Toronto: Butterworths, 1996 at 276–79; 292–96.
- Bird, Stephen and John Zauhar. *Recreation and the Law*. Toronto: Carswell, 1992 at 52–54.
- Fridman, G.H.L. *The Law of Contract in Canada*. 4th ed. Toronto: Carswell, 1999 at 593–637.
- Hanna, Glenda. *Outdoor Pursuits Programming: Legal Liability and Risk Management*. Edmonton: University of Alberta Press, 1991.
- Law Reform Commission of British Columbia. *Report on Recreational Injuries: Liability and Waivers in Commercial Leisure Activities*. Vancouver: The Commission, 1994.
- Linden, Allen M. *Canadian Tort Law*. 7th ed. Toronto: Butterworths, 2001 at 474–78.
- *Occupiers' Liability: Recreational Use of Land*. Edmonton: Alberta Law Reform Institute, 2000 (February 2000. Final Report No. 81).
- Opie, Hayden. *Compensation for Physical Injury Sustained by Participants in Sport*. LL.M. Thesis, University of Toronto, 1985 at 217–19.
- Osborne, Philip H. *The Law of Torts*. 2d ed. Toronto: Irwin Law, 2003 at 102–7.
- Spencer, Mary. *Report of the Task Force on Bungee Jumping*. Toronto: Ministry of Consumer and Commercial Relations, 1993.

Articles
- Bark, W.D. "Waiver — Release — Hold Harmless Agreements" in *Sports in the Courts*. Toronto: Canadian Bar Association — Ontario, 1987.
- Bowal, Peter. "For the Thrill of One's Life: Legal Liability for Shattered Adventures" (1999) 23:5 L. Now No. 27.
- Campbell, Colin L. "Warnings, Disclaimers, Consents: Preventive Measures and Legal Strategies to Reduce the Potential Exposure" in *Recreational Facilities Liability: Maximizing Protection, Minimizing Exposure*. Toronto: Canadian Institute, 1993.
- Kligman, Robert D. "Tort Liability for Sports Injuries" (1989) 1 C.I.L.R. 153.
- Neumann, Jeffrey J. "Disclaimer Clauses and Personal Injury" (1991) 55 Sask. L. Rev. 312.
- Olah, John A. "Sports Liability: The Operator's Nightmare" in *Sports in the Courts*. Toronto: Canadian Bar Association — Ontario, 1987.

- Tomlinson, J.D. and G. Grant Machum. "The Contractual Waiver of Liability in Ski Resort Negligence Claims" (1997) 15 Can. J. Ins. L. 49.

Encyclopedia

Canadian Encyclopedic Digest. 3d ed. Vol. 31. Toronto: Carswell, 2000. "Sports," § 96.

Case Law Digests

Canadian Abridgment. 2d: Vol. R29: Negligence — Defences (V) — Exculpatory clauses (2) (Negligence, V.2).

Canadian Abridgment., 2d: Vol. R29: Negligence — Defences (V) — Volenti non fit injuria (6) — Sporting events (g) (Negligence, V.6.g).

Canadian Abridgment. 2d: Vol. R29: Negligence — Occupier's Liability (VI) — Particular situations (3) — Amusement or other public parks (a) (Negligence, VI.3.a).

Canadian Abridgment. 3d: Vol. 27: Contracts — Construction and Interpretation (VII) — Disclaimer clauses (9) (Contracts, VII.9).

E. COMMENTS ON THE SAMPLE RESEARCH MEMO

The drafting of the memo represents the fourth and fifth stages of the FILAC legal research process discussed in Chapter 1, section B (i.e., analysis and conclusions). What is not shown here are the detailed notes that must be taken by the researcher when reviewing the primary sources of law in Step 4 of the Legal Research Checklist.

In addition, what is not explicitly evident in the materials above is the circular or iterative nature of the legal research process. The very nature of this process reinforces the value of being as thorough as possible in following the various steps in the Legal Research Checklist since, even if you perhaps miss an obvious source in one of the steps, there is a good chance you will stumble across the reference to the source in another stage of the process. A few examples of this occurred while conducting the research for the hypothetical problem in this chapter:

- A footnote in the *Canadian Encyclopedic Digest* referred to some relevant journal articles that were not uncovered the first time the *Index to Canadian Legal Literature* was searched.
- The *Index to Canadian Legal Literature* disclosed several relevant book titles (although these were already found during the "book search" phase), as well as revealing that there was a "Sports" title in the *Canadian Encyclopedic Digest*, something that may not have been obvious to a researcher using the encyclopedia for the first time.
- Once cases were found in various books and journal articles, it was then possible to "repeat" the book research by reviewing the "Table of Cases" in those books to check for possible additional commentary on those cases. It was also possible to re-run the journal index searches on those case names to look for case comments on those cases.
- If the initial legislative research did not uncover regulations governing bungee jumping in Ontario, it may well have been that Internet searches would have uncovered references to bungee safety codes, which should then prompt the researcher to repeat the legislative research to verify the existence of these regulations.

The point here is to realize that the effective researcher will pick up on clues and references and not be shy to re-visit or repeat earlier steps in the research process. At a certain point, when the same references and cases start to re-appear consistently, that may be a good sign that you have come close to exhausting the research for that topic.

The form of the sample memo ended up being more like the type of legal research memo written in law school for a course where a hypothetical problem is assigned to a law student. Many law firm legal research memos, for example, are not always so deeply footnoted and may not contain an Appendix of resources consulted (although lists of resources consulted can be useful to give assurance to the reader that standard materials were not overlooked). In addition, some law firm memos might be organized more along the lines of numbered "legal issues" as opposed to using the headings used in the sample research memo (summary of research findings, facts and assumptions, academic commentary, etc.). Because the issues were so straightforward in this problem, it was felt to be unnecessary to use a separate, bolded heading called "Issues." In more complex problems, it can often be useful to list the issues and answer each issue individually, in order.

Here are some additional comments on the sample memo:

- Most readers want to know your conclusions right away; hence, the "Summary of Research Findings" is the first major section of the memo. This results in the "Analysis" section later in the memo is somewhat repetitive, but by this stage, the reader can quickly skim the details if he or she is satisfied with the information by that point.
- The summaries of cases are also somewhat repetitive but many lawyers who read memos like to get a sense of what the relevant cases are about and to get some (but not too many) quotations from actual decisions. Initially, I had not planned on setting out the summaries of cases into two broad categories (cases where the waiver was enforced and cases where the waiver was not enforced), but this seemed like a practical way to convey the information. Alternatively, a chart might have been used for this purpose.
- You will see that I weaselled out of actually drafting a proposed plain language release (I often made my students do this when I used this problem as an assignment since it was a good exercise for them to draft a waiver in plain English). In reality, the lawyer asking for this research would also likely ask for a sample waiver. I tried to be somewhat helpful at least by identifying several good sources for sample waivers.
- I also waffled on the issue of whether waivers signed by parents on behalf of their child would be enforceable, in part because I was not expecting this issue to arise and I was surprised that the law appeared to be as uncertain as it did on this point. Waffling is not always a bad thing since the lawyer (and client) may not have appreciated hours of research on this issue if it turned out that the client

in fact already limited its operations to adults only. I therefore felt that briefly identifying the issue was sufficient, inviting the lawyer to ask for more research on this sub-topic, if relevant.

- If this were an academic research problem assigned in law school, it might be that the analysis would discuss the academic literature in more detail. Some of this discussion appears to be critical of the waiver decisions and the lack of consistency in their holdings (between *Crocker* and *Dyck*, for example). For this memo, however, I felt it was not too misleading to set out the cases without identifying this academic debate since the lawyer reading the memo wants practical answers, not a scholarly discussion.

- The memo is ridiculously long. In reality, because the law on these issues is relatively straightforward, it is unlikely that the client would be willing to pay for such a lengthy memo or detailed research. The memo ended up being so long in part because it is being published in a book and will be "frozen in time" for all readers of this book to read. As such, I felt the need to be more thorough than I might otherwise have been had I been writing this memo in a real-life situation.

There is no right or wrong way to organize a memo so long as the method used is logical and has some flow to it. Writing a memo can be a very organic process and the writer of the memo may very well change his or her organization, ideas, and even conclusions as to what the state of the law is as the memo is being drafted and revised.

Finally, equally important to what is expressed in the legal memo is what is contained in the legal research folder. Ideally, the researcher has a file containing detailed and dated notes showing what resources were consulted, what online searches were conducted (and on which databases), and what cases and legislation were consulted. Such notes, especially if the Legal Research Checklist is followed, go a long way to defeating allegations of legal research malpractice and ensuring high quality legal research results.

GLOSSARY

[Words in boldface within the definitions are defined elsewhere in the Glossary]

Abridgment: In legal literature, a summary or digest of a court case. Many publishers provide compilations of these summaries or digests organized by topic or theme. A well-known case law digest in Canada is Carswell's *Canadian Abridgment*, available in print, on CD-ROM, and on WestlaweCARSWELL (by subscription), which has summaries of Canadian court decisions, organized by topic. Quicklaw has an online digest service in its CCS database. See Chapter 2, section D for more information on abridgments.

Bill: A draft piece of legislation introduced in the applicable legislature. Most often, it is the ruling party that introduces draft legislation, but members of the opposition can also introduce bills; however opposition bills generally do not pass the requisite three readings needed to become law if they are too controversial. Bills can be public (if they are of general application) or private (if they only affect one organization or entity). A bill must pass all three readings and come into force prior to the proroguing of the legislature to become law. See also **Prorogued**.

Bluebook: This is the colloquial name of the legal **citation** guide used in the United States. Its formal name is *The Bluebook: A Uniform System of Citation* (published by the Harvard Law Review Association and revised regularly).

Boolean operators: Search commands used by Internet search engines and commercial online legal databases to allow the researcher to combine keywords. The typical Boolean operators are AND, OR, and NOT. Some search engines also allow the NEAR command (such as "wiretap NEAR unauthorized") or proximity searches, typically using the "within" command placing the words "within" so many words of each other ("wiretap /3 unauthorized"). Check the "search tips" provided with most search engines to create more precise search strategies.

Case comments: Structured "critiques" or comments on recent cases of significance. They are discussed in detail in Chapter 11, section D.

Catchwords: Legal publishers sometimes add **headnotes** or summaries of facts and law to court cases that they publish. Above the headnote and usually after the **style of cause** (the names of the parties to the lawsuit), the publisher may add "catchwords" (often in italics) that are the keywords by which the publisher has "tagged" or identified a particular case. Browsing through the catchwords can be a quick way of getting an idea of the relevancy of the case.

C.I.F. or CIF: In legal research parlance, C.I.F. stands for "coming into force" and is used by **Queen's Printers** to indicate in a Table of Public Statutes when an amendment to the statute comes into force. Example from the *Statutes of Canada* Table of Public Statutes: CIF, 1995, c. 45 in force 01.03.96 see SI/96-23. The foregoing example tells the reader that Chapter 45 of the 1995 *Statutes of Canada* is in force on 1 March 1996, as per a government order registered as SI/96-23 (which can be found in the *Canada Gazette Part II*).

Citation, legal: Most people don't like legal citation, but it is important. It refers to the numerous technical rules for citing cases, legislation, and other law-related materials. Some of these rules can be memorized or remembered; most of them must be checked by consulting the McGill Guide, the standard legal citation guide in Canada, more formally known as the *Canadian Guide to Uniform Legal Citation*. See also **Bluebook**, **McGill Guide**, and **Neutral citation**.

CJ: "Canadian Judgments," commonly called CJ, is the largest global database on Quicklaw of Canadian case law. If one wants to do the most exhaustive search of Canadian case law on Quicklaw, choose the CJ database.

Competent lawyer: A recent report by the Competence Task Force of the Law Society of Upper Canada (discussed in Chapter 1, section

A(1)) concluded that legal research and writing were fundamental skills of a competent lawyer.

Cookies: In Internet vocabulary, cookies are strings of computer-level information communicated between your Web browser and the Web site you are visiting, assuming you have "enabled" your browser to accept cookies. If your Web browser is so enabled, your computer will store information in a document called "cookies.txt" about the sites you have visited. When you next visit the same sites, information from your "cookies.txt" file will be used to help identify you and your preferences to the site you are visiting. Cookies are discussed in more detail in Chapter 5, section O.

Defendant: The person being sued by the **plaintiff** in a civil lawsuit. In the **style of cause** *Smith v. Jones*, one can assume that Jones is the defendant being sued by Smith (but this is not necessarily always the case since Smith could have originally been a defendant, and if Smith lost at trial and there was an appeal decision, the appellant in some **jurisdictions** is sometimes the first named party in the **style of cause**).

Dictionaries, legal: Provide simple definitions of law-related words, including more difficult legal or Latin phrases. They are discussed in more detail in Chapter 2, section E(1). See also **Words and phrases**.

Ejusdem generic: Literally "of the same kind." A rule used in statutory interpretation that presumes that a general term following a list of specific terms will be limited to the more specific term — in other words, the general term will be defined to be "of the same kind" as the more specific preceding terms. See Chapter 3, section F(4) for an example.

Electronic footprint: Internet and Web browser technology results in data being created every time one "surfs the net." There are a variety of "electronic footprints" that one can leave when using a Web browser. Chapter 5, section O discusses electronic footprints in more detail.

Expressio unius est exclusio alternius. Literally "to express one thing is to exclude another"; also known as the implied exclusion rule. This rule suggests that if the legislature left something out, it intended to do so since if it had wanted to include something it would have expressly set it out. See Chapter 3, section F(4) for an example.

Factum: A written argument or brief filed with the court that is used by a lawyer to argue a motion or case before a judge. Most **jurisdictions** have relatively strict rules regarding the contents and form of a factum. Chapter 11, section F discusses factums in more detail.

Field or **segment**: Most online commercial legal databases organize information, whether it be a case, a **statute**, or a journal article, into fields (on LexisNexis, they are called segments). You may not automatically see or recognize the fields when you look at the information on the screen, but you should realize the advantage of being able to search on particular fields in order to make your search results more precise. Examples include searching for cases by a particular judge, searching for cases before or after a particular date, and searching for cases involving a particular person or company.

FILAC: This refers to the five-step approach to legal research identified by Maureen Fitzgerald (and discussed in more detail in section Chapter 1, section B). The five letters in the acronym stand for the five stages of the legal research process that researchers should address: Facts, Issues, Law, Analysis/Application, and Conclusions.

Forms and precedents: Sample agreements and court documents produced commercially by legal publishers or privately by lawyers and law firms. Most forms and precedents use a "fill in the blank" approach, requiring users to use their own judgment in properly adapting the form or precedent to suit the particular transaction for which it is being prepared.

Gazette. An official publication of the government (provincial or federal) through which the government publishes new **regulations** and announces other official government action, including proclamation dates for new legislation.

Generalia specialibus non derogant. Literally "the general does not detract from the specific." This maxim suggests that courts prefer specific provisions over provisions of general application where the provisions are in conflict. See Chapter 3, section F for an example.

Governor General in Council or **Lieutenant-Governor in Council**: The Queen in Canada is represented federally by the Governor General and provincially by the various Lieutenant-Governors. In legal research parlance, you will often see in **statutes** the phrase that the "Governor General in Council" or "Lieutenant-Governor in Council" be empowered to enact **regulations**. This does not mean these representatives of the Queen are themselves drafting regulations; instead the task is effectively left in the hands of Cabinet and committees of Cabinet who would carry out the regulatory-making powers and submit the necessary paperwork to the Governor General (or Lieutenant-Governor, provincially speaking) for signature.

Hansard: The official verbatim transcripts of Parliamentary debates in Canada (federal and provincial) and England. In Canada, Hansard debates are now available through the Web sites of the applicable government (see Table 5.10 in Chapter 5, section G for a list of the Canadian federal and provincial government Web sites).

Headnote: A summary of a case provided by the publisher. A headnote typically provides a brief summary of the facts, the ruling by the court, and a summary of the reasons of the court in support of its ruling.

HeinOnline: An Internet subscription database available at <http://heinonline.org> that has, among other things, hundreds of full-text law journals available in PDF format, usually from the first volume of the journal. It has great historical coverage.

Invisible web: Also known as the "deep web." The invisible web refers to Internet information not found by normal search engines, such as Google, and is located on a company's proprietary server instead of the free World Wide Web. There are special Web sites, discussed in Chapter 5, section C, that help identify the invisible web.

ISP (Internet Service Provider): A company that provides individuals or organizations access to the Internet through a subscription. Increasingly in Canada, ISPs offer a flat monthly rate for unlimited access (7 days a week/24 hours a day) to the Internet. ISPs are competing with each other to also provide faster Internet access through digital lines or cable modems.

JOUR: The acronym for the global journal database on Quicklaw. If you search in this database, you will be conducting the most exhaustive search of full-text journal articles on Quicklaw. On WestlaweCARSWELL, the full-text journal database is JLR (Journals and Law Reviews). LexisNexis also has a global full-text law journal database.

Journal indexes: Journal indexes should be used to help identify relevant journal articles. Most indexes are organized by topic or keyword, author, and title. In Canada, there are two primary journal indexes: the *Index to Canadian Legal Literature* (available in print and online) and the *Index to Canadian Legal Periodical Literature* (available in print only). Journal indexes are discussed in more detail in Chapter 2, section B.

Judicial history: The judicial history of a case refers to the course or path the case has taken through the court system, from a trial decision, to a court of appeal, and possibly to the Supreme Court of Canada (note that not every trial decision gets appealed). One of the reasons you "note up" a case is to ensure the case you are reading has not been reversed or varied on appeal. See also **Judicial treatment** and **Noting up**.

Judicial precedent: See *Stare decisis*.

Judicial Treatment: The judicial treatment of a case refers to how subsequent judges have applied, distinguished, or otherwise considered the case. Shown as "Summary of Judicial Consideration" on Quicklaw's Quickcite database.

Jurisdiction: At one level, jurisdiction refers to a set boundary or territory; hence, "Canada" is a jurisdiction with specific borders and defined geographic space. Jurisdiction also refers to a notion of juridical power; hence, one can speak of "federal" or "provincial" jurisdiction (based on the division of powers in the *Constitution Act, 1867*) or whether, for example, a small claims court judge has jurisdiction (i.e., legitimate power) to hear a defamation claim.

Legalese: The jargon used by some lawyers, especially in the old days (e.g., WHEREFORE BY THESE PRESENTS . . . at the start of an Agreement). It is to be avoided.

Library of Congress Subject Headings (LCSH) and Classification: Legal materials (typically books) need to be organized on the shelf to allow for the orderly retrieval of information. The Library of Congress in Washington, D.C. has a system for organizing material by topic that is used by major libraries throughout the world. Library of Congress Subject Headings are a controlled vocabulary used to describe the topic of a book. Thus, all books in a law library that relate to human rights law in Ontario will be assigned the subject heading "Human rights — Ontario" and searching in an online library catalogue on that specific subject heading will retrieve *all* books on that subject held by the library. Related to these subject headings are Library of Congress call numbers that are assigned to a book depending on the book's topic. The "Law of Canada" is usually assigned the starting letters "KE" followed by a number that relates to the topic (KE 850 would likely be a book on Canadian contract law). Some Canadian law libraries, however, use the "KF" letters to organize their Canadian legal materials (KF is ordinarily the "Law of America" and when Canadian law libraries use KF for Canadian materials, it is referred to as "KF Modified").

Listservs or **online discussion groups**: These groups are organized by many topics and allow one to register or subscribe using e-mail. Once one has subscribed, messages can be sent and received to all subscribers to the group. This allows for the exchange of information and ideas. Law-related listservs are discussed in more detail in Chapter 5, section K.

McGill Guide: The McGill Guide is the colloquial name given to the *Canadian Guide to Uniform Legal Citation* (Carswell), the standard reference book in Canada to cite legal materials. The McGill Guide is discussed in detail in Chapter 1, section C.

Netletters: Online newsletters published by Quicklaw on a variety of topics. These netletters, prepared by experts in their fields, provide regular (usually weekly) updates of all developments within a particular area of law for the preceding period.

Neutral citation: A fairly new method of citing cases by the case name, case number, and level of court. It is "neutral" citation to the extent that this basic citation would remain the same even if a commercial legal publisher later reported the same case and assigned its own publication's citation to the case. Neutral citation is discussed in more detail in Chapter 1, section C.

Noscitur a sociis: Literally "one is known by one's associates". This maxim suggests that courts should look to the common features of words linked by "and" or "or" and limit the interpretation of those words to fit within the scope of those terms. See Chapter 3, section F(4) for an example.

Noting up: The process of verifying or updating your legal research. You can, and should, note up cases, legislation, and any information found in a looseleaf book where supplemental information is provided. You note up a case for two reasons: (1) to ensure it has not been reversed on appeal (you check its **judicial history**) and (2) to see how later courts may have interpreted your case (you check its **judicial treatment**). You note up legislation to ensure that the provision you are looking at has not been amended or repealed. See also **Judicial history** and **Judicial treatment**.

Order-in-Council: An official decision or order made by Cabinet. Orders-in-Council are officially issued by the Governor General at the request of Cabinet at the Federal level.

Parallel citation: Multiple citations for the same case. In other words, important cases are often reported by more than one publisher in various case law reporters. That case will therefore have multiple citations. Each of those citations is referred to as a parallel citation since it leads you to the same case (albeit in different sources).

Plaintiff: The person who initiates a civil lawsuit by suing the defendant. In the **style of cause** *Smith v. Jones*, one can assume that Smith is the plaintiff being sued by Jones (but this is not necessarily always the case since Smith could have originally been a defendant, and if Smith lost at trial and there was an appeal decision, the appellant in some **jurisdictions** is sometimes the first named party in the style of cause).

Primary legal resources: Traditionally, those sources of law, such as legislation and the decisions of courts and tribunals, which have the power to directly affect people's legal rights.

Proclamation: An official announcement by the government, often through the **Governor General** or the **Lieutenant-Governor**. Some statutes will state that they come into force on proclamation. In these situations, the government will announce the proclamation date in the applicable *Gazette*.

Prorogued: When Parliament is prorogued, it means that a session has been formally ended and all Parliamentary business, including sittings of Parliament and draft **bills**, is at an end. Unless the government specifically states, prior to proroguement, that a bill will be carried over to the new session, all bills are said to "die on the Order paper" at the time Parliament is prorogued.

Queen's Printer: Traditionally a branch of government that acted as the government's official publisher and that published legislation on behalf of the government. In recent years, there has been a move by some governments to either privatize their publishing or to require their publication branches to show a profit.

Quicklaw: Quicklaw <http://www.quicklaw.com> was one of the first companies in the world to create online, searchable databases of information. Since the 1970s, Quicklaw has grown in depth and ease of use to include not only Canadian cases, legislation, journal articles, textbooks, and news, but also to include law-related material from the United States, the United Kingdom, Australia, Africa, and the Caribbean.

Regulations: Legislation enacted by the government ordinarily only where a particular statute authorizes the government to enact such regulations. Since the **statute** usually speaks of delegating the power to enact regulations to a Minister, to Cabinet or to an appropriate statutory body, regulations are often referred to as delegated legislation. See also **Statutory instrument**.

Royal Assent: The symbolic but necessary formal approval of all federal or provincial legislation by the Queen given on her behalf by the **Governor General** (federally) or the applicable **Lieutenant-Governor** (provincially). Approval is by way of signature.

Secondary legal resources: Background material (such as textbooks, journal articles, encyclopedias, and case law digests) used to help locate **primary legal resources** (such as cases and legislation). Secondary legal resources are discussed in Chapter 2.

SOR: Stands for "Statutory Orders and Regulations" and refers to federal regulations (enacted since the most recent Consolidated version of the regulations) in the *Canada Gazette Part II*. In French, it is abbreviated DORS and stands for "Décrets, ordonnances et règlements." Example: SOR/98-176 refers to the *Hazardous Products (Glazed Ceramics and Glassware) Regulations*, and it was enacted in 1998 as Regulation 176.

Standing order: The arrangement made between a legal publisher and its customer for the customer to automatically be sent the new edition or the new annual version of a publication.

Stare decisis: Literally "to stand by things decided," *stare decisis* is a rule that requires judges to follow or obey the rulings of other judges higher in the judicial hierarchy and is similar to the concept of a binding judicial precedent. When the facts in Case A are similar to Case B, the judge in Case B must follow the ruling in Case A if the judge in Case A is from a higher court in the same **jurisdiction**.

Statute: A written law debated and voted upon by elected officials. Statutes can be amended or repealed, so it is critical to ensure that one is consulting an up-to-date version of the statute. Statutes are discussed in more detail in Chapter 3.

Statutory instrument: A regulation or other order or rule created by the government (see Chapter 3, section E for a more formal definition). In England, the term is used instead of regulation. In Canada, the term statutory instrument is broader than the term regulation. See also **Regulation** and **SOR**.

Style of cause: The names of the parties in a lawsuit. A style of cause in a civil lawsuit could be *Smith v. Jones* (meaning, most likely, that someone named Smith is suing someone named Jones). In a criminal matter, a style of cause in Canada could be *R. v. Williams*, in which the "*R.*" stands for *Regina*, being the symbolic name in which all prosecutions by the government against an accused are brought. (If there is a

King in power, the "*R.*" stands for *Rex*); in the foregoing example, Williams would be the accused, the person being tried by the government. The style of cause is usually always italicized. In online commercial databases, such as Quicklaw, one can usually search for cases by the style of cause in the "case name" field.

Taxing officer: A court official (sometimes a Master, sometimes a judge, and sometimes a person specially designated as a taxing officer). This court official is given power to determine what costs, if any, a successful party is entitled to after a lawsuit has finished. Taxing officers can also settle "fees" disputes between a lawyer and his or her own client. In the context of legal research, there are a number of cases, discussed in Chapter 1, section A(2), where the taxing officer has allowed a successful litigant to recover the costs incurred to conduct online searches on commercial online legal databases such as Quicklaw.

Time bomb: For law-related CD-ROMs, a "time-bomb" is a security feature built into the software by the publisher to disable or disallow the reading of data from the CD-ROM after the expiry of the license period for which the customer has paid for the CD-ROM.

Unreported decision: A decision of a judge that has not been published in a print case law reporter. Most decisions in Canada are in fact unreported and are only available either from the original court file or from a commercial online legal database, such as Quicklaw, LexisNexis, or WestlaweCARSWELL.

URL (Uniform Resource Locator): A URL (pronounced either "you are ell") or an URL (pronounced "earl") is a Web site's Web address (i.e. http://www.irwinlaw.com).

Words and phrases: Words and phrases dictionaries are arranged alphabetically and contain words and phrases as they have been defined or considered by the courts. Unlike law dictionaries, which usually only provide one or two definitions, words and phrases dictionaries attempt to provide multiple examples of how the words and phrases have been defined, often organized by level of court or by topic. See also **Dictionary, legal**.

TABLE OF CASES

INDEX

ABOUT THE AUTHOR

Ted Tjaden, LL.B., M.I.St. is the Coordinator of Information Services at the Bora Laskin Law Library, and Adjunct Professor in the Faculty of Law at the University of Toronto. He holds a cross appointment in the Faculty of Information Studies. Professor Tjaden teaches both introductory and advanced legal research at the Faculty of Law and a graduate course legal librarianship in the Faculty of Information Studies. Prior to joining the University of Toronto he was a research lawyer and librarian at the Toronto firm of Gardiner Roberts. He holds a bachelor of law degree from Queen's University and a Master's degree in Information Studies from the University of Toronto.